FOR TEACHERS IN ELEMENTARY AND SECONDAR

Ruth E. Grout, M.P.H., Ph.D.

PROFESSOR EMERITUS, SCHOOL OF PUBLIC HEALTH AND
COLLEGE OF EDUCATION, UNIVERSITY OF MINNESOTA

SCHOOLS

Health
Teaching
in Schools *Fifth Edition*

W. B. SAUNDERS COMPANY

Philadelphia — London — Toronto —

W. B. Saunders Company: West Washington Square
Philadelphia, Pa. 19105

12 Dyott Street
London, WC1A   1DB

1835 Yonge Street
Toronto 7, Ontario

Health Teaching in Schools

ISBN 0-7216-4316-7

Print No.:   9   8   7   6   5   4

Preface to the Fifth Edition

This new edition, like its predecessors, has been written for prospective teachers and those now teaching at both elementary and secondary levels. I hope, too, that administrators, curriculum consultants, nurses working in schools, and other education and health personnel concerned with strengthening health education will find help from these pages.

The book attempts to provide a rational approach to planning and carrying out health instruction. In early chapters, a discussion of health needs of children and youth, and of home, school, and community, directs the teacher's attention to the particular needs of the pupils and the community he serves. These needs, as described, suggest the broad concepts which should provide the framework for an organized approach to health instruction. A chapter in which health education is viewed in the light of changing educational theory and practice is followed by one on planning for health education in school and classroom. The teacher is introduced to elements of planning and given specific guides for selecting and organizing content of health instruction and for determining learning experiences. Then come chapters on methods and materials applicable to health instruction. At the heart of the book are chapters which contain practical, proved ideas for carrying out health teaching at kindergarten, lower elementary, upper elementary, junior high school, and senior high school levels. Later chapters deal with individualized health instruction, evaluation, and our valued co-workers in health education.

Emphasis throughout the book is on teaching which is directed toward improved health behavior of children and youth, and improved health conditions in the home, school, and community. The focus is on the school as an integral part of the community, and on school health instruction as an inseparable part of the total school curriculum.

The greater portion of this fifth edition has been completely rewritten. The chapters on health needs have been extensively redrafted to incorporate the most recent data available as well as to reflect changing emphases in such areas of concern as obesity, smoking, use of alcohol, mental health, sex education, safety, and environmental health. Additions and changes have been made throughout the book to bring out more clearly than in previous editions the interlocking of needs, objectives,

v

content, learning experiences, and evaluation. Increased attention is given to adapting health teaching to the socio-cultural and economic conditions found in different communities.

The chapters on methods of health instruction and on instructional materials include recent innovations; those which contain specific suggestions for classroom teaching have been enriched with many fresh examples illustrating how up-to-date methods and materials can be applied. These examples have been selected from contributions of teachers and school systems throughout the country.

The teacher may study the book in the order in which it is written or turn to its separate parts as the situation demands. A detailed index is included to assist one in locating the material he is seeking on a specific subject.

Over the years, many people have contributed directly or indirectly to the contents of this book. Teachers, health workers, students, and professional associates have influenced immeasurably the points of view expressed. Indebtedness is acknowledged to the following members of the faculty of the School of Public Health, University of Minnesota, who have reviewed portions of the book and offered valuable suggestions for this revised edition: Allyn Bridge, M.D., Associate Professor, Maternal and Child Health; Norman A. Craig, M.P.H., Associate Professor, Health Education; Leonard M. Schuman, M.D., Professor, Public Health Administration and Epidemiology; Ruth Stief, Assistant Professor, Maternal and Child Health (Nutrition); and members of the environmental health faculty. Deep appreciation is also extended to the following members of the faculty in the College of Education, University of Minnesota, for their critical review of parts of the manuscript: Ronald Lambert, Ph.D., Associate Professor and Chairman of Elementary Education; Neville P. Pearson, Ph.D., Associate Professor, Audiovisual Education; and Helen M. Slocum, Ph.D., Professor, Department of Physical Education for Women, and Chairman, School Health Education Program. Special gratitude goes to my sister, Julia R. Grout, Professor Emeritus, Duke University, for her helpful comments on the manuscript of this fifth edition. Particular acknowledgment is made to the school systems and organizations which have generously furnished information on their programs, loaned pictures from their files, or permitted the use of copyrighted materials. Finally, to Miss A. Evelyn Munro and Mrs. Lois Brama goes a special word of appreciation for their invaluable assistance in the preparation of this revision.

Ruth E. Grout

Contents

CHAPTER SIX

CHAPTER SEVEN

1

NATURE OF HEALTH EDUCATION IN THE SCHOOL AND COMMUNITY

Throughout the world people are seeking better health and better education. Never before have such high priorities been given to these two attributes. From the smallest village to the most complex urban center, new hopes exist for improving the health of individuals, families, and communities. At the same time education which is suitable to the locality and the times has become a matter of major importance. Vast resources, both human and financial, are now directed toward bringing about better health and better education at local, state, regional, national, and international levels. In the midst of these changes, schools are confronted with new demands as well as new opportunities to contribute to the health of children and the homes and communities of which they are a part.

Despite phenomenal progress on all health and education fronts, a wide gap exists today between health knowledge and the practical application of that knowledge. Research has taught us much about such fields as mental health, nutrition, the control of water and air pollution, and accident prevention. But we have not yet made sufficient use of this increased knowledge. Many essential health services, such as immunization clinics, school health services, and rehabilitation activities, are not supported adequately or, when available, used fully, despite their recognized value. Legislation and regulatory measures which are needed for adequate health protection, as in control of basic sanitation, often lack adequate public support.

Theories and practices of education have barely made their imprint on many school and adult health programs. Though en-

1

couraging progress has occurred in recent years, much yet needs to be done to use the powerful force of education so that the fullest impact of health research, services, and legislation will be felt on the lives of children, parents, and the community at large. Education is increasingly recognized as an essential part of all health efforts—education which will evoke understanding, support, and willing participation of the people themselves.

The World Health Organization has defined health as a "state of complete physical, mental, and social well-being and not merely absence of disease and infirmity." Though one is at a loss to define education in such precise terms, in countries where democracy is held at a premium educational efforts in general are directed toward helping people develop their potentialities as individuals and as responsible members of society. A person who has fully developed his individual potentialities and who possesses and applies the values, knowledge, and actions demanded of good citizenship is indeed an educated person.

WHAT IS HEALTH EDUCATION?

The term "health education" means many things to many people. Numerous individuals and groups have tried to define it. Some definitions focus on health education as an educational force or a process by which agents of education—teachers, parents, nurses, or community health workers—exert their influence on individuals in such ways as to affect their health behavior. Thus school health education is defined as "the process of providing or utilizing experiences for favorably influencing understandings, attitudes, and practices relating to individual, family and community health."[1]

Another way of viewing health education is to consider both the educational forces and the behavioral changes in individuals. Health education, then, may be thought of as the translation of what is known about health into desirable individual and community behavior patterns by means of the educational process. According to this definition, three interrelated elements make up the health educational process: the basic health concepts (what is known about health), the ultimate health goals (desirable individual and community behavior patterns), and the educational process (translation by means of the educational process). In any health education endeavor, each of these parts is essential. For effective results, all need to be combined with proper balance into a unified whole.

---

[1] Health education terminology. Journal of Health–Physical Education–Recreation, *33*:28 (Nov.) 1962. (Report of the Joint Committee on Health Education Terminology.)

The Joint Committee on Health Problems in Education of the National Education Association and the American Medical Association has recently prepared a statement on what health education is and is not. This statement focuses essentially on health education as "an academic field and subject"; it merits attention in view of the many conflicting and confusing approaches to health education within school systems today. According to the Joint Committee:[2]

Health Education Is:	*Health Education Is Not:*
education for health; education for healthful living of the individual, family, and community.	*hygiene of yesteryears.* It is not "blood and bone" hygiene, nor is it physiological hygiene.
an academic field and subject. All of its content and objectives are intellectual and academic in nature. Its content must have meaning and purpose to the students now as well as in the future.	*anatomy or physiology or both of these combined.* These fields serve as its foundation, but do not contribute the major concepts of its body of knowledge. They are necessary as background to understand health concepts applied to living.
a relatively new discipline. The natural (biological), the behavioral, and the health sciences provide its foundation.	*a pure science, but an applied science.* It is an applied science concerned with man's understanding of himself in relation to health matters in a changing society.
Facts, principles, and concepts pertaining to healthful living constitute its body of knowledge.	
The body of knowledge identified, organized, synthesized, and utilized in appropriate courses and experiences is sequentially arranged to form the discipline.	*physical education.* Health education and physical education are separate and distinct fields. They have similar goals, are closely related, but their activities and the conduct of activities are completely different. Sound physical education programs properly conducted contribute to the health of the individual.
It is derived from sociology, psychology, educational psychology, and the behavioral sciences — its purpose is to favorably change health behavior (knowledge, attitudes, and practices).	
a needed approach to bridge the gap between scientific health discoveries and man's application of these discoveries in daily life.	*physical fitness.* It contributes to the total fitness of man. It is not synonymous with muscle fitness.
	driver education. Health education is related to driver education through its safety area. Driver education is but one facet of safety.
an integral part of the curriculum at every level and an essential element in the general education of all students.	
the educational component of a school, college, or university health program (instruction, services, and environment).	*a requirement course organized to deal with legal provisions of alcohol, narcotics, and fire prevention.* These are essential problems that should be incorporated with other basic problems to provide a structured course or program.

---

[2] Joint Committee on Health Problems in Education of the National Education Association and the American Medical Association: Why Health Education. Washington, D.C., and Chicago, The Associations, 1965, pp. 1–2.

Health Education Is:	*Health Education Is Not:*
contributing to the well-educated individual by providing meaningful health experiences which can change health behavior. (Educational Policies Commission, The Purposes of Education in an American Democracy, 1938)	*rainy day or incidental instruction.* Health education must be carefully planned and incorporated in the curriculum; taught in a wholesome learning environment in which pupil activities can be carried out, particularly through problem-solving situations under the guidance of professionally prepared health educators.
best achieved by developing the rational powers of man (critical thinking), enabling him to make wise decisions and solve personal, family, and community health problems. (Educational Policies Commission, 1961)	*just grooming practices such as tooth brushing and combing the hair.* Health education has gone far beyond grooming.
based upon and improved through basic and applied research.	
best conducted by professionally prepared health educators from accredited colleges and universities.	

AIMS OF HEALTH EDUCATION

A now classic statement on the aims of health education comes from the World Health Organization:

> The aim of health education is to help people to achieve health by their own actions and efforts. Health education begins therefore with the interest of people in improving their conditions of living, and aims at developing a sense of responsibility for their own health betterment as individuals, and as members of families, communities, or governments.[3]

Health education thus conceived reflects the dual role of education as stated earlier in this chapter. On the one hand, it is directed toward the development of individuals who are physically, emotionally, and socially equipped to gain full satisfaction from life as individuals and as contributing members of society. On the other, it aims to improve health conditions of communities and to strengthen health responsibilities of governments.

Education for health begins with the start of life and extends throughout the span of existence, in the home, at school, and in the community. Although it has unique characteristics in each of these settings, health education encompasses all educational efforts related to the health needs of people and their communities, needs that are by-products of life itself. This book stresses the health education of school children; its interrelationships with all other health education efforts are nevertheless constantly kept in mind.

---

[3] Expert Committee on Health Education of the Public: First report. World Health Organization Technical Report Series No. 89. Geneva, Switzerland, World Health Organization, 1954, p. 4. (Copies may be ordered from Columbia University Press, International Documents Service, 136 S. Broadway, Irvington on Hudson, N.Y. 10533.)

Figure 1. Health education begins within the family unit. (Courtesy of the Cleveland Health Museum, Cleveland, Ohio.)

HEALTH EDUCATION IN THE HOME

The home is the very foundation upon which society is built and of all social institutions exerts the greatest influence. The values children place on healthful living and the degree to which they carry out desirable health practices are determined in large measure by factors within the home.

Cultural values, religious beliefs, the emotional climate of the home, and the nature of family relationships are among the factors that can influence a child's health behavior. So, too, can the attention parents give to child care during infancy and preschool years. While some place high value on health care, others relegate it to a position of little importance, not only during these early years but also throughout the child's school life. The funds and facilities available for carrying out good health practices also have an effect.

Within the home, parents are the principal educators. Most of their health education is done informally in the give and take of family relationships. Families needing help may seek advice from family physicians and dentists or from health counseling services now available in many communities. The public health nurse is often the keystone of such family health service. Teachers, counselors, and other school personnel play important parts, too, in helping parents with their health educational problems.

HEALTH EDUCATION IN THE SCHOOL

Health education of the school-age child supplements and reinforces efforts at home. At the same time health education should be an inseparable part of the total school curriculum. Just as each child grows and develops as a whole with a synchronization of his physical, emotional, and intellectual capacities, so, too, should the curriculum for that child be a unified whole. When the school blends health education in proper balance with all other educational efforts, children will be neither overtaught nor undertaught in this field. Moreover, the curriculum as a whole will be the richer for it.

School health education (including safety education) takes its place in the general curriculum through the following:

Individual Health Counseling

Teachers, nurses, physicians, guidance counselors, and others who are in direct contact with individual children and their parents have opportunities for much individual health teaching. No school health program can function on a sound basis without this personal health guidance. Every child at one time or another needs special help with his own particular problems, and every parent would benefit by such counseling. Although this book deals primarily with group teaching, the importance of individualized instruction in the classroom, in the nurse's and the physician's offices, or in the home must be kept in mind. A separate chapter (Chapter 10) in this book is devoted to a discussion of individualized health instruction.

Informal Health Teaching (and Learning) in Relation to Daily Experiences

We do some of our most effective health teaching informally as problems arise that need attention or as school or community events arouse interest and discussion. Many teachable moments occur in the daily life at school. The following examples illustrate situations that lend themselves well to informal health teaching and learning:

1. The health examination: preparation for, assistance with, and follow-up.

2. The school lunch program: assistance in planning school lunch menus and selection of a well-balanced meal.

3. An accident or illness at school or in the community: consideration of what caused it and how it could have been prevented, as well as how to prevent a similar occurrence.

4. The adjustment of the physical environment at school for comfort and health: assistance with the arrangement of furniture and shades for good lighting; proper use of handwashing facilities and toilets.

5. Care of pets at school: observation and discussion of the biological needs and behavior of these animals that may be compared with human needs and processes.

6. Athletic activities: sense of well-being from participation; safe and hygienic use of equipment; avoidance of overfatigue.

7. Laboratory and workshop activities: use of protective devices; storage of chemicals; safe handling of tools and machinery.

8. Human relations incidents: showing respect for others; helping the handicapped child.

Systematic Health Instruction

As valuable as informal learning is, we cannot depend upon it as the only way to teach health; too much would be omitted or inadequately taught. Carefully planned health instruction is needed. Teachers commonly provide for planned instruction through:

1. Separate health courses or classes scheduled according to a definite plan.

2. Health units incorporated in other parts of the curriculum, such as the sciences, physical education, home economics, social studies, and language arts (writing, literature, and the like).

3. Planned integration of health concepts and health education activities throughout the curriculum, as, for example, the inclusion of a study of home lighting in a unit on housing.

HEALTH EDUCATION IN THE COMMUNITY

Health education on a community-wide scale assumes many forms. Planned community health education, frequently called public health education, is commonly conducted through activities of health departments, voluntary health agencies, schools, youth organizations, and other community groups reaching young people and adults alike.

Though its scope is broad and its methods varied, community-wide health education is concerned with the application of sound health principles and practices in many aspects of community life. It seeks to elicit understanding of and support for essential health services and to foster healthful conditions wherever people live and work together, such as in neighborhoods, institutions, and industry. It adheres to the goals already stated—individuals and communities working actively and creatively toward better health. Community-wide health education most frequently takes the following forms.

Individual Counseling

Through the use of the face-to-face interview, physicians, dentists, public health nurses, and many other types of health workers provide much valuable health guidance in their contact with people in homes, schools, offices, and clinics. An interview, properly conducted, strengthens the individual's ability to think through and deal with health problems.

Group Instruction

Groups organized for health and safety instruction form a part of the large and growing adult education movement. Parents, industrial workers, clinic patients, and members of youth and civic organizations are among those benefiting by this form of group learning. Through meeting together in classes and informal discussion groups, they develop an understanding of problems of common interest, as well as attempts to find solutions to those problems.

Use of Mass Media of Communication

Through newspapers, radio, television, printed materials, mass meetings, and similar media of communication, agencies disseminate facts about health problems and services and stimulate action in health matters. Health information and publicity services are important parts of community-wide health programs aimed at large numbers of people. To be effective, these services must go hand in hand with other forms of education which more intimately touch the lives of the people whose understanding and action are solicited.

Community Action Programs

In many urban and rural areas people increasingly are banding together to deal with such problems of mutual concern as neighborhood development, agricultural improvements, conditions aggravated by poverty, and a myriad of other issues and needs. Health problems are often the focus of such community organization efforts, and as people study, plan, and act on health matters much valuable education can result. Health education of the population is frequently their aim. Moreover, community organization for health can in itself be a very effective method of educating those engaged in community health action, since it provides the means whereby people gather facts, make decisions, and commit themselves to fostering indicated health improvements. Further, people thus committed may in turn influence others with whom they are in contact.

Informal Health Education

A summary of health education at work in the community would not be complete without mention of the informal type of health education that goes on in ordinary contacts among people. Within the home, much health education occurs in the day-by-day give and take of family relationships. Outside the home, the "grapevine" is increasingly being recognized as an important medium for health education. The housewife who has taken her young children to an immunization clinic and, over the back fence or coffee cup, convinces her doubting neighbor that immunizations are important, is providing health education of a sort. The businessman member of a citizens' committee on education who learns about the inadequacy of school health services, and who with his friends over a meal discusses ways to improve the services, is not only conveying health facts but may also be engendering health action. Those engaged in school and community health education would do well to pay greater heed to these less tangible, but nonetheless important, means of health education that influence attitudes, spread information (and, unfortunately, misinformation also), and call forth action.

NEED FOR UNIFICATION IN HEALTH EDUCATION

Unification in health education is essential for at least two reasons. First, the individual needs a consistent pattern in the health education he experiences in the home, at school, and in the community at large, not only during school years but also over a span of years.

Second, unification is important because many health problems are community-wide in their scope and consequently require community-wide action for their adequate solution. For example, if there is need for fluoridation of community water supplies, families, schools, and the community at large have stakes in the solution of the problem, for the community as a whole has a civic responsibility to fluoridate its water supply. Parents, whose children would benefit by fluoridation, need to know its value and need to be encouraged to engage in community action programs toward its realization. Schools can develop an understanding of the importance of fluoridation through disseminating information and providing opportunities for children to take part in community education efforts. Health education is needed on a community-wide basis to secure widespread understanding and support for this and other important health measures.

HIGHLIGHTS IN THE DEVELOPMENT OF HEALTH EDUCATION[4]

Health education as it is known in the United States today is largely the result of developments in public health and education since 1850. The year 1850 marks the beginning of public health as

---

4 Portions of this section have already appeared in somewhat different form in the following article: Grout, R. E.: Health education today in the light of yesterday. The Yale Journal of Biology and Medicine, 19:573–580, 1947. The Journal kindly granted permission to reprint this material.

an organized movement in this country. During this year a plan for a comprehensive public health program, including a program of health education, was published in the form of the "Report of the Sanitary Commission of Massachusetts."

The year 1850 also marks the date when tax-supported public schools became a reality in most of the northern states. Prior to the nineteenth century, education was available only to the privileged few. The early schools were church schools with religious teaching as their dominant purpose. The child was thought of as a passive entity to be molded according to the will of his superiors. No recognition was given to his developmental needs and little to his preparation for useful citizenship. Health education as we know it could have no place in such a system. With the establishment of plans for a true public health program and for universal public education, the foundations were laid for education in health.

Developments Before 1850

Recognition of the importance of health dates back many centuries. Even before the beginning of the Christian era, this recognition was shown in the philosophy and beliefs of the Chinese and Jews. The Greeks, through their great philosophers and in their modes of life, gave expression to beliefs in the close relationship between health and other aspects of life. Juvenal, the Roman satirist and poet, in the second century A.D., wrote the classical statement, *Mens sana in corpore sano* (a sound mind in a sound body).

From the early days of the Christian era on into the Middle Ages, there was no place for the care of one's health under a philosophy that accepted the body as an enemy of the spirit. With the revival of learning, the beginnings were laid once again for the concept that health is essential to human welfare.

John Locke, famous seventeenth century English philosopher, whose book *Some Thoughts Concerning Education* has become a classic, wrote:

A Sound Mind in a Sound Body is a short, but full description of a happy State in this World. He that has these two, has little more to wish for; and he that wants either of them will be but little the better for anything else. Men's Happiness or Misery is most part of their own making. He, whose Mind directs not wisely, will never take the right Way; and he, whose Body is crazy and feeble, will never be able to advance in it.

This is followed by rules of hygiene applied to children, summarized in Locke's own words:

And thus I have done with what concerns the Body and Health, which reduces itself to these few and easy observable Rules. Plenty of open Air, Exercise, and Sleep, plain Diet, no Wine or strong Drink, and very little or no Physick, not too warm and strait Cloathing, especially the Head and Feet kept cold, and the Feet often us'd to cold Water, and expos'd to wet.

And further:

The Method of Teaching Children by a repeated Practice, and the same Action done over and over again, under the Eye and Direction of the Tutor, 'till they have got the Habit of doing it well, and not by relying on Rules trusted on their Memories, has so many Advantages, which Way ever we consider it, that I cannot but wonder (if ill Customs could be wonder'd at in any Thing) how it could possibly be so much neglected.[5]

A century later, Catharine E. Beecher, founder of Hartford Female Seminary, Hartford, Connecticut, and a leader of thought in her time, wrote about the education of mothers and teachers:

What is the profession of woman? Is it not to form immortal minds, and to watch, to nurse, and to rear the bodily system, so fearfully and wonderfully made, and upon the order and regulation of which, the health and well-being of the mind so greatly depend? . . . The restoration of health is the physician's profession, but the *preservation* of it falls to other hands; and it is believed that the time will come, when woman will be taught to understand something respecting the construction of the human frame; the philosophical results which will naturally follow from restricted exercise, unhealthy modes of dress, improper diet, and many other causes, which are continually operating to destroy the health and life of the young.[6]

Lemuel Shattuck, a layman who drafted the "Report of the Sanitary Commission of Massachusetts," was in fact an educator in the modern spirit when he wrote:

Every child should be taught, early in life, that to preserve his own life and his own health and the lives and health of others, is one of his most important and constantly abiding duties. Some measure is needed which shall impel children to make a sanitary examination of themselves and their associates, and thus elicit a practical application of the lessons of sanitary science in the every-day duties of life. The recommendation now under consideration is designed to furnish this measure. It is to be carried into operation in the use of a blank schedule, which is to be printed on a letter sheet, in the form prescribed in the appendix, and furnished to the teacher of each school. He is to appoint a sanitary committee of the scholars, at the commencement of school, and on the first day of each month, to fill it out, under his superintendence. . . . Such a measure is simple, would take but a few minutes each day, and cannot operate otherwise than usefully upon the children, in forming habits of exact observation, and in making a personal application of the laws of health and life to themselves. This is education of an eminently practical character, and of the highest importance.[7]

---

[5] Locke, J.: Some Thoughts Concerning Education. 6th Ed. London, A. J. Churchill, 1709, pp. 1, 33, 66.

[6] Beecher, C. E.: The profession of a woman. In Bailey, E.: Young Ladies Class Book. Boston, Gould, Kendall, and Lincoln, 1839, pp. 201–203.

[7] Report of the Sanitary Commission of Massachusetts. Boston, Dutton and Wentworth, 1850, pp. 178–179. (A facsimile edition of this book was published by the Harvard University Press, Cambridge, Mass., in 1948.)

Developments from 1850 to World War II

During these years of great expansion in education and public health, several developments took place that have had a direct bearing on health education.

Child Study Movement

Among the most significant developments, yet perhaps the slowest to leave its imprint, was the introduction into this country of the educational theories of Rousseau, Pestalozzi, Froebel, and Herbart. Education up to this time had been largely a system for the transmission of knowledge. In theory, and gradually in practice, it now sought to understand child needs and to meet these needs through suitable educational methods.

Through the eighties and early nineties a child-study movement was inaugurated among educators, with the systematic study of physical needs as one part of the program. Since the twenties and early thirties, no program of education or health education has been considered sound unless it first seeks to understand the needs of the individuals being taught and then attempts to meet these needs through psychologically sound methods and authentic information.

Temperance Movement

The teaching of physiology and hygiene was made mandatory in many states around 1880, on the wave of a powerful propaganda movement sponsored by temperance interests. The basic purpose of this legislation was to require instruction on the effects of alcohol and narcotics, but most of the laws were so worded that this instruction became part of a broader teaching program. School textbooks of the period 1890 to 1918 reflected this movement.

Developments in Physical Education

Physical education is another development of major significance which began between 1880 and 1890. The early programs stressed calisthenics to help counteract the effects of sedentary life and to develop physical efficiency. By 1910, legislation for the inclusion of instruction in physical education in schools had become widespread. Many laws specified the teaching of health habits.

Physical educators united to form a professional association in 1885. This group has taken an increasing interest in health education. In 1937 the American Physical Education Association became a department of the National Education Association under the name of the American Association for Health, Physical Education, and Recreation. The membership of this association has expanded so that today it includes numerous professional groups that are concerned with health.

Establishment of School Medical Inspections and Other School Programs

A further movement of importance in the development of health education was the establishment of school medical inspections. Begun in the United States in 1894 in Boston, Massachusetts, largely for the purpose of controlling contagion, this program has gradually expanded to become an inclusive program of health appraisal and counseling in which parents, teachers, nurses, physicians, and other health workers participate.

Other programs initiated during this period that have helped to further the scope of school health education include the school lunch program, safety education, and programs dealing with emotional health needs.

Early Programs for Child Health Improvement

Among the greatest contributions to the growth of school health education were the nation-wide educational efforts initiated by medical and health authorities to lessen infant mortality and to improve child health. In 1909 the American Association for the Study and Prevention of Infant Mortality was formed, which, first under its original name, and later as the American Child Hygiene Association, carried on aggressive programs of education for better child care for 13 years.

In 1915, tuberculosis associations developed the "Modern Health Crusade" on a national basis, using numerous devices to catch pupil interest, such as health stories, plays, posters, ceremonies, and routines. These tuberculosis associations had begun their educational activities for the public at large in 1904, with the formation of the National Association for the Study and Prevention of Tuberculosis. This group has been credited with popularizing the concept that education of the people on a large scale is an indispensable part of public health.

With the start of World War I, the health of school children became a matter of major national concern. One important result of this awakened interest was the formation of the Child Health Organization in 1918 for the purpose of promoting school health education. The term "health education" was proposed for the first time in 1919 at a conference of leaders of health and of education called by this organization.[8] The first fellowships for the preparation of teachers in health education were awarded by this organization in 1920.

In 1923 the American Child Hygiene Association and the Child Health Organization merged to form the American Child Health Association. Until its dissolution in 1935 this group exerted wide influence, especially in school-child health. Among its most significant projects were conferences on health education which did much over the years to weld together the forces of public health and education that often were following divergent courses. When the American Child Health Association was dissolved, its sale of publications and correspondence services were transferred to the National Education Association and the American Public Health Association.

The Second White House Conference on Child Health and Protection in 1930, like the First Conference in 1909, added its share toward creating a better understanding of health education. Its printed reports have been used widely through the years.

Early School Health Demonstrations

We should also mention the several school health demonstrations which proved that health education could change behavior. One of the first of these was launched in 1914 in a school in the Locust Point section of Baltimore, Maryland. Other experiments were numerous in the twenties and thirties. Among the better known were the demonstrations conducted in Mansfield and Richland County, Ohio, under the auspices of the American Red Cross from 1922 to 1925; in Malden, Massachusetts, from 1922 to 1923 and later, with aid from the Department of Biology and Public Health, of the Massachusetts Institute of Technology; in Fargo, North Dakota, from 1923 to 1927 through grants from the Commonwealth Fund; and in Cattaraugus County, New York, from 1931 to 1938, with the financial assistance of the Milbank Memorial Fund.

Early Cooperative Programs

School-community cooperation in health education has been an ideal of leaders in public health and education for many years. On a national scale, machinery for such cooperation was established to a limited degree through the early child health organizations previously mentioned. In 1911 the Joint Committee on Health Problems in Education of the National Education Association and the American Medical Association was formed. This Committee has

---

[8] Jean, S. L.: Health education: some factors in its development. News Letter, School of Public Health, University of Michigan, June, 1946, p. 4.

helped to harmonize policies of the professions in respect to school health. Its publications are standard references today.

The National Conference for Cooperation in Health Education, organized in 1940, provided another channel for inter-agency planning. Its members, who were representatives from national agencies, both official and nonofficial, met periodically, and were responsible for several publications, including *School Health Policies,* which have been used widely in the development of school health programs.

Developments in Public Health Education

While health education had been expanding within school systems, its growth was even greater in the community at large. During the first two decades of the present century, several voluntary health agencies sprang into being which had as one of their primary purposes the dissemination of information in the field of health. Among these early groups were the National Association for the Study and Prevention of Tuberculosis, mentioned earlier; the Society for Sanitary and Moral Prophylaxis, organized in 1905; the National Committee for Mental Hygiene, created in 1909; and the American Society for the Control of Cancer, formed in 1913. In 1914, the New York City Health Department became the first official health agency to establish a bureau of health education. Other official bodies soon followed. In 1922, health education workers in public health agencies had become numerous enough to form a section of their own in the American Public Health Association.

One of the first community-wide action programs which attracted national attention was started in Hartford, Connecticut, in 1938. Coordinated programs had been established previous to this time but were focused largely on the school-age child. The Hartford program, using modern methods of community organization, sought to unite the whole community in a program of study and action.

Developments from World War II to the Present

World War II, like its predecessor, was responsible for an acceleration of programs in many fields, including those of education and health. Selected developments that have influenced health education in this period are summarized here.

Developments in Education

In recent years educational activity has been greatly intensified. The tremendous knowledge explosion and demands for more and better qualified personnel in many areas of human endeavor are among factors that have brought almost insurmountable pressures on our educational systems. Change is the characteristic of the day, change that is occurring so fast that few can grasp the full meaning of many developments. Two directions in which change is evident are discussed briefly here.

Curriculum movements.   Three distinct but interrelated cycles of curriculum development are either currently in operation or discernible for the future.[9] The so-called curriculum reform movement, under way since about 1951, with its emphasis on subject matter and its nationally prepared curriculum materials (as in mathematics and science) is an example of a development that has already been put into practice. More recently, school leaders have been exerting efforts to obtain a balance in school offerings from which a "total curriculum" can emerge. This movement is resulting in a redefinition of educational goals, a variety of attempts to better interrelate knowledge, and, inevitably, a conflict among the numerous subject fields, each seeking time and recognition in the curriculum. Pervading, and at times overriding, these two developments is the persistent recognition that education must be humanistic, that is, that it must be concerned with human interests and values. Each cycle has added and will continue to add new dimensions to curriculum development programs.

From time to time educational authorities have set forth statements on education which have not only reflected trends of the period but also have influenced educational thought and practice. In 1961 the Educational Policies Commission issued such a statement in its publication "The Central Purpose of American Education." The commission, accepting the fact that the school is only one of many agencies involved in education, stated that the unique and central role of the school is that of helping individuals develop their rational powers so that they may be able better to achieve their personal goals and meet their obligations to society. Applying this point of view to health education, the commission stated:

Health, for example, depends upon a reasoned awareness of the value of mental and physical fitness and of the means by which it may be developed and maintained. Fitness is not merely a function of living and acting; it requires that the individual understand the connections among health, nutrition, activity, and environment, and that he take action to improve his mental and physical condition.[10]

In 1963, the National Education Association through its Project on Instruction issued several reports intended as guides for

[9] Goodlad, J. I.: Direction and redirection for curriculum change. In Curriculum Change: Direction and Process. Washington, D.C., Association for Supervision and Curriculum Development, 1966, pp. 1–14.

[10] Educational Policies Commission: The Central Purpose of American Education. Washington, D.C., National Education Association, 1961, p. 5.

the improvement of instruction in schools. The recommendations contained in these reports have already had an appreciable impact on schools, and as they are implemented through the activities of the NEA's Center for the Study of Instruction their influence should continue to spread. Throughout these reports there are many implications for health education. To quote one passage:

> Urbanization, changed social conditions, and technological advances have created new health problems as well as benefits, both for individuals and for the community. Their satisfactory solution depends on popular knowledge of scientific information and fundamental principles in the area of health as well as on the work of health specialists. The school, as the only social institution that reaches all children and youth, has responsibility for teaching the basic information and for helping young people develop the habits and attitudes essential for healthful living. Effective health education begins in early childhood and continues as a cumulative program through the elementary and secondary school years. It stresses the application of rational thought processes to health problems as well as the teaching of essential knowledge.[11]

Federal support programs for schools. Over the years the federal government has assumed increasing responsibility for strengthening the schools of our nation. A useful volume outlining the many federal programs for schools has recently been published.[12] This volume points out that the money now available is "seed money" that is intended to stimulate more active self-help efforts at every level of educational endeavor.

Within a three-year period in the early 1960's, Congress enacted 24 pieces of legislation directed at improving American education. The most far-reaching of these recent acts was the Elementary and Secondary Education Act of 1965. Through this act funds are provided for the expansion of educational programs for disadvantaged children in low-income areas and for the expansion of library resources, including textbooks and audiovisual materials. Other parts of the act provide for local and regional education centers through which innovations in school practices can be developed and tested. Thus, for the first time, federal funds are available for a wide spectrum of school improvements, including improvements in health education.

The Economic Opportunity Act of 1964 is another far-reaching piece of legislation which has made possible, through the Office of Economic Opportunity, the distribution of funds to local communities for use with economically deprived groups. The best known project under this act is Project Head Start, which has provided enriching school-centered experiences for preschool children and

---

11 NEA Project on Instruction: Deciding What to Teach. Washington, D.C., National Education Association, 1963, pp. 113–114.

12 Office of Education, U.S. Department of Health, Education, and Welfare: Education '65; A Report to the Profession. Washington, D.C., U.S. Government Printing Office, 1966, 100 pp.

Figure 2. Some social conditions present special health problems. (From California's Health, Vol. 23, Nos. 10–11, 1966. Photo by Norman Breslow.)

low-income families. Not only have thousands of young children benefited from Project Head Start but so have mothers recruited from poverty areas who have served as aides in Head Start programs. In many communities, the project has already demonstrated ways of making more meaningful for these children the year-round educational experiences provided by the school. Moreover, it is said that many aides have benefited greatly by the project and in fact have developed into neighborhood leaders active in parent-teacher groups and other neighborhood organizations. Health services and health education have been featured prominently in Head Start programs.

Developments in School Health and Health Education

When one is in the midst of change it is sometimes difficult to sort out those developments which are of long-term significance and those that are of passing importance only. So it is in the field of school health and health education. Since World War II there have been persistent efforts on many fronts to strengthen school health programs. Some of these efforts have been instigated by educational leaders and some by health and medical groups. Most have become cooperative endeavors involving both educational and health interests. A few of the better known developments are discussed briefly here.

Physical fitness programs.   During World War II, and for a period following the war, much stress was placed on physical fitness. Conferences were held, guides produced, and a special President's Council on Youth Fitness was formed. Though such programs initially stressed total fitness, they are today more closely identified with fitness through physical activity than with fitness through application of sound health practices. Health education efforts mounted in the name of physical fitness are now being replaced by other developments more readily discernible as health education.

Cooperative programs.   Today there is hardly a school health program that does not in some way involve cooperative planning and action among school and community groups. At the national level, the Joint Committee on Health Problems in Education of the National Education Association and the American Medical Association is still active. The National Conference for Cooperation in Health Education remained active until its disbandment in 1961. In 1951, the National Council of Chief State School Officers and the Association of State and Territorial Health Officers published a significant statement on "Responsibilities of State Departments of Education and Health for School Health Services." These two very influential administrative bodies have continued to pool their resources on problems of mutual interest. Cooperative programs at state levels have added other milestones to joint planning and action. These state-level programs have been further nurtured at the national level by biennial conferences on physicians and schools sponsored by the American Medical Association.

The Midcentury White House Conference on Children and Youth held in 1950 and the 1960 White House Conference on Children and Youth have provided documents of value to those engaged in school health education. The 1960 conference was noteworthy for its preconference activities in the separate states where people from many organizations and walks of life participated in a study of existing conditions and services and drew up plans for future action, many of which have implications for health education.

In 1964, the National Health Council initiated steps to stimulate its member organizations—voluntary groups, governmental agencies, and professional associations—to become more active in supporting improved school health education. A task force was formed, a national conference was held, and in 1966 a brochure was published.[13]

Selected activities of professional organizations. Three organizations have been singled out here for their recent efforts to strengthen school health and health education.

THE AMERICAN ASSOCIATION FOR HEALTH, PHYSICAL EDUCATION, AND RECREATION. In 1959, the Health Education Division of the American Association for Health, Physical Education, and Recreation held an important planning conference to chart long-range action for the advancement of health education in schools and colleges. In 1960, the division formed six commissions to implement the recommendations of the conference. Of immediate possible interest to the readers of this book is the work of the Curriculum Commission.

The Curriculum Commission set for itself the task of identifying concepts related to selected health problems which were believed to be of special importance in the 1960's and 1970's and of significance to children and youth as well as to adults. In consultation with health authorities, the commission worked for several years to develop these concepts and to gather data supporting them. A document containing the concepts and supporting data was published in 1967 as a source of help to curriculum workers, teachers, and others engaged in effecting health curriculum changes.[14]

In 1967, the Health Education Division entered a new phase in its efforts to improve school health education by convening a Na-

---

[13] Health Education in Our Schools Today: The Need for Agency Action. New York, National Health Council, 1740 Broadway, 1966, 15 pp.

[14] Health Concepts; Guides for Health Instruction. Washington, D.C. American Association for Health, Physical Education, and Recreation, 1967, 49 pp.

tional Conference for School Health Education Curriculum Development. Over 180 people attended the conference which dealt with new approaches to curriculum change and recommendations for implementing change at regional and state levels.

THE AMERICAN SCHOOL HEALTH ASSOCIATION.   The membership of this group consists of school physicians, school nurses, health educators, and others engaged in school health activities. It has kept members posted on new developments in health education through its *Journal of School Health.* One full issue of the *Journal* was devoted recently to the subject of "Growth Patterns and Sex Education."[15]

THE AMERICAN ACADEMY OF PEDIATRICS.   The Academy has recently added its contribution, too, through a publication of a report prepared by its Committee on School Health.[16] Though the report is intended primarily for physicians, it contains much helpful information for teachers and other educators. The report gives solid support to school health education.

The School Health Education Study.[17]   This project was initiated in 1961. In the first phase of the study, a nation-wide survey was made of health instructional practices in public schools. The survey revealed important omissions and unnecessary repetition of health content and learning experiences and far too many situations in which health instruction was nonexistent or wholly inadequate. Phase one also included an inventory of student health behavior which was made in a sampling of school systems throughout the country. Again, conditions were found that pointed to the need for improving health education programs and practices.

The School Health Education Study entered its second phase in 1963, with focus on developing experimental curriculum materials for health education. Through the work of writing teams, assisted by educational leaders and teachers in try-out centers, the study has produced a plan for the structuring of the health curriculum by means of the conceptual approach[18] and is currently developing a series of instructional guides and other teaching-learning materials for use in schools.

The first phase of the study has helped to dramatize the plight of school health instruction today. Powerful voices are now being heard among school administrators, health administrators, and others in support of more adequate attention to school health education.

---

15 Growth patterns and sex education; A suggested program—kindergarten through grade 12. Journal of School Health, *37* No. 5a (May) 1967, 136 pp. (Special issue)

16 Report of the Committee on School Health of the American Academy of Pediatrics. Evanston, Illinois, The Academy, 1966, 128 pp.

17 School Health Education Study. Washington, D.C., School Health Education ˌ Study, 1507 M Street, N.W., Room 800, 1964, 74 pp.

18 Health Education: A Conceptual Approach to Curriculum Design. St. Paul, Minn., 3M Education Press, Box 3100, 1967, 141 pp. (By the School Health Education Study.)

Though at this writing it is too early to determine the effects of the second phase of the study, indications are that the health concepts developed by this group (and by the Curriculum Commission of the American Association for Health, Physical Education, and Recreation mentioned earlier) have given health education a visibility not previously attained.

Developments in Public Health and Medical Care

In recent years, unprecedented growth has occurred in the business of providing health and medical care to our population. The reasons are many. People are demanding more and better health services. Medical knowledge which can be translated into improved health and medical care programs has expanded at a phenomenal pace. New health legislation now makes possible services and facilities never before available to wide segments of the population. In 1965 alone, at least 15 new pieces of health legislation were passed by Congress, more than in any other single year in the history of our country.

Though significant health developments are too numerous to outline here, several which have opened new areas for emphasis in school health education are mentioned. Intensified efforts are now directed toward immunization of all children. In many states, special community-wide education programs are now focused on such problems of importance to young people as education in sex and family life, consumer health, use of alcohol and narcotics, and venereal disease control. Millions of dollars in federal, state, and local funds are being spent on hospital facilities for the acutely and chronically ill, on health centers for preventive and control services, and on rehabilitation centers for the handicapped. Medicare and Medicaid, which became realities in 1965, have introduced a whole new concept of health care. One of the most critical challenges of the times is that of providing enough qualified manpower to deliver the services for which funds and facilities are increasingly available. Thus, education on the career opportunities in health and medical fields has become a matter of national concern.

In the midst of these developments, public health education is showing steady growth. As new community health programs develop, the educational components of these programs are more carefully identified and planned than formerly. Better balanced health education services are also evident. Although health workers in earlier years were often satisfied to limit health education to the use of publicity techniques, today they are seeking ways to involve people in action programs within which a variety of educational procedures are appropriately combined. Individuals and groups in communities are banding together in health committees and councils to solve common problems. Sometimes these groups are organized to deal with specific problems, such as tuberculosis, mental health, or safety; sometimes they deal with a variety of health needs.

A striking feature of present-day community health work is the growth of volunteer activities. Thousands of youths and adults are engaged in useful services within health organizations, hospitals, health centers, and neighborhoods. Not only is important work being accomplished, but also a core of informed and dedicated citizens is being developed to extend further needed community health improvements.

Growth of International Health Programs

Programs of community betterment, initiated by the people themselves, are becoming realities in different parts of the world. As a result of such self-help endeavors many newly developing countries are taking great strides in the control of diseases and the provision of health facilities and personnel. Health education is an important part of these programs. Though the countries themselves assume primary responsibility for their own health improvements, they are assisted in numerous ways by international agencies. The United States, through its Agency for International Development (AID), provides direct help on a bilateral basis, as do other countries with well-developed resources. On a multilateral basis, that is, by the combined resources of many countries acting through the United Nations and its specialized agencies, other developments are taking place both within nations and between nations. Special mention should be made of the work, often on a cooperative basis, of the World Health Organization (WHO), the Food and Agriculture Organization (FAO), the United Nations Children's Fund (UNICEF), and the United Nations Educational, Scientific and Cultural Organization (UNESCO).

Since 1949, WHO has had a section on health education which provides assistance, on request from individual nations, in the development of programs of health education. It works closely with other international agencies, such as those in education, agriculture, and labor, and encourages similar relationships within nations so that health education is properly related to the larger efforts that are being made for improving community life. Through WHO's stimulation expert committees have met and issued reports on health education.[19]

School health has been a subject of international concern. In

---

[19] For example, Expert Committee on Health Education of the Public: WHO Technical Report Series No. 89. Geneva, Switzerland, World Health Organization, 1954, 41 pp.

1951, a WHO Expert Committee on School Health Services issued a report which has served as a guide for school health programs throughout the world.[20] In 1960, a Joint WHO/UNESCO Expert Committee published a report on teachers' preparation in health education.[21] A more recent joint endeavor was the publication of a source book on *Planning for Health Education in Schools.*[22]

Professional and voluntary bodies are now organizing on an international scale. Among those which have given special attention to school health education are the World Confederation of Organizations of the Teaching Profession, the International Council on Education for Teaching, and the International Council for Health, Physical Education, and Recreation.

SUMMARY

Health education as set forth in this chapter is seen as an essential component of health efforts in home, school, and community, and as an integral part of the total school curriculum. Though its emphases have changed through the years as developments have occurred in the fields of health and of education, its persistent goal has been that of helping people "to achieve health by their own actions and efforts." School health education, soundly conceived and developed, supplements and reinforces health education in the home and unites with health education endeavors in the community.

REFERENCES

The Changing American School. The Sixty-fifth Yearbook of the National Society for the Study of Education. Part II. Chicago, The University of Chicago Press, 1966, 319 pp.

Dwork, R. E.: Social innovations and health education. Journal of Health–Physical Education–Recreation, *38*:19–21 (April) 1967.

Head Start Child Development Program: A Community Action Program for Young Children. Washington, D.C., Office of Economic Opportunity, 1966, 64 pp.

Jean, S. L.: The development of health education in the U.S.A. Health Education Journal (London), *17*:36–48 (March) 1959.

---

[20] Expert Committee on School Health Services: WHO Technical Report Series No. 30. Geneva, Switzerland, World Health Organization, 1951, 36 pp.

[21] Joint WHO/UNESCO Expert Committee on Teacher Preparation for Health Education: Technical Report Series No. 193. Geneva, Switzerland, World Health Organization, 1960, 19 pp.

[22] Planning for Health Education in Schools. London, Longmans, Green & Co., Ltd., 48 Grosvenor St., 1966, 157 pp. (A study undertaken by Professor C. E. Turner on behalf of UNESCO and WHO.)

Joint Committee on Health Problems in Education of the National Education Association and the American Medical Association: Health Education. 5th Ed. Washington, D.C., and Chicago, The Associations, 1961, 429 pp.

Means, R. K.: A History of Health Education in the United States. Philadelphia, Lea & Febiger, 1962, 412 pp.

National Committee on School Health Policies of the NEA and the AMA: Suggested School Health Policies. 4th Ed. Chicago, American Medical Association, 1966, 54 pp.

Oberteuffer, D., and Beyrer, M. K.: School Health Education. 4th Ed. New York, Harper & Row, 1966, pp. 3–45.

Sliepcevich, E. M.: Echoes from the past. Journal of School Health, *30:*205–211 (May) 1960.

Turner, C. E., Sellery, C. M., and Smith, S. L.: School Health and Health Education. 5th Ed. St. Louis, The C. V. Mosby Company, 1966, pp. 3–36.

Willgoose, C. E.: Health Education in the Elementary School. 2nd Ed. Philadelphia, W. B. Saunders Company, 1964, pp. 1–19.

2

HEALTH NEEDS OF THE GROWING CHILD AND YOUTH: A BASIS FOR HEALTH EDUCATION

In health teaching, decisions must constantly be made on what to teach. The field of health is so vast it cannot possibly be covered fully in a school curriculum. Moreover, health needs and concerns differ widely among children. Teachers and curriculum builders alike must choose the content of health instruction so that it has meaning and value at any one time, as well as over a span of time as children progress through school years.

Health needs of growing children and youth, as well as of their homes and communities, form the basis for decisions on the selection of health content. In this chapter health needs of the school-age child are summarized with special reference to their implications for health teaching. In Chapter 3, the needs of the home, school, and community are likewise summarized.

Each child has his own assortment of health needs and problems which require individual attention. Individual problems may range from momentary difficulties, like a cut finger, to conditions requiring long-term adjustments, like chronic heart disease. Many needs, however, are common to large numbers of children and youth and vary only in their detailed manifestations at different maturity levels and in different kinds of communities. Some are related directly to the life processes, such as eating and sleeping. Others are related to physical, social, and cultural environments. All who are concerned with children must be aware of the individual needs of the child and deal with them with regard for the child's best welfare.

The common needs, however, can form a basis for selecting the major concepts and the content of health teaching of children in groups.

HOW A TEACHER CAN FIND OUT ABOUT CHILDREN'S HEALTH NEEDS

A teacher may identify the health needs of the children she teaches in a number of ways. Study of general data as given in this chapter is just a start. Specific procedures can be followed to obtain pertinent information about each child and each group of children. Among these procedures are observation, interviews and conferences, and study of records and reports.

Observation

A teacher who is living and working with children day in and day out is in a favorable position to observe their appearance and behavior. Among distinguishing signs of health are an abundance of vitality; bright, clear eyes; lustrous hair; good muscle tone; clear skin; good teeth; a hearty appetite; freedom from illness; freedom from correctable defects; a wholesome outlook on life; and ability to get along well with oneself and with others. Such a state of health is seldom the possession of any single individual. Consequently, careful observation of a classroom group is essential in order to find those children with deviations serious enough to require individual attention by teacher, parents, physician, or other specialized health personnel.

A generation ago it was common practice for teachers to make formal inspections of children each morning as they entered the classroom or as the teacher moved up and down the aisles. Such procedures were defended because of the prevalence of epidemics, skin infections, general uncleanliness, and other poor conditions. Ignored was the fact that illnesses or other deviations demanding immediate attention could occur during the day; ignored, too, was the effect that such openly conducted inspections could have on a child's emotional health.

Today teachers are encouraged to make observations informally and unobtrusively and to be alert at all times to factors in a child's appearance or behavior which may suggest that something is wrong. Wheatley and Hallock[1] point out that a teacher who needs to develop skills of observation can acquire them step-by-step. He might

---

[1] Wheatley, G. M., and Hallock, G. T.: Health Observation of School Children. 3rd Ed. New York, Blakiston Division, McGraw-Hill Book Company, 1965, pp. 9–10.

Figure 3. One can learn much about a child by talking with him. (Courtesy of the National Education Association.)

first look for just one thing in all the children, such as evidences of undue fatigue, until this particular observational skill is developed; he then might study one child carefully for any signs of departure from normal health and gradually extend such observations to the other children. As background for these observations, one should be familiar with the general growth and development characteristics of the age level of the children being taught. Information contained in Table 5 near the end of this chapter and in Chapters 8 and 9 should be helpful in this respect. One should also be familiar with the appearance and behavior of each child when he is well. Such knowledge will make a teacher more sensitive to conditions in the child which may suggest ill health, as for example, dull eyes, breathlessness, fatigue, or such personality changes as short temper and uncooperativeness. These signs may appear at any time during the day, and may occur while the child is working, resting, or exercising.

Interviews and Conferences

A teacher can learn much about a child by talking with the child himself or with parents, physicians, nurses, guidance counselors, social workers, and others who are in direct contact with the child. In conversations with the child, one can often learn about personal health habits and attitudes, such as food likes and dislikes and sleeping and play habits, as well as emotional problems and home life. Conferences with parents may reveal health problems or conditions not readily identified through observation alone, as, for example, the presence of diabetes or chronic heart disease. Health and related personnel may know of emotional, social, and economic problems, as well as physical health problems, that may affect the child's performance at school and his relationships with others. The nurse working in the school who also has contact with the home is often a key person in drawing a teacher's attention to health needs of specific children. Regular conferences with the nurse should be arranged for this purpose.

Records and Reports

In most school systems, teachers have access to a health record for each child. Health records are sometimes kept as separate records and sometimes as part of cumulative records. Well-kept records will reveal such conditions as defects that need correction, the status of immunizations, and evidences of faulty behavior patterns. These records will be passed along with the child as he moves through the different stages in his schooling and will have space for teachers to record their own observations. In some schools, the records are kept in the classrooms or by the homeroom teachers; in others, they are filed in the principal's office or health room. Wherever they are filed, teachers should review them periodically. Well-kept records that are readily accessible to teachers can provide much useful information for individual counseling and for determining those conditions which are common enough among a class as a whole to warrant group instruction.

HOW HEALTHY ARE OUR CHILDREN AND YOUTH?

The health of our children and youth has never been better than it is today. Improved health services are preventing many adverse conditions, detecting others before they become serious, and finding ways to bring more children under care. Modern medicine and surgery are saving the lives of many children and rehabilitating many more. Health education of children, parents, and community is producing results. Despite important gains in child health, however, far too many children and young people are not living at a level of optimum health and are not benefiting from preventive measures now available.

Deaths Among School-Age Children and Youth

Since World War II there has been a steady reduction in deaths from most causes which formerly accounted for loss of life among the school-age group. Moreover, the death rates for this group are far below those for the population as a whole. Table 1 compares death rates per 100,000 population for selected age groups, and by sex, for 1950 and 1965. It will be noted that rates in 1965 are con-

Table 1. *Death Rates Per 100,000 Population for Selected Age Groups, by Sex, United States, 1950 and 1965**

	1950			1965		
Age Group (years)	Both Sexes	Male	Female	Both Sexes	Male	Female
5–9	61.7	71.0	52.2	43.6	50.5	36.5
10–14	58.1	70.7	44.9	40.7	51.3	29.9
15–19	108.6	140.7	76.5	95.1	135.6	53.8
All ages	963.8	1,106.1	823.5	943.2	1,088.4	803.3

* Data provided through the courtesy of The National Center for Health Statistics, Public Health Service, U.S. Department of Health, Education and Welfare, Washington, D.C., March 1967.

Table 2.   *Deaths from Selected Causes by Selected Age Groups,
United States, 1965**

Cause of Death	Total	Age Group (years)		
		5–9	10–14	15–19
All causes	32,799	8,954	7,721	16,124
Accidents	17,016	3,911	3,480	9,625
Malignant neoplasms	3,846	1,449	1,116	1,281
Congenital malformations	1,552	667	455	430
Influenza and pneumonia	1,174	476	347	351
Homicide	976	120	129	727
Suicide	789	1	103	685
Vascular lesions affecting central nervous system	473	102	158	213
Chronic and unspecified nephritis and other renal sclerosis	335	57	101	177
Diabetes mellitus	181	39	76	66
Chronic rheumatic heart disease	178	11	34	133
Appendicitis	166	60	58	48
Asthma	164	38	57	69
Meningococcal infections	147	75	35	37
Acute nephritis and nephritis with edema including nephrosis	122	43	34	45
Deliveries and complications of pregnancy, childbirth, and the puerperium	119	—	3	116
Rheumatic fever	110	40	48	22
Measles	76	64	9	3
Tuberculosis, all forms	66	14	14	38
Acute poliomyelitis	20	5	7	8

* Data provided through the courtesy of The National Center for Health Statistics, Public Health Service, U.S Department of Health, Education and Welfare, Washington, D.C., March 1967.

siderably lower than those in 1950. In 1965, however, the death rate for ages 15 to 19, though lower than in 1950, was more than double that for each of the younger age groups but about one tenth of the rate for all ages of the population. Also to be noted is the much higher death rate for 15- to 19-year-old males.

Selected causes of death in 1965 are listed in Table 2. Accidents head the list and are responsible for over one half of the deaths at ages 15 to 19 years. Other leading causes are cancer (malignant neoplasms), congenital malformations, influenza and pneumonia, homicide, and suicide. Though the same conditions head the list of leading causes of death in 1950, the actual death rates for selected causes and age groups as found in Tables 3 and 4 present a more accurate picture of changes which have occurred in the 15-year period between 1950 and 1965.

Though each reader will wish to make his own comparisons, mention is made of a few of the most striking changes between 1950 and 1965. Death rates from accidents have decreased for ages 5 to 9 and 10 to 14, but have increased for ages 15 to 19. Homicide and suicide rates have increased to a startling degree.[2] Congenital

---

[2] In actual numbers, during 1965 a total of 789 children committed suicide in contrast to 321 in 1950, and of these, 103 in 1965, as against 37 in 1950, were only 10 to 14 years old.

Table 3. *Death Rates Per 100,000 Population for Selected Causes and Age Groups, United States, 1965**

Cause of Death	Age Group (years)		
	5–9	*10–14*	*15–19*
All causes	43.6	40.7	95.1
Accidents	19.1	18.4	56.8
Malignant neoplasms	7.1	5.9	7.6
Congenital malformations	3.3	2.4	2.5
Influenza and pneumonia	2.3	1.8	2.1
Homicide	0.6	0.7	4.3
Suicide	0.0	0.5	4.0
Vascular lesions affecting central nervous system	0.5	0.8	1.3
Chronic and unspecified nephritis and other renal sclerosis	0.3	0.5	1.0
Rheumatic fever and chronic rheumatic heart disease	0.2	0.4	0.9
Diabetes mellitus	0.2	0.4	0.4
Appendicitis	0.3	0.3	0.3
Asthma	0.2	0.3	0.4
Meningococcal infections	0.4	0.2	0.2
Acute nephritis and nephritis with edema including nephrosis	0.2	0.2	0.3
Deliveries and complications of pregnancy, childbirth, and the puerperium	—	0.0	0.7
Measles	0.3	0.0	0.0
Tuberculosis, all forms	0.1	0.1	0.2
Acute poliomyelitis	0.0	0.0	0.0

* Data provided through the courtesy of The National Center for Health Statistics, Public Health Service, U.S. Department of Health, Education and Welfare, Washington, D.C., March 1967.

Table 4. *Death Rates Per 100,000 Population for Selected Causes and Age Groups, United States, 1950**

Cause of Death	Age Group (years)		
	5–9	*10–14*	*15–19*
All Causes	61.7	58.1	108.6
Accidents	22.8	22.6	49.0
Malignant neoplasms	7.4	5.9	7.9
Congenital malformations	2.6	2.1	1.9
Influenza and pneumonia	3.6	2.6	3.1
Homicide	0.5	0.6	3.9
Suicide	0.0	0.3	2.7
Vascular lesions affecting central nervous system	0.4	0.5	1.1
Chronic and unspecified nephritis and other renal sclerosis	0.9	1.0	2.0
Rheumatic fever and chronic rheumatic heart disease	2.2	4.0	4.6
Diabetes mellitus	0.4	0.7	1.2
Appendicitis	1.0	1.0	1.2
Asthma	Not Available		
Meningococcal infections	0.6	0.4	0.4
Acute nephritis and nephritis with edema including nephrosis	0.7	0.7	0.9
Deliveries and complications of pregnancy, childbirth, and the puerperium	—	0.1	2.7
Measles	0.5	0.3	0.2
Tuberculosis, all forms	1.7	2.0	7.4
Acute poliomyelitis	2.6	2.3	1.7

* Data provided through the courtesy of The National Center for Health Statistics, Public Health Service, U.S. Department of Health, Education and Welfare, Washington, D.C., March 1967.

malformations also show an increase. Decreases in death rates have been greatest for those conditions for which there are now improved methods of prevention or treatment. Acute poliomyelitis has all but disappeared. Tuberculosis, measles, rheumatic fever, and chronic rheumatic heart disease now take far fewer lives, as do diabetes and kidney conditions.

Extent of Illnesses and Impairments Among School-Age Children and Youth

Despite important strides in child health care, many children of school age are burdened with illnesses and impairments that keep them from functioning at their optimal level. Some adverse conditions result in absences from school or even in hospitalization. Others are so prolonged that they require special educational facilities or home care. Too many of these conditions have existed undetected before the child entered school, and too many go undetected or untreated throughout the school years.

Complete nation-wide statistics on illnesses and impairments are not available. Because physicians are not required to report such conditions, accurate data are difficult to secure. We must therefore rely upon findings of special studies to gain some idea of the extent and seriousness of health problems of the school-age child.

The most comprehensive information available about health conditions of the general population has been gathered over a period of years through visits to households. Recent data from this National Health Survey are contained in a publication of the Children's Bureau entitled *Health of Children of School Age*, along with selected data from other studies.[3] A few items of special importance to teachers are summarized here.

Acute illnesses are very prevalent among school-age children. In the year ending June 1961, the National Health Survey found 169,892,000 acute conditions among children under 15, amounting to three episodes of acute illness per year for every child. More than half of these conditions were categorized as respiratory. Acute conditions resulted in an average of four days per child lost from school during one year.

Chronic conditions are also widespread. For the period July 1959 through June 1961, the National Health Survey data showed that almost one child in every five under the age of 17, or 18 per cent of children in that age group, had at least one chronic condition. Hay fever, asthma, and all other allergies along with sinusitis, bronchitis, and other respiratory diseases accounted for almost half of all the chronic conditions for children under age 17.

---

[3] Health of Children of School Age. Children's Bureau Publication No. 427–1964. Washington, D.C., U.S. Government Printing Office, 1964, 31 pp.

	1960	1970
Epilepsy (under 21)	360,000	450,000
Cerebral palsy (under 21)	370,000	465,000
Mentally retarded (under 21)	2,180,000	2,720,000
Eye conditions needing specialist's care including refractive errors (5–17)	10,200,000	12,500,000
Hearing loss (under 21)	360,000–725,000	450,000–900,000
Speech (5–20)	2,580,000	3,270,000
Cleft palate–cleft lip	95,000	120,000
Orthopedic (under 21)	1,925,000	2,425,000
Congenital heart disease	About 25,000 born each year, of whom 7,000 die in the first year	
Emotionally disturbed (5–17)	4,000,000	5,400,000

The study showed that not only do children live through several episodes of acute illness before they enter school, but they also begin to accumulate chronic diseases which will increase as they get older.

Estimates of the number of handicapped children in the nation are startling. Though precise data are not available, the foregoing estimates for 1960 and the projected figures for 1970 indicate the immensity of the problem:[4] It is said that by standards of education about 12 per cent of children of school age are in need of special education because of handicapping conditions.

Data from examinations of selective service registrants have provided additional information on the health status of our youth. A report of the President's Task Force on Manpower Conservation on January 1, 1964, states that 15 per cent of all males were disqualified for military service between August 1958 and June 1960 for medical reasons. Though many of the conditions that cause rejection (e.g., epilepsy, diabetes, and certain orthopedic disorders) cannot be prevented with our present knowledge, many others are preventable or treatable, such as eye and ear defects and hernias. The many psychiatric disorders, high on the list of causes for medical rejections, merit special concern by medical authorities and educators.

In later sections of this chapter disabling conditions are discussed further. The teacher who would learn about the health status of his particular group, however, must gather facts locally, as suggested earlier in this chapter.

SPECIFIC HEALTH NEEDS

The growth and development of the child and the maintenance and improvement of his health are dependent upon meeting certain

---

[4] Health of Children of School Age. Children's Bureau Publication No. 427–1964. Washington, D.C., U.S. Government Printing Office, 1964, p. 6.

basic needs. Needs that are common to all age levels are discussed in this chapter under the following headings:

Food and Eating
Elimination of Body Wastes
Exercise and Play
Sleep, Rest, and Relaxation
Prevention of Handicapping Defects

Prevention and Control of Illness and Disease
Safety
Mental Health
Development of Healthy Sexuality
Other Needs

These needs are further analyzed by age levels in Table 5 as well as in Chapters 8 and 9.

Food and Eating

Food is the source of nutrients required for body building, production of energy and warmth, and maintenance of health. Nutrition authorities recommend that a healthy person select his daily diet around the following four food groups. Adherence to this flexible daily food plan helps assure adequate quantities of all nutrients required for health and growth.

A Daily Food Guide[5]

Milk group (Some milk for everyone)
    Children   3 to 4 cups
    Teen-agers   4 or more cups
    Adults   2 or more cups
Meat group (Two or more servings)
    Beef, veal, pork, lamb, poultry, fish, eggs
    As alternates—dry beans, dry peas, nuts
Vegetable-fruit group (Four or more servings)
    A citrus fruit or other fruit or vegetable important for vitamin C
    A dark-green or deep-yellow vegetable for vitamin A at least every other day
    Other vegetables and fruits, including potatoes
Bread-cereal group (Four or more servings)
    Whole grain, enriched, or restored

People in our country are, on the whole, eating well, according to findings of medical studies on nutritional status and surveys of food consumption made throughout the United States from 1947 through 1958 by over two hundred professional nutrition investigators. Foods eaten by both boys and girls up to age 12 in all regions were estimated to be adequate, except that intake of calcium was slightly low for girls. Between the ages of 13 to 20 years, boys were

---

[5] Food for Fitness. U.S. Department of Agriculture Leaflet No. 424. Washington, D.C., U.S. Government Printing Office, 1963.

eating enough of all nutrients except vitamin C, but the girls in this age range showed intake that was seriously low in calcium, iron, thiamine, and ascorbic acid and somewhat low in calories and protein. Such overall average estimates can be deceiving, however, for they conceal diet deficiencies of specific individuals or groups of individuals. Actually, many children in our country still have diets that are far from adequate.[6]

Children and youth could eat better even when good food is at hand. This fact is borne out by diet studies of 5,771 public school pupils in Austin, Minnesota, a community of about 30,000 persons located in the midst of one of the most extensive food-raising sections of the country. In an analysis made during early February, 1958, of the information obtained in a three-day survey of food consumption by pupils, about one quarter of the diets were classified as "poor," with the junior high school group reporting the highest per cent of "poor" diets. Fewer than one half of the pupils reported having recommended amounts of citrus fruits and "other fruits and vegetables." Although 60 per cent of the pupils in this dairy region reported that they drank an average of three cups of milk a day, the study showed a different pattern for each sex. Milk consumption by girls decreased with grade in school to the point at which only 42 per cent of senior high school girls were drinking the recommended amounts. Milk consumption by boys remained fairly constant through junior high school and then increased so that in senior high school 76 per cent of the boys were drinking the recommended amounts.[7]

Another study, conducted among school children in Iowa, showed that diets were plentiful in meat, potatoes, sweet desserts, table fats, and cereals, but inadequate in milk and vitamin-rich fruits and vegetables. More than half the teen-age girls had very poor diets, with the most conspicuous deficiency among the over-size girls who apparently preferred calorie-rich foods to those rich in calcium and vitamins.[8]

More recently, and as a part of a larger study, an analysis was made of dietary records kept by about 1,000 boys and girls from ninth through twelfth grade within the Berkeley (California) Unified School District. Their eating patterns during a four-week period have been described as follows:

The average nutrient intake for boys almost met or exceeded the Recommended Dietary Allowances of the National Research Council, which is a generous

6 Morgan, A. F., Editor: Nutritional Status U.S.A. Bulletin 769. Berkeley, Calif., California Agricultural Experiment Station, 1959, 131 pp.

7 Stief, R.: Nutrition studies. From Austin (Minn.) School Health Study. American Journal of Public Health, 52:303–305 (Feb.) 1962.

8 Eppright, E. S., and Roderuck, C.: Diet and nutritional status of Iowa school children. American Journal of Public Health, 45:464–471 (April) 1955.

yardstick. The average intake for the girls was low in iron and calcium. . . . Calorie intakes varied a great deal from person to person and from day to day for the same person. Most of the calories consumed by the boys came from the meat group, followed closely by dairy products, then cereal products, and desserts and sweets. For the girls the chief suppliers of calories, in descending order, were dairy products, the meat group, desserts and sweets, and the cereal group. In general the obese teenagers ate less than the non-obese and their diets were lower in nutrient value. They were more likely to skip meals, did less snacking, and ate fewer fruits and vegetables. Most of the teenagers snacked, some many times a day, and the snacks made varying contributions to the nutrient value of their diets. For the student who snacked, the choice of snacks would often determine the quality of the diet.[9]

Among other findings of the study, about 60 per cent of the girls said they wanted to lose weight while in fact, according to their measurements, only about 17 per cent needed to do so. The majority of both sexes expressed interest in modifying their size, shape, fatness, or leanness. While the boys wanted to gain weight or muscularity and to do it through exercise, the girls wanted to lose weight or dimensions and, as first choice, to do it through dieting.

The generally poor showing among teen-age girls has led to intensified efforts to improve the quality of nutritional intake of this important group. Dr. Pauline Stitt has aptly said: "What of the adolescent girl? For whom is she eating? For herself and how many unborn children or even unborn generations? . . . Whoever provides good nutrition for an adolescent girl may unwittingly influence multitudes, not only through the care and replenishment of the girl's own physical resources, but through awakening her to awareness of good nutrition, so that at a later time she may guide and protect those who come into her life."[10]

Obesity is a special problem requiring individualized attention. Medical authorities agree that the causes of obesity are complex and not fully understood, and that treatment or management is often difficult. Many obese children have problems of psychological or social adjustment. Lonely, frustrated, and distressed by their appearance, they may sit around all day and seek satisfaction through eating. Not all obese young people consume more calories than their peers; they usually are more inactive, however. Obese children often have parents who are overweight. This may be due partly to genetic predispositions and partly to family and cultural food patterns, as well as to cultural attitudes toward obesity. In some societies, for example, obesity is considered a sign of affluence.

Pediatricians stress that in counseling obese children, better

---

9 Shapiro, L. R., Hampton, M. C., and Huenemann, R. L.: Teenagers: their body size and shape, food, and activity. Journal of School Health, *37*:167–168 (April) 1967.

10 Stitt, P. C.: Growth and development expectancies as feeding guides. School Lunch Journal, *16*:56 (March) 1962.

results may be obtained by encouraging increased physical and social activity as well as regulation of diets. Such attention should be given from the earliest evidences of obesity in an effort to prevent the more persistent obesity of later years. A young person must have the motivation to lose weight. Without motivation, his attempts to lose weight under pressure may result in failure and aggravate his difficulties. Schools can foster better balance in food intake through education and school feeding programs. They can provide outlets for satisfying social activity and relationships. They should not attempt to conduct reducing classes, however. Obesity is too complex a condition to deal with in this manner, and the potential harm to individuals could be considerable. For many obese children, medical counseling will be needed.

We have ample evidence that in our educational efforts we must emphasize how to make intelligent selection of food, both in quality and quantity. Young people must have enough information so that in regulating their diets they avoid the trap of diet fads. Nutrition education in the classroom should be linked with the school lunch program which gives children opportunity to practice good eating habits. In many instances the root of correction lies in family education, with careful thought given to the economic, psychological, social, and cultural patterns that lead to poor food habits. Education of the pupils themselves will be more effective as it becomes synchronized with family and community education.

Elimination of Body Wastes

Waste products of the body, including products of metabolism and unused food materials, must be removed regularly through the organs of elimination, which include the lungs, skin, kidneys, and intestines.

Elimination of wastes such as urine through the kidneys and feces through the intestines is a highly variable process, both as to frequency and amount. Sometimes teachers forget this fact and try to make all children conform to the same toilet routines. There are differences between children, and day-to-day differences in the same child depending upon how much water or food has been taken, or upon emotional or other factors.

Nausea, vomiting, diarrhea, constipation, and other digestive disturbances are not uncommon among children and youth. Temporary upsets are often caused by overeating, or by excitement or fatigue. Since digestive disturbances can mean symptoms of other more serious conditions such as appendicitis or intestinal infections, they should not be taken lightly, especially if they are very severe or prolonged.

There are several health education implications in the foregoing facts. To allow children to use the toilet whenever they indicate a need is an informal educational procedure which contributes to good habit formation. Instruction on elimination processes themselves, and on factors that contribute to good elimination, provides a rational basis for the development of good toilet habits. Moreover, a friendly and informal classroom, in which children are free from undue tensions, helps to prevent digestive and elimination disturbances caused by emotional factors.

Instruction on cleanliness of the skin should include information on the need for bathing to remove wastes of the body that are excreted through the skin. When these excretions are allowed to accumulate, they produce undesirable odors and contribute to poor skin conditions. Such instruction is especially pertinent for young people troubled with acne.

Exercise and Play

Healthy children are always active. Exercise is one of their most fundamental needs. Exercise improves muscle tone, which influences posture and the processes of elimination, and helps to develop strength and endurance. Activity is especially important in controlling obesity. Exercise through games, sports, and rhythm develops coordination and useful skills. The satisfactions derived from coordinated body movement, skills learned, and the experience of playing with others promote mental and emotional health.

Natural opportunities for healthful exercise occur less frequently than in the past. With more children riding to school than walking and with fewer home chores to be done, a positive effort must be made to provide organized physical activity. The extent of the problem is shown in findings of the Berkeley study referred to in the section on food and eating. The average boy in grades nine through twelve spent amounts of time during a day in different classes of activity as follows:[11]

Activity	Time Spent
Sleep	8 hours, 57 minutes
Very light	10 hours, 5 minutes
Light	3 hours, 16 minutes
Moderate	1 hour, 21 minutes
Strenuous	21 minutes

These data are based on four separate seven-day records. The average girl varied only slightly from this pattern of activity. Further, it was shown that for students who tended to be physically lethargic, the physical education class made a considerable difference in the

---

11 Shapiro, L. R., et al.: Teenagers: their body size and shape, food, and activity, p. 168.

amount of activity reported. Influence of the physical education class was also evident when comparing the amount of activity during the school year and in the vacation period.

Good programs of physical education under proper leadership are more important than ever. They not only can help provide the physical activity needed for growth and development but can also contribute to the social, emotional, and moral fitness of our children and youth.

Exercise and play in the out-of-doors provide opportunity for children to be exposed to sunlight, which is needed for growth and health. Sunlight helps the body to produce vitamain D, a substance which aids the body in its use of calcium and phosphorus, essential for development of teeth and bones and for good general health. Sunlight also contributes to a feeling of well-being.[12]

Sleep, Rest, and Relaxation

Everybody needs sleep. In children, too little sleep or rest interferes with nutrition and thus with growth; it accentuates fears and muscular tics, produces extreme discomfort, and contributes to fatigue. Within a wide range of individual differences, sleep requirements for school-age children are said to be:[13]

Age	Hours of Sleep
5 years	11–13
10 years	10–12
15 years	9–11
20 years	8–9

Sleep habits, for good or bad, will have been developed long before school years. Some of the conditions that help in the development of good sleep habits are regularity in retiring hours; a quiet, relaxing period before going to bed; comfortable bed clothing; and good attitudes toward sleep.

The growing child needs periods of rest and relaxation, which should be properly alternated with periods of work and active play in accordance with his individual requirements.

Fatigue is an all-too-common condition among both elementary and secondary school pupils. Children who are under emotional strain, who habitually have too little sleep, who are overactive or malnourished, and whose bodies are weakened by infection are easy victims of fatigue. Children should be taught how to relax and to

---

[12] For further reading see: Exercise and fitness. Journal of Health–Physical Education–Recreation, 35:42–44, 82 (May) 1964. (Joint Statement from American Medical Association and American Association for Health, Physical Education, and Recreation.)

[13] Sleep and Children. A Report of the Joint Committee on Health Problems in Education of the National Education Association and the American Medical Association. Washington, D.C., National Education Association, 1956, p. 12.

take responsibility for securing enough rest and sleep under favorable conditions.

Prevention of Handicapping Defects

A great many children are victims of handicapping defects which lower physical efficiency and cause poor emotional, social, and scholastic adjustment. The most common defects are discussed here.

Vision

Good vision is of limitless value to children, yet large numbers of children have eye conditions needing special care.[14]

Refractive errors, that is, farsightedness, nearsightedness, and astigmatism, account for the greatest percentage of eye defects. Some eye disorders are the result of infections, injuries, and irritations, but application of modern medical knowledge has greatly decreased the number of cases of blindness caused by these factors.

Eye fatigue is a common difficulty observable in the school-age child. It may or may not be associated with an eye defect. Poor visual habits, failure to wear proper glasses when they are needed, faulty lighting, and doing fine work such as sewing or reading small print all contribute to eye fatigue.

The relationship of television to eye fatigue is of considerable interest to teachers. Conditions which aggravate eye fatigue include pictures which are indistinct, grainy, or with light bands; too great a contrast between illumination in the room and on the screen; and length of viewing. Rest periods are needed to minimize the fatigue.

Young people need to be taught how best to care for and to protect their eyes. The teaching should deal with maintenance of good body health and nutrition; protection from infections and injury; practice of good eye hygiene, including good reading habits under proper lighting conditions; and use of glasses when needed. Periodic eye examinations are essential and may be linked directly to the educational program.

Hearing

Good hearing is needed to keep one in active touch with people and events. Poor hearing, on the other hand, may make a

---

[14] For a summary of available data on the extent of eye difficulties, see Wallace, H. M.: Health Services for Mothers and Children. Philadelphia, W. B. Saunders Company, 1962, pp. 384–385.

Figure 4. Periodic hearing tests can be educational. (Courtesy of the Chicago Public Schools, Chicago, Illinois.)

child seem dull and inattentive, and may eventually lead to serious emotional disturbances, retardation in school, and speech defects. There are many children under 21 years of age with impaired hearing.[15]

Hearing impairments may be temporary or permanent. Temporary hearing loss is common among school children and frequently is caused by an accumulation of wax in the ears or by the common cold, which temporarily produces stoppage of the passages that lead from the throat to the middle ear.

Modern methods used to detect hearing loss have uncovered large numbers of children who have permanent hearing impairments which are frequently caused by infections, especially of the middle ear, and by injuries to the ear drum or other parts of the ear. Among other causes of hearing loss are heredity and damage produced by such diseases as measles, mastoid infection, scarlet fever, and congenital syphilis. Neglect of any ear difficulties may result in permanent damage to this delicate organ. Recent studies have shown that prolonged exposure to excessive noise may result in permanent hearing loss in adults.

We need to instruct children on how to prevent unnecessary infections or injuries to the ears, and on the importance of seeking early medical care for ear infections. There should be developed in children an awareness that wax should be removed, and an understanding of how to have it removed safely. They should also learn the precautions to be taken to protect the ear in sports, such as swimming and diving.

Periodic hearing tests may be used, not only to discover early hearing losses, but also as an educational device to arouse children's interest in the care of ears and in the importance of seeking medical advice when indicated.

Teeth

Sound teeth are a great asset. They contribute to a pleasing personal appearance and help in the proper chewing and digestion of food. Missing or irregular teeth may cause speech defects; they may also cause unpleasant facial expressions and, in severe cases, deformity of the jaw.

Data accumulated from many studies throughout the country show that children who reach school age average three or more decayed primary teeth, while less than four per cent of high school pupils are free of dental decay.[16]

---

[15] For a summary of available data on the extent of hearing impairments, see Wallace, H. M.: Health Services for Mothers and Children. Philadelphia, W. B. Saunders Company, 1962, pp. 395–396.

[16] Dental Health Facts for Teachers. Chicago, Ill., American Dental Association, 1960, p. 11.

The causes of dental caries (dental decay) are not known with certainty. Some of the factors believed to be causes are as follows: the action of bacteria in the mouth which thrive in the presence of carbohydrates, especially sweets; malnutrition, including deficiency of fluorides; lack of care; and heredity.

On the basis of our present knowledge, dental education programs for all school-age groups should stress four main points in the prevention and control of dental caries, namely, timely dental care; eating the right kinds of food; cleanliness; and use of fluorides, a chemical that reduces dental decay.

Visit the dentist.   Children should be encouraged first of all to visit the dentist regularly and often. The most recent data from the National Health Survey,[17] however, indicate that about 50 per cent of all children under 15 years of age have never visited a dentist. Those in the highest family income group have a rate of dental visits about five times as high as those of corresponding age in the lowest family income group. While only 5 per cent of dental visits in the high income bracket were for extractions, 32 per cent of the visits in the lowest income bracket were for that purpose.[18] Though some improvements in dental care through dental visits can be expected as a result of the dental education of the school-age child, the problem goes far deeper and must be attacked on a community-wide basis as well. Intensified parent education is needed to initiate dental visits during preschool years. Dental health programs need to be established for medically indigent families, and the public must be awakened to the extent and the seriousness of the problem and the importance of providing adequate dental health care for all children.

Proper foods.   A proper diet is important for sound teeth for a twofold reason. During the development of the temporary and permanent teeth, and until the child reaches age thirteen, a good diet helps to build sound teeth. Throughout the period of growth, good general nutrition is essential for normal growth and development, including the development of teeth. The second reason why diet is important is that a diet too rich in carbohydrates may foster the growth of decay-producing bacteria, as mentioned earlier. Thus, children who habitually suck candy, chew gum, consume soft drinks, eat rich pastries, and otherwise crowd their diets with sweets are creating a condition in their mouths which is favorable to the growth of bacteria. An educational program for most children will need to stress reduction of sweets in the diet.

---

[17] Medical Care, Health Status, and Family Income. National Center for Health Statistics Series 10, No. 9. Washington, D.C., U.S. Government Printing Office, 1964, pp. 34, 36–37. (Data from National Health Survey, Public Health Service.)

[18] For a helpful summary of recent data see Dental disease, a continuing health problem. Currents in Public Health, 7:1–4 (March) 1967. (A publication of Ross Laboratories, Columbus, Ohio.)

Cleanliness.   Good oral hygiene through proper tooth brushing, though having limited value in the prevention of caries, should nevertheless be encouraged. Everyone knows that clean teeth look better and feel better than teeth that are neglected. In addition, children should be taught the importance of having teeth cleaned at the dentist's office once or twice a year. The dentist will remove tartar and other accumulated deposits or stains.

Fluorides.   The most recent development in the prevention and control of dental decay is the use of fluorides. Fluorides may be applied directly to the teeth by the dentist at appropriate ages. They may also be added at low cost to public water supplies and thus reach all children drinking from the supplies in amounts sufficient to reduce decay. Some dentifrices also contain beneficial fluorides. Fluorides are especially effective during the formation of the teeth, or from birth to eight to ten years of age. Children who are older at the time fluoridation starts may benefit to a lesser degree. Studies extending over a ten-year period in New York State[19] and Michigan[20] show convincingly that the caries rate among children aged six to nine who had been drinking fluoridated water all their lives was about 60 per cent lower than among children in comparable communities in which the water was not fluoridated. Some reduction in caries also occurred among older children whose teeth had already been calcified when fluoridation started. It should be remembered that benefits from fluoridation gained during the growth period last through adulthood. More and more communities are fluoridating their water supplies. They are receiving active support from the medical and dental professions, public health authorities, and many civic groups. The participation of schools in educational efforts for fluoridation is needed.

Orthopedic Defects

Children with orthopedic defects, that is, defects of bones, muscles or joints, have various degrees of incapacity for normal body activity.

Poor posture is a common orthopedic defect in school children. Attempts at correction are often based on the assumption that there is a standard type of posture to which every child can be made to conform through proper posture training. Commonly accepted standards of good posture are being questioned today by many pediatricians. It is now generally agreed that posture is an indi-

19 Hilleboe, H. E., et al.: Newburgh-Kingston caries-fluorine study—final report. Journal of the American Dental Association, *52:*290–325 (March) 1956.

20 Arnold, F. A., Jr., et al.: Effect of fluoridated public water supplies on dental caries prevalence. Tenth year of the Grand Rapids–Muskegon study. Public Health Reports, *71:*652–658 (July) 1956.

vidual characteristic. Each age group during the period of growth and development has its characteristic posture pattern. Moreover, each child has his own pattern; that is, he will sit, stand, and walk his own way. A well child naturally has manifestations of good posture; he holds himself fairly straight, but not necessarily in rigid conformity to the standards often pictured in health books.

Children may have poor posture for several reasons, the most common of which is fatigue. As we have seen earlier, posture can be affected by such conditions as inadequate sleep, malnourishment, or emotional strain. Sometimes poor posture is caused by transient mannerisms which will disappear if no one pays attention to them. At other times it is caused by specific local physical strains, such as those incurred from carrying a newspaper bag or from doing heavy farm work. It may be caused by skeletal diseases such as bone tuberculosis and osteomyelitis, or by nervous and muscular disorders such as cerebral palsy. It cannot be overemphasized, however, that the greatest percentage of postural defects are those associated with fatigue, which is common in the thin, nervous child who lacks proper nourishment and care. Poor posture, then, is usually a symptom rather than a cause of a difficulty, and should be handled accordingly. Grave injustice is done to children in overstressing the mechanical correction of poor posture without giving proper attention to determining and removing its underlying causes.

Health instruction for the prevention or correction of poor posture, as for so many other health needs, should concern itself with teaching the principles of good nutrition, accident prevention, and the maintenance of physical and emotional health in general. Physical education may go beyond this and under proper medical guidance help children to correct many faulty posture habits.

Much could be written about other orthopedic defects which cripple thousands of children and which are too often neglected in school health programs. The tremendous advances in medical science and rehabilitation services now make possible the prevention or correction of many of the defects. Because of early correction, fewer cases of prenatal defects, i.e., club foot and wryneck, are seen at school than in the past. Osteomyelitis (a bone infection), rickets (a nutritional disease), and tuberculosis of the bones and joints are now infrequent. Crippling poliomyelitis has left its mark, but virtually no new cases are appearing because of widespread use of oral vaccines. Though cerebral palsy, a condition caused by brain damage, cannot be cured, much can be done to help children with cerebral palsy to live happy, productive lives. Permanent bone and joint damage from accidents and injuries can be prevented, or minimized, with modern medical treatment.

Health instruction in connection with orthopedic defects must vary with the condition. When the defect is permanent the child must be helped to accept the condition and to learn how to live effectively with it. In an increasing number of school systems, handicapped children, except for the severely disabled, are kept in the regular classroom for as much of the day as possible. Teachers must help the child's associates to understand his special needs and accept him as a regular member of the group. There is a vast amount of educating to be done within schools and communities to publicize not only the resources needed but also those now available, or potentially available, for special education, medical care, and rehabilitation of the handicapped.

Prevention and Control of Illness and Disease

Disabling illnesses and diseases interfere with the child's growth and development. Acute conditions may cause only temporary disability, but sometimes, as in the case of measles, they may permanently damage the body. Chronic illnesses such as rheumatic fever are even more likely to do permanent harm. No attempt will be made here to describe in detail the many illnesses and diseases that beset childhood and adolescence. This information can be secured from other sources. Neither will all the factors involved in communicable disease control be described. It is assumed that the reader is familiar with these factors through previous study. Rather, a brief summary will be given of a few illnesses and diseases of special importance among school-age children and of the contributions that health education can make to their prevention and control.

Acute Illnesses and Diseases

The common cold. The cold, prevalent at all ages, causes much discomfort and absenteeism. When a cold is not properly cared for, secondary infections may follow, among which are bronchitis, sinusitis, pneumonia, and middle ear infections. On the other hand, several specific diseases, for example, measles, whooping cough, mumps, and diphtheria, may be ushered in by symptoms that resemble a cold. Allergic conditions and asthma may at times be mistaken for a cold.

A child with a cold should stay at home until the acute stage is over in order to protect himself from the hazards of further infections. There is no known method for the prevention of colds. The way in which cold viruses spread makes it impossible with our present inadequate knowledge to keep people from having colds. Education, therefore, should be directed toward proper care of a

Figure 5. Learning how to live with a handicapping condition. (Courtesy of the National Education Association.)

cold and toward maintaining good general health as a means of withstanding the effects of a cold.

Other childhood diseases. Rapid changes are occurring in the prevention and control of many of the childhood diseases which over the years have taken their toll in illness and death. Science is discovering new vaccines or other immunizing agents which give promise of virtually eliminating many of these diseases. Throughout the country intensive programs are now in progress to immunize children of all ages against smallpox, diphtheria, whooping cough, tetanus, poliomyelitis, and, most recently, measles. Further, German measles and mumps may soon be added to the list if experimental vaccines now being developed with encouraging results become available.

Continuing education is needed to maintain immunization levels. Immunizations during infancy are not enough; they must be followed periodically by further immunizations because we lose our immunity. Thus, schools as well as health agencies have a constant task of stressing the importance of immunizations to both parents and children. Moreover, school-age children and youth can assume some responsibility as citizens in promoting participation of others in immunization programs.

We cannot be complacent in our efforts to keep these diseases in check. Serious outbreaks have occurred when communities became negligent in maintaining immunization levels. Diphtheria and smallpox are two deadly diseases now thought by many to be no longer a threat in the United States. Yet, as recently as 1956, Detroit, long known for its excellent public health program, reported an outbreak of over 150 cases of diphtheria, most of which were in unimmunized children. Smallpox outbreaks have occurred in the United States until recently. Even in Western European countries which are sophisticated in regard to health, 63 cases and 12 deaths of this dread disease occurred in late 1961 and early 1962, mostly in England and Germany. Introduced by travelers from areas of the world where smallpox still exists among the population, the disease was spread to others not recently protected by vaccination. In 1967, smallpox again appeared in Europe, spread from an outbreak in India.

Chronic Illnesses and Diseases

Cancer. Cancer (malignant neoplasms) is the leading cause of death from disease among children of school age. Over one third of these deaths are due to leukemia, for which a cure has not yet been found. Many schools include units of study on cancer, not only because this is a disease that can afflict young people but also because school-age youth are today often in families with older people who have cancer. Instruction which stresses the importance of early diagnosis and treatment and presents the hopeful aspects of cancer control can do much to allay fear now and in the future.

Rheumatic fever and rheumatic heart disease. In recent years, an extensive nation-wide program of education has been conducted for the prevention of rheumatic fever. Emphasis is on vigorous treatment and prevention of streptococcal infections, an underlying cause of the disease. If effective drugs are adequately used when streptococcal infections occur, rheumatic fever can be prevented. When the same drugs are taken regularly following an acute attack of rheumatic fever, the chance of a recurrence is greatly diminished. According to authorities, about one third of those who become afflicted with rheumatic fever recover completely, another third have some heart damage but lead normal lives, and one third have such serious heart damage that their activities must be curtailed. Education must give emphasis to early diagnosis and treatment of streptococcal infections so as to cut down initial attacks and recurrences. Children who have had the disease and have recovered need intelligent guidance in their activities and in the use of controlling drugs so they may return to normal living. Though much progress has been made in recent years in reducing rheumatic fever and rheumatic heart disease, much remains to be done.

Tuberculosis. Formerly the leading cause of death from disease during adolescence, tuberculosis no longer holds this position. Modern methods of control and treatment and generally higher living standards are important factors in its decline. In this country, a nation-wide program is directed toward finding all hidden cases of tuberculosis and putting these cases under treatment. Tuberculin testing of school children, chest x-ray studies of positive reactors, and also x-ray screening of adults in populations having high rates are part of this program. So, too, are efforts to educate people in the prevention and control of tuberculosis. That these efforts are producing results is attested by data provided by the National Center for Health Statistics of the Public Health Service (see Tables 2 to 4). In 1950, 1,230 children aged 5 to 19 died of tuberculosis. In 1965, only 66 children in the same age group died of the disease. In the age group from 15 to 19 years, tuberculosis death rates per 100,000 children dropped from 7.4 to 0.2 during the same period while deaths dropped from 790 to 38.

Venereal diseases. Syphilis and gonorrhea, diseases transmitted almost exclusively through sexual intercourse, are on the increase in the United States. The greatest percentage increase is among teen-agers. In a New York City study of 600 adolescents attending social hygiene clinics,[21] it was found that those most likely to become infected came from impoverished homes, were frequently early school dropouts, and, especially the boys, promiscuous. Homosexual activity was reported by 115 youths, mostly boys. When asked what they did in their spare time, 509 of these young people replied, "Nothing." The parents of these adolescents were interviewed about the illness of their children and, contrary to common belief, showed concern and frequently asked for help in dealing with the problem.

Venereal diseases, though more common among certain groups, as suggested earlier, can be found among young people from all social and economic levels, and are increasingly becoming recognized as symptoms of "psychic distress in a world of changing values" which can be attacked at their roots only by reaching into the very fiber of our society. These diseases can, however, be brought under greater control than at present by more intensive case finding (including the tracing of contacts), treatment, and education.

Control efforts in the past have been hampered by widespread ignorance as to the dangers of venereal diseases and by fear of condemnation on the part of infected persons should infection be disclosed. Fortunately, a phenomenal change is taking place in the willingness of schools, health authorities, parent groups, and the press to engage actively in educational efforts to inform young people and adults about venereal diseases and to encourage immediate treatment should infection be suspected. Vast amounts of educational material to aid in this task are now available from local, state, and federal health agencies.

Within schools, venereal disease education should be introduced as a part of education on communicable diseases at both junior and senior high school levels. The subject should be treated scientifically and objectively, and the sexes, in most schools, should not be segregated for such instruction. As with other communicable diseases, instruction should cover cause, effect, transmission, treatment, prevention, and what the individual and community must do for control. Scientific facts about the disease should be stressed especially during junior high school years to reach potential dropouts who might otherwise not receive basic information. During senior high school years the social and public health aspects should be given attention. Instruction on venereal diseases could be included in health and biology courses, and the social aspects could be dealt with not only in these courses but also in social studies and literature classes. Many educators believe that the subject does not belong

---

[21] Deschin, C. S.: Teenagers and Venereal Disease. Distributed by the American Social Health Association, 1740 Broadway, New York. (Reprint from July–August 1962 issue of Children.)

in units on family life education and sex education, which have other objectives.

Safety

Many lives are needlessly lost and many people are incapacitated for useful work because of accidents and injuries. Bodily injury may cause crippling, emotional and social disturbances, sickness, or even death.

Accidents lead all other causes of death among school-age children. In 1964, a total of 7,400 children from ages 5 to 14 were killed by accidents.[22] The four leading causes of accidental deaths at this age were, in order of importance: motor vehicle accidents, 3,430; drownings, 1,467; fires and burns, 726; and firearms, 422. In the same year and for the same age range, the national accident rate per 100,000 children was 19.1, less than half of what it was in 1922 (40.0), the year safety education was introduced in the schools. Comparable figures are not available for ages 15 to 19, but in the age range from 15 to 24 years, total accidental deaths mounted to 17,420, with 12,400 listed as motor vehicle accidents.

Deaths from accidents are only a part of the picture. For every child killed by an accident, many more are injured or incapacitated. Through the cooperation of a large number of schools in different parts of the country, figures are now available for school jurisdiction accidents. In the 1965–1966 school year, the rates of school jurisdiction accidental injuries per 100,000 student days were as follows:

	Boys	Girls
Kindergarten	6.67	3.93
Grades 1–3	6.68	4.01
Grades 4–6	9.86	6.56
Grades 7–9	18.67	9.35
Grades 10–12	24.22	8.64

The tremendous increase in accident rates at junior and senior high school levels, especially among the boys, is of special concern to educators. Of concern, too, are the location and types of accidental pupil injuries under school jurisdiction. The following list of such injuries in elementary and secondary schools during the 1964–1965 school year has been taken from a more detailed list of estimates prepared by the National Safety Council.

---

[22] Unless otherwise stated, figures in this section are taken from: Accident Facts. Chicago, Illinois, National Safety Council, 1966, 96 pp., or from data provided the author by the Council.

Location and Type	Total	Boys	Girls
Total school jurisdiction	830,000	570,000	260,000
Shops and laboratories	42,000	35,000	7,000
Building (general)	125,000	75,000	50,000
Grounds (unorganized activities)	160,000	110,000	50,000
Grounds (miscellaneous)	55,000	35,000	20,000
Physical education	300,000	200,000	100,000
Intramural sports	15,500	12,000	3,500
Interscholastic sports	71,500	70,000	1,500
Special activities	4,000	1,000	3,000
Going to and from school (motor vehicle)	22,000	12,000	10,000
Going to and from school (not motor vehicle)	35,000	20,000	15,000

According to the National Safety Council, this pattern of school jurisdiction accidents changes but little from year to year. The Council has not attempted to collect data on the number of non-school jurisdiction accidents of school-age children because the number of reports is so low the data would have little value. Nevertheless, it is estimated that there are "no fewer than two non-school jurisdiction for each school jurisdiction accident." From reports that are available, home accidents led the list by a wide margin among elementary school children.

In 1962 and 1963, the Minnesota Department of Health conducted an eleven-month study of physician-attended injuries in Brown County, Minnesota, using data supplied by 22 physicians. More than one half of the accidents occurred to persons under the age of 25 years. Nearly one half (626 out of 1423) took place in or about the home, with more girls and women injured than boys and men. However, 60 per cent of the accidents outside the home were among boys and men. About eight out of ten persons injured at places of recreation were males, and over six out of ten were less than 25 years of age.[23]

Special mention should be made of bicycle accidents. In 1965, 62 per cent of the lives lost in bicycle accidents associated with motor vehicles were of children in the 5 to 14 age range. During the same year about 25,500 children in this age range were injured in bicycle-motor vehicle accidents. When one adds to these figures the unrecorded bicycle accidents due to all causes it is clear that the problem of safety in bicycling is serious. Once again a large portion (over 80 per cent) were under 16 years of age and were males. The National Safety Council attributes many of these accidents to lack of knowledge or skill. A study conducted by the Council revealed that many teachers, parents, and occasionally policemen tell children that they should ride on the left side of the street. Data show, however, that riding on the left side is definitely more

23 Rosenfield, A. B.: Epidemiology of accident morbidity. Minnesota Medicine, 50: 267–272 (Feb.) 1967.

hazardous than riding on the right side. On this point, much public education is needed.

The title of this section of the chapter is "Safety," yet up to this point stress has been laid only on what happens when safe practices are not followed. The need for safety is evident; the ways to attain safe living among children of school age is a matter of conjecture. One would not deprive youth of the joys of adventure nor would one wish to instill unnecessary fears. Is it possible that educational efforts should place greater emphasis on developing skills so that potentially dangerous acts are performed with minimum hazard? Young people could profit by learning what skills are acquired and what precautions are taken by professional athletes and drivers to minimize dangers of accidents and injuries.

The data presented here indicate that safety education in schools must deal with both school and non-school accidents. Though such education must take place through all 12 years of schooling, a particularly critical time would appear to be during the upper elementary years, when accident rates begin to go up noticeably, and before the junior and senior high school years, which show a startling increase in accidents. Special attention should be given to instruction in home safety and bicycle safety. Development of individual responsibility during unorganized activity periods at school should be encouraged. School boards, administrators, faculty and students should analyze causes for the large number of school-related accidents and make the necessary corrections. Driver education, already popular in many schools, needs further development. Each school and locality should study its own accident situation and determine the most apparent needs of that locality. This would make a worthwhile project for the older students. Basic first-aid instruction should be provided for all children beyond the intermediate grades.

Mental Health

In our increasingly complex society we are becoming aware as never before of the importance of good mental health. The following statement, which introduces a recent publication on *Mental Health in the Schools,* presents a point of view which is fundamental to an understanding of mental health needs of children and adults alike:

Mental health includes the ability to manage one's self and one's environment in an effective and growth-producing way. One of the most significant contributions of the behavioral sciences today is the idea that one's feelings about self are the basic determinant in mental health. The mentally healthy person is possessed of a sense of self-esteem, insight, and self-acceptance. When a realistic perception of self is added to a realistic perception of the world, the possibility of effective and productive interaction is reasonably assured. The mentally healthy person's relationships with people and the world produce certain constructive consequences. Two consequences are especially significant to the school. First, the mentally healthy person perceives reality with minimal distortion and is able to communicate these perceptions effectively. Second, the possession of self-esteem contributes to intellectual functioning.[24]

Many factors in home, school, and community life affect the mental health of children and youth. The emotional climate of the family and school influences the image children have of themselves. A child needs to feel that he is loved and respected and that he belongs. Yet society does not always provide readily for these needs. Conditions which may contribute to maladjustments are family mobility, one-parent families, excessive academic pressures, racial disturbances, and uncertainty about military service or future job opportunities.

With encouragement and understanding, many children can make their own adjustments with a minimum of difficulty. When the adjustment is too difficult, emotional disturbances and behavior problems arise. These problems reveal themselves in a variety of ways, depending upon the individual and the situation in which he finds himself. He may become overaggressive or sullen, timid or withdrawn. He may lose appetite or sleep, or his physical health may become impaired in other ways. His school work may suffer.

Many emotional problems are too deep-rooted to be solved through regular classroom procedures. They require careful individual study and attention and, at times, psychiatric help. Yet there are ways in which teachers can contribute to the improved mental health of children. Direct contributions, particularly during adolescence, may come through class discussions of students' adjustment problems. Indirect contributions may be made in the day-by-day relationships through both work and play that build up respect for each child's personality and that give recognition to individual and group accomplishments. In dealing with the hostile young person, a teacher should realize that the behavior is not usually directed against the teacher personally, but rather is a response which the child has learned through earlier experiences with difficult situations. It is the teacher's task to help the child relearn responses that are socially acceptable; punitive action may only aggravate the situation.

Development of Healthy Sexuality

Every human being is endowed with masculine or feminine qualities which need development in ways that will contribute to

---

[24] Mental Health in the Schools. Washington, D.C., Council of Chief State School Officers, 1201 16th St., N.W., 1966, p. 1. (Prepared by The Association of State and Territorial Health Officers, The Association of State and Territorial Mental Health Authorities, and The Council of Chief State School Officers.)

Figure 6. Proper sex role identification is important in developing responsible individuals. (Courtesy of Leonard McCombe, Life Magazine, Time, Inc.)

desirable human relationships. At birth each child brings into the world those unique physical characteristics which distinguish the individual as male or female. Distinctive psychological characteristics are learned from adults who influence the child's beliefs and actions according to the culture of which they are a part. Through infancy and early childhood these characteristics need special nurture so that the masculine and feminine roles appropriate to the culture are developed. As experience is added on experience, and the child moves through adolescence into adulthood, sexual characteristics are expressed in ever more distinguishing ways. It is toward their healthy expression in all forms of human relationships that sex education in schools today must be directed.

Sex education, though dealing in part with human reproduction and the physical, psychological, and social aspects of sex and marriage, must go beyond the mere scientific approach to these subjects. In word, and by example, teachers need to help children and youth identify their masculinity and femininity and learn how to act as responsible males and females. Sex education so conceived permeates the school day as children live and work together. It is enhanced or distorted depending upon the teacher's attitudes and example.

In the early elementary grades, young children can grasp the wonders of birth and life as they share experiences over the arrival of a new brother or sister or raise animals in the classroom. They may talk about family life and what is expected of fathers and mothers; they may learn a suitable vocabulary. In neighborhoods where there are many one-parent families, with the result that some children are exposed only to a mother, and perhaps a female teacher, special ways should be found to help boys identify as males and assume masculine roles.

In upper elementary grades, direct instruction on human physiology can be given. Boys and girls are interested in their bodies and by the fifth grade need to understand about human reproduction. Among both boys and girls interest in sex is increasing. Some girls will start menstruating at this time.

During junior high school years special units on the subject should be introduced in health classes. In addition, through the study of biology, literature, and social studies, concepts can be developed toward strengthening the understanding of sexuality and its place in the wholeness of life. Instruction should include a study of biological and emotional changes associated with puberty and such problems as boy-girl relationships, dating, and human reproduction in greater depth than at an earlier period.

By senior high school years, and earlier in some areas, young people are ready to be instructed as adults. In many communities they are exposed to adult sex practices among their peers or older

Table 5. *Summary of Health Needs and Interests of the Growing Child and Youth*

	Kindergarten (Age 5)	Grades 1-3 (Ages 6-8)	Grades 4-6 (Ages 9-11)	Grades 7-9 (Ages 11-14)	Grades 9-12 (Ages 14-18)
Growth in height and weight	Yearly gain: 4-6 pounds; 1-3 inches in height	Yearly gain: 3-6 pounds; 1-3 inches in height	Gains in height and weight slow and steady. By 11, some show rapid growth	Pubescent spurt with wide variations in growth patterns. Usually rapid physical growth in girls, 11-14; in boys, 12-16	Rapid growth in early period, with leveling off at about 16 for majority
Eating	Usually eats 2 good meals a day. Breakfasts often poor. May need help in eating, 1600 calories daily energy requirement	Well child, good eater. Breakfasts often poor. Habits of poor eater improve, 2100 calories daily need	Well child is a good eater. May be concerned about food and its preparation, 2200 calories daily for girls; 2400 calories daily for boys	Needs large intake of right foods. Dietary excesses common. 2500 calories for girls; 3000 calories for boys	Food excesses and picky appetites present problems. 2300 calories for girls; 3400 for boys
Elimination	Needs help and supervision in establishing elimination habits. Usually 1 bowel movement daily	Habits become better established	Good control over bowels and urination	Laxative and cathartic habit may develop. Faulty eating, irregular regimen, emotional strain may aggravate elimination difficulties	See grades 7-9
Exercise and play	Needs variety of exercises for motor skills and for general body development	Has much energy. Experiments with new motor skills. Likes imaginative play and dramatizations. Likes to collect things	Tends to overexercise. Older child interested in organized games, constructive projects. Sex differences appear in recreational activities	Exercise needed for proper development, but too great exertion during rapid growth may cause overfatigue. Abilities and capacities vary widely. Increased interest in team play and sports	Interest in skilled sports, organized and individual. Greater confidence in abilities. Girls may begin to lose interest in vigorous activity

Table 5. *(Continued)*

	Kindergarten (Age 5)	Grades 1–3 (Ages 6–8)	Grades 4–6 (Ages 9–11)	Grades 7–9 (Ages 11–14)	Grades 9–12 (Ages 14–18)
Sleep and rest	Needs 11–13 hours of sleep. May take nap or quiet rest	Needs 11–12 hours of sleep. Can take responsibility for bedtime schedule. Tires easily	Needs 10–12 hours of sleep. Good sleeper. Often does not have enough sleep. Tires easily	Tires easily. Needs at least 9–11 hours of sleep	Many need 9 or more hours of sleep
Eyes and ears	Usually farsighted; fine work tiring. Has frequent ear injuries and infections	Rapid eye development and control. Increased need for glasses. Eye accidents a problem. Middle ear infections	Gains fuller control of eye movements; increased need for glasses. Has fewer earaches	Vision and hearing defects increase. Interest in care of eyes	See grades 7–9
Teeth	All 20 deciduous (first) teeth in; permanent ones forming	4 six-year molars (first permanent) erupt. Continued calcification of non-erupted permanent teeth	Permanent teeth appearing; 9–10, the first and second bicuspids; 11, the cuspids	Permanent teeth continue to replace deciduous ones. Needs to keep teeth in good repair	All permanent teeth except third molars (wisdom teeth, 17–21 years) are in. Regular dental care is important
Posture	Sits and stands with trunk erect. Tires with sitting	Posture satisfactory if health is good. By 8, child is aware of posture	Is likely to slouch and assume unusual postures	Postural difficulties increase with body changes. May have good balance in activity, but poor posture in repose	Posture problem continues, but may be less serious than earlier
Illness and disease	Childhood diseases common; stomach-aches frequent; colds fewer than in earlier years	6-year-old has colds and communicable diseases. With age, illness decreases	Period of good health with fewer diseases and infections. Child begins to take responsibility for preventing disease	Relatively free of diseases. Minor ailments; some have emotional basis. Not interested in disease	Cancer is major cause of death from disease. Shows increased interest in disease prevention and control

Accidental injuries	Accident risk increases	Eye injuries, falls, drownings, automobile and bicycle accidents increase	Accidents increase in each grade. Need for some supervision and safe recreational facilities to minimize accidents resulting from dangerous play	Accidents continue to lead all causes of death, as in earlier years. School accidents increase	Accidents reach peak in this period. Motor vehicle accidents mount
Mental health	Poised, self-contained; likes routine, small responsibilities	Transition to school life may cause emotional problems. Aggressive at 6, less so by 8; fears and worries at 6, decreased by 8; self-centered at 6, more social at 8. Growing independence. Likes praise and approval	9-year-old is well organized. Enjoys satisfaction of achievement, likes hard work, challenging tasks. Occasional emotional outbursts	Biological change accounts for many emotional problems. Tensions often manifested by overaggression, withdrawal, illness, menstrual disorders. Personal appearance important. Concern over grooming and skin conditions. Needs adult understanding and recognition; needs identification with group	Continued emotional problems. Needs to feel worth in group and family. Psychoneurotic conditions increase. Delinquency, smoking, drinking problems arise. Personal appearance important
Sex adjustments	Sex interests center in babies or animals and animal reproduction	At 6 is curious about sex differences and general sex information. By 8 wants specific information. Notices opposite sex. Adores babies	9-year-old is interested in own body. Wants to have questions answered. At 10 and 11, sex differences are marked; little companionship between sexes. Well organized girl is more mature than boy of same age	Puberty presents problems. For girls, menstruation and secondary sex characteristics appear. Puberty is reached during latter part of period, or later, for boys. Sex organs develop, and secondary sex characteristics such as changes in voice and development of hair on face. Acne is common. Changes trouble the adolescent. Interest in opposite sex develops	At puberty interest in opposite sex begins. This interest is intensified during adolescence. By latter part of this period, many young persons are contemplating marriage and the establishment of a home and family. Want adult information on their sex roles. Some have first-hand sex experiences. Should be helped to develop an interest in procreation

brothers and sisters. Some are themselves having sexual relationships. Adolescent pregnancies are on the increase, and early marriages compound the problem of how to provide suitable sex education for these near-adults. However, it is generally agreed that attention should be given to preparation for marriage as well as responsibilities and adjustments in marriage, including planning for parenthood. Unfortunately, many teachers do not yet feel qualified to handle the subject with objectivity and understanding. For them, special help should be sought. In some universities and health departments there are specialists ready and able to assist teachers with their sex education efforts through counseling and short courses.[25]

The question is often raised whether the school should attempt sex education at all. It is pointed out that such education should preferably be the responsibility of the home. Unfortunately, a majority of our young people get their sex information outside of the home, from such sources as their peers and the mass media. If this group, deprived of help from the family, is to be adequately instructed, a major responsibility must indeed fall upon the school. For those fortunate children who come from homes doing a good job of sex education, the school, through its accessibility to audio-visual materials and its experience in group instruction, is in a strategic position to enhance and reinforce the teachings of the home. For all others, it has the potential for providing the quality of sex education that may help to counteract faulty or distorted education from other sources.[26]

Other Needs

In previous editions of this book, the four areas discussed in this section: smoking and health, alcohol and health, consumer health, and occupational health, were included in the next chapter under the general heading of "Adult Health." In our changing times, young people still in school are now increasingly faced with decisions in these four areas. Consequently, these subjects are discussed here where they are now more appropriate, though it should be recognized that they remain matters of great concern for many people throughout their lives.

---

25 For a recent article on the subject see Calderone, M. S.: The development of healthy sexuality. Journal of Health–Physical Education–Recreation, *37*:23–27 (Sept.) 1966. See also, Growth patterns and sex education. A suggested program—kindergarten through grade 12. Journal of School Health, *37* No. 5a (May) 1967, 136 pp. (Special issue.)

26 For further discussion see Kirkendall, L. A., and Calderwood, D.: The family, the school, and peer groups; sources of information about sex. Journal of School Health, *35*:290–297 (Sept.) 1965.

Smoking and Health

Smoking is a habit which frequently starts during the early teens. Studies made before 1964 show that from age 12 on, the number of those who smoke increases so that by the senior year in high school from 40 to 55 per cent of children have been found to be smokers. Rates vary from one part of the country to another and from school to school. There are more and earlier smokers in cities than in the country, for example. By age 25, it has been estimated that as many as 60 per cent of men and 36 per cent of women smoke. From the knowledge now available, the years from the early teens to the age of 20 are critical ones during which a majority of later smokers develop the habit.

Current knowledge points to the fact that cigarette smoking is the most important cause of lung cancer in men and women and that the longer a person smokes and the more cigarettes he smokes daily, the greater the risk of developing lung cancer. Chronic bronchitis, emphysema, and coronary artery disease (the main kind of heart disease) are also linked with cigarette smoking. Smoking is an expensive habit, though for many a pleasurable one. Once started it is a difficult habit to break. There appear to be a variety of psychological and social reasons why people start the habit and continue it as well as why they find it difficult to stop. Many young people seem to start smoking to gain status with their peers, to develop self-esteem and an acceptable self-image, as well as to cope with painful feelings of inadequacy. There is a strong association between parents' and children's smoking habits, though the reasons for this correlation are not yet fully clear.

In 1964, the Advisory Committee to the Surgeon General of the Public Health Service issued a report on *Smoking and Health*.[27] This important report, which brought together under one cover the accumulated knowledge on the subject drawn from many studies, has triggered a nation-wide educational movement, an important part of which is directed toward the school-age child, especially in intermediate, junior and senior high school years. Much yet needs to be learned about the behavioral aspects of smoking. As such knowledge increases, we may hope to give better focus to our educational efforts.

In teaching young people it is generally agreed that stress should be given not only to the health aspects of smoking but also to the psychological, social, and economic aspects. In most states material is now available to help teachers with this difficult task. In the fall of 1966, a program to keep seventh and eighth graders

---

[27] Smoking and Health. Report of the Advisory Committee to the Surgeon General of the Public Health Service. Public Health Service Publication No. 1103. Washington, D.C., U.S. Government Printing Office, 1964, 387 pp.

from smoking was initiated by the National Congress of Parents and Teachers in cooperation with the National Clearinghouse for Smoking and Health of the Public Health Service. In announcing this program, the Surgeon General of the Public Health Service stated that "more than 4,000 young people each day try smoking for the first time, and half of the nation's teenagers are regular smokers by the age of 18. The earlier the child begins smoking, the greater will be his risk of premature death in later years."

We are entering a new era in our anti-smoking activities. Estimates of the U.S. Department of Agriculture indicate that though domestic consumption of tobacco in 1966 was at a record, per-capita use was below the record of 1963. Could we hope that concerted educational efforts among children and adults, if continued at the present pace, or increased, could lead to further decrease in consumption and to the further protection of health and the saving of life?[28]

Alcohol and Health

Increasing use of alcohol as a beverage among the people of the United States has resulted in a situation which demands special attention by schools. Many young people are exposed at an early age to adults who drink. They are faced with decisions as to whether they themselves will drink and if so, on what occasions. Though divergent beliefs and practices exist, ranging from total abstinence to excessive drinking, the general tenor of the times is such that drinking in moderation has become an accepted practice in many homes and social gatherings. The task, then, which falls upon the schools is to provide young people with facts about alcohol which will help them to make decisions for their own good and that of others. The task is not an easy one for the teacher who holds strong beliefs himself for or against the use of alcohol as a beverage. Yet if dealt with objectively, the facts will speak for themselves more convincingly than the propaganda of the past, which often seriously distorted the truth.

Studies show that the first exposure of young people to drinking is usually at home. For some, it is limited to wine drinking as a family ritual; for others, it may be "tasting" under parental control. The first "for real" drink is likely to take place among peers in an attempt to play an adult role. Maddox states that nearly every young person has used an alcoholic beverage at least once by the time he has finished high school. He may have started to use it,

---

28 For further reading on developments see Davis, R. L.: Progress and problems in smoking education—one year after establishment of the National Clearinghouse for Smoking and Health. Journal of School Health, *37*:121–128 (March) 1967.

however, by ages 13 to 14 years. Estimates on the number of young people who drink vary widely from community to community. In some communities as many as six to eight out of ten adolescents have been found to be users while in other communities it is as few as three or four out of ten. Young people tend to consider alcohol as a social beverage rather than as a drug and are more concerned with what it does for them than what it does to them.[29]

In teaching about alcohol, emphasis should be given not only to the physiological effects but also to psychological, social, and economic effects. The most complete source of help to the teacher currently available is *Alcohol Education for Classroom and Community* referred to in the previous paragraph.[30] A few points only are mentioned here.

The physiological effects of alcohol on the body are complex and not fully understood. Changes may occur in vision and hearing, in muscular control, and in judgment. Serving as a depressant or an anesthetic, alcohol can release inhibitions and lead to behaviors which are deleterious to the drinker as well as to those around him. A person becomes intoxicated when the blood-alcohol level is high. The point of intoxication varies widely among individuals and is dependent upon the amount a person drinks, his rate of drinking, and the volume of his blood. Large doses of alcohol can be poisonous to the body and seriously impair body functions. Continued, excessive use of alcohol may lead to alcoholism, an illness of great proportions in the United States today.

The use of alcohol is increasingly recognized as a social problem with ramifications in many aspects of living. Some people drink as an escape from anxieties and frustrations; other drink because it is the socially acceptable thing to do. Such reasons for drinking are evident among teen-agers as well as adults. Though many people can control their drinking, others drink to the point of intoxication and even alcoholism. Intoxication can be a disturbing and serious problem among young people whose physical and emotional balance has not yet been fully established; it can lead to socially unacceptable behavior, to accidents, and even to death. According to the National Safety Council, drinking may be a factor in as many as one half of the fatal motor-vehicle accidents and in 13 to 15 per cent of non-fatal accidents.[31]

Among young people who will soon be old enough to drive special interest can be engendered in the effect of alcohol on driving.

---

[29] Maddox, G. L.: Adolescence and alcohol. In McCarthy, R. G. (Editor): Alcohol Education for Classroom and Community. New York, McGraw-Hill Book Company, 1964, pp. 32–47.

[30] See also, Health Concepts; Guides for Health Instruction. Washington, D.C., American Association for Health, Physical Education, and Recreation, 1967, pp. 10–12.

[31] Accident Facts. Chicago, Illinois, National Safety Council, 1966, p. 52.

To quote from Diehl:

> Nervous control and motor coordination are definitely reduced by alcohol. Grim evidence of this is the large number of automobile accidents which occur to drivers who have been drinking. Moderate amounts of alcohol interfere with attention, concentration, memory, judgment, and reason. Speed of performance is slowed and errors increase. Even while the driver under the influence of alcohol thinks he is doing his best, he is making more mistakes than usual. By paralysis of critical judgment his self-confidence is increased; he takes chances he would never dream of taking when sober. Alcohol slows reactions, interferes with judgment, and disturbs neuromuscular control. Drinking, therefore, is a serious hazard for anyone driving an automobile.[32]

It is exceedingly important that the relationship between alcohol and driving be stressed in health classes as well as in driver-education classes and other appropriate parts of the curriculum.

The economic effects of alcohol can provide a subject for study among senior high school students. The U.S. Department of Commerce, the Internal Revenue Service of the U.S. Treasury Department, and state or local liquor control bodies have data on production and consumption of alcoholic beverages which would bear analysis by the more mature student. Investigation of possible economic effects within neighborhoods and homes familiar to young people may help to accentuate the high cost of drinking. Students may study, for example, expenditures for liquor, wine, or beer; or they may estimate economic losses resulting from the abusive use of alcohol. Legal aspects, too, should be studied by senior high school students, as should also the steps being taken in communities by health, welfare, and educational agencies to cope with the alcohol problem.

Consumer Health

All of us at one time or another are purchasers of goods and of services. If we are to buy wisely from the standpoint of health and safety, we must be able to judge which products and services will be beneficial to us and which may be harmful or useless. The Food and Drug Administration states that the informed consumer is the one best able to

> Buy foods wisely.
> Use drugs safely and effectively.
> Protect children against poisonings in the home.
> Choose health services carefully.
> Avoid phony cures and fake medical devices.
> Steer clear of frauds and cheats.
> Think critically about claims in labeling and advertising.
> Evaluate information about foods, drugs, cosmetics, food additives, and
>   pesticides.

---

[32] Diehl, H. S.: Healthful Living. 7th Ed. New York, McGraw-Hill Book Company, 1964, p. 173.

Participate in governmental processes such as the setting of food standards. Assist others in getting the most benefit from consumer protection laws enacted by Congress.

BE A WISE CONSUMER.[33]

Education in consumer health should start with the young child. When he has money to spend for pleasure, he may be helped to weigh values in what he buys. If he is given money for his lunch, for example, he may be taught how to spend it wisely. As he grows in maturity, he needs to learn of the federal, state, and local laws and regulations that have been established to protect the consumer in the purchase of foods and drugs. He should know how to locate dependable medical, dental, and nursing services. He should be able to apply knowledge acquired in respect to personal and environmental health in the purchase of personal services and of household goods.

The use of potentially habit-forming drugs has greatly increased among some young people in recent years. Information now available from the Food and Drug Administration and other sources about the use and abuse of drugs should be a subject of study by senior high school years.[34]

Today medical quacks of all kinds are bombarding the public with glowing promises of the benefits of their methods or products. Millions of dollars are spent annually by a gullible public on worthless and sometimes harmful "cures." Easy victims of this quackery are people suffering from chronic diseases that resist medical treatment, such as arthritis and cancer. The American Medical Association, the Federal Food and Drug Administration, the Post Office Department, the Federal Trade Commission, as well as state and local health departments and medical associations are carrying on a nation-wide movement to fight against these "gangsters of the scientific world."

School children can become an important part of this movement to protect the public. They can gain skill in evaluating the barrage of advertising in the name of health. Armed with sound information on health and disease acquired in their school studies, children themselves can embark upon a plan of education among their families and friends.[35]

---

[33] On cover of packets of material of the Food and Drug Administration, U.S. Department of Health, Education, and Welfare, 1965.

[34] See, for example, Drug Abuse: Escape to Nowhere. A Guide for Educators. Washington, D.C., National Education Association, 1967, 104 pp. (Published by Smith Kline & French Laboratories in cooperation with the American Association for Health, Physical Education, and Recreation.)

[35] For further information, see FDA Packet A, Consumer Protection—Foods and FDA Packet B, Consumer Protection—Drugs, Cosmetics. Washington, D.C., U.S. Government Printing Office, 1965; also, Education for consumer protection. Journal of Health–Physical Education–Recreation, *36*:23–32 (Feb.) 1965.

Occupational Health

Occupational health problems should be made a subject of study for the more mature students. Of special importance will be the problems associated with the students' own employment experiences during out-of-school hours and in the summertime. General personal health on the job, as well as avoidance of unsafe or unhealthful practices should be subjects of special value to young people in the different kinds of job training programs, such as food-service courses, now offered in many school systems.

All students, however, regardless of their present needs or future occupational plans, will benefit by knowing something about the common health and safety hazards in industry, in office and store employment, and in farm work. Among the types of industrial hazards that would make appropriate subjects for study are dangers associated with hand and machine tools, electricity, flying particles, chemical substances (e.g., solvents, carbon monoxide), and noise. The importance of good personal health in the avoidance of accidents and in the reduction of absenteeism should be stressed. Instruction on proper lifting, pushing, and pulling is desirable.

Students should know of the problems associated with office and store employment, including foot trouble from long periods of standing, and how these problems can be counteracted by proper hygienic practices.

Health and safety problems on the farm that are worthy of study include such matters as water sanitation; milk sanitation; washing facilities; farm accidents, such as those caused by animals and machinery; and exposure to excessive heat or to poisonous plants, snakes, and insects.

SUMMARY

Every young person has certain basic health needs that are outgrowths of his physiological and emotional development and of his mode of living. These needs must be met satisfactorily if growth is to proceed in orderly fashion. It is not enough to do things for the child in the name of health. He himself should learn at his level of understanding what these needs are and should share in efforts for meeting them. Needs common to all school-age levels are summarized in this chapter. They suggest the direction of health-teaching efforts both from the standpoint of concepts to be developed and problems to be solved.

REFERENCES

Acute Conditions; Incidence and Associated Disability, United States, July 1964–June 1965. National Center for Health Statistics Series 10, No. 26.

Washington, D.C., U.S. Government Printing Office, 1965, 61 pp. (Data from National Health Survey.)

Anderson, G. W., Arnstein, M. G., and Lester, M. R.: Communicable Disease Control. 4th Ed. New York, The Macmillan Company, 1962, 606 pp.

Breckenridge, M. E., and Vincent, E. L.: Child Development. 5th Ed. Philadelphia, W. B. Saunders Company, 1965, 485 pp.

Children and Youth in the 1960's. Survey papers prepared for the 1960 White House Conference on Children and Youth. Washington, D.C., Golden Anniversary White House Conference on Children and Youth, Inc., 1960, 340 pp.

Cohen, D. H., and Stern, V.: Observing and Recording the Behavior of Young Children. New York, Teachers College Press, Teachers College, Columbia University, 1958, 86 pp.

Control of Communicable Diseases in Man. 10th Ed., 1965. New York, The American Public Health Association, 1740 Broadway, 1965, 282 pp. (An official report edited by J. E. Gordon.)

Facts on Quacks; What You Should Know About Health Quackery. Chicago, American Medical Association, 1967, 32 pp.

Harper, P. A.: Preventive Pediatrics. Child health and development. New York, Appleton-Century-Crofts, 1962, 798 pp.

Health Concepts; Guides for Health Instruction. Washington, D.C., American Association for Health, Physical Education, and Recreation, 1967, 49 pp.

Health Education: A Conceptual Approach to Curriculum Design. St. Paul, Minn., 3M Education Press, Box 3100, 1967, 141 pp. (By The School Health Education Study.)

Health problems revealed during physical activity. Journal of Health–Physical Education–Recreation, 36:6, 8 (Sept.) 1965. (Statement authorized by the American Medical Association's Committee on Exercise and Fitness.)

How Children Develop. Revised Ed. Columbus, Ohio, The Ohio State University, 1964, 68 pp. (Prepared by the faculty of University School, College of Education.)

Interdepartmental Committee on Children and Youth: Children in a Changing World. Washington, D.C., Golden Anniversary White House Conference on Children and Youth, Inc., 1960, 84 pp. (A book of charts.)

Jenkins, G. G., Shacter, H., and Bauer, W. W.: These Are Your Children; How They Develop and How to Guide Them from Birth through Adolescence. 3rd Edition. New York, Scott, Foresman and Company, 1966, 371 pp.

Johns, E. B., Sutton, W. C., and Webster, L. E.: Health for Effective Living. 4th Ed. New York, McGraw-Hill Book Company, 1966, 540 pp.

Joint Committee on Health Problems in Education of the National Education Association and the American Medical Association: Health Appraisal of School Children. 3rd Ed. Washington, D.C., and Chicago, The Associations, 1961, 49 pp.

Miller, B. F., and Burt, J. J.: Good Health; Personal and Community. 2nd Ed. Philadelphia, W. B. Saunders Company, 1966, 508 pp.

Nemir, A.: The School Health Program. 2nd Ed. Philadelphia, W. B. Saunders Company, 1965, 418 pp.

Policy Statement on Family Life and Sex Education. Springfield, Illinois, Office of the Superintendent of Public Instruction, 1967, 24 pp. (Developed by The Illinois Sex Education Advisory Board.)

Recommended Dietary Allowances. 6th Revised Ed. Publication 1146. Washington, D.C., National Academy of Sciences, National Research Council, 1964, 59 pp. (A report of the Food and Nutrition Board.)

Report of the Committee on the Control of Infectious Diseases. 15th Ed., 1966. Evanston, Illinois, American Academy of Pediatrics, P.O. Box 1034, 1966, 185 pp.

Report of the Committee on School Health of the Academy of Pediatrics. Evanston, Illinois, The Academy, P.O. Box 1034, 1966, 128 pp.

Research Related to Children. Children's Bureau Bulletin 19. Washington, D.C., U.S. Government Printing Office, 1966, 247 pp. (Prepared by Clearinghouse for Research in Child Life.)

Schiffer, C. G., and Hunt, E. P.: Illness among Children. Children's Bureau Publication No. 405–1963, reprinted 1966. Washington, D.C., U.S. Government Printing Office, 1966, 107 pp. (Data from U.S. National Health Survey.)

School Health Education Study. Washington, D.C., School Health Education Study, 1507 M. Street, N. W., Room 800, 1964, 74 pp.

Strasser, M. K., Aaron, J. E., Bohn, R. C., and Eales, J. R.: Fundamentals of Safety Education. New York, The Macmillan Company, 1964, 453 pp.

Turner, C. E.: Personal and Community Health. 13th Ed. St. Louis, The C. V. Mosby Company, 1967, 448 pp.

U.S. Department of Agriculture: Consumers All. The Yearbook of Agriculture 1965. Washington, D.C., U.S. Government Printing Office, 1965, 496 pp.

HOME, SCHOOL, COMMUNITY HEALTH NEEDS: A BASIS FOR HEALTH EDUCATION

Home, school, and community provide the setting within which children grow and develop. Conditions which exist in these environments can influence children's health and well-being and must be understood by teachers who would make their health instruction vital and effective. In this chapter selected health factors in home, school, and community are summarized with special reference to their implications for health teaching. Examples of ways in which teachers may utilize the environment as a basis for health instruction are given in Chapters 8 and 9.

We are becoming increasingly aware of the wide variations which occur from home to home and community to community. Even within a specific school or school system, differences in economic, social, and cultural backgrounds can be so marked as to make adaptations in health instruction necessary. Each teacher and each school must understand conditions within families and neighborhoods and make necessary adjustments in content and methods of health instruction.

HOW A TEACHER CAN FIND OUT ABOUT HOME, SCHOOL, AND COMMUNITY HEALTH NEEDS

Information contained in the following sections of this chapter may provide a foundation for identifying home, school, and community health needs. This information must be supplemented by specific data which can be obtained by such procedures as observation, interviews or conferences, and study of records and reports. Though the discussion of these approaches to study of needs is focused on local conditions, it should be pointed out that study should not be limited to the immediate environment only. We live today in a world community, and environmental conditions at state, national, and even international levels should be subjects of study as well. Observation of these broader needs may not be possible; information about them, however, can be obtained from written and verbal reports of people familiar with them and from the many special studies and publications now available.

Observation

Home visits provide a fruitful way of learning firsthand about the home environment. In some areas, the community is so small and compact that teachers living within it have easy access to homes for both professional and social reasons. In many communities, however, the nurse or social worker in the school is the person more likely to have direct home contacts.

Among conditions which should be observed on home visits are provisions for carrying out health and safety practices, such as availability of sanitary facilities, and space for food preparation, sleeping, and playing. Attention should also be directed toward evidence of special problems which may affect the physical or emotional health of the children, as, for example, poverty, family illnesses, and overburdened mothers carrying full responsibilities for the home. Positive factors should be noted, too, such as cultural characteristics which give a distinctive quality to family living, and the almost universal efforts on the part of parents to provide well for their children.

Within schools, observations of the physical environment can be made informally in the classroom or through tours of the building under the trained eyes of qualified personnel. Environmental health specialists of the health department, the nurse working in the school, and even the school custodian may point to factors in the physical environment that are conducive or detrimental to child health. Teachers themselves, aided by social workers, nurses, or guidance counselors may become sensitive to factors in the social and emotional environment of the school, such as undue work pressures, tensions among pupils or faculty, and faulty scheduling that can affect learning and health.

Within the neighborhood observations can be made of many environmental factors that affect favorably or adversely the health and safety of the inhabitants. These observations can also be made on a more extensive scale. Housing, traffic patterns, cleanliness of food establishments, handling of solid waste disposal, and street lighting are but a few of the indicators of the community's sense of responsibility toward its own health and safety.

Interviews and Conferences

The child, the parent, the nurse, and the social worker are among the best sources of information about factors in the home that may affect child health. Much can be learned in the informal day-by-day conversations with children. Discussions with parents during home visits or at parent-teacher meetings can bring forth useful information. In some schools, regular parent-teacher conferences at the school are arranged. Supporting the teacher with ready information about home conditions may be the nurse and other special service personnel just mentioned and, in many instances, personnel of the local health and welfare departments. A new teacher may need to learn the channels of communication which have been developed for the use of these sources of help. In some instances he may find it necessary to initiate his own channels.

Within the school, information about all aspects of school health needs and programs is available, simply for the asking, from many sources, such as administrative and supervisory personnel, teachers, nurses, social workers, and other special service personnel. Teachers' meetings, health council activities, and other planned conferences may provide special opportunities for learning about school-related health needs.

For an understanding of community-wide health needs, teachers may seek contact with the numerous health agencies and organizations in the area. Chapter 12 of this book is devoted to a discussion of the help available from many of the more readily accessible co-workers in health education.

Records and Reports

Data on family health problems and needs, and on the economic, social, and cultural factors which may affect family health, are increasingly available from health and welfare agencies. The school, too, may have made studies of the families it serves. Agencies and organizations such as those discussed in Chapter 12 may also have useful data on family health. The teacher would do well to explore possible sources through the school nurse or local health authorities.

Records and reports on school health needs are most likely to be found in the administration office or the school health services office. Special studies on school health conditions may be conducted from time to time for the purpose of drawing the attention of school authorities or the community to needs requiring their attention. These studies can often be useful to individual teachers as background for their own understanding of the school, as well as being a basis for classroom teaching.

Public health departments at local and state levels regularly assemble records and reports on the state of the community's health. Health departments and other community agencies may conduct special studies to highlight special needs, such as those related to water pollution, air pollution, housing, and safety. The nurse, or local health authorities when they are available, should be helpful to the teacher in locating information on community health needs and problems.

HEALTH NEEDS IN THE HOME

In most cultures the family is the basic unit for decision making in matters of health. The individual needs of children, as discussed in the preceding chapter, must be viewed within a family setting, for it is within the family that children receive their physical, psychological, social, and emotional nurturing. Though in Chapters 2 and 3 certain health needs have been discussed separately, their interrelatedness must be kept constantly in mind. Today, as James has pointed out, "we have made man into a series of chapter headings." Rather, he states, we must view each individual as "belonging to one family and having one set of many problems."[1] To deal with any one of the problems or needs in isolation from other problems and needs is to create a separateness that is untenable. Mary is a case in point.

Mary lived with her family in a rented duplex house. Her father, a nonskilled worker, received a modest income, which, under ordinary circumstances, provided enough for the family's basic needs. Her mother worked irregularly as a short-order cook at a nearby lunch counter. Mary's sixth grade teacher began to notice changes in Mary. She was often absent and when at school seemed tired and distracted. Her health record showed uncorrected visual and dental defects; her appetite in the lunchroom was poor.

---

[1] James, G.: Poverty as an obstacle to health progress in our cities. American Journal of Public Health, 55:1769 (Nov.) 1965. (Presented as part of a symposium on "Poverty and Public Health—New Outlooks.")

The nurse working with the school visited Mary's home in an effort to be of help. There she found an invalid grandfather who had come to live with the family during the past year. The nurse learned that Mary returned home from school each day to care for the grandfather and two preschool children. Her absences, too, were said to be for the same reason. A series of illnesses and other reverses in the family had drained the family's financial resources; there never seemed to be enough left to secure glasses and dental care for Mary. Obviously, the root of Mary's difficulties lay not in herself alone, but in the total family situation. Help for Mary's problems would require help for the family as a whole.

Needs of the Family as a Unit

Human Relations in the Family

Becoming a successful member of a family requires patience and understanding. Personal desires of parents and children alike must often be submerged for the welfare of the group. Members of the family must share responsibilities as well as joys. They must learn ways of living and working together harmoniously.

The social and emotional patterns of family living have a profound influence on an individual's personality and actions throughout life. Even the young child reacts to the conditions about him. If he lives in a happy, well adjusted family, he himself is likely to be happy and well adjusted. If he is reared in an atmosphere of strife, the insecurities that such conditions engender may develop in him serious behavior problems.

Many families are on the move today. Migrant workers move with the crops. Others, though less mobile, go from rural to urban areas, from cities to suburban communities, from state to state, and even from country to country. No one understands fully what effect this mobility has on children and youth. Doubtless, many of the changes are for the good. Suburban living may result in more comfortable and spacious homes and more opportunity for outdoor life. On the fringe of some cities, however, "rural slums" are developing where families live in small, overcrowded houses and in communities still lacking the facilities and services essential for healthful living. Moreover, the farther the family is from the city where the father works, the less the children will see of him. Moving from one community to another may mean better family income and more contented parents, but it creates problems of school and social adjustment for the children. Teachers can lessen the impact of family mobility by helping newly arrived children make adjustments and by providing opportunities for neighborliness among children and parents alike.

Another problem growing in importance is that of the working mother. The effect of her long absences from home is a subject of serious study. Though this is a problem about which children have little choice, it should be taken into account in health teaching.

Recent attention to pockets of poverty within both urban and rural areas has increased our awareness of the effects that deprivation can have on family stability. Poverty breeds problems, and for many of the families the problems are multiple. A *Profile of Minneapolis Communities* compiled by the Community Health and Welfare Council dramatizes the situation. Within the central community, where family incomes were the lowest for the city, the rate of juvenile delinquency was the highest of all sections as were the rates of divorce and illegitimacy. The delinquency rate of children under 18 living in broken homes, that is, without both parents in the home, was highest in this area. So, too, was the rate of child neglect. Mobility was the greatest, too, with about 70 per cent of the population age five and over having moved during the previous five years as compared with about 50 per cent for the city as a whole.[2]

Young people on entrance to marriage carry with them many hopes and desires, or, conversely, many fears and uncertainties. These feelings are conditioned to a large degree by their past experiences as members of a family unit. Too often they start a new home ignorant of the elements that lead to successful family life.

Instruction on the social and emotional factors that make home life a bulwark of strength should be incorporated in the curriculum throughout the school years. Through group projects and discussions, young children may learn what part each member of the family plays in contributing to family solidarity. They may learn and carry out simple home responsibilities. At the senior high school level, direct instruction on family relationships should be given either as a separate course or through units introduced in already existing courses. Emphasis should be placed on responsibilities involved in marriage and parenthood, and on the emotional factors that guide people's lives together in a home.

Preparation for Parenthood

Much of what has been written thus far in this and the previous chapter bears directly or indirectly on preparation for parenthood. A young person who has good physical and emotional health and who understands, believes in, and applies principles of healthful living is laying the bases for responsible future parenthood. The

---

2 Profile of Minneapolis Communities; An Inventory of Social Characteristics and Social Problems in the City of Minneapolis. Minneapolis, Minnesota, Community Health and Welfare Council of Hennepin County, Inc., 1964, 144 pp.

Figure 7. Preparing for parenthood—a home economics student practices child care. (Courtesy of the Minneapolis Star.)

person who has developed a healthy sexuality, who possesses some understanding of the processes of human reproduction and the psychological and social aspects of sex and marriage, and who respects the integrity of the home, is gaining insights which may help to guide behavior as a parent in later years. Added to such knowledge and understanding should be an appreciation of the importance of health supervision and good prenatal care throughout pregnancy for the protection of the health of the pregnant mother and the child to whom she will give birth.

Infant care, with focus on parental responsibilities toward helping each infant develop physically, emotionally, and intellectually, provides a worthwhile subject of study for the older student. Young people who baby-sit may apply this knowledge immediately and use their experiences as subjects for discussion during class sessions. Care of the preschool child can also be a subject for study in health and home economics classes. In projects of health career clubs, youth organizations, and other groups, young people may have opportunities to test their knowledge of child care through practice under supervision, as may those who assist with Head Start programs and similar community child care projects.

First Aid and Home Care of the Sick

Sickness is a common invader of the home and requires intelligent handling both as a safeguard to the patient and as a protection to the other members of the family.

Injuries and sudden illness demand knowledge of what to do until the doctor arrives. Sometimes the doctor's arrival is delayed for hours, and knowledge of first-aid procedures may actually save a life. In certain areas of the country, especially in rural districts, medical and nursing services are inadequate, and hospital facilities are at a distance. Home care of the sick throughout an illness then becomes a necessity in order to meet the patient's daily wants. Even when facilities and services are at hand, many phases of care fall upon the family.

There are various elements of home care that should be common knowledge. These include early recognition of illness; first-aid and emergency treatment in times of sudden injury or illness; care of a bedridden patient; how to carry out the doctor's orders, as in giving simple treatments and medication; feeding of the patient; care of the convalescent and such special cases as patients with communicable diseases.

First aid and home care of the ill have long been recognized as important fields of study at the adult level. Older pupils, too, will benefit by such instruction. Illness in the home is often a personal problem for the school child. He may become ill himself, but even more important, he is likely at some time to share the same home with an ill person and perhaps also share in the patient's care. Courses or units of work in first aid, medical self-help, and home nursing are becoming increasingly popular during junior and senior high school years. Units may also be introduced in the intermediate grades.

Problems of the Chronically Ill and the Aging

As people live longer, students are increasingly in contact with the chronically ill or aging. Moreover, through press, radio and television they are exposed to information pertaining to the health, social, emotional, and economic needs of this growing segment of our population requiring special care. In view of these inevitable exposures, it would seem pertinent that during school years students gain some understanding of the needs of the chronically ill and aging and of programs now developing for their care.

Chronic illnesses lead in the causes of incapacity and death. Included in these illnesses are heart disease, stroke, cancer, diabetes, arthritis, and the variety of ailments associated with declining years. Contrary to common belief, such chronic illnesses as heart disease, cancer, and diabetes occur also in children. Though the student need not dwell on chronic disorders for an extended period, a realistic knowledge of them and of the problems they present can help him to understand and be sympathetic toward those requiring special care. Needs and possibilities for rehabilitation and control of chronic conditions could also be fruitfully studied. If such study is handled in a constructive way, a bulwark against unnecessary fears as well as a sense of hope may be established.

Rapid strides have been made in studying and acting on problems of the aging. Medicare, housing, recreational programs, and other special services are increasingly available to the older members of our society. They provide appropriate subjects for study in health and social problems classes. Young people may carry some responsibility for the care of older people in their families; through work experience programs and health career projects they may also provide care. As members of youth organizations and other groups they may participate in community service projects for the elderly—in hospitals, nursing homes, and recreation centers. They could, as a part of such service, profitably study the special needs of older people and think through ways in which they themselves can relate effectively to those they are helping.

Needs Related to the Physical Environment

Housing

Good housing contributes to good health. Poor housing, on the other hand, has long been associated with poor health. Although poor housing alone cannot be held responsible for the many ills that beset people who live under crowded conditions, few persons would deny that a connection exists between the two. Families living in substandard housing have more sickness. Accidents mount. Infant mortality, as might be expected, is higher in some areas where there is overcrowded living. Juvenile delinquency increases and mental illness may be a by-product.

New housing developments and rehabilitation of old housing, now occurring in many cities, provide a positive approach to the study of health and housing. Children and families who have recently moved into new developments may be helped to appreciate the advantages of safer, more healthful homes. The health and social aspects of poor housing also provide worthwhile subjects for study. All children should share in home and community efforts for housing improvements. In this section of the chapter, only three aspects of healthful housing are discussed. Doubtless many others would come up in an intensive study of the subject.

Heating and ventilation.   Proper conditions of temperature and humidity are among the basic needs of people. Simple principles of home heating and ventilation and ways in which people can provide healthful atmospheric conditions at home should be included in the education of the school child. They might learn, for example, the advantages and disadvantages of the most common types of home heating and air conditioning systems. They should understand why different members of the family require different room temperatures for comfort, and why babies and old people need more heat than school children and young adults.

Lighting.   Good home lighting adds much to the comfort and efficiency of members of the family. Good lighting also prevents unnecessary eye strain. Every home needs light of the right amount and quality to provide these desirable effects. Amounts of light required range from 10 to 50 foot-candles, depending upon the kind of activity. Light should be distributed evenly through rooms; glare and shadows should be avoided.

Problems of home lighting present an interesting study for school children, who may learn ways in which they themselves can contribute to better home lighting, such as by helping in the arrangement of existing facilities or in simple redecoration of rooms to bring about lighting improvements.

Sanitation.   In recent years millions of new homes have been built; yet far too many of these homes do not have connections with municipal water or sewerage systems. This lack of modern sanitation in many of our suburban areas and other new developments is becoming a national disgrace. The attractiveness and safety of our home surroundings are further menaced by the growing accumulation of litter, or solid wastes, the disposal of which often presents difficult problems for the householder. The neighborhood dump, the pile of rubbish behind the hedge, and the litter-strewn yards and sidewalks are all too common. Except in sparsely settled rural areas where each household must provide its own sanitary facilities, concerted community action is needed to correct these adverse conditions.

When new developments lack community water supplies and sewerage systems, sanitation needs can become a subject for study in the school. Moreover, school children may be instrumental in initiating clean-up drives; they may also be participants in these drives as well as in year-round efforts to keep their home surroundings safe and healthful.

In urban areas the need shifts from the provision of new facilities to the proper use of those on hand. The water supply may come from a safe municipal source, and sewage may be discharged into a satisfactory municipal system. Solid waste collection services and public incinerators may be available. Yet within the home, much of the protection afforded by these community, provisions is lost through ignorance or carelessness. Poor home plumbing is an illustration. When faucets or other water inlets are so installed that they lie below the spill line of a lavatory, tub, or toilet fixture, contamination of water supplies may occur by water rising above the inlet and entering the water supply by back siphonage.

Home swimming pools are becoming commonplace in some communities. When improperly installed, used, or maintained, they may be little better than an open sewer. Before installing a pool, one should check state or local health and safety regulations. Reputable swimming pool construction companies know the regulations for construction and operation, as well as the specifications for filtering systems and chemicals for treating the water. Family and friends using the pool should establish rules for themselves regarding sanitary precautions as well as safety measures to be observed. (See section on home and farm safety in this chapter.)

These problems of sanitation suggest topics for special study among students. A fruitful activity would be the investigation of sanitary conditions in the homes of a community and the planning of a course of action for the provision of better facilities or for more hygienic use of facilities at hand.

Control of Pests

Homes are a common haunt of certain pests. Many pests are capable of transmitting diseases, and all of them are a great annoyance to people.

Rats. In some sections of the country, rats may harbor fleas that may infect human beings with one form of typhus fever. Rats also are responsible for the transmission of plague, food infections, and other diseases. Rats are best controlled by the rat-proofing of buildings to exclude the rodents from nesting places and food; by elimination of harborages, such as hidden places within buildings and rubbish piles; and by protection of food, such as garbage, grain piles, and rotting vegetables and fruits. Poisons and traps are temporary measures of control which are also sometimes used. Rat control measures provide constructive study for students. When given training and opportunity, students may even assist in carrying out these measures.

Houseflies.   These pests are not only a nuisance, but they may also transmit intestinal diseases, such as dysentery and other diarrheal disorders. The basic method of controlling flies is elimination of breeding places, such as manure and garbage; a secondary method is screening. The use of DDT (or other insecticides) to supplement these methods is now common practice. Under supervision, school children may take an active part in control measures.

Mosquitoes.   Certain types of mosquitoes transmit malaria and yellow fever. Though these diseases are practically nonexistent in the United States today, the mosquitoes that transmit them can be found in some areas. Constant vigilance is needed on the part of health authorities to prevent reintroducing these diseases from countries where malaria and yellow fever still exist. Mosquitoes also carry the viruses of encephalitis to man as well as to livestock, pets, and other animals. Methods of mosquito control vary with the kind of mosquito and with the locality in which it is found, but drainage of surface waters and filling are common methods for eliminating breeding places. Acceptable and potent insecticides are now also considered effective in the destruction of mosquitoes. Children should familiarize themselves with the control measures used in their own communities, such as the work of "mosquito control districts," and cooperate whenever possible in these activities. They may also be interested in the world-wide efforts of international agencies to eradicate malaria in all countries.

Bedbugs and lice.   These insects thrive under conditions of crowding and uncleanliness. Though bedbugs are not definitely known to spread disease, they are open to suspicion and should be destroyed.

There are three types of human lice: namely, head lice, pubic lice, and body lice. Though all types may cause much discomfort, only the body lice are important in the transmission of disease. Body lice transmit typhus fever and trench fever. Remarkable results in the destruction of lice have been obtained through dusting of clothing and the body with DDT powder, but from the standpoint of prevention and control, general habits of cleanliness are first in importance.

Insecticides, including DDT, have been mentioned several times. These are highly useful chemicals when applied under proper controls; they are very dangerous when used improperly. Children should learn the dangers of improper use.

Food Handling and Food Storage

Good food is more than nutritious food; it must also be safe to eat. Food infections (e.g., salmonella infections) or food poisonings (e.g., staphylococcal poisoning) occur when a person consumes food that has become contaminated by disease-producing bacteria or poisons. Salmonella organisms can be present in raw meat, poultry, eggs, and dairy products. Thorough cooking destroys the organisms. Animal feeds may be contaminated with salmonellae and can provide a means for the spread of infection from animals to man. Bacteria need food, warmth, and moisture for growth. Such foods as salads, casserole dishes, cream puffs, and custards, when left standing at room temperature for a comparatively short time, provide a most favorable environment for the growth of bacteria.

Perishable food should be stored until ready for use at a temperature of 45° F. or less, depending upon the type of food. Modern electric refrigeration or well insulated ice boxes make this possible. In homes that lack refrigeration, food should be consumed immediately after preparation. An all too common practice in many homes is to prepare food and then let it stand at room temperature until it has "cooled off." This is done even when ample refrigeration is present. In the case of such perishable foods as those mentioned earlier, it is better to refrigerate them at once, in order to inhibit the growth of any disease-producing organisms that may be lodged in the food. Moreover, the food should be refrigerated in small quantities to allow for adequate cooling. For example, if a large amount of potato salad is to be refrigerated it should be placed in several small containers rather than in one large container.

Quick-frozen foods are popular today. They should be stored at sub-freezing temperatures until ready for use and should never be refrozen because spoilage takes place rapidly after the food has thawed. With modern methods of packaging, our foods look better but are often kept too long and with increased risk of becoming contaminated.

Home canning of food presents other problems. Improperly canned foods may contain the organisms that cause botulism, a highly fatal disease. The spores of this organism are found in the soil and contaminate the food while it is growing. They are especially common in far western states. If canning temperatures are not high enough or if the canning process is not of sufficient length, the spores may grow and the food will become unsafe for consumption. Tasting and smelling are not safe criteria for determining whether or not food has been contaminated. To avoid the risk of poisoning from this organism, food should be canned under pressure and for a long enough period to destroy the spores. Home-canned food should also be boiled thoroughly before eating as a double assurance that the food is safe to eat.

Insecticides and agricultural chemicals, now widely used, may contaminate food. Special care is needed in the home and in agricultural production to keep these substances out of food.

Opportunities are numerous throughout the school day for learning about and applying safe food-handling and food-storage practices. When food is prepared by pupils for school parties, picnics, camp-outs, or other events, good food-handling practices can be applied. Young people in training for work in restaurants or other food-service industries should be taught how to handle food to minimize contamination. If children bring lunches to school they may work out with teachers and school authorities sanitary methods for handling and storing the food until ready to eat. Observation of, or participation in, school lunch services provides another opportunity to study the subject. Home and farm practices should be subjects for study and practical application of good practices, too.

Home and Farm Safety

The physical environment at home should be safe as well as healthful. Serious and fatal home accidents occur most often in the yard, with kitchen, stairs, living room, porch, and bedroom accidents following in close order. Falls are by far the greatest cause of serious accidents.

Leading fatal home accidents of young people are distributed as follows:[3]

0–4 years		5–14 years		15–24 years	
Suffocation, mechanical	950	Fires, burns	550	Fires, burns	250
Suffocation, ingested		Firearms	300	Firearms	250
objects	850	Falls	100	Poisons, solid or liquid	130
Fires, burns	1,250	Poison gases	30	Poison gases	190
Falls	400	Suffocation, ingested		Suffocation, ingested	
Poisons, solid or liquid	300	objects	40	objects	40
		Poisons, solid or liquid	30	Falls	50

[3] Accident Facts. Chicago, Illinois, National Safety Council, 1966, pp. 82–83. (Estimates for 1965.)

Startling indeed is the large number of deaths due to handling of firearms. Instruction in the proper storage and use of firearms thus appears to be of great importance, especially in rural areas. Some states have special programs of youth education through sportsmen's clubs. Public opinion is growing toward the restricted sale of firearms. Young people could profitably discuss this trend.

Deaths from poisonous substances, especially in very young children, are attracting wide attention today. For every fatal home-poisoning accident there are hundreds of nonfatal ones. Drugs and medications (such as candy-like aspirin) head the list of substances responsible for the poisoning. Home cleaning fluids containing carbon tetrachloride or benzene are damaging to the body when inhaled. But there are many other chemicals in use in and about the home that are potentially dangerous, such as insecticides, fertilizers, and weed killers. The home hobby fad has introduced into the home new substances that should be kept away from children. A number of localities have set up poison control centers where information is available on the many poisonous substances.

Power mowers maim thousands of children and adults each year. Over one half of the injuries are to feet and hands, which, through careless operation, are caught in the machine. Flying particles thrown by the whirling blades account for many other injuries.

Accidents which occur to farm residents bear special mention. Farm people are subject to the same kind of accidents as other people, but because of the special conditions of farm living certain hazards are greater. Tractor accidents cause about 1,000 deaths annually, and studies indicate that more than one fourth of the victims are under 20 years old. Farm fires not only cause great economic loss but also loss of lives. Other special hazards on farms which may lead to injury or death include farm machinery and tools; conditions that may lead to falls; wells and ponds; and pesticides as well as other chemicals. In one study, the largest number of permanent disabilities was found to be caused by parts of the body being caught in machinery.

Home accidents cause approximately 29,000 deaths each year and result in injuries to millions of other people. Nearly one third of all fatal accidents in the nation occur in or about the home. State and local health departments, agricultural agencies, and other groups are taking an increased interest in home accidents and may have local data. The immensity of the problem should make a study of the local situation by school children an especially practical undertaking.

Young people should be encouraged to help correct accident hazards at home and on the farm and provide protection for younger children. It is not enough merely to survey the situation—action to remove hazards and improve practices is essential.

HEALTH NEEDS IN THE SCHOOL

Children have a stake in what is happening at school. They may share in the various school health procedures, such as the provision of a healthful school environment and the intelligent use of school health services. The many health problems that arise in the day-by-day living at school form a basis for much valuable health education.

Healthful Living at School

Throughout the nation attention is being drawn as never before to the importance of providing school surroundings which are beneficial to learning and to the general welfare of children. New buildings are being constructed to replace obsolete structures and to meet the needs of a rapidly expanding school population. Old buildings are being renovated. The teacher and his relationships with children are under scrutiny. For these and other reasons, safe and healthful school living is a timely subject for school study.

The school building is the child's abode for many of his waking hours. It should provide the best there is for safe, comfortable, and healthful living. Water supplies should be safe; sewage should be properly disposed of; lighting, ventilation, and seating in the classroom should promote rather than hinder good health; sanitary lunchroom facilities should be available; and shops, gymnasiums, showers, locker rooms, and swimming pools should be constructed and operated according to sound health and safety standards.

Although provision of healthful housing conditions at school is primarily an administrative responsibility, there are nevertheless many things that the children themselves may do to bring about improvements both in the facilities and in their use. A study of the conditions that surround them, as through the use of check lists and participation in projects for the betterment of school housing, may provide content for much health education.

Provision of a safe and healthful physical environment is only one part of a program of healthful living. The attitude of the teacher toward the children is an extremely important factor in the daily life at school. A teacher who is sympathetic and understanding, yet firm when necessary, and who treats the children with respect, is a good influence. In contrast, the teacher who is emotionally disturbed and who nags and scolds the children can create an atmosphere that is adverse to study and to happy living. Relationships among children are equally important. Children need to work out together ways of living and working harmoniously throughout the school day.

Provision and Use of School Health Services

School health services have been defined as "The procedures used by physicians, dentists, nurses, teachers, etc., designed to appraise, protect, and promote optimum health of students and school personnel." To be more specific, "Activities frequently included in school health services are those used to: (1) appraise the health status of students and school personnel; (2) counsel students, teachers, parents and others for the purpose of helping school-age children get treatment or for arranging education programs in keeping with their abilities; (3) help prevent or control the spread of disease; (4) provide emergency care for injury or sudden sickness."[4]

Health Appraisal and Health Counseling

Health appraisal has been defined as "The evaluation of the health status of the individual through the ultilization of various organized and systematic procedures such as medical and dental examinations, laboratory tests, health history, teacher observation, etc."[5]

Health counseling, on the other hand, may be thought of as a "method of interpreting to students or their parents the findings of health appraisals and encouraging and assisting them to take such action as needed to realize their fullest potential."[6]

At every turn in the health appraisal and health counseling program there is opportunity for health education. Health guidance given to individual students and their parents is in itself health education. Group instruction is appropriate and essential in preparation for and as follow-up after health appraisal activities, such as tests for vision, hearing, weight and height, and the medical examination itself. In preparing for the tests or the medical examination, we can help pupils understand the purposes of the procedures and what the examiner will do. Pupils may be introduced to the use of the audiometer, the stethoscope, and the x-ray film.

Health problems discovered through the various procedures, when common enough to become group problems, may provide content for valuable group instruction. For example, in most schools, tests or examinations will reveal a sufficient number of children with dental and visual defects to warrant group instruction on these problems. Students may help to find ways of securing corrections, and they may explore the broader aspects of prevention and control.

---

4 Health Education Terminology. Journal of Health–Physical Education–Recreation, *33*:27–28 (Nov.), 1962. (Report of the Joint Committee on Health Education Terminology.)
5 *Ibid.*
6 *Ibid.*

Care and Education of Handicapped Children

Within most school systems some children need special care and education because of handicapping conditions. Many of these children can be taught in regular classrooms for a large part of the time if adequate provisions are made for their special needs. Others may require special class instruction for all or part of the day, and still others may need education in special schools. A few will be homebound on a temporary or permanent basis.

No attempt will be made here to suggest the kinds of teaching required for the different types and degrees of disability. The teaching of handicapped children demands special skills and training.

A classroom teacher who has a handicapped child in his room will need to learn from the nurse, special teacher, or other appropriate personnel just what will be required to help the child to live comfortably and safely and to adjust emotionally to his condition. So far as possible, the child should be treated like the other children and helped in every way to become a well adjusted member of the group. The group, in turn, may need help in accepting the child.

Prevention and Control of Communicable Diseases

The school's part in communicable disease prevention and control should be closely integrated with home and community programs. Teachers are in a strategic position to observe children throughout the day for signs or symptoms of disease. Any suspicion of disease should start a chain of action which will include isolation of the child, notification of the parents, and a report to health authorities according to predetermined plans. Parents should be instructed as to signs and symptoms of disease and on the importance of keeping children at home when a disease is suspected. Drivers of school buses should also be given instructions on communicable diseases; when qualified, they may even be given the authority to exclude children from buses when the children show evidence of illness.

Children should have a share in all these aspects of communicable disease control. They should know how to tell when they are ill and should be taught to cooperate in informing parents and teachers of illness. They should also learn the importance of following the doctor's orders during an illness. They should know who in their school and community is in charge of the communicable disease control program and should learn to support the measures advocated, such as those discussed in Chapter 2.

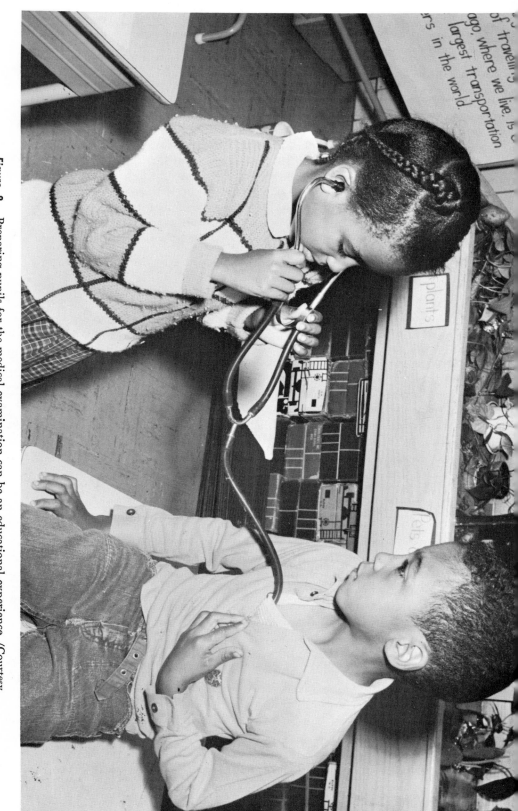

Figure 8. Preparing pupils for the medical examination can be an educational experience. (Courtesy of the Chicago Public Schools, Chicago, Illinois.)

Care of Emergencies

Just as the home must be prepared to meet sudden illness or injury, so, too, must the school, including both school personnel and children. In an efficiently run school there will be written policies in regard to emergency care, including policies for the rendering of first aid, isolation of children with communicable diseases, notification of parents, methods of getting children home, and procedures for securing medical care in case of a serious emergency. Children as well as their parents should know what these policies are. They may, within limitations, even help to formulate the policies. A study of policies should be included in every health instruction program.

COMMUNITY HEALTH NEEDS

Over and above community needs that have been dealt with earlier in this chapter are certain needs associated with the health and welfare of the community as a whole. These include needs related to environmental health; general measures for disease prevention and control; community safety; disaster preparedness; and personnel and facilities for health and medical care. Each of these needs will be discussed with special reference to its implications for school health education. Illustrations that are chosen in no way represent a complete coverage of even the most essential needs about which a community, including its school children, should be concerned.

Environmental Health [7]

Water Supplies and Sewage Disposal

For years, the city dweller has given little thought to the source of his water supply or to the sewage-disposal methods used by his community. These matters, which were of direct concern to our forebears a century or less ago, have been considered to be beyond the need for attention by the individual citizen. But changes are occurring that can no longer leave us complacent.

Each year there are increasing demands for water as our population grows and our living standards rise. Yet with each year, the supply of safe and usable water is decreasing. Thousands of communities in the United States today need new or improved public water supplies as well as sewerage systems. Thousands of others

---

[7] For a more complete summary of concepts on environmental health, see Health Concepts; Guides for Health Instruction. Washington, D.C., American Association for Health, Physical Education, and Recreation, 1967, pp. 24–33.

must give greater heed to potential or actual causes of pollution, such as harmful chemicals in household wastes, and waste products from industry which find their way into our water supplies. Add to this the many homes in rural areas which need new or improved facilities, and the unknown number of schools whose systems should be improved, and one recognizes a problem of great national concern.

In this area of needed community health improvement, education is the principal weapon of attack. Communities must learn to recognize the importance of good sanitation and must be willing to provide funds to install and maintain adequate systems. Students should investigate needs in their own community and take part in promotional programs for improvements.

Food Sanitation

Food sanitation touches closely upon the lives of every individual in the community. Long before food reaches homes, schools, or other eating places, it may be exposed to contamination by a variety of means unless it is properly protected and handled.

Problems of food handling in stores, restaurants, and other eating places have attracted much public attention in many sections of the country. Health authorities and managers of food establishments are working together to improve food-handling practices; the public is being aroused to demand better protection for the food it buys. Principles involved in food handling in homes apply also to food handling in public places. Students, who often help in food purchases, and who may sometimes work in stores and public eating places during out-of-school hours, should understand and apply good food-handling practices.

Milk is one of the most easily contaminated of foods. Disease germs which cause such human diseases as undulant fever, tuberculosis, septic sore throat, and salmonellosis may pass from an infected cow or goat into the milk and produce infection in a person unless the germs have been destroyed by pasteurization before consumption. Contamination may also take place as a result of unclean handling of milk during the various processes through which it passes from animal to consumer. Improper storage and refrigeration of milk will provide conditions which favor the growth of harmful bacteria which may have entered the milk from infected cows or human beings.

Sanitary milk control starts with the elimination of all infected animals. Intensive programs over a period of years have resulted in almost complete elimination of cattle infected with tuberculosis. Similar programs are now being directed to the eradication of livestock infected with the germs which produce brucellosis (undulant fever) in man. A collateral program is vaccination of calves against brucellosis.

Safe milk is milk which not only comes from healthy animals, but also is produced under the highest standards of cleanliness. Milk, to be safe, must be adequately pasteurized. An example at point is the effect of pasteurization on brucellosis. As recently as 1950, as many as 50 per cent of the cases were from unpasteurized milk. Today, brucellosis is largely an occupational disease of slaughterhouse workers, farmers, and others who handle infected carcasses.

Facts on food sanitation should be in the possession of every school child old enough to know what they mean. They provide a field of fruitful study for urban and rural children alike.

Air Pollution and Radiation Exposure

Air pollution has become a matter of national concern. Outside air, especially in metropolitan areas, is becoming increasingly contaminated with smoke, dust, and gases—products of our modern way of life. These pollutants come from the fuels we burn in homes and factories, from automobile exhaust, and from the production and processing of materials in mines and factories.

Evidence is accumulating that polluted air can affect health. Though much research must yet be done to demonstrate relationships between air pollution and specific diseases, it is known that illnesses and deaths have occurred among people with chronic respiratory diseases, such as asthma, on days when the atmosphere has been heavily laden with smog. A most dramatic instance that illustrates this relationship took place in London, England, in 1952. When heavy smog settled on London, so many more deaths than usual occurred that a special study was made, with the conclusion that about 4,000 deaths were precipitated by the smog. Studies also show that emphysema and other chronic diseases of the lungs are increasing as industrialization increases. The young scientist in high school will find air pollution control a fascinating field in which he himself may wish to carry on experimentation. He can seek help for such study from specialists now in many city and state health departments as well as in universities.

Radiation exposure is a subject of much current discussion and research. In actual fact, man has been exposed to radiation throughout his life on earth. Cosmic radiation and naturally occurring radioactive substances in water, soil, and atmosphere have been sources of external exposure, while water, food, and air have been sources of internal exposure. With development of the atomic and nuclear bombs, as well as the wide development and use of radioactive materials in medicine, industry, agriculture, and research, the potential for radiation exposure has increased. The extent of damage from exposure depends not only on the kind of radiation involved but also on the dose and period of exposure, as well as other factors. With proper application of safety precautions, radiation can be used without hazard to individuals. Developments in the use of radioactive materials and in methods employed to prevent exposure can provide interesting subjects for classroom study.

General Measures for Disease Prevention and Control

The prevention and control of childhood diseases referred to previously, though of special importance at school age, is only one part of the community's communicable disease control program with which children and adults alike should learn to cooperate. The community as a whole must be constantly alert to possible disease outbreaks and properly protected from their damaging effects.

Health education is needed to put more widely into practice measures known to be of value in the prevention and control of disease. Schools should join actively with public health departments in such community-wide efforts. Education is essential, as we have already mentioned, for the conduct of successful immunization programs, and for the eradication of insects and animals which may transmit disease germs harmful to human beings. Lack of organized health services often hampers measures for disease prevention and control. Even when personnel are on hand, people must be willing to cooperate with necessary procedures. Persuasion through education is a far better weapon than enforcement.

Community Safety[8]

Accidents of the school-age child and accidents that occur in homes, on farms, and at school have already been discussed. Other types of accidents that are of community-wide concern include motor vehicle accidents, accidents in and around water, industrial accidents, and a miscellaneous group of accidents that occur through a variety of causes. Special mention is made here of motor vehicle accidents and accidents in and around water.

In 1965, motor vehicle accidents caused 49,000 deaths and were responsible for an estimated 1,800,000 disabling injuries. By far the greatest number of fatal accidents occurred in rural areas while the greatest number of nonfatal accidents occurred in urban areas. Collisions between motor vehicles top the list when fatal accidents are

---

[8] Data in this section are taken from Accident Facts. Chicago, Illinois, National Safety Council, 1966, 96 pp.

classified by types. Nearly one third of the fatal accidents involved vehicles which were being driven too fast for existing conditions. As mentioned in the previous chapter, drinking may be a factor in as many as one half of the fatal motor vehicle accidents. Though in 1965 seat belts had been installed in about one half of all passenger cars, there was estimated to be only about 30 per cent usage of these belts. A National Safety Council study of fatal accidents indicated that the fatality rate of users of seat belts was nearly three fourths lower than that of nonusers. When motor vehicle accidents are analyzed by frequency of accident involvement according to age, the highest frequencies are in the under 20 and the 20–24 age groups. Within recent years there has been a great increase in motorcycles, including motor scooters, motorized bicycles, and motorized tricycles. Between 1964 and 1965 motorcycles increased by 31 per cent, but deaths of motorcycle riders increased by 41 per cent. It becomes clear from these data that school and community-wide education toward greater skill and responsibility in driving is imperative on a continuing basis at all times.

As more and more people take to the water, instruction in water safety grows in importance. Home and community swimming pools have become popular, as have small craft of all types. Swimming and boating can be highly pleasurable sports; they are, nevertheless, dangerous sports unless proper precautions are taken. Drownings rank second among causes of fatal accidents in the 5 to 14 age group and fourth for all age groups. Though there are no comparable data on nonfatal water accidents, it is apparent that they far exceed fatal accidents. Conditions which may result in accidents around swimming pools include overcrowding; running on wet, hard surfaces; and jumping and diving in shallow water or crowded spots. Wires or power lines, as well as lighting equipment and electric appliances used in and about the pool, can be very dangerous. Swimming alone or without life guards present at public pools and beaches may lead to drownings which could have been avoided. Failure to follow recognized rules or procedures has led to unnecessary deaths and accidents of Scuba divers and skin divers.

In 1965, over 1,000 people were killed in water transport accidents—from falls, burns, etc., as well as drownings. Three fourths of the drownings involved boats with capacity of less than ten persons. Studies have shown that most boating accidents happen with small pleasure boats and that most victims are inexperienced boatmen or nonswimmers. Schools should not only teach safety measures in and around water; they should also teach skills in swimming and handling of small craft as well as rescue and survival techniques. They may be aided in this task by various community organizations.

In health and safety instruction young people should be given an opportunity to investigate the most frequent causes of accidents in the locality in which they live and to consider the community's responsibilities for preventive and control measures. All students, before they leave school, should have acquired basic skills in first aid.

Disaster Preparedness

Floods, tornadoes, hurricanes, blizzards, epidemics, explosions, and fires, as well as nuclear attacks, can create situations in which full mobilization of community resources, such as food, shelter, and medical care, become a realistic necessity.

Designated governmental and quasi-governmental (American National Red Cross) authorities have specific duties to perform when disaster strikes. The success of their efforts is dependent upon widespread citizen cooperation. Well-directed citizen action in turn is dependent upon education of all the people, including the school-age child.

On national, state, and local levels, manuals for school use are now available. Many suggest appropriate learning experiences for the different grade levels. Pupils have a right to be taught in accordance with the recommendations of these manuals and in line with local community needs.

Personnel and Facilities for Health and Medical Care

Better health for the country through better services is a problem of national concern. As pointed out in the first chapter, much progress has been made in providing health and medical services for the elderly and the poor, and much new legislation is resulting in a wide variety of new services for the population as a whole. A compelling and persistent problem, however, is finding the funds on an individual and community basis to pay for the ever increasing costs of health and medical care. An equally compelling problem is finding the personnel to provide the basic preventive and corrective services once such facilities as hospitals, clinics, nursing homes, and laboratories are available. Added to the dilemma is poor use of the services and facilities. Even when they are provided, many families do not know when or how to use them or fail to use them wisely.

An intelligently informed public is basic to securing individual and community understanding and support for essential preventive and protective services. Community education is the key. Education must begin with the school child but must extend into the community at large if needed improvements are to occur. Education on health careers and on the economics of health care should be an integral part of the school program.

SUMMARY

There are many health needs associated with family living, school experiences, and community development that children may study with profit. Some of the more outstanding of these needs that may touch intimately the lives of children during school years have been summarized in the preceding pages. Suggestions have also been given as to how children may be helped through education to contribute to meeting their needs.

There is a great unexplored field for total community cooperation in the solution of community health problems through the educational process. The school should utilize every opportunity for identifying itself with such community efforts. In so doing, its own program will grow in vigor, and its children will have experiences in citizenship that are of lasting value.

REFERENCES

Anderson, G. W., Arnstein, M. G., and Lester, M. R.: Communicable Disease Control. 4th Ed. New York, The Macmillan Company, 1962, 606 pp.

Anderson, W. J.: Design for Family Living; A Guide from Childhood to Old Age. Minneapolis, T. S. Denison & Company, Inc., 1964, 384 pp.

Byrd, O. E.: Health. 4th Ed. Philadelphia, W. B. Saunders Company, 1966, 441 pp.

Cauffman, J. G., Petersen, E. L., and Emrick, J. A.: Medical care of school children: factors influencing outcome of referral from a school health program. American Journal of Public Health, 57:60–73 (Jan.) 1967.

Cities in Crisis; the Challenge of Change. Welfare Administration Publication No. 20. Washington, D.C., U.S. Government Printing Office, 1967, 47 pp.

Conant, J. B.: Slums and Suburbs. New York, McGraw-Hill Book Company, 1961, 147 pp.

Control of Communicable Diseases in Man. 10th Ed., 1965. New York, The American Public Health Association, 1740 Broadway, 1965, 282 pp. (An official report edited by J. E. Gordon.)

Diehl, H. S.: Healthful Living. 7th Ed. New York, McGraw-Hill Book Company, 1964, 691 pp.

Gabrielson, I. W., Levin, L. S., and Ellison, M. D.: Factors affecting school health follow-up. American Journal of Public Health, 57:48–59 (Jan.) 1967.

Harrington, M.: The Other America; Poverty in the United States. Baltimore, Penguin Books, Inc., 1965, 186 pp.

Health Concepts; Guides for Health Instruction. Washington, D.C., American Association for Health, Physical Education, and Recreation, 1967, 49 pp.

Health Education: A Conceptual Approach to Curriculum Design. St. Paul, Minn., 3M Education Press, Box 3100, 1967, 141 pp. (By the School Health Education Study.)

Irelan, L. M., Editor: Low-Income Life Styles. Welfare Administration Publication No. 14. Washington, D.C., U.S. Government Printing Office, 1966, 86 pp.

Johns, E. B., Sutton, W. C., and Webster, L. E.: Health for Effective Living. 4th Ed. New York, McGraw-Hill Book Company, 1966, 540 pp.

Joint Committee on Health Problems in Education of the National Education Association and the American Medical Association: Health Appraisal of School Children. 3rd Ed. Washington, D.C., and Chicago, The Associations, 1961, 49 pp.

Joint Committee on Health Problems in Education of the National Education Association and the American Medical Association: Health Aspects of the School Lunch Program. 2nd Ed. Washington, D.C., and Chicago, The Associations, 1962, 30 pp.

Joint Committee on Health Problems in Education of the National Education Association and the American Medical Association: Healthful School Living. Washington, D.C., and Chicago, The Associations, 1957, 323 pp.

Joint Committee on Health Problems in Education of the National Education Association and the American Medical Association: School Health Services. 2nd Ed. Washington, D.C., and Chicago, The Associations, 1964, 414 pp.

Kerber, A., and Bommarito, B.: The Schools and the Urban Crisis; A Book of Readings. New York, Holt, Rinehart and Winston, Inc., 1965, 367 pp.

Man—his environment and health. American Journal of Public Health, 54:1–83 (Jan.) 1964. (Part II—a special issue on the subject.)

Miller, B. F., and Burt, J. J.: Good Health; Personal and Community. 2nd Ed. Philadelphia, W. B. Saunders Company, 1966, 508 pp.

National Committee on School Health Policies of the NEA and the AMA: Suggested School Health Policies. 4th Ed. Chicago, American Medical Association, 1966, 54 pp.

Nemir, A.: The School Health Program. 2nd Ed. Philadelphia, W. B. Saunders Company, 1965, 418 pp.

Rosenau, M. J.: Preventive Medicine and Public Health. 9th Ed. by F. Maxcy and P. Sartwell. New York, Appleton-Century-Crofts, Inc., 1965, 1070 pp.

School Health Program; An Outline for School and Community. Public Health Service Publication No. 834. Revised August 1966. Washington, D.C., U.S. Government Printing Office, 1966, 7 pp.

Shaver, J. A.: The learning environment. Journal of School Health, 37:226–231 (May) 1967.

Shostak, A. B., and Gomberg, W.: New Perspectives on Poverty. Englewood Cliffs, N.J., Prentice-Hall, Inc., 1965, 185 pp.

Smolensky, J., and Haar, F. B.: Principles of Community Health. 2nd Ed. Philadelphia, W. B. Saunders Company, 1967, 515 pp.

Strasser, M. K., Aaron, J. E., Bohn, R. C., and Eales, J. R.: Fundamentals of Safety Education. New York, The Macmillan Company, 1964, 453 pp.

Straus, R.: Poverty as an obstacle to health progress in our rural areas. American Journal of Public Health, 55:1772–1779 (Nov.) 1965.

Turner, C. E.: Personal and Community Health. 13th Ed. St. Louis, The C. V. Mosby Company, 1967, 448 pp.

Yerby, A. S.: The disadvantaged and health care. American Journal of Public Health, 56:5–9 (Jan.) 1966.

4

EDUCATIONAL CONCEPTS AND PRACTICES: A BASIS FOR HEALTH EDUCATION

One who would do effective health teaching must not only take health needs into account, but also consider how health education can interrelate with education as a whole. What, for example, are the aims of education in general and how may health education contribute to attainment of these aims? How do people learn and how can theories of learning be applied to health education? What curriculum changes are occurring and how may these changes affect health teaching? Though these and other questions cannot be discussed in detail, in this chapter a brief examination is made of selected points having implications for health teaching.

AIMS OF EDUCATION AND OF HEALTH EDUCATION

Each of us who is seriously concerned with the education of children and youth needs to think through what our children should be, do, and know as a consequence of their schooling. The many new demands on schools today make it increasingly difficult for us to see clearly in what directions we are or should be going. No longer does the child-study approach to education provide sufficient direction; yet knowledge of the children and youth we teach and the environment of which they are a part is of great importance in determining aims. No longer can schools limit their goals to teaching facts and more facts unrelated to broader concepts and principles; the growing body of knowledge is too great and the problem of selection too difficult. No longer can educators ignore human needs and man's struggle for identity in an ever more complex world community; education is a part of culture and must change as culture changes. Foshay has stated:

> Our task in curriculum work, therefore, is greatly complicated by the opportunities and perils of our times. We have to come to a deeper knowledge of the child we teach and of the man we hope he will become than we have ever known, in order that we may properly take into account the nature of organized knowledge in the service of the society we would have. It is in the unity of these three—the child, the society, and organized knowledge—that future excellence in the schools will be found.[1]

Over the years, educators have attempted to determine broad aims of education. As Foshay has implied, these aims reflect the kind of society we live in and the people's expectations of schools. In 1918, the Commission on the Reorganization of Secondary Education established the following as the seven principal aims of education: good health, command of fundamental processes, worthy home membership, vocation, civic education, worthy use of leisure, and ethical character. In 1938, the Educational Policies Commission set forth a series of objectives under four major headings: self-realization, human relationship, economic efficiency, and civic responsibility. The commission has redefined and refocused its statement in light of changing conditions in schools and society. To quote from its 1961 report:

> The purpose which runs through and strengthens all other educational purposes—the common thread of education—is the development of the ability to think. This is the central purpose to which the school must be oriented if it is to accomplish either its traditional tasks or those newly accentuated by recent changes in the world. To say that it is central is not to say that it is the sole purpose or in all circumstances the most important purpose, but that it must be a pervasive concern in the work of the school. Many agencies contribute to achieving educational objectives, but this particular objective will not be generally attained unless the school focuses on it. In this context, therefore, the development of every student's rational powers must be recognized as centrally important.[2]

In Chapter 1 the reader will find statements on the aims of health education as set forth by the World Health Organization. An attempt is made here to show in parallel columns the relationship between specific objectives of education and those of health education. The objectives of education, outlined in the left-hand column, have been adapted from a list prepared by the Educational

---

[1] Foshay, A. W.: A modest proposal for the improvement of education. In What Are the Sources of the Curriculum? A Symposium. Washington, D.C., Association for Supervision and Curriculum Development, NEA, 1962, p. 13.

[2] Educational Policies Commission: The Central Purpose of American Education. Washington, D.C., National Education Association, 1961, p. 12.

Policies Commission. The equivalent objectives for health education are outlined in the right-hand column. Although all of the aims are broad, and their attainment can be expected only over a span of many years, during a child's school years, he should be able to make important progress toward their realization. However, if broad objectives are to have meaning in the life of a child, they must be translated into attainable goals at a given point of time and with a specific child or group of children in mind. Suggestions for the refinement of objectives are given in Chapter 5.

Objectives of Education (Adapted from "The Purposes of Education in American Democracy")	*Objectives of Health Education as Related to General Objectives of Education*
1. Optimum development of the individual	1. Optimum development of the individual with special reference to physical and emotional development
a. To use wisely the fundamental tools of learning	a. To use wisely the fundamental tools of learning in the field of health
(1) Speech	(1) To speak articulately and intelligently on matters of health
(2) Reading	(2) To read selectively and understandingly in the field of health
(3) Writing	(3) To write simply and accurately on health matters
(4) Numbers	(4) To be reliable in one's interpretation and translation of health data
b. To develop powers of listening and observation	b. To show discrimination in what one listens to in the field of health. To use powers of observation wisely to broaden comprehension of health problems and principles
c. To maintain and improve health	c. To develop and practice desirable health behavior
d. To use leisure time wisely	d. To participate in a variety of wholesome and healthful recreational and leisure-time activities
e. To appreciate beauty	e. To appreciate the aesthetic values of healthful living, including cleanliness and sanitation
f. To develop a philosophy which gives self-direction to life	f. To make emotional adjustments which enable one to face life realistically and to develop ability for self-direction in one's own health behavior
2. Betterment of human relationships	2. Betterment of human relationships, particularly from the standpoint of health
a. To develop ability to consider	a. To contribute to the maintenance

Objectives of Education	*Objectives of Health Education as Related to General Objectives of Education*
the well-being of others	and improvement of health of friends, neighbors, members of the family and of local, state, national, and world communities
b. To enjoy a rich, sincere, and varied social life	b. To find emotional satisfactions in daily relationships in the school, home, and community
c. To cooperate with others in work and play	c. To work cooperatively, rather than competitively, with others in the solution of health problems
d. To observe the amenities of social behavior	d. To apply acceptable rules of conduct in respect to health practices. To recognize the emotional health values of consideration toward others
e. To appreciate the family as a social institution	e. To understand and appreciate the biological and emotional bases for unified family life
f. To conserve family ideals	f. To understand the physical and emotional health problems associated with marriage, homemaking, and parenthood, and to work out ways of handling these problems in immediate and future family situations To work for economic and social conditions which will contribute to health and happiness in the home To make adjustments required to conserve the integrity of the family
g. To develop skills in homemaking	g. To develop such skills as food preparation, care of the sick, child care
h. To maintain democracy in the home	h. To use democratic methods in making physical and emotional health adjustments in the home
3. Economic efficiency in the production and consumption of goods and services	3. Application of health facts and principles in respect to economic efficiency in the production and consumption of goods and services
The Producer a. To know the satisfaction of good workmanship	a. To recognize and experience the physical and emotional health satisfactions associated with appropriate work
b. To choose intelligently an occupation suited to the individual's capacities	b. To recognize and accept one's health assets and liabilities, and to use them as one guide in finding a suitable occupation

Objectives of Education	*Objectives of Health Education as Related to General Objectives of Education*
c. To succeed in a chosen vocation; to make adjustments for maintaining and improving efficiency	c. To have a wholesome emotional attitude toward work To understand the health and saftey hazards associated with a chosen vocation and to be prepared to cooperate in control measures, or to take steps to prevent or avoid the hazards
d. To appreciate the social values of work	d. To appreciate how work may contribute directly or indirectly to human health and happiness

The Consumer

a. To plan the economics of one's own life	a. To budget so as to provide the essential requirements for health maintenance
b. To use judgment and efficiency in buying	b. To recognize quackery and nostrums in the field of health To refrain from purchasing drugs or health cures of unknown value To use only dependable resources for health and medical care
c. To take appropriate measures to safeguard one's interests	c. To take aggressive steps in educational and legislative programs which safeguard the health of the consumer

4. Civic responsibility	4. Civic responsibility, especially in respect to health
a. To have a sense of social justice and understanding, and to act to correct unsatisfactory social conditions	a. To recognize that optimum health is the right of every individual and to work for adequate community programs for health maintenance and improvement
b. To respect honest differences of opinion	b. To keep emotionally balanced when associated with people who hold different opinions
c. To have respect for the law	c. To have an attitude of respect for health laws, and to seek improvement or change in any laws of which one does not approve
d. To be economically literate	d. To be aware that many health problems have their roots in economic and social ills, and to work actively for conditions that will increase effectiveness of human resources
e. To be a cooperative member of the world community	e. To be aware of the interdependence of nations in respect to matters of health and disease; to recognize the contribution of other countries in this field; and to make one's own contribution in the world community

Objectives of Education	Objectives of Health Education as Related to General Objectives of Education
f. To accept civic duties	f. To take active part in school and community efforts for health improvement
g. To accept and apply democratic ideals	g. To have experience in democratic solution of health problems, in school, home, and community

There is economy of effort as well as strength through reinforcement when teachers develop health education with recognition of the wider values that may be obtained. To illustrate, the elementary school child who tells or writes about his visit to the dentist's office is not only fixing in his mind a desirable health practice and perhaps verbalizing fears, but he is also learning to use the fundamental tools of speaking or writing. The boy who comments on how good it feels to be clean is not only appreciating the aesthetic values of healthful living, but he is also in a small but practical way appreciating beauty itself. Learning home nursing helps to meet specific health needs; it also contributes to better family living and ultimately to the improvement of human relationships. Experience in evaluating commercial advertising on health and medical care may result in refusal to use harmful nostrums or "cures." It will also help make one a more intelligent consumer of goods and services in general. Participation by students in community programs for health betterment, such as in the promotion of a safe water supply, may make the community a healthier place in which to live. Such experiences will, in addition, be excellent preparation for civic responsibility.

A leader in health education who was formerly a county school superintendent once stated that she had shifted to the field of health education because she felt that it offered greater opportunity than any other field to improve education as a whole. Whether or not the reader agrees with this point of view, he could scarcely deny that health education teems with opportunities to attack vital problems which have their ramifications in every phase of living. Chapters 8 and 9 describe many examples of efforts to teach health with larger goals in mind.

THE LEARNING PROCESS AND HEALTH EDUCATION

Health education, as we have already seen, seeks to bring about improvements in what people actually feel, think, and do about health. As Ruskin once said of education as a whole, "Education does not mean teaching people what they do not know. It means teaching them to behave as they do not behave." If we are to attempt to help people toward behavior changes, we must try to gain some understanding of how behavior changes take place, or, as commonly stated in education, how learning occurs. For insight on human behavior and its changes, the teacher will find profitable reading in books on the psychology of learning and in the fields of philosophy, anthropology, sociology, social psychology, and child development. In this brief discussion, a few points only will be summarized with special reference to health education.

The Nature of the Learning Process

Learning is an active process occurring through the learner's own efforts. In learning, reactions within the learner and interactions between the learner and his environment may have both an emotional and a rational basis. At the risk of oversimplifying this highly complex subject, one may regard the learning process as made up of three principal elements, namely, the motivation to learn; the goal response or the end product of learning; and, in between, the things to be mastered, or, in other words, the things that stand in the way of reaching the desired goal.

These three elements are best illustrated in terms of learning a specific skill. Let us suppose that a high school girl wants to learn to paddle a canoe so that she can go on a canoe trip with her friends. In this situation the motivation to learn is the desire to go on the trip. The goal response is the actual fruition of her wishes, that is, taking the trip safely by canoe. Between these two are the things to be mastered, that is, the skills she must acquire in the manipulation of the canoe and the rules of the water she should know in order that the canoe trip may be made with ease and safety.

Learning is, of course, not usually so simple, but in all effective learning, interests and purposes hold a prominent place. Most children do not learn health for health's sake, but rather as a means toward goals important to them. In the illustration just used, the learning of water safety was coincidental with learning to handle the canoe for the trip.

As learning takes place, or, in other words, as a person undergoes behavior changes, he moves through several discernible though not fully understood stages. Early stages may be identified as awareness, interest, and desire. Desire may be followed by conviction, and, if conditions are right, conviction will ultimately be followed by action and repetition until the change becomes a part of the person's beliefs and practices. In health teaching we at times are concerned primarily with helping children to become aware of, and to develop interest in, a particular health practice or situation. Thus, we teach pupils in primary grades about the work of the nurse in the school so that they may know who she is and view her as a friendly person ready to help when they need her help. More often, however, we try to evoke in pupils desires and convictions which will result in beliefs and practices of immediate and lasting value.

To gain further insight into the learning process, we may note different degrees of responses on the part of pupils within learning situations. Some pupils do not respond at all. So-called "hard to reach" persons are the subject of much serious study today. Other pupils may respond only at the verbal level. They can talk about a subject and can parrot material taught to them, but that is as far as they go. Still others may show appreciation of a desirable health measure to the point at which they will promote the measure, yet do nothing about it themselves. A student reporter for the school newspaper, for example, may write a very convincing article about better selection of food in the school cafeteria, but may then go to the corner drugstore for his noon-hour meal of potato chips, soft drink, and candy.

Change in immediate action, such as is demanded in intensive community health programs, is another degree of response. In an immunization program, for example, children may go willingly to be immunized simply because of the pressures of the program or because it is the thing to do. Such momentary behavior change, though desirable, is often not lasting. When repetition of a practice is needed at a later date, as is the case with some immunizations, further extrinsic stimulation may be required to continue the desired practice. "Dropouts" in immunization programs which demand several "shots" with intervals between are a perplexing problem to health authorities. So, too, are failures to carry out on a continuing basis many other important health measures.

Change that is lasting, that becomes a part of a person's beliefs and practices, or is internalized, is the most frequently sought in our health education efforts and yet is the most difficult to bring about. Such change is governed by conviction based on knowledge and understanding; it is the outgrowth of decisions made by the individual himself. Let us look now at some of the factors that influence behavior change.

Factors That Influence Learning

Values

People hold to certain values which influence their perceptions and actions. Values are often deeply rooted in the culture or develop out of the circumstances under which people live. They are among the marks which distinguish one community or one individual from another. Conflicts in values often stand in the way of essential health progress. Willard has stated:

> The philosophy of social responsibility, that society has an obligation to those who are underprivileged and need help, that organization is essential for effective action, is inevitable in a highly interdependent, industrialized and urbanized society. It implies a value system that is in conflict with another value system which has been traditional in the United States. This latter system emphasizes the responsibility of the individual, the importance of personal initiative, free enterprise, and the economic profit motive. . . .
>
> The conflict between these two value systems contributes to many of our problems. Although the social conscience of our nation has been changing rapidly since the great depression of the thirties, there remains a significant public attitude based upon the Elizabethan poor law philosophy, that the poor are poor and the sick are sick because they did not assume personal responsibility or exhibit the initiative and gumption to take care of themselves. . . .[3]

With such attitudes, too many teachers and health workers have been blind to the values held by those whom they serve, values that must be understood if communication with such people is to be meaningful. We are beginning to recognize, for example, that many of our urban and rural poor, long bound by the desperate conditions under which they live, may be oriented to the present, suspicious of "outsiders," and preoccupied with the basic demands of existence. Values growing out of such circumstances are the subject of increasing attention by educators, sociologists, anthropologists, psychologists, and other social scientists.

In somewhat different vein, teachers can gain perspective for health teaching through being sensitive to the values held by the age groups with which they work. The value system of teen-agers is a case in point. Many teen-agers have money to spend and spend it—on clothes, cars, records, cosmetics, and other luxury items. They have their own language and their own modes of dress which vary with class backgrounds. The values they give to scholastic competence and intellectual pursuits likewise differ with backgrounds and locality. Magazines written for them, and to which they write copiously, reveal them to be shy and uncertain, yet wanting to be popular; to be concerned with overweight, underweight, and acne, and wanting to be attractive. They are preoccupied with sex. They imitate or borrow from adult culture, but are rebellious toward adult controls. Their values are their own. When they become a part of the labor force, however, or seriously assume responsibilities as students in college, they no longer reflect a teen-age culture; they are, in truth, young adults following an "adult-made pattern."[4]

---

[3] Willard, W. R.: Report of the National Commission on Community Health Services; Next Steps. American Journal of Public Health, *56:*1829–1830 (Nov.) 1966.

[4] For further discussion on the subject, see Teen-age culture. The Annals of the American Academy of Political and Social Science, *338:*1–136 (Nov.) 1961. (See especially Bernard, J.: Teen-age culture: an overview, pp. 1–12.)

An important task of education is to discover the values that are held important by pupils and to guide thinking and action in order to develop worthwhile values that are forceful enough to bring about desirable changes. Some educators feel that children can best acquire a set of workable values by actually living through concrete, practical situations that require an expression or a definition of values. Dr. Alice Miel has said:

> From the standpoint of process it would seem desirable that groups attempt to arrive at common values less by intellectual discussion before launching an enterprise and more by undergoing together many experiences involving valuation throughout the process. Only as values are lived will they come to have real and deep meaning to those who hold them. Only as they come to be deeply held can values exert a strong motivating force and genuinely influence the direction of efforts. If values are deemed important enough, they will prompt the holders to search for ways of realizing them.[5]

In the field of health, each child at his own maturity level may be helped to arrive at his own set of values by thinking them through in relation to concrete, practical situations and then applying those values in practice in accordance with his decisions. As one example, pupils in a sixth grade discussed the following questions while studying qualities that make a good member of the school community:

> How can we judge whether we are good members of the school community?
> Who is responsible for safe and healthful living at school?
> What can we do for more harmonious relationships in our classroom and on the school grounds?

As a group, these pupils decided to offer their services to the school principal for help on the playgrounds and in the lunchroom. As individuals, they made progress in showing greater tolerance toward each other. A very shy pupil was gradually drawn into group activities; a new pupil from a displaced family was made to feel at home.

Education can and does call forth changes in values. The responsibility that falls upon us as educators is considerable, however, as we disturb people's traditional patterns of feeling and thinking in order to substitute new ways. We must fully understand our own motives and at all costs preserve the individuality, the dignity, and the feeling of self-respect among those with whom we deal.

Perceptions

Perception plays an important part in learning. People perceive things in the light of their knowledge, experience, and value systems. If a person perceives something in a specific way, that is the way it is from his viewpoint, though it may be perceived quite dif-

---

[5] Miel, A.: Changing the Curriculum; A Social Process. New York, D. Appleton-Century Company, Inc., 1946, p. 37.

ferently by another person. Such selective perception must be taken
into account in health teaching. To illustrate, in many parts of
the world where food is more difficult to obtain than in our own
country, children of many families eat frequently, picking up food
as they can. Nutrition education stressing three meals a day would
have little meaning to children in such situations. Lantis suggests
that our young people are falling into similar patterns of eating.[6]
With the products of the vending machine and refrigerator age, the
working mother, and the habit of eating out, they too eat "here and
there, now and then." Does this suggest that for such young people
perceptions of what constitutes a balanced daily diet may likewise
be changing? Does it also suggest that teachers may need to redirect
their teaching on food selection?

   We all know people who respond to health and safety teachings
with the "it-can't-happen-to-me" attitude or who do not even allow
themselves to be exposed to such teachings. We recognize here the
child who likes dangerous adventure and daring, who completely
ignores efforts to help him live more safely; for him, the need for
being cautious just does not apply. Some of us refuse to install or
to use seat belts in passenger vehicles. We reject as too disagreeable,
or too improbable, the idea that we ourselves could be responsible
for a dangerous act that could result in injury or death. Should we
in our educational efforts, then, stress what *can* be perceived—that
an accident might occur through someone else's actions?

   In an extensive study of a rural community in New York State,
Koos identified three more or less distinct sub-cultures from the
standpoint of behavior patterns relating to health. Each group had
its own perception of illness and its own standards for seeking
medical care. Koos concludes:

   In the last analysis the health of the community is based upon the ideas,
ideals, attitudes, and behavior patterns of the individual and his family, for these
determine what he will or will not, can or cannot, expect or accept from those
who make his health their professional concern. Perception in all aspects of illness and health must be seen as varying from one stratum in the social hierarchy
to another. . . . These class related differences are differences in perception, and
from perception stems acceptance or rejection of what is professionally known to
be necessary for health.[7]

Readiness

   Readiness is basic to learning. Readiness is determined to a
large extent by the degree of maturity a person has reached, by his
native endowments, by his background, including his previous ex-

   [6] Lantis, M.: The child consumer. Journal of Home Economics, *54*:370–375 (May)
1962.
   [7] Koos, E. L.: The Health of Regionville. New York, Columbia University Press,
1954, pp. 156–157.

periences, by the way he perceives things, and by such emotional factors as anxiety or self-confidence. Thus, the student who has matured to the point at which he can think about abstractions is more likely to care about the social consequences of ill health than is the young child who sees ill health only as an obstacle to doing something immediate that he wants to do. Or girls in a child-care class who are doing baby-sitting may be more ready to find out about proper ways of feeding and playing with children than girls for whom child care is not yet a problem.

In health education, as in all other education, teachers must start at the children's level of development, experiences, and value systems, and see that they have additional experiences in keeping with the characteristics of each particular individual or group. With some children a teacher may demand less, while with others he may demand more.

Timeliness

Closely linked to readiness is the factor of timeliness in teaching. Every person has realized the potency of "striking while the iron is hot." Special community health programs, new legislation, an epidemic, or a seasonal event are typical of situations that may create interest in a particular health problem and make the teaching of that problem timely.

Motivation

Motivation has long been recognized as important for learning. Teachers must be ever alert to those "springs to action" within children and youth, at times utilizing them as a starting point in teaching, at times arousing them when they are latent or apparently lacking. In general, motivations are part and parcel of interests, feelings, or strivings within individuals which lead them on to action. Teachers may provide incentives which tap or arouse motives, but motivation itself comes from within a person.

Motives are classified in different ways by different authorities. Selected motives of special importance to consider in health teaching are discussed briefly here.

Basic organic needs. Food, water, sleep and rest, elimination, activity, sex, and protection from physical harm are among the basic physiological needs of all human beings. Striving for their fulfillment provides powerful motivation for much health learning. For example, the desire of adolescents to be attractive to the other sex, one of the strongest motives at this age level, may form the basis for a great deal of beneficial health teaching.

Need for belonging and affection. All people need the affection of those who are important to them. Moreover, they need to feel that they belong, that they are accepted as human beings. When needs for belonging and affection are thwarted, psychological and social maladjustments may develop. Teachers who recognize this deep-rooted motivation in young people and who provide for its expression in classroom relationships are contributing positively to the children's emotional health.

Need for self-esteem.   People want to feel important, to have self-confidence, and to gain the approval of others. Most children develop a real sense of personal worth if given a chance to act independently and creatively in appropriate situations and to take part in significant undertakings. Health projects which involve useful service in the community can help to satisfy this need for self-esteem. The desire for social approval, for acceptance, can be a strong force toward overcoming faulty health attitudes or habits. Often it is enough to commend a child for some health improvement—to recognize his progress toward some health goal, such as diet regulation in the case of an obese child. Social approval is such a powerful motivating force, however, that we must watch that it is not abused. It can become a dangerous force when children with unequal opportunity for achievement are allowed to compete with one another, as through a classroom display of achievement charts on health.

Desire for new experiences.   The desire for freedom from boredom moves people toward change. Such desire may be directed into constructive channels, but, undirected, may result in restless, unproductive, or even destructive activity. The field of health provides many opportunities for new and worthwhile explorations, as will be seen in Chapters 8 and 9.

Innate interests.   Some young people have definite interests, as for example, the desire to become a physician or nurse. These interests can be used as a starting point for much valuable health learning.

Self-actualization.   The need for self-fulfillment is a compelling force in the lives of many. Even in children and youth, it may become evident among those whose special interests or talents lie deep in science, sports, the arts, or other accomplishments. Self-set goals may have strong motivational value for health learning. To illustrate, the boy who aspires to be an athlete will work diligently for years to qualify for a particular skill or sport and will be willing to carry out health practices that will help him to reach his goal. Though health workers recognize that good health itself contributes to an individual's capacity to live to the fullest, we too often have failed to make this relationship meaningful to children and adults alike. Ways of improving school health education toward this end are discussed in later chapters.

Motivations change as children grow and mature. Motivations at the different age levels and their implications for health teaching are summarized in Chapters 8 and 9.

Instruction

In this discussion of the learning process, the focus has been on the pupils—on their values, perceptions, and motives. It has become clear, however, that the extent to which pupils will change their behavior under the influence of the school depends in considerable measure on the ability of the teacher to understand the motives of the pupils and on his skill in using these motives as a guide in his instructional efforts.

Through instruction, experiences are provided with which pupils interact. The teacher, aided by pupils, selects, organizes, and applies concepts, content, and methods of instruction in line with the needs and interests of the pupils as well as the demands of each learning situation; he locates and uses resources in the form of people and materials. The remaining chapters of this book contain many practical suggestions to help the teacher in performing these functions.

THE CHANGING CURRICULUM—IMPLICATIONS FOR HEALTH TEACHING

At the frontiers of education today, both citizens and school leaders are reassessing the school's place in society with an intensity not equalled in recent years. Major issues focus not only on the central purpose of the school but also on what to teach and how to organize for instruction. At the writing of this fifth edition we cannot discern clearly what the schools of tomorrow will be like. Many conflicting points of view have been set forth on this matter. Schools of today, however, are undergoing rapid changes, and a few of these changes which have special implications for health teaching are mentioned here. The reader is directed to the references at the end of the chapter for a fuller discussion of these and other changes.

Re-emphasis on the Individual

We in this country have committed ourselves to universal education. Over the years we have built a complex system of general education which many feel has served us well. In theory, and often in practice, we have attended to the needs of individual children. As our schools bulge with increased enrollments, as more and more children stay in school for a greater number of years, as costs of education increase, and as mass education techniques are introduced, many thoughtful educators have feared that the needs of individual children would be submerged to the needs of the masses.

New and powerful voices are being heard on behalf of the gifted child, the handicapped child, the delinquent child, the disadvantaged child, and the potential dropout. Accelerated programs, special classes, and individual counseling services are increasingly available for these pupils with special needs. But what of the *average* child who likewise has needs and interests, perhaps less spectacular but nevertheless requiring individualized attention for the full development of his potential? At last, he too is commanding the attention of leaders in education.

A growing emphasis on creativity is one manifestation of this renewed concern for the individual. Miel sees creativity as a way of responding that is available to all human beings and that enables them to cope with increasingly complex problems, conditions, and opportunities. By relating things that were previously unrelated, by coming forth with new products of the creative process, whether ideas or materials, the individual gains new joy in living, increased self-esteem, and greater personal growth. In the process he may also contribute to society's needs.[8]

Health needs of children, as discussed elsewhere in this book, by their very nature demand individualized attention. Perhaps less recognized, but nonetheless important, is the potential in the health field for fostering creativity. The creative student with scientific ability can find in medicine and public health great unexplored areas for experimentation and investigation which, when pursued, may give satisfaction to himself and perhaps contribute also to the welfare of mankind. The creative individual with a sensitivity toward people can find in the vast range of social services boundless opportunities to contribute to the well-being of others. Numerous examples are given in later chapters of worthwhile service projects for students in hospitals, health centers, and other community endeavors. To help the teacher plan and carry on individualized health instruction, a special chapter (Chapter 10) on the subject is found later in this book.

Re-examining the Functions of the School

A considerable controversy exists today as to the school's responsibilities in regard to instruction. This controversy is complex and involves numerous issues. Two issues are mentioned here be-

---

[8] Miel, A., Editor: Creativity in Teaching. Belmont, California, Wadsworth Publishing Company, Inc., 1961, pp. 6–7.

cause of their implications for health teaching, namely, establishing priorities for the school and selecting and organizing curriculum content.

Establishing Priorities for the School

With the great extension of knowledge and the growing competition for the student's time and energies, the question is legitimately raised whether the school should assume full responsibility for helping pupils to achieve generally accepted goals of education, or whether it should share responsibility with family, church, and other agents of education. The Educational Policies Commission, in arriving at its statement on the central purposes of education, states:

> . . . The American school must be concerned with all these objectives if it is to serve all of American life. That these are desirable objectives is clear. Yet they place before the school a problem of immense scope, for neither the schools nor the pupils have the time or energy to engage in all the activities which will fully achieve all these goals. Choices among possible activities are inevitable and are constantly being made in and for every school. But there is no consensus regarding a basis for making these choices. . . .
> Furthermore, education does not cease when the pupil leaves school. No school fully achieves any pupil's goals in the relatively short time he spends in the classroom. The school seeks rather to equip the pupil to achieve them for himself.[9]

If recent statements of several policy forming groups are indicative of the future, we shall see a growing movement of the school into the community and the community into the school—an extension of the pupil's horizons as he moves outside the four walls of the school and a sharing of educational responsibilities as he is helped in the task. This interplay is already occurring in many communities through pupil participation in community-centered projects and through the use of resource people in and out of the classroom. Such changes will leave more time for the schools themselves to help the individual develop the rational powers which "involve the processes of recalling and imagining, classifying and generalizing, comparing and evaluating, analyzing and synthesizing, and deducing and inferring. These processes enable one to apply logic and the available evidence to his ideas, attitudes, and actions, and to pursue better whatever goals he may have."[10]

If applied to health teaching, this would mean that the school must provide the needed health information, help locate and use appropriate resources for learning, give children the opportunity to develop their rational powers as just suggested, and guide them

---

[9] Educational Policies Commission: The Central Purpose of American Education. Washington, D.C., National Education Association, 1961, p. 2.
[10] Ibid., p. 5.

toward making wise health decisions which they can apply in their daily lives. Many examples of such learning opportunities, both within and beyond the classroom, are given elsewhere in this book.

An important ramification of school-community relationships is the extension of pupil interests and activities into the world community. Pupils today do not only study about current world events, but they actually enter into international relationships. They live and study with exchange students from other lands, and a few of the more fortunate are themselves exchange students. They correspond with overseas friends and may even travel to other lands. Through such organizations as the Red Cross and UNICEF, students provide direct services to children in other parts of the world. World health problems are now their problems and are essential subjects for study.

Selecting and Organizing Curriculum Content and Learning Experiences

The school in transition is experimenting with many new patterns of organization for instruction. Teachers are increasingly enriching subject-matter curricula by developing their teaching activities around broad concepts and principles and by providing opportunity for pupils to participate in a wide variety of activities. Emphasis is on discovery, inquiry, and independent study. Teaching is moving away from the presentation of isolated facts which may quickly become obsolete in these rapidly changing times.

The elementary school has long accepted a curriculum focused on the needs and concerns of children. In newer, experimental programs, flexibility is the order of the day. Flexibility is found in the arrangement of learning experiences and in the use of instructional resources. Children are grouped in a variety of ways, according to their abilities and the progress they have made in their studies. Teachers set aside large blocks of time for experimentation and for a deeper search into the meanings of things being studied than can be accomplished when the day is broken into many short periods in which children jump from one subject area to another. Time is provided for individual work, with careful attention to progression in learning for each child, so that growth, not stagnation, occurs.

Special mention should be made of the attention being given at the elementary level to compensatory education for the culturally deprived child.[11] Small-sized classes, use of teaching methods and materials which are suitable to the culture, and employment of teachers trained to work with these children characterize current efforts to improve instruction for this group. In recognition of the

---

[11] Bloom, B. S., Davis, A., and Hess, R.: Compensatory Education for Cultural Deprivation. New York, Holt, Rinehart and Winston, Inc., 1965, 179 pp.

Figure 9. Developing one's rational powers. (Courtesy of Lamar Junior High School, Austin, Texas.)

fact that basic needs, such as food, sleep and rest, clothing, and medical care, can influence a child's capacity to learn, schools in areas of high concentration of the culturally deprived are joining increasingly with other community agencies in efforts to help parents and the children themselves secure these essentials for health and learning. In teaching and in rendering service, the focus is on satisfying immediate goals for this group whose conditions of living have resulted in present, rather than future, orientation in the solving of life's problems.

At the secondary level, proponents of change are deeply concerned with the development of curricula which will provide interest and challenge to the wide variety of youth in high schools today. Compensatory education for the culturally deprived is gaining acceptance in secondary schools as well as elementary. Work-study programs, tutorial help, and encouragement of "peer societies" are among curriculum adaptations recommended for this group. In some communities, special youth programs now exist for disadvantaged young people to help them with personal adjustments and to prepare them for earning a living. Examples of such programs include the Neighborhood Youth Corps for in-school youth from families of low income and Work Opportunity Centers where hard-core school dropouts can receive special training. These programs are highly individualized. In most communities they are tied in with ongoing community activities.

In many subject areas, especially those already well established in schools, new curricula have been prepared at national, state, and local levels. Of the three sources of curricula mentioned earlier in this chapter, the child, society, and an organized body of knowledge, the source which has most frequently formed the basis for the new curricula has been an organized body of knowledge. Outdated content has been brought up to date, scholars in the respective fields have had a part in curriculum revision, and packaged materials have been prepared to guide teachers and pupils. As changes occur, one finds more flexible scheduling, team teaching, variable-sized groups ranging from large to small, as well as individualized instruction and experimentation with new methods of teaching. Master teachers, televised lessons, machine teaching, and other innovations enter into this revolutionized organization for instruction.

Critics of these new programs point to their overemphasis on organized bodies of knowledge and their inadequate attention to the child and society. Though millions of dollars have been spent in the development of new curricula in such fields as the physical and biological sciences and mathematics, some fields have not been dealt with at all. Broad objectives of education have been overlooked, the critics point out, with the result that the total curriculum is too often out of balance. Fortunately, many leaders in education recognize the need for putting the pieces together in a manner meaningful to students and useful to society. One may expect further experimentation and greater attention to evaluation in the years to come.

It is too early to assess the effect of these and other attempts at change on the physical and emotional health of students. One may wonder, however, if in mass instruction programs, in use of teaching machines and other impersonal approaches, there is not danger that the individual student and his health needs may be overlooked. Yet in the specialized programs now available for the disadvantaged, new opportunities exist for attention to the health problems of young people who especially need help.

The impact of recent curriculum developments is being felt in health education as such. As mentioned in Chapter 1, two national groups have each developed series of health concepts intended to serve as guides for health instruction. National, state, and local groups are preparing new curriculum materials and experimenting with new curriculum designs. Through such intensified efforts, educators are increasingly identifying health education as a separate discipline with its own body of knowledge. However, little progress is evident in interrelating health education with other disciplines, such as the biological and social sciences, to assure its proper place in total curriculum development.

In health teaching, the dangers of overemphasis on content and the consequent neglect of the child and society seem remote. Health education by its very nature deals with people and their environment; its organized body of knowledge is drawn from the health needs of the child and the society of which he is a part. Yet if the content is to be translated into improved health behavior, more attention needs to be given to conditions existing in a particular situation and to more dynamic methods for health teaching.

SUMMARY

The school of today is reassessing its role in society. Major issues focus on the central purpose of the school, on what to teach, and how to organize for instruction. Re-emphasis is being placed on the individual—on how he learns and how his full potential may be developed. Increasingly, teaching-learning experiences are organized around broad concepts and principles, and foster inquiry and independent study. Specialized programs for the disadvantaged child are now appearing. These changes are having a profound effect on health education, its direction, its content, and its organization.

REFERENCES

Bruner, J. S.: The Process of Education. Cambridge, Massachusetts, Harvard University Press, 1961, 97 pp.

Cardinal Principles of Secondary Education. Bureau (U.S. Office) of Education Bulletin No. 35, 1918. Washington, D.C., U.S. Government Printing Office, 1937, 32 pp. (A Report of the Commission on the Reorganization of Secondary Education.)

The Changing American School. The Sixty-fifth Yearbook of the National Society for the Study of Education. Part II. Chicago, The University of Chicago Press, 1966, 319 pp.

Conant, J. B.: The American High School Today. New York, McGraw-Hill Book Company, 1959, 140 pp.

Curriculum Change: Direction and Process. Washington, D.C., Association for Supervision and Curriculum Development, NEA, 1966, 59 pp.

Educational Policies Commission: The Purposes of Education in American Democracy. Washington, D.C., The Commission, 1938, 157 pp.

Gardner, J. W.: Self-Renewal; The Individual and the Innovative Society. New York, Harper Colophon Books, Harper & Row, 1965, 141 pp.

Goodlad, J. I., Von Stoephasius, R., and Klein, M. F.: The Changing School Curriculum. New York, The Fund for the Advancement of Education, 477 Madison Avenue, 1966, 122 pp.

Knutson, A. L.: The Individual, Society, and Health Behavior. New York, Russell Sage Foundation, 1965, 533 pp.

McClure, R. M.: Instructional trends in the United States. In New Dimensions in Curriculum Development; the Proceedings of the Second International Curriculum Conference, Toronto, Canada, 1966. Toronto, Ontario, Canada, Ontario Curriculum Institute, 344 Bloor Street, W., 1966, pp. 13–14.

Means, R. K.: The school health education study: a pattern in curriculum development. Journal of School Health, *36:*1–11 (Jan.) 1966.

NEA Project on Instruction. Washington, D.C., National Education Association. Deciding What to Teach, 1963, 264 pp. Education in a Changing Society, 1963, 166 pp. Planning and Organizing for Teaching, 1963, 190 pp. From Bookshelves to Action, 1964, 32 pp.

New Curriculum Developments. Washington, D.C., Association for Supervision and Curriculum Development, NEA, 1965, 106 pp. (A Report of ASCD's Commission on Current Curriculum Developments.)

New Insights and the Curriculum. Yearbook 1963. Washington, D.C., Association for Supervision and Curriculum Development, NEA, 1963, 328 pp.

Olsen, E. G., Editor: School and Community. 2nd Ed. Englewood Cliffs, N.J. Prentice-Hall, Inc. 1954, 534 pp.

Paul, B. D., Editor: Health, Culture and Community. New York, Russell Sage Foundation, 1955, 482 pp.

Perceiving, Behaving, Becoming. Yearbook 1962. Washington, D.C., Association for Supervision and Curriculum Development, NEA, 1962, 256 pp.

Saylor, J. G., and Alexander, W. M.: Curriculum Planning for Modern Schools. New York, Holt, Rinehart and Winston, Inc., 1966, 534 pp.

Schools for the Sixties: A Report of the NEA Project on Instruction. New York, McGraw-Hill Book Company, 1963, 217 pp.

Taba, H.: Curriculum Development; Theory and Practice. New York, Harcourt, Brace & World, Inc., 1962, 526 pp.

Theories of Learning and Instruction. The Sixty-third Yearbook of the National Society for the Study of Education. Part I. Chicago, The University of Chicago Press, 1964, 430 pp.

Trump, J. L., and Baynham, D.: Focus on Change; Guide to Better Schools. Chicago, Rand McNally and Company, 1961, 147 pp.

Tyler, R. W.: Implications of behavioral studies for health education. Journal of School Health, *33*:9–15 (Jan.) 1963.

Westby-Gibson, D.: Social Perspectives on Education: The Society—The Student—The School. New York, John Wiley & Sons, Inc., 1965, 481 pp.

5

PLANNING FOR HEALTH EDUCATION WITHIN SCHOOL AND CLASSROOM

Planning for health education takes place at several levels. The most important planning occurs within the classroom at the instructional level. More remote from students, but nevertheless essential, is the planning within schools and school systems which nurtures and gives direction to classroom planning. An even more remote, but invaluable, aid to local planning is that at state and national levels by education authorities, professional organizations, and special curriculum groups.

Never in the development of health education has greater attention been given to planning than today. Mention has already been made of several cooperative efforts at the national level which have broadened the approach to health education and have resulted in the formulation of broad concepts and the production of new curriculum materials. In a number of states, departments of education are assuming responsibility for the development of improved resource materials and are setting new and strengthened standards for health teaching. Local school systems, too, are involved in health curriculum activities. In some instances planning is directed toward a broad health curriculum; in others it is focused on special subject areas, for example, smoking and sex education. As planning is intensified, and more and more curriculum materials are available, those who are closest to the classroom—the individual teachers and the schools themselves—must take stock of their particular needs and resources and find ways of directing their planning for health education into timely yet well-balanced learning experiences. This chapter is intended to help local planners in this task. Elements of planning are first discussed, followed by suggestions for school-wide planning, and then for planning within the classroom.

Underlying the remarks in this chapter are certain beliefs about health education which have been set forth in previous chapters. They are summarized here for emphasis:

1. Health education is concerned with the development of individuals who are physically, emotionally, and socially equipped to gain full satisfaction from life as individuals and as contributing members of society. It aims also to improve the health conditions of communities and to strengthen the health responsibilities of governments.

2. In health education, full consideration needs to be given to psychological, sociological, cultural, and economic factors which influence health behavior.

3. Health education should be based on scientific health knowledge which is selected and applied toward meeting needs of individuals and of society.

4. Health education within schools must be an integral part of the total school curriculum and an essential element in the general education of all students.

5. Health education within the schools must be a continuum with health education in the home and community so that there is a consistent movement toward common goals, not only during school years but over a span of years.

ELEMENTS OF PLANNING FOR HEALTH EDUCATION

Numerous elements need to be taken into account when planning for health education. The elements suggested here present a logistics which may help to give direction to planning undertaken by curriculum groups as well as by classroom teachers.

Collecting Information Essential for Planning

At least two principal kinds of information are important in the early stages of planning, namely, information on health needs and conditions and information on resources and limitations.

Health Needs

The health needs of growing children and youth are discussed in some detail in Chapter 2. Selected needs, interests, and beliefs inherent in the growth pattern for five different age groups are outlined in Table 5 (page 59) and are further developed in Chapters 8 and 9. Home, school, and community health needs are highlighted in Chapter 3. In both Chapters 2 and 3, specific suggestions are given for helping the teacher to find out about needs. In using the material in these chapters as a basis for local planning, it must be recognized that needs vary widely from child to child, from community to community, and even from period to period. Needs are often culturally, socially, economically, or politically determined. To illustrate, at the present writing, high priorities are being given nationally to the special needs of poverty areas, to problems of the environment such as water and air pollution, to improved family living, and to smoking and health. Locally, not only these but other problems may be receiving special attention. Consequently, generalizations in the chapters just mentioned may not always apply to a particular group or community. They can, however, form a starting point for analyzing local situations.

Resources and Limitations

Before a local planning group or an individual teacher can progress very far with plans for improving health instruction, an effort should be made to learn about resources which could be used not only during the planning stages, but also in implementing those plans. Among resources within the situation that should be considered are teachers and curriculum planners with related interests. Special mention should be made of those who are now working on biological science and social studies curricula since the content and emphases in these fields are, at many points, closely related to the content and emphases in health education. Other resources include health personnel and agencies, material resources, funds, and individuals within the community who could make special contributions. More remote from the local situation, but nevertheless potentially helpful, are state and national curriculum groups which have identified important concepts and have developed a variety of methods and materials for classroom use.

Factors which may foster or impede progress must be understood, since they set limits within which planning can proceed. Mention has been made before of the psychological, socio-cultural, economic, and political factors which reflect the general character of a community and influence decision making within it. Other factors include the manner in which children and the community have reacted to previous efforts toward change. If there is much "burnt-over timber," as Ronald Lippitt once put it, then relighting of this timber may indeed be a frustrating task.

Establishing Objectives

When enough information has been gathered on needs, resources, and limitations to proceed with plans, the next step is to prepare objectives which are sufficiently clear-cut to give direction to the selection of content and learning experiences as well as to the evaluation of results. Though at all stages the broad purposes of education and of health education should be kept in mind, the time comes when specific, workable objectives must be prepared.

In arriving at objectives for health instruction, decisions must first be made, with the help of pupils, regarding desired behavior changes in the pupils themselves or improvements in that part of the environment over which they have some control. In other words, we must determine what we hope the learner will be doing as a result of instruction and under what conditions he will be doing it. We are then ready to formulate objectives that are essential for giving direction to further planning and action. Mager, in his book *Preparing Instructional Objectives,* points out that each objective should be stated so that it not only identifies the behavior which is desired but also defines conditions under which the behavior is to occur. He warns against the use of words in statements of objectives which are open to many interpretations like "to understand," "to appreciate," and "to believe." More precise, and therefore more helpful in guiding instructional efforts, are words like "to identify," "to solve," "to differentiate," and "to be able to."[1] Let us use a hypothetical example to illustrate how a teacher might arrive at a set of objectives.

In a suburban community many children ride bicycles to school as well as for pleasure. Accidents had been so frequent, especially among the 5 to 14 year olds, that a teacher in the upper elementary grades decided to develop a unit on bicycle safety. In preparation, he found that many of the children had been riding on the left side of the street and had been careless in their riding habits. He learned from national data that bicycle riders are at fault in four out of five accidents, the most common violations being not having the right of way, improper turning, disregarding stop signs and signals, riding in the center of the street, riding against traffic, ridng too fast, carrying an extra rider, and riding abreast.[2]

On the basis of this information, a teacher might prepare objectives for the unit. He might anticipate that as the unit progresses the children themselves would set goals for their improved behavior —an anticipation reflected in the objectives. A few objectives he might develop are:

1. The pupil is able to list the circumstances under which bicycle accidents occur most frequently in the United States.

2. The pupil is able to analyze and compare with national data those circumstances leading to bicycle accidents within his own community during the past three months.

3. The pupil identifies at least one possible procedure in relation to each local accident which, if followed, might have prevented the accident.

---

[1] Mager, R. F.: Preparing Instructional Objectives. Palo Alto, Calif., Fearon Publishers, 1962, 60 pp.

[2] Taken from an unpublished statement of the National Safety Council.

4. The bicyclist improves his bicycle-riding practices. (Note: this objective should be spelled out by each pupil in terms of needed improvements in his own practices.)

5. The pupil joins with others in school- and community-wide efforts to reduce bicycle accidents.

6. The community establishes a bicycling club which, among its functions, carries on bicycle safety programs.

7. The community provides a bicycle lane around a lake within its boundaries.

8. Bicycle accidents in the community decrease.

The first objective is directed toward the acquisition of knowledge and classification of information. It is stated more precisely than had it been worded "to know" or "to understand." The second and third objectives, if they are to be realized, demand critical thinking, while the fourth and fifth focus on actual changes in pupil practices. The sixth, seventh, and eighth objectives are long-term, but may be gradual outgrowths of an educational program initiated in this classroom, providing, of course, that other activities are arranged on a school- and community-wide basis. Though none of the objectives mentions changes in values, attitudes, interests, knowledge, or understanding, such changes could well be by-products of activities prompted by the specific objectives just proposed.

Selecting and Organizing the Content of Health Instruction

At some point in the planning process decisions must be made on what to teach and how to organize the content of instruction. This is a most difficult task, yet one that can be facilitated if the earlier elements of planning have been thoughtfully developed. Curriculum groups seriously engaged in working out effective plans for health instruction would profit by reading current literature on curriculum planning, such as that listed at the end of this and the previous chapter. A few general points are mentioned here. Others are included in later sections of this chapter.

Relating Health Content to the Growth Pattern

No satisfactory way has yet been devised to select and arrange content with full assurance that it is appropriate for each age level. Fortunately in the field of health there are certain helpful indicators. Many health needs persist throughout life, but they manifest themselves in different ways at different maturity levels. Interests, too, shift with the years. Consequently, it is possible to approach problems from a variety of angles and with an increasing degree of complexity as children progress through school, thus lending novelty, freshness, and greater depth to the content of learning. For example, dental health instruction in the early years at school may

Figure 10. Teaching bicycle safety—a bicycle inspection. (Courtesy of Florida State Board of Health.)

focus on getting acquainted with the dentist and with the care of the six-year molar. In the middle grades, teachers may capitalize on the gang spirit in enlisting pupil participation in organized attempts to secure dental corrections. In senior high school, students may be encouraged to engage in community-wide action programs for provision of adequate dental care.

In selecting the content of health teaching it is important to know where children at different age levels stand in respect to their relationships with others and with the world around them. Are they wrapped up in their family and immediate neighborhood, or have they broadened their interests to include national or even international affairs? With exposure to television and increased mobility, this latter point may occur at an earlier age level with many children than formerly. Yet among the culturally deprived, horizons may be very limited indeed. Then, too, what is their response toward authority? Do they accept without question the precepts of their parents and teachers, or have they reached the stage of wanting to know the reasons why, or wanting to act independently? As the child grows in maturity, he progresses in his ability to grasp concepts and to handle situations of increasing complexity. By gaining even an elementary insight into the steady sequence of growth, schools may be able to arrange their curricula, and teachers may be helped to direct their health education content, along lines that are in harmony with the child's maturity and experience level.

The Conceptual Approach

One approach to the selection and organization of content is the conceptual approach, an approach which is now receiving wide attention. In this approach an attempt is made to extract and synthesize from a large body of health knowledge those concepts or "big ideas" that should provide the framework for an organized approach to health instruction. It is not the intention that concepts be taught as such, but rather that they help to give direction to the selection of objectives, content, methods, and materials of instruction which, when applied, may result in pupils developing their own concepts. To illustrate, a concept developed by the Curriculum Commission of the AAHPER Health Education Division is quoted here with its supporting data and is discussed briefly in terms of its possible help to teachers (the concept is in italics):

Family members experience physiological, psychological, and sociological problems and make adjustments as they progress through part or all of a family cycle.

Each family grows and lives out the family cycle in its own unique way.

Health influences individual and family living throughout the family cycle.

Family living is enhanced when individuals understand and accept individual differences in patterns of growth and development.

Communication is likely to be more effective when family members use a socially acceptable vocabulary concerning sex and reproductive functions.[3]

An elementary teacher might see in this concept a number of possibilities for health instruction which would provide content and experiences through which the children could begin to evolve their own concepts concerning family relationships. For example, in a deprived community where there is a need for the child of elementary age to share in the care of younger members of the family, dramatizations or role-playing of family situations, includings the care of infants and preschoolers and the carrying out of routine health procedures, could lead to discussions of responsibilities which the children themselves could assume in the home. Comparisons between ways in which families with diverse backgrounds meet their daily health needs might be another approach. At the secondary level, family health problems associated with poverty, or health conditions affecting family life in different parts of the world, could be studied in ways that would enhance the pupils' comprehension of the ideas contained in this concept. Lest this concept be developed only at the intellectual level, experience in caring for younger children could be obtained by an arrangement with nursery schools, hospitals, or rehabilitation centers, and family problems associated with conditions existing among these children could be studied in some depth.

The Curriculum Commission, in determining health concepts as guides for health instruction, turned to both research and program experts in the different health areas for help in determining the concepts students should possess by the time they had progressed through 12 grades of school. Then came much work in refining the concepts. Problem areas around which concepts were developed by the commission are: accident prevention, aging, alcohol, disaster preparedness, disease and disease control, the economics of health care, environmental conditions, the evaluation of health information, family health, international health, mental health, nutrition, and smoking.[4]

The School Health Education Study, in arriving at the list of concepts that is serving as a basis for the development of a wide range of curriculum materials, worked through a writing team, tryout centers, and the use of experts not only in the health field but also in curriculum and supervision.[5]

State and local curriculum groups are also developing health

---

[3] Health Concepts; Guides for Health Instruction. Washington, D.C., American Association for Health, Phiysical Education, and Recreation, 1967, p. 38.

[4] *Ibid,* 49 pp.

[5] Health Education: A Conceptual Approach to Curriculum Design. St. Paul, Minn., 3M Education Press, Box 3100, 1967, 141 pp. (By the School Health Education Study.)

curriculum materials around broad concepts. These and the national materials can be very helpful in enabling teachers to grasp the larger structure of health knowledge and in providing a framework from which teachers can select and arrange content and learning experiences pertinent to the problems of the children and the locality.

Relating Health Content to Other Areas of Learning

One of the important tasks of all schooling is to help pupils see things in their larger relationships. One way of helping them to see the relationships of health concepts and principles to the broader purposes of education is to tie in health content whenever possible with the content of other subject areas. It should be pointed out that such a move is sound only to the extent that the related areas, such as the social studies, sciences, physical education, and language arts are geared to the maturity levels of the pupils, to their personal needs, and to the needs of society. Possibilities for such interrelationships are many. For example, in an elementary classroom, the children may be studying about man's adjustments to the different types of environments around the world. In the social studies, living conditions in different types of communities may be studied; in science, different climates and their effect on man may be emphasized; and in health, the effects of housing conditions, climate, and foods grown in these regions on the health of people may be explored.

At the senior high school level unified teaching has received less emphasis. Teachers might well give serious thought, however, to better coordination of teaching content, if not to complete unification. For example, in consumer education, the cost of desirable and adequate preventive health services and medical care could be investigated at the same time that studies are being made of actual consumer expenditures. Whether such health problems would be studied in a separate health course or as a part of another course would depend upon teacher qualifications and the way the curriculum is organized.

At both elementary and secondary levels, planning is the key to success in efforts to tie in health teaching with teaching in related areas of learning. Without careful planning the results will be spotty and ineffective.

Providing for Continuity and Progression

Nothing is more deadening to children than a constant repetition of health facts presented in much the same way year in and year out. In some school systems, as the children move from teacher to teacher, or even as they stay with the same teacher in small schools, health teaching too often revolves around a few continuing problems. The School Health Education Study, conducted on a national scale, revealed that of topics widely accepted as essential content areas, only five—accident prevention, cleanliness and grooming, dental health, food and nutrition, and exercise and relaxation— were generally offered throughout the elementary and secondary school years. Moreover, much of what was being taught was repetitious and unrelated to needs and problems at different levels of development. Certain content areas were universally neglected: consumer education, noncommunicable diseases, international health activities, sex education, and venereal disease.[6]

Though the study was conducted from 1961 to 1963, and since then new curriculum materials have been developed around many neglected content areas, there is reason to believe that much more needs to be done in a systematic way to assure growth in learning through building continuity and progression into school- or system-wide curriculum plans.[7]

Some schools have attempted to chart concept or content emphases, indicating grades where a subject might be dealt with in some depth and other grades where it might be treated through incidental instruction. Though this plan may assure coverage, at least on paper, it does not assure that teachers will follow the plan or that desirable and timely learning experiences will result with a particular group of pupils. Some schools have been known to use a plan whereby teachers record and pass along with the children as they go into the next grade a summary of what has been taught during the year. Others depend upon frequent meetings of teachers for exchange of such information. In one city system, four feeder elementary schools and a junior high school are getting together on an area basis to consider not only continuity in the curriculum but also ways of dealing effectively with area problems. Long-term plans call for concerted action with community agencies, including health agencies.

Regardless of school-wide efforts, the individual teacher must make a conscious attempt to find out what his pupils have previously learned in health and what their future learning may be. Only with such knowledge can new approaches to old problems be introduced and pupils' comprehension of health concepts and extension of health experiences be assured. Though no fully satisfactory way has been found to build desirable continuity and progression into health

---

[6] For further discussion, see Conner, F. E.: Focus on health. Journal of School Health, 37:4 (Jan.) 1967.

[7] For general suggestions, see especially, NEA Project on Instruction: Planning and Organizing for Teaching. Washington, D.C., National Education Association, 1963, 190 pp.

teaching (or, for that matter, into other forms of instruction), the various experiments being conducted now by a wide variety of curriculum groups give promise of improvements in the future.

Determining Appropriate Learning Experiences

Up to this point in the discussion of the logistics of planning for health instruction, attention has been directed toward collecting information essential for planning, establishing objectives, and selecting and organizing the content of instruction. These steps lead naturally to the next step, that of determining learning experiences which are appropriate to each situation. In the past there was a tendency in many classrooms toward indiscriminate selection of learning activities. A teacher would hear of a trick or device that he felt would lend novelty or interest to his teaching and would try it out with little or no thought for the needs, objectives, or content of instruction. Today there are too many pressures on schools, and on the children themselves, to perform in such a haphazard and ineffective manner. Methods and materials for health instruction must be carefully selected so that they not only lend novelty and interest to learning, but also give meaning to health content and contribute to desired behavior changes.[8]

Objectives as a Guide

Specific objectives which have been determined on the basis of needs provide the principal keys to the selection of learning experiences. In other words, how we proceed with our health teaching should be decided by what we hope to accomplish with a particular individual or group in a given situation. Let us see how this approach might operate in the hypothetical project on bicycle safety described earlier in this chapter under the discussion of objectives. The first four objectives are repeated here, along with suggested learning experiences that might be appropriate in connection with them.

Objective 1. The pupil is able to list the circumstances under which bicycle accidents occur most frequently in the United States.

To accomplish this objective, pupils would need to explore available literature on bicycle accidents, i.e., through library research or correspondence. They would need to decide how they would wish to list the circumstances for greatest value in their study—for example, by location, age, sex, and nature of violations. Learning experiences, then, would include collection and classification of data.

---

[8] In Chapter 6, the reader will find described numerous methods and techniques for health teaching along with a discussion of circumstances under which each method might be used effectively. Chapter 7 deals with instructional materials and their use in health education. Chapters 8 and 9 contain a wide array of learning experiences taken from actual classroom situations.

Objective 2.   The pupil is able to analyze and compare with national data those circumstances leading to bicycle accidents within his own community during the past three months.

For this objective, pupils would need to decide where the local data might be found, and how the data could best be collected, analyzed, and compared with national data. Visits to offices of agencies which might have the data, interviews, study of back issues of local newspapers, and discussion on what constitutes their community are among activities indicated in this learning situation. Group problem solving could hold a prominent spot at this stage; critical thinking would be demanded as well as synthesis of data.

Objective 3.   The pupil identifies at least one possible procedure in relation to each local accident which, if followed, might have prevented the accident.

At this point, further knowledge of the causes and prevention of bicycle accidents would be necessary. Learning experiences might include study of literature, review of films, and consultation with police. In some instances a visit to the site of the accident might give further clues. Actual accident scenes could be simulated with models for further clarification. Through such experiences pupils would be in a position to deduce possible preventive steps.

Objective 4.   The bicyclist improves his bicycle-riding practices.

Though this objective, directed toward actual change in practice, might be an outgrowth of the previous activities, specific learning experiences directly related to the objective should be incorporated in the project. For example, bicyclists might keep individual records of their daily riding experiences, including hazards they faced and how they avoided them. They could practice under supervision on a cycling trip; engage in competitive races in which they are judged on their skill and on their ability to handle the bicycle safely; or take a bicycle safety test. Then, too, they might be encouraged to discuss at home and among friends the need for better traffic control, not only to establish more firmly in themselves the need for safe riding but also to arouse public opinion toward improving traffic conditions for bicyclists.

From this illustration, it is evident that a variety of methods and materials may be required to meet a particular objective. Examples of appropriate learning experiences for different types of objectives are given in the following paragraphs.

Development of values, attitudes, and interests.   These attributes are at the heart of learning; without them few desirable behavior changes of lasting worth would take place. Yet, as Taba has pointed out,

Feelings, values and sensitivities are matters that need to be discovered rather than taught. . . . This means that the provisions for these objectives must include opportunities for direct experiencing of some sort and materials which affect feelings. A much more conscious use is needed of the experiences of students, of literature, and of other materials which reproduce life in its full emotional meaning and which express and affect feelings and values.[9]

There is some truth to the statement that "values and attitudes are better caught than taught." The teacher who is liked by his

---

[9] Taba, H.: Curriculum Development; Theory and Practice. New York, Harcourt, Brace & World, Inc., 1962, p. 224.

pupils subtly and often unconsciously influences the pupils around him through this behavior. In health teaching, however, favorable attitudes and values, as well as genuine interests, are more likely to emerge when pupils deal with live, vital health problems of the day and the times. Examples of learning experiences which may foster identification with timely needs include problem solving, use of case materials, role-playing, and community service. Pretesting at the beginning of a project may help to arouse interest, as may also the viewing of a film or undertaking a field trip. Exploration of literature depicting the great discoveries in the health sciences and the contributions of health services to the betterment of humanity may stir the emotions and open up new horizons for exploration.

Development of knowledge and the ability to think critically. Sound health knowledge is fundamental to intelligent health behavior. So, too, is the ability to think critically in matters related to health. Facts are best remembered and applied when their usefulness is clear to the learner. The ability to think critically is best developed in situations which give exercise to this ability. Individual and group problem solving experiences, as well as experimentation, help young people to acquire meaningful information and to develop the ability to think critically. Collecting, organizing, applying, and evaluating data in simulated or real situations help to give reality to the facts learned and to increase the powers of inquiry. Teaching around broad concepts can aid pupils in seeing the interrelatedness of health knowledge with their own lives and with the welfare of their families and communities.

Development of desirable health action. Improvement in health behavior is the ultimate goal of all health teaching. Learning experiences, then, which lead to desirable action are of utmost importance in health education.

Since attitudes and values held by pupils determine to a large degree their motivations toward improved health practices, and since, moreover, sound health knowledge and critical thinking are needed for intelligently directed health behavior, the learning experiences mentioned previously should be kept firmly in mind at this point. However, other learning experiences may be essential for the development of specific practices or skills.

"Learning by doing" is a cliché which applies aptly here. Home nursing skills, first-aid measures, safe automobile driving, are but examples of practices that demand special instructions and practice under supervision. In daily life, opportunities abound for learning through direct experience, as on the playground or within the lunchroom. Participation in school and community service activities likewise gives pupils a chance to learn through overt acts. Audiovisual materials provide other means of teaching practices and skills.

Developing a Detailed Plan of Operation

With the preceding steps well under way, a teacher or group is ready to draw up a plan of operation. In many instances plans will be directed toward developing an intensified educational effort around a specific need and through the cooperative efforts of all concerned. Such plans should include decisions on (1) specific groups to be reached (grade groups, parents, and so forth); (2) approaches to be used; (3) concepts and content to be developed; (4) methods and materials to be used; and (5) evaluation procedures to be followed. In other words, there would be an effort to synthesize the various steps discussed in the preceding sections of this chapter. In some instances the plan might involve preparing resource units or setting up a broad design for program emphasis and development for the academic year. Whatever direction a plan takes, it should take into account the timing of various steps and the allocation of responsibilities. It should remain flexible—anticipating changes, facilitating changes, and adapting to changes as needed.

Carrying Out a Plan of Action

An individual or group is ready to carry out a plan of action only when the preceding steps have been carefully developed. Sometimes, however, the demands of the moment make it necessary to start action before plans are fully formulated. Moreover, in a field as dynamic and changing as that of health, no preconceived plan can or should be followed without changes as circumstances dictate. Nevertheless, a thoughtfully prepared plan, flexible enough for adaptation and change, gives purpose and direction, and when successfully pursued, gives the sense of accomplishment so essential for continuing efforts.

Evaluating Results

Evaluation is an essential part of any program that seeks to bring about change. In health teaching there should be constant evaluation to determine whether progress is being made in reaching established goals. Evaluation procedures are discussed in Chapter 11.

SUGGESTIONS FOR SCHOOL-WIDE PLANNING

This section offers specific suggestions for school-wide planning toward improved health education offerings. Though principal focus is on planning within a single school, many of the suggestions are equally applicable to system-wide planning.

Make Health Education Planning an Integral Part of Overall Curriculum Planning

If health education objectives are to become one with general education objectives, and if health education is otherwise to be in harmony with total education, then planning for health education must be dovetailed with overall curriculum development.

The individual classroom is the place to begin such coordinated planning. In the elementary school the classroom teacher, either alone or through team teaching, will carry the major responsibility. In the secondary school subject matter teachers will need to discover such opportunities individually or in cooperation with other teachers.

On a school-wide basis, one person or a group of persons with special interest and qualifications in health education should be given the responsibility for seeing that health education is so related. For example, when committees have been set up to work on curriculum problems, it is logical to expect that in most situations one committee will be formed to deal with health instruction. In addition, there should be health education representation on many of the other curriculum committees so that health education concepts and learning experiences are introduced where they fit naturally. Such a coordinated approach is becoming increasingly necessary as more schools examine alternative curriculum plans in attempts to decide which plans to adopt, or, in some instances, to adapt to their own situations. As these decisions are being made, health education should have its place along with other disciplines; it should not be fitted into an already overcrowded curriculum as an afterthought, as is sometimes the case. But planning is necessary, and that planning must be guided, when possible, by professionally qualified health educators.

Involve All School Personnel in Health Education Planning

There are many reasons why all school personnel should share in health education planning. Health problems are not respecters of subject matter lines. They appear wherever children are living and working, and that means in every phase of school life. Problems of healthful living that require education for their solution are as likely to arise in the commercial room, where such elements as lighting, posture, and fatigue affect work, as in the elementary classroom. In industrial shops there are problems involving the use of dangerous materials and equipment, as well as those of lighting and fatigue, which require the understanding and application of health and safety principles and practices by teachers and by pupils. On the play field and in the science laboratory, health and safety precautions demand constant attention.

The incorporation of health concepts and content into various subject matter fields has already been discussed. Teachers whose fields offer special opportunities for health instruction should be particularly active in planning on both a long- and short-term basis. In long-term planning, attention needs to be given to discovering unnecessary overlapping of health emphases, as well as gaps in health instruction, and to the allocation of responsibility for covering essential health concepts and content. Short-term planning could lead to concerted efforts to deal effectively with problems of current importance in the school or community.

Provide for Pupil Participation in Planning Activities

The value of pupil participation in planning as a motivational device has already been mentioned. Planning by pupils not only in the classroom but also on a school-wide and system-wide basis can be an important experience in citizenship. Young people should be made to feel that they are a part of what goes on around them and should have the chance to share with others in the solution of problems that concern them. Often their contributions will lend a quality of freshness which they alone can bring.

Pupils may begin to serve on committees early in the elementary years. It is never too soon to start this direct training for citizenship. Student councils or committees provide an important channel for pupil participation in planning and action. General student councils may deal with health problems along with other school problems, or health and safety councils may be set up as distinct groups to deal exclusively with health and safety matters.

Make Health Education Planning an Integral Part of Total Planning For Health in Both School and Community

If health education is to bring about actual health improvements, it must relate to health needs as outlined in previous chapters. It must also relate at every possible point to the regulatory and service aspects of health programs being conducted in both the school and community. Many problems are often of such magnitude that they could not possibly be solved by any single approach or by any single group. A simultaneous broadside attack on them by edu-cational and health forces through service, education, and regulation (if necessary) is essential. The contributions of parents, public health workers, private physicians and dentists, teachers, children, volun-tary health agencies, and the community at large are needed for their successful solution.

In the following discussion of planning between school and health personnel, no attempt is made to consider all the adminis-trative problems involved. The administration of school health pro-grams is ably handled in other publications.[10] Neither is there an attempt to distinguish between school health personnel and com-munity health personnel. In some communities, particularly in rural areas and certain large cities, they are the same. Other communities have two separate services. Regardless of the administrative struc-ture, school and community health personnel have the responsibility for thinking and acting coordinately if the total health program is to be performed with efficiency and effectiveness.

Ways in which those concerned with health education in a school can plan with those concerned with other aspects of the total health program are discussed here.

Informal Planning

Informal planning is often a natural by-product of an under-standing relationship between school and health personnel as indi-viduals. A cup of coffee or a lunch together, a chat at a parent-teacher meeting, a picnic, or a game of golf all help to bridge the gaps which sometimes exist between people with common interests. Under such relaxed conditions many good ideas are likely to be exchanged or new ones developed. With each person learning to appreciate the other's special assets and potential contributions, the foundation is laid for cooperation of a professional nature.

Informal planning may also take place as special problems come up that need attention. Those most concerned may get together and continue to work together until the need is met. For example, as a result of district reorganization based on school attendance, one elementary school in a middle-class neighborhood of a large city had added to its pupil population a sizable group of children from a nearby poverty area. Their presence created problems of physical and emotional adjustment and demanded, among other changes, a recasting of school health services and adaptations in health instruc-tion efforts. To facilitate these changes, school personnel met in-formally for several sessions with health and social welfare personnel

---

10 See, for example, Oberteuffer, D., and Beyrer, M. K.: School Health Education. New York, Harper & Row, 1966, pp. 299–525.

Figure 11. A senior high senate participates in planning. (Courtesy of University High School, University of Minnesota.)

serving the poverty area, as well as with representatives of a neighborhood action group in the poverty area.

Nurse-Teacher Conferences

Nurse-teacher conferences provide an excellent opportunity for health education planning. Teachers and nurses have long been recognized as the key people in any school-community health program. They are the workers closest to the children and adults, and they render the most direct services. In some instances the nurses may be working full time in the school; in others, they may be serving both the school and the surrounding community. Planned conferences between individual teachers and nurses help to give the teacher the substance for her health instruction, either individualized or group, and the nurse, the information she needs for pupil and family health counseling.

Joint planning should take place informally whenever a need arises. In addition, there should be a scheduled time for joint planning at least once a year, preferably more often. In practice, however, such planning is far from being realized. Many communities today lack the services of qualified public health nurses and many other communities must spread their services so thin that there is little time for the kind of help the schools need or want. Even when a nurse is available to the school, her time is not always used to good advantage. In too many schools she is kept busy acting as a truant officer, bandaging fingers, or making out records. As a result she has little time left to follow up the needs of individual children in home and classroom, or to provide consultative services to teachers.

Staff Meetings

Staff meetings of school personnel furnish another opening for coordinated planning in health education. These staff meetings may be system- or school-wide, departmental or grade meetings. Each health worker, particularly the nurse working in the school, should be considered a part of the school staff and should be invited to attend staff meetings regularly, whether or not the worker is a full-time employee of the school system. Her presence makes it possible for her to gain a better understanding of the school's program and how she may fit her own activities into it. Moreover, when problems arise that have a bearing on health, she will be there ready to answer questions or to contribute her part to the solution of the problems. Both school and health personnel benefit from such meetings together.

Case Conferences

Case conferences on physical and emotional health problems of individual children have become a valued procedure in some schools as a part of the guidance or counseling program. The conferences are particularly useful in secondary schools in which several teachers deal with the same pupil each day. Conferences may be held periodically, as well as when special problems come up. The teachers concerned, the nurse, the community social worker, the visiting teacher, the guidance counselor, and sometimes the school physician should join in these sessions. By such planning together, the work of the teaching and health staffs is more consistently performed and the pupils benefit from the concerted attack. Moreover, all gain insight into problems in such ways that their educational activities are improved.

Health Councils

School and community health councils (or committees), or combined school-community councils, have been formed in many communities to facilitate coordinated planning and action. Since membership on these councils usually includes both school and health personnel, the combined efforts of these two groups can accomplish much.

Within an individual school, a council may be composed of representatives from the teachers, parent groups, and the student body, as well as the school nurse, a physician, and one or more members of the administrative staff. The school lunch manager, the head custodian, and representatives of official and voluntary health agencies closely affiliated with the school may also serve on the council.

In general, school health councils carry on a variety of activities directed toward the improvement of health conditions in the school. They may help to identify new resources for health teaching and to develop new materials, such as resource units. They may sponsor school- or community-wide health education efforts and arrange for in-service education of teachers and other school personnel.

Individual school health councils may have the backing and stimulus of system-wide councils. The larger councils often serve the important function of recommending school health policies to boards of education. They sometimes engage in system-wide curriculum development.

In recent years neighborhood action bodies have been springing up in many urban and rural areas; these consist of groups of citizens who are concerned with the welfare of the community in which they live. The potential for health planning within these groups is tremendous. Schools would do well to foster such efforts at "grass roots democracy" and join actively with local leaders in working toward improving neighborhood health conditions.

Organizing a school health council. A health council, valuable as it may be, should be formed only when there is widespread feeling that one is needed. Councils established only because it seemed to be the thing to do have been notoriously unsuccessful. Several satisfying experiences in working together informally on specific projects are often necessary before a need for a council is felt. Some groups may prefer to operate indefinitely without one. In lieu of a formal council, they may instead set up specific task forces to accomplish specific functions and then disband a task force when its job is finished. There is merit in this task-oriented approach. Whatever plan is worked out for coordination of efforts and resources, it needs constant support from administrators and health education specialists at every stage in its development and operation.

If a school or school system decides to establish a council, it must feel its way and create an organization which is custom-built to its own situation. No set procedure can be outlined here. However, the following elements are often found in the development of councils:

1. An individual (or a group) decides that something needs to be done about something. He talks the problem over with one or two others, among whom will be the school administrator.

2. A temporary committee is organized to study the problem. This group may work informally for some time.

3. The problem is brought up for consideration at a staff meeting.

4. A representative body, often temporary, is established to plan further toward action.

5. There is periodic referral back to the staff for guidance and a gradual involvement of staff and others in the problem-solving situation.

6. Appropriate action takes place with wide participation of all concerned.

7. In time, and as a result of these and other similar experiences, a permanent body may form.

Seminars, Work Conferences, and Workshops

These vehicles for joint study, planning, and action give opportunity for people with similar interests to work together informally. Some last for only one or two sessions, while others extend over periods of several days to several weeks.

Some school systems sponsor week-end conferences in which health problems may be discussed. Teachers who work alone and community teams engaged in curriculum development find these conferences of special value. Through them, new leadership may be found and new programs introduced.

A few states now arrange for selected teachers to have experience with local health departments during the summer months, and with extra reading and conferences, to receive academic credit for the experience at a neighboring university or college.

Bulletins and Newsletters

Although not strictly an instrument for planning, the bulletin or newsletter facilitates planning by keeping lines of communication open among those responsible for the development of programs. Through the bulletin ideas are exchanged and current happenings are described. Bulletins and newsletters are of many types, ranging from house organs used primarily within the school or school system to publications distributed beyond the school. They need not be elaborate; a simple mimeographed sheet can convey much useful information and give recognition to work well done. Its publication could be the function of a school health committee.

Seek Community Assistance in the Planning Process

A school that is truly a community school will turn to the community of which it is a part for help in its health education planning. Mention has already been made of the assistance that may be obtained from community health workers and neighborhood action groups. Parents and other citizens may likewise give service in the planning. They see problems from a realistic angle, unhampered by professional bias, and they often have a keen sense of what is practical and workable. Besides, they are much more likely to give support to measures if they have had a part in their making. Fully as important, a group of community citizens planning along with the school on matters of school concern may in turn take aggressive steps to do something about similar problems in the community. The possibility of their permanency in a community also adds stability to a program.

Community assistance may be sought through informal contacts with individuals or groups, or there may be more organized efforts at joint planning, as through groups composed not only of school and health personnel, but also of community representatives. Local citizens' committees for better schools, now found in thousands of communities, are also potential sources of help.

Make Planning a Continuous Process

This principle applies in all forms of curriculum development. It is based on the realization that teachers are constantly confronted with new problems and new conditions which need to be considered as they arise. It is based also on the realization that regular participation in planning contributes to the constant growth of those involved. Most important of all, constant planning helps to give continuity to a program.

Foster Widespread Leadership

Administrative Leadership

The satisfactory planning and execution of health education programs are dependent upon proficient leadership at every level. Upon the school administrator rests the basic responsibility for the provision and development of a sound program, properly integrated with the total school program and with community activities. Without his constant and intelligent support, the efforts of others are likely to fall on barren ground and die through lack of proper nurture. His wise leadership is a first essential in any program.

Leadership of Teaching and Health Personnel

In elementary schools the classroom teacher is a leader of great importance. She is with the children, guiding their total development day in and day out, and consequently is in a unique position to relate health teaching to the daily living problems of the children. In secondary schools each teacher, too, is a potential leader, as has been suggested, though some teachers naturally may take greater leadership than others because of the subjects they teach and the services they render. Among those who have a large obligation for the direction of health education are teachers of physical education, biology, home economics, and social studies, guidance counselors, and teachers of special health courses. In both elementary and secondary schools, especially in larger communities, there are others who should take leadership because of the positions they hold. These include the nurses, physicians, dentists and dental hygienists, social workers, and other special personnel working with the schools.

Health Educators

There is a growing recognition of the need for a wider kind of leadership than one would expect most administrators, teachers,

Figure 12. Parent-teacher groups can contribute to planning. (Courtesy of PTA of Chelsea Heights School, St. Paul, Minnesota.)

and health workers to give, even when they are banded together in an effectively functioning committee. Someone especially equipped in health education should be available to help stimulate and assist with health education activities. Thus, a new kind of professional health worker has come into existence, known usually as a health educator, health coordinator, health director, or health education consultant, whose responsibility it is to see that the health education job gets done. Health educators are most commonly employed by school systems, health departments, or voluntary health agencies such as tuberculosis associations. Sometimes they are employed jointly by these groups.

The health educator within a single school may teach health classes and may also serve as a link between the school and the community in health matters of common concern, particularly those involving education. He may facilitate the working together of school administrators, other teachers, health workers, and parents toward the realization of a well balanced program of service and education.

Health educators employed by a school system provide consultant services to schools and do on a larger scale, and for the system as a whole, many of the things the health coordinator for a single school does within his realm of influence.

Community-wide health educators, often called public health educators, are discussed in Chapter 12.

In some schools, teachers from the staff are appointed to carry on health coordination functions. Usually these people have teaching responsibilities in addition to the work of health coordination. Teachers with interest and leadership abilities should be encouraged to prepare themselves further for such responsibilities through additional professional training.

Leadership from Within the Community

One of the crying needs in community life today is the development of leadership from among the people themselves. From the standpoint of school health, this leadership will reinforce and supplement that of professional workers. Too often a school planning group will function actively under the direction of a dynamic teacher or nurse only to disintegrate completely when that person leaves the community. Leadership from within the community itself lends stability and continuity to school health programs.

Focus on Planning Toward Action

When people work together in a school or community situation, there is always need for finding common ground on which

to function. This process involves group discussion, sometimes over·
a considerable period of time. The difficulties come when that discussion stays at the level of generalizations. Group planning is much
more likely to result in action if it evolves around efforts to solve
specific problems in specific situations, or, in other words, if it
focuses on the job to be done and how to do it.

PLANNING PROCEDURES IN THE CLASSROOM

The teacher who feels even the slightest responsibility for
health teaching must lay broad and flexible plans and then plan
further with his pupils for experiences that are meaningful to them.

Much of the material that has been presented thus far provides the broad foundations for classroom planning. The focus now
is on how the classroom teacher can plan and carry out health
teaching activities with a specific group of children during a specific
school year. Many of the suggestions are applicable also to curriculum groups that are concerned with more extensive planning problems.

General Guides for Developing a Year's Plan

In planning for health teaching, most classroom teachers find
themselves caught between two forces. On the one hand, they are
operating within the large framework of a curriculum determined
by the state or local community or school. On the other, they are
confronted with pupil needs and interests which demand attention.
How, then, can they link the two into a workable and effective
program? How much advanced planning should they themselves
attempt and what should be the nature of this planning? Though
these and other similar decisions will be made to a large extent
within the local situation, a few general suggestions may help.

Set Up a Broad Plan at the Beginning of Each School Year

In health teaching the teacher cannot depend on a haphazard
program which follows merely the inspiration or the dictates of
the moment. Without a plan worked out early in the year, such
teaching, if not completely neglected, is likely to be aimless and
ineffective.

If there is a system- or school-wide curriculum pattern, the
teacher will first of all wish to familiarize himself with the recommendations applying to his grade level or subject. These are often
outlined in curriculum guides or other readily available curriculum

materials. Experienced teachers will have this information at hand. Those new to a system, however, should secure it before school starts in the fall.

During the first days of school the teacher will need to find out all he can about the pupils he will teach and, if he is new, the communities in which they live. His next step is to set up a basic plan which will give attention to the most important needs of pupils and community within the overall curriculum pattern. It is hoped that while doing this he will work with other teachers and will be guided, too, by such considerations as are outlined in this chapter.

So far, much of the planning will have been done without the help of the pupils themselves. As soon as it is feasible, however, the pupils should be brought into the planning, too.

Keep the Plan Flexible

In the course of a year, unforeseen developments may occur which will suggest the need for redirection of health teaching. Even the best laid plans may need revision as a program unfolds and unexpected events take place. Moreover, a flexible program allows for readjustments as pupils are drawn into the planning.

Concentrate on a Few Problems Each Year

Many teachers prefer to concentrate on two or three especially significant health problems each year with a thoroughness which will assure actual health improvements. It is far better to select a few timely problems and work on them to the point of accomplishment than to touch upon many in a superficial, unproductive manner. This does not mean the neglect of opportunities for informal teaching as needs arise. It does mean, however, that teaching is likely to be better focused and more effective.

Give Special Attention to Sequence of Learning Activities

Dr. Fannie Dunn once commented:

At my country home I have cans of meats, vegetables and fruits arranged on shelves by varieties. Whenever I want something to eat I take down the cans I need to make a meal. Perhaps it will be tongue, peas and fruit salad for one meal, or maybe dried beef, corn and peaches. I never eat up all the meat just because it happens to come first on the shelf and then all the vegetables because they are sitting next to the meat. So with good teaching. Instructional materials suitable for a particular group at a given time are taken from different sources and arranged in sequences that make sense to that group even though they're not organized and arranged that way in a curriculum guide or textbook.

In determining the concepts to be developed, the units to be taught, or the major activities to be undertaken in health education, it is well to begin with the problems of most urgent need and to relate them to things for which pupils have shown, or are likely to show, the greatest interest and concern. A group may then move on into other activities as readiness for them has been developed. Timeliness, too, is a factor which may influence sequence. In making choices, continued attention needs to be given to the introduction of new experiences, or to fresh approaches to old problems, so as to assure growth in learning. Giving heed to readiness, timeliness, and new experiences is in accord with what is known about learning.

Avoid Both Overemphasis and Underemphasis on Health

Disproportionate attention to health education prevails in some classrooms. Teachers who lay too great a stress on health often defeat their own purposes. With everything pointing to health, the children become so saturated that they may rebel as did a boy who remarked one day, "There are two things I don't want to hear anything more about; one is George Washington and the other is health."

Neglect, rather than overemphasis, is more common. Neglect may occur when teachers think of health education as something apart from the rest of the curriculum, perhaps as a subject required by law and remote from the daily living problems of pupils. To them health education is just another subject to be taught, a subject that eats into precious time that could be used more profitably in other pursuits. Neglect also occurs where there is a so-called integrated program for health but no planning for it. In such a haphazard situation "what is everybody's business soon becomes nobody's business."

Provide for Integrated Learnings That Are Natural, Not Forced

An overenthusiastic teacher tends to bring a health slant into all teaching with the results that are often artificial and meaningless. For example, while nutrition is being studied in some classrooms, arithmetic problems will deal with foods, and poems will be composed and songs will be sung on the subject.

True integration occurs only within an individual. Educators point to the need for discovering "integrative threads" (e.g., concepts and objectives) which are common to several subject areas and then, through a variety of learning experiences, helping students to understand how these concepts or objectives can be operative in the different subjects. To illustrate, the School Health Education Study has identified as one of its concepts that *"Food selection and eating patterns are determined by physical, social, mental, economic and cultural factors."* This concept is sufficiently broad to be suitable for development not only in health classes but also in social studies, language arts, science, and other classes. It could, moreover, be extended to include an understanding of the effects of the various factors (physical, social, mental, economic, and cultural) on other human living patterns, as for example, patterns of family relationships or patterns for obtaining medical care.

Enrich Pupil Learning Through Relating Classroom Teaching to Pupil Health Experiences in the Community

Youth organizations, voluntary health agencies, health departments, hospitals, and other community agencies are increasingly providing health-related experiences for young people. Some youth serve as volunteers, engage in service projects, or enter into community-wide programs for health improvements. Others, as those in a variety of vocational training or work experience programs, may serve as food handlers or as workers in various health institutions, clean-up programs, or similar projects.

Some student projects are arranged through the school, others are conducted independently of the school. Regardless of their sponsorship, they provide excellent background for a form of classroom teaching that is not now being explored in most classrooms. The innovative teacher, by encouraging young people to share their community health experiences with classmates, would find in these experiences excellent case study material for class discussion and for further investigation through interviews or other contacts with health authorities. Though confidential information would need to be handled carefully, in most instances the projects would be sufficiently impersonal to allow for such study. They not only would lend vitality to class work but also might help to broaden the comprehension of students.

Use Textbooks Wisely

Today, textbooks are generally considered most useful when they serve as references and help provide answers to problems upon which children are working. The teacher who follows a textbook religiously from cover to cover does not get full value from the book. He may in fact inhibit real learning.

Most modern health textbooks provide motivating materials

and present health facts in an appealing form. They can become a useful resource in teaching when used as a supplement and not as the entire substance of teaching.

Make Optimum Use of Teaching Guides and Resource Units

Teaching guides can give much practical help to the teacher. The modern guide suggests general directions for teaching but leaves the teacher free to develop his own teaching plans with the children themselves and in coordination with the plans of other teachers.

Resource units may furnish valuable ideas for teaching. A good resource unit can help the busy teacher by suggesting expected outcomes, outlining key concepts and facts, and presenting a wealth of activities from which teacher and pupils may select those that will be most helpful in their particular situation. Resource units in health may be developed by teachers locally. Some units on special health subjects are available from various state and national health and educational agencies.

Regardless of the type, these various teaching aids are better used as guides than as crutches.

Locate and Use Other Resources

Teaching is enhanced when a wide variety of resources is used. The health educator, the public health nurse working in the schools, or a materials resource committee may be of great assistance to the teacher in locating suitable resources, particularly in the form of people and materials.

Some teachers have set up files of information so that when a new project is being planned they can find out quickly what resources may be available on that project. In such a file a teacher might gradually accumulate under various headings (e.g., nutrition, disease control, and community health services) the names and addresses of people or agencies upon whom he may call for help, references to journal and magazine articles, titles and sources of films, and possibilities for field trips. Pamphlets, pictures, and newspaper clippings may be kept in a separate file under similar headings.

Provide for Evaluation as the Program Develops

Evaluation is such an important part of all program development that a separate chapter (Chapter 11) has been devoted to the subject. It is mentioned here only as a reminder of its importance.

Involve Pupils in the Planning

In organizing learning experiences, a teacher may be guided by his own ideas of what is important and also by those things which seem important to pupils. When the aims of teacher and pupil are not identical, ways must be found to combine them into a workable plan in harmony with sound principles of learning and in line with the larger goals of health and education. Let us use an example to see how this might be done.

A high school teacher of a social studies class in a rural community has decided that it is important for his students to understand the organization and operations of a local public health department as well as some of the problems involved in securing adequate public health services in the county. The subject is in line with the broad objectives of the course and is an important problem in this particular community. When a discussion of public health services is started, however, the students seem much more concerned about the lack of a hospital and the shortage of doctors, because these are conditions which they have often heard their parents discuss.

In deciding what to do, the teacher may follow one of several courses. He may proceed with his original plan or he may start with the expressed interests of the students and, as study proceeds, work toward an understanding of the need for preventive care. Still another alternative is to work out cooperatively with the pupils just what they will take up. If the teacher follows the first course, he may need much teaching skill to develop a receptivity on the part of the students so that they will learn effectively what is being taught on public health needs. If he follows one of the other plans which provide for student participation, the chances are that needs as both teacher and students see them will be more successfully dealt with. Moreover, the students will have grown in their ability to make decisions of their own.

How to Plan a Teaching Unit

Many of the suggestions already proposed for the planning of a year's program may, with adaptations, be applied to planning for a unit. Unit planning, however, involves additional specific procedures which will be presented briefly here. More complete information on unit planning may be found in current books on educational methods.

Regardless of the amount of pupil participation in the planning of the unit, there is definite need for the teacher to make certain preparations himself before the unit is started. In unit planning, as in broader planning, the teacher must first of all consider the pupils, their needs and interests, and their readiness for the contemplated study. Consideration should also be given to the problems involved and how they reveal themselves in the community or in the larger setting where their importance is significant. Thought, too, should be given to concepts which are pertinent. In sound planning, the unit itself will have been selected in the light of these factors.

After giving proper thought to all the elements in the situation, the teacher is ready to develop a written plan. This plan may take numerous forms. The form presented here is offered, not to serve as a model, but rather to suggest the items that should be included.

I. Title of unit, preferably stated in the form of a problem or question.
II. General objectives of unit, stated in terms of student accomplishment.
III. Suggested approaches (how the unit may be introduced).
IV. Body of unit:

Problems, interests, and needs	Specific objectives	Concepts and content	Teacher and pupil activities (Learning experiences)	Materials

V. Plan for evaluation.

It is well to state a unit in the form of a problem or question. This will help to give focus and meaning to the unit. For example, a unit on "Water" could mean almost anything, whereas one on "How to Improve Our Sources of Drinking Water" suggests a focal point for further planning.

A teacher should determine in advance the broad objectives of the unit and consider how the unit might be introduced. Problems, interests, and needs, as discovered in an analysis of the situation, provide the keys to specific objectives, concepts, content, activities or learning experiences, and materials. These may be listed in outline form or set up side by side as just illustrated.

Teachers and pupils together need to decide how they will gather the essential facts, what resources they will use, the time schedule they will follow, the division of responsibility, and other details involved in a shared project. As they progress they should evaluate what they are learning from the unit and modify their plans as the need for modification is indicated.

SUMMARY

Planning is essential in school health education. The most significant planning occurs in individual classrooms, but planning is also needed on a wider scale so that health education is thoroughly unified with the total school curriculum and with community life. Teachers, pupils, parents, health workers, and others in the school and community should share in planning activities. Leadership is needed, most particularly leadership of administrative personnel, qualified health educators, and coordinating bodies.

In all planning, orderly procedures are required for effective attainment of goals. The logistics of planning include collecting information essential for planning, establishing objectives, selecting and organizing the content of health instruction, determining appropriate learning experiences, developing a detailed plan of operation, carrying out the plan, and evaluating results.

Within individual classrooms, teachers need to lay broad, flexible plans for health teaching and then plan further with their pupils for experiences that are meaningful to them. It is better to select a few timely problems and work on them to the point of accomplishment than to touch upon many without results.

REFERENCES

Fleming, R. S.: Curriculum for Today's Boys and Girls. Columbus, Ohio, Charles E. Merrill Books, Inc., 1963, 662 pp.

Fodor, J. T., and Dalis, G. T.: Health Instruction: Theory and Application. Philadelphia, Lea & Febiger, 1966, 176 pp.

Hill, W.: Unit Planning and Teaching in Elementary Social Studies. Office of Education Bulletin 1963, No. 23. Washington, D.C., U.S. Government Printing Office, 1965, 82 pp.

Hull, V., Krippene, B., and Porter, F.: Manitowoc Story. A Team Approach to a School Health Study. Fond du Lac, Wis., Wisconsin State Board of Health, District Office No. 3, 1966, 48 pp.

Landes, R.: Culture in American Education: Anthropological Approaches to Minority and Dominant Groups in the Schools. New York, John Wiley & Sons, Inc., 1965, 330 pp.

Lippitt, R.: Processes of curriculum change. In Curriculum Change: Direction and Process. Washington, D.C., Association for Supervision and Curriculum Development, NEA, 1966, pp. 43–59.

Mayshark, C., and Shaw, D. D.: Administration of School Health Programs. St. Louis, The C. V. Mosby Company, 1967, 482 pp.

National Committee on School Health Policies of the NEA and the AMA: Suggested School Health Policies. 4th Ed. Chicago, American Medical Association, 1966, 54 pp.

National Conference on Coordination of the School Health Program: Teamwork in School Health. Washington, D.C., American Association for Health, Physical Education, and Recreation, 1962, 32 pp.

NEA Project on Instruction. Washington, D.C., National Education Association.
Deciding What to Teach, 1963, 264 pp.
Education in a Changing Society, 1963, 166 pp.
Planning and Organizing for Teaching, 1963, 190 pp.
From Bookshelves to Action, 1964, 32 pp.

Planning for Health Education in Schools. London, Longmans, Green & Co., Ltd., 48 Grosvenor St., 1966, 157 pp. (A study undertaken by Professor C. E. Turner on behalf of UNESCO and WHO.)

Responsibilities of State Departments of Education and Health for School Health Services. Revised Edition. Washington, D.C., The Council of Chief State School Officers, 1959, 52 pp. (A policy statement approved by The Council of Chief State School Officers and The Association of State and Territorial Health Officers.)

School Health Education Study. Washington, D.C., School Health Education Study, 1507 M Street, N.W., Room 800, 1964, 74 pp.

Warren, R. L.: Studying Your Community. New York, Russell Sage Foundation, 1955, 385 pp.

CHAPTER

6

METHODS OF HEALTH INSTRUCTION

In determining appropriate learning experiences, attention must be given to the selection of instructional methods which
will lead to desirable behavior changes. We know that what we teach
is of utmost importance. We realize, however, that the processes
of instruction are likewise important. When appropriately selected
and used, good teaching methods bring life and meaning to the
course content and help pupils to move toward desirable goals. Both
must go hand in hand, the content providing the substance of health
teaching, the methods, the means.

The bases for selecting and using methods have been developed
in previous chapters.[1] Briefly summarized, methods should be
selected and used so that they

1. Contribute to meeting instructional objectives.
2. Take into consideration what is known about learning.
3. Contribute to growth in learning.
4. Relate to the culture.
5. Make effective use of available resources.
6. Provide for individual differences.
7. Foster active involvement of pupils.
8. Provide for economy in learning.
9. Contribute to the wholeness of learning.

During the latter part of the nineteenth century and the first
two decades of the twentieth, teaching methods gave little or no
recognition to children's real motives as a basis for learning. In

---

[1] Also, in Chapters 8 and 9 many practical examples are given of methods used in
actual classroom situations. The reader will be helped in locating examples of the use
of specific instructional methods by turning to the index.

health instruction, children simply read from their health texts and recited back to the teacher what they had learned, with little attention to actual health problems.

As a reaction against this trite and ineffective kind of teaching, a movement to make health teaching more attractive was started about 1915 to 1920 under the leadership of voluntary health agencies. Interest catching devices such as the health crusade, health clowns and fairies, and health songs, plays, rhymes, and posters were introduced. Dr. C-E. A. Winslow once characterized this period as the "sing-a-song-and-eat-a-carrot" stage in health education. "Blue ribbon" and "gold star" children vied among themselves and displayed their accomplishments in lavish health parades. The children's enthusiasm often mounted to great heights, with much good doubtless accomplished. Observers recognized, however, that "interesting children" was sometimes confused with "entertaining children," and though immediate results in health habit improvement might be spectacular, long-term results were less evident.

More discerning observers also saw dangers, particularly in the techniques that involved competition. Sometimes children were put in unfair rivalry with their more fortunate classmates who were constitutionally healthier than they or who had better home advantages for carrying out health habits and correcting physical defects. Health competition sometimes encouraged dishonesty. One took a bath the night before one was checked on bathing, but baths were unnecessary before holidays or weekends. A child might, of course, report toothbrushing twice a day, if it meant helping to earn a gold star, even though he did not possess a toothbrush or its substitute.

Today the picture is changing. Modern educational psychology is pointing the way to a more dynamic type of health teaching that gives recognition to the motives and interests of individuals as well as to much broader concepts of educational goals and ways of reaching them.

PROBLEM SOLVING

Health teaching, on a one-to-one basis and with groups, often takes the form of problem solving. This method is especially well adapted to health education. Problem solving provides a rational approach to decision making and to action; it is in harmony with health education goals. Problem solving methods applicable to individualized health instruction are discussed at length in Chapter 10. This section is limited to a discussion of group problem solving.

Group problem solving may range from informal day-by-day activities centered around concerns of the moment to extensive and elaborate problem units. As an illustration of the first method, there may be too many minor accidents and too much fighting on the playground. These incidents are discussed, and the children think through and apply ways of having just as much fun with less risk. A more extensive group problem solving situation might arise as a group concerns itself with smoking and health. Pupils would not only need to find out how smoking can affect health but also think through what the consequences may be for themselves as they weigh decisions on whether or not to start smoking, or to stop smoking, if the habit has been established.

Steps in Problem Solving

These steps may be identified as follows:

Selecting a Problem for Attention

The pupils, with the help of the teacher, may select a problem related to some real life situation at school, in homes, or in the community.

Defining the Problem

Definition involves a clear statement of the major problem and of the smaller problems that are a part of the larger. Students may need to interview others, read extensively, and think creatively before they are able to define the problem clearly and precisely. With added knowledge and insight they may find it necessary to modify what they originally believed the problem to be. During this stage they will need to put "fences" around the problem, refining it and limiting it to the point at which its solution is manageable within their capacities and with the resources at hand.

Collecting Data

In this phase of problem solving, pupils will assemble pertinent information from different sources. They may decide to work out a plan whereby they share responsibility for collecting data. Some facts will be readily available while others will require further study and investigation. This is a phase in which interviewing, reading, discussing, and selecting will figure prominently. It is the stage in which pupils must learn to distinguish between fact and opinion, sound and unsound sources, complete and incomplete information, as well as accurate and inaccurate data. Some time is required for this phase.

Analyzing and Interpreting Data

At this point critical thinking comes into active play. The findings are studied thoroughly for their implications and their value in solving the problem. Limitations are noted. Classification and reclassification of findings as related to major and subordinate problems occur with the elimination of the irrelevant. During this stage, pupils and teacher may need the help of technical personnel, such as physician, nurses, sanitary officers, or health educators so that interpretations are sound.

Drawing Conclusions

This procedure naturally follows the steps just described. Judgment enters the picture here. Previous experiences of the pupils and the values they hold will be reflected in the conclusions they draw. Once again, students may benefit by help from health personnel or others with special knowledge of the problem.

At this point several alternative choices may present themselves, as would be the case, for example, in arriving at conclusions on the consequences of smoking. Pupils need to be cognizant of these alternative choices and of their consequences.

Applying Conclusions to the Solution of a Problem or to a Plan of Action

This is the crucial stage in problem solving. Some pupils may go no further than to talk about a problem. Others may gain greater understanding of and insight into a situation when they have worked through the steps of problem solving. When the problem situation is oriented toward action, orderly progression through these steps may lead to actual decision making and commitment on the part of individuals or the group to act on the measures indicated. If health teaching is to accomplish its goals, this last outcome is often to be desired.

Evaluating Results

Evaluation should be an integral part of every step in problem solving. Whenever pupils think critically and test their choices and decisions against objectives during the different stages of the process, they are indeed evaluating. In addition, evaluation may help the pupils gain some appreciation of the problem solving process itself as well as of related learnings from the experience. The teacher, too, needs the evaluation as a basis for future planning.

Creating a Favorable Climate for Problem Solving

If problem solving is to facilitate learning, a climate favorable for its development is essential. When children are deeply involved in problem solving, feelings may run high; at one moment there may be the excitement of discovery; at another, the frustrations and disappointments of uncertainty and disagreement. The teacher who is accustomed to formal classroom procedures can become disturbed by these responses and in his anxiety hamper rather than release creative thinking and action. Concerned lest the group does not accomplish what he believes they should, he will too often make decisions for the pupils, shaping their thinking rather than allowing them to think for themselves. The following suggestions are offered for the teacher who would like to gain confidence in creating an environment in the classroom which fosters problem solving.

1. Start with a few simple problems as they arise in daily living or in routine studies.
2. Encourage pupil questioning and respond to the questions willingly and with genuine interest. When possible and pertinent, use the questions as a starting point for group problem solving.
3. Raise questions yourself which will help pupils to explore the meaning of things.
4. When problem situations arise, hold back on your own answers; instead, encourage pupils to clarify problems and delay arriving at answers or decisions until facts have been assembled and alternative solutions considered.
5. Be accepting of pupils' suggestions yet prepared to lead them toward further exploration if so indicated.
6. Encourage pupils to discover problems themselves, to try out their ideas on others, and to be willing to accept differing points of view.
7. Allow enough freedom in both physical and mental activity to facilitate ready communication among pupils.
8. Help pupils to recognize that not all problems are soluble—that often, however, progress can be made by working on them.
9. Develop the pupils' faith in their ability to face and solve problems commensurate with their maturity level and background of experience. They may not always do it your way, but with your help they can grow in their ability to think and act independently and with confidence and conviction.[2]

How a Problem-Centered Unit Was Planned and Carried Out

A problem-centered unit is described and analyzed here to illustrate how steps in problem solving can be followed in a learning situation. This unit was developed with a biology class

---

[2] Adapted from Gross, R. E., Muessig, R. H., and Fersh, G. L., Editors: The Problems Approach and the Social Studies. Number Nine, Revised Ed. Washington, D.C. National Council for the Social Studies, 1960, pp. 27–29.

in a rural high school and was concerned with "How Is Milk in Our Town Protected?"[3]

Selecting a Problem for Attention, and Defining the Problem

Marge M., Jane B., Ted A., and Dick E. were fellow students in biology in Our Town. One day, while on the topic of nutrition, a lively discussion arose. Milk was the first of foods, of course. But just how well protected was Our Town's milk supply? Were herds tested? Yes, some students were pretty sure of that. For what? No one really knew for sure. Were barns inspected? Dick, a farmer's son, nodded a vigorous yes. By whom and how often? That was a harder question. Was milk pasteurized? Were dairy plants inspected? Did Our Town have an adequate milk ordinance?

The biology class decided there were a lot of things it didn't know . . . things that good citizens should know. "Let's really find out!" said Ted—and Marge and Jane and Dick agreed. So did Mr. H., their biology instructor. . . .

Collecting Data

So . . . Our Town's biology class decided it needed a committee to find out the facts. Mr. H. quickly named it: the four students who had asked the most questions. And almost as quickly they went to work. Each of them went out to a different grocery, each bought three bottles of milk. They took them into the high school laboratory, poured out samples. Eleven of the twelve samples stood the test with flying colors. But one of them was sour. Somewhere there was improper sanitation or handling, permitting bacteria to grow. Where?

"You said, 'Let's find out the facts,'" Mr. H. reminded them. "Suppose you go down and see Mr. T., the health officer."

So Jane and Dick went down to the other end of Main Street. Chet T. . . . ran Our Town's biggest garage. The health officership . . . well, that was just a side line . . . taken on as a favor for Our Town's village board because nobody else wanted to be bothered.

"Our Town's milk supply, was it adequately protected?"

"Son," Chet told Dick, "I'm no doctor, I'm no chemist. . . . You go talk to somebody who really knows!" . . .

"Let's go to Madison, they'll surely know there!" said Marge. One Saturday they set off. The State Health Officer . . . told them about the State Health Department's year-round program of health education on the nutritive values of milk. But milk sanitation, he said, was mainly the job of the Wisconsin Department of Agriculture. . . .

They then called upon the Director of the Department of Agriculture, who told them about the staff of dairy inspectors who regularly visit dairies through the state and about the tests used to protect the state's milk supply. He also gave them the story of how bovine tuberculosis was conquered in Wisconsin. He then arranged for one of the inspectors to take the students to a model dairy barn where they saw at first hand the clean handling of milk throughout the milking process.

---

[3] From It happened in biology. The Crusader (Wisconsin Anti-Tuberculosis Association), *41*:2–13 (Jan.) 1949. This story is based on an actual situation described by Warren H. Southworth, University of Wisconsin.

Analyzing and Interpreting Data

When the four fact-finders . . . returned to Our Town, they had a lot to tell their classmates about what the State of Wisconsin does to protect and improve Wisconsin milk. They had a lot to tell their parents.

One thing they brought back was more vivid in their minds than anything else. . . . Many precautions should be taken and are taken. But to err is human. To guard against a breakdown anywhere along the line, every community should be protected by a standard milk ordinance, which includes licensing of producers and distributors, precise definitions of terms, and proper regulations regarding production, distribution, and sanitation.

Drawing Conclusions

Did Our Town have such an ordinance? No, it didn't. Did it need one? There was little doubt in the minds of Our Town's high school students, their teachers, their parents when the four fact-finders had told what they had learned.

Applying the Conclusions to the Solution of a Problem or to a Plan of Action

Soon Chet T., the local health officer, took the matter in hand. He secured a standard milk ordinance, and with the backing of the community, presented it to the village board.

There was some discussion, of course; there were even one or two members who had to be shown. That was right and proper . . . the due democratic process.

But the facts presented, the need shown, Our Town's village board to a man said "Aye."

"We've got a fine town, fine kids," said Cliff T., village president. "And we mean to keep 'em fine!"

A Unit on "Solving My Problems"

The teen-ager is faced with a myriad of problems, for which he must find solutions. Many of his problems are not easily solved. Helping the teen-ager to become proficient in using problem-solving methods is one of the most important tasks of the school. The degree to which each youth learns how to solve every-day problems will have a direct bearing on his success in life.[4]

This statement introduces a unit for eighth grade students in the Columbus Public Schools. Only one portion of the unit is presented on the pages immediately following. The other two portions, on "Improving Study Habits" and "Evaluating Advertising," give pupils a chance to test their ability to solve problems. A pretest covering the whole unit is omitted. Teacher objectives for the unit are listed at the top of page 166.

---

[4] Solving My Problems; Unit I for Grade 8. Columbus, Ohio, Columbus Public Schools, 1961. Committee Contributors: Donald Richardson and Richard Dodge.

Contents	Fact-Finding Sources	Pupil Activities
Introduction: Man as a thinking animal will always have problems. How he solves his problems is the important issue.	*Basic Readings:* Building Health, pp. 76–88. Into Your Teens, pp. 41–54. Science 2, pp. 4–10. Teen-agers, pp. 46–48. You and Your Problems.	
A. SCIENTIFIC THINKING	A. SCIENTIFIC THINKING	A. SCIENTIFIC THINKING
1. What is the definition of a problem?	1. *Book:* Into Your Teens, pp. 36–39.	
a. (A situation that causes some anxiety and for which there is no ready answer without research and thinking.)		
2. What do some people do to avoid facing problems?	2. *Book:* Building Health, pp. 386–388. *Film:* "The Procrastinator" (290). Also available from the Ohio Department of Education, Division of Audio-Visual Education.	2. *Class Discussion:* Ask pupils to name specific ways that people avoid solving problems. Use the headings outlined in the content column.
a. Take flight because they are afraid (to play make believe; to daydream, to become sick, or to forget).		
b. Want to fight because they are angry.		
c. Compensate (to try more or less unconsciously to make up for what we feel that we lack).		
d. Rationalize (unconsciously to give untrue excuses or explanations for our behavior).		
e. Project (to give untrue excuses and to place the fault on someone or something else).		

Contents	Fact-Finding Sources	Pupil Activities
A. SCIENTIFIC THINKING	A. SCIENTIFIC THINKING	A. SCIENTIFIC THINKING
f. Give negative responses (nearly always to answer "no" to suggestions and invitations; to resent criticism).		
g. Have a temper tantrum (a flare of temper marked by violent actions and words).		
3. Why is it dangerous for you to avoid facing your problems? a. You will lead an unrealistic life. b. You will become continually dependent on others. c. You may get hurt physically, socially, and mentally.		
4. What is a fact? (A proven statement)	4. *Small Poster and Diagram:* "Fact and Fable." Central Ohio Heart Association. *Film:* "How to Judge Facts." Ohio Department of Education, Division of Audio-Visual Education. *Leaflet:* "Fears, Fact and Fable." Central Ohio Heart Association.	4. *Discussion:* What is the difference between a fact and a fable? What is a superstition? Why has man lived by superstitions in the past?
5. What are some common superstitions? (Examples) a. Walking under a ladder. b. Black cat crossing your path.	5. *Film:* "Science and Superstition" (20). Also available from the Ohio Department of Education, Division of Audio-Visual Education.	5. *Oral and Written Committee Report:* The superstitions of sport personalities. What is the origin of common superstitions?

Experiment:

List superstitions and facts suggested by pupils. Make a chart and determine how many believe and how many do not believe or doubt these statements. Check the validity of these statements by experimenting. Report results of experiments to the class. For example, if a pupil carries a rabbit's foot does it bring him good luck? Will a person who breaks a mirror have bad luck?

6. *Written Report to be Given Orally in Class:*

What are the signs of the Zodiac? Use an encyclopedia or an almanac for reference.

7. *Individual Reports to be Given Orally:*

Have pupils bring in several horoscopes from the daily newspapers and prepare a report about their findings.

Discussion:

Have pupils list, define, and discuss the fake scientists who prey on people.

6. *Book:*

Building Health, pp. 77–78.

6. Why are some people superstitious?

a. Because of the stories their families and friends have handed down to them.
b. Because of the influence fortunetellers, astrologers, and others have had on their lives.
c. Because of the influence certain literary stories have had on their lives.
d. Because they are afraid.
e. Because the truth is unknown to them.

7. Who are some people who take advantage of your superstitions for a profit?

a. Fortunetellers.
b. Palm and tea-leaf readers.
c. Mediums.
d. Mystics.
e. Astrologers.
f. Witch doctors.

Contents	Fact-Finding Sources	Pupil Activities
A. SCIENTIFIC THINKING	A. SCIENTIFIC THINKING	A. SCIENTIFIC THINKING
8. How are "fads" similar to superstitions? a. In origin. b. In scientific support.		8. *Interview:* What "fads" are now popular? Interview teachers, parents, and fellow pupils. *Discussion:* How do you react to popular fads? What limitations should be apparent? *Written Report:* Have each pupil select one health fad and analyze it scientifically.
9. What problems do superstitions and unhealthy living sometimes cause an individual? a. Loss of good personal health, especially mental anguish. b. Loss of money.		9. *Discussion:* What is the relationship between superstition and unhealthy living?
10. How does a scientist differ from a charlatan? a. The scientist is open-minded. b. The scientist does not jump to conclusions (thinks critically). c. The scientist is curious. d. The scientist is discriminating. e. He is accurate. f. He is tolerant of the opinions of others.	10. *Books:* Science 2, pp. 7–9. Building Health, pp. 79–88.	10. *Written Report:* List the traits of a scientist. Tell why each of these traits in important.

11. What is the right way to find answers to your problems?
(Use the scientific method in solving your problems.)

a. Define the problem.
b. Collect facts about the problem.
c. Reach a tentative conclusion.
d. Check the tentative conclusion.
e. Reach a final conclusion.
f. Do something about it.

11. *Book:*
Building Health, pp. 388–391.

Film:
"What Is Science?" (17)

Booklet:
You and Your Problems, pp. 3–8, 36–40.

11. *Discussion:*
What is the scientific method?

Problem Solving:
By using the steps involved in the scientific method, solve a problem which confronted a scientist.

Examples:
Walter Reed and the transmission of yellow fever.
Jonas Salk and the polio vaccine.

Written Report:
Assign pupils the responsibility of listing specific resources to which they could go to gather data in solving a problem.

Discussion:
Under what general categories could these resources be grouped?

Teacher Objectives

Knowledge

To help pupils understand the scientific method of problem solving.
To assist pupils in learning how to study and how to take a test.
To acquaint pupils with unscientific appeals in health advertising.

Attitudes

To encourage pupils to develop a sensible and an analytical approach to the solving of everyday problems.
To help pupils appreciate the importance of developing good daily study habits.
To aid pupils in evaluating advertising related to health.

Behavior (habits and skills)

To help pupils practice scientific methods of problem solving.
To assist boys and girls in establishing effective study habits.
To encourage teen-agers to use good judgment in purchasing.

DISCUSSION METHODS

Discussion is woven inextricably within the fabric of our democratic living. In schools, discussion may assume many different forms, a few of which are described below as they apply to health teaching.

Lecture-Discussion

This term is used for lack of a better one to cover a wide range of presentations combined with discussion. Encompassed within it are presentations not only by lecture, but also by tape, films, television, or similar forms of communication. A presentation by the teacher, by an outside resource person, or by a pupil can help to arouse interest in a subject and set the stage for discussion, problem solving, or other types of pupil activity. Case materials, unfinished stories, and critical issues are often handled in this way. Presentations can help pupils gain skill in listening and, when given in the form of talks by the pupils themselves, skill in verbal communication.

A number of schools throughout the country are employing a new form of instructional organization that consists of large-group instruction coordinated with individual study and small-group discussions. The lecture method is frequently used to present material before the large groups of pupils who are assembled in a single room. If several smaller rooms are used the lecture is relayed to the separate rooms by means of closed-circuit television.

Open-circuit television (broadcasting) is also used in a similar manner.

Numerous lecture-discussion techniques are possible depending upon the purposes of the situation. A lecture may be combined with a buzz session, a panel discussion, a symposium, or questions and answers and general discussion. The talk itself is often strengthened by the use of visual aids, such as overhead projectors, displays, films, slides, or filmstrips.

In one fifth grade classroom a pupil reported on a special library study he had made of health problems in the space age. He used photographs and newspaper clippings to illustrate his points and documented his material well. His talk was followed by a question period, the questions being formulated by small clusters of pupils arranged in buzz groups.

A senior high school health class studying problems of water safety invited a speaker from the local safety council to tell the class about water safety problems as he saw them. His lecture was followed by a panel discussion in which selected pupils participated. Their discussions focused on what they and others could do to make waterways in their community safer for recreation.

Presentations which are intended to stimulate problem solving should contain only enough information to clarify points and to direct thinking into appropriate channels. A film or a talk which presents a problem situation or a critical issue can be used in this way. Unfinished stories are sometimes used as starters for discussion, especially in elementary schools. In one community where an influx of migratory workers was expected during the summer months, a fourth grade teacher prepared her children for their new neighbors by telling a story of a child from a migratory family who had arrived in a community only to find he was rejected by children of his age. She followed the story with the question, "What would you do if such a child came into your neighborhood?" The lively discussion which followed led to new insights on the part of pupils regarding the needs of migratory children and to some practical plans for making life happier for those children soon to arrive in the community.

A *symposium* is a variation of the lecture-discussion technique. In a symposium, several people give speeches in sequence concerning a broad subject, each speaker presenting an aspect of the subject. The audience may respond with questions or comments. Symposia are suitably used in assembly programs as well as in classrooms or other gatherings when a subject is of such scope that no one person can wisely present all aspects of it. Presentation of different points of view by several people is often more stimulating than a "one-man show."

Informal Discussion

Informal discussion has been used in classrooms for years. At almost every stage in group problem solving, discussion is important. It provides opportunity for the impact of one mind on another, for the pooling of experiences, and for the creation of concepts and plans that result in attainments impossible by any other means. In community life as well as in the classroom, discussion has become an essential procedure for democratic living.

Discussion is not an end in itself; its value lies in the understanding it brings and the action it engenders. Certain conditions are likely to bring more productive results from discussion than others. A few of these are:

1. The teacher, or appointed student leader, is a facilitator, and not a master. He tries to liberate the best that is in a group, rather than to impose upon the group the best that is in him.
2. The group sets its own goals of accomplishment and its own course toward reaching the goals.
3. The contributions of each member are respected by all in the group.
4. Wide group participation is encouraged.
5. Each member, at some time and in some way, holds a leadership role.
6. Focus is on problems to be solved rather than on shortcomings of the members.
7. Discussion is rooted in sound knowledge.
8. Discussion leads to decision.
9. The physical environment within which discussion takes place is comfortable and conducive to informality.

Children in a Florida school had been working in the garden that their class had planted at school. Since mustard, turnip greens, lettuce, onions, and radishes were ready to eat, they decided to prepare lunch for themselves the next day, using the vegetables from the garden. The following discussion ensued. It is reported here in detail since it illustrates how this method of health teaching can lead to change in attitudes and action.

"I believe I won't come tomorrow then," Keith said. "I just hate all kinds of greens."

Some others, less outspoken, agreed with him.

"I believe you'll like these tomorrow," said Miss Brown, smiling at them. "Don't decide against the luncheon until it is planned. . . . You might miss something, you know."

"All right, I guess I'll have to be open-minded about it," Keith quipped. . . .

"Now, how shall we serve these?" she asked.

They finally decided to cook the mustard and turnip greens together and to have tossed salad, using lettuce, onions and radishes. Then their planning "bogged down."

"What might help you now?" Miss Brown asked.

"Oh, the Food Chart," Iva answered. After a look at the chart she said, "We don't have any meat, fish, eggs or milk."

"What would be good to serve with greens?"

Mary replied, "My mother nearly always serves poached eggs."

"We'd better boil ours," Betty added. "It's hard to pick up a poached egg without breaking it."

"We can have milk to drink," Bill contributed.

"I think we are beginning to have a very well-balanced meal. Do we need anything else?" Miss Brown continued.

"Dessert, we don't have a dessert," Elizabeth said.

"Let's have candy," Martha, with a sweet tooth, suggested. "No," Katie said, "This is going to be a real health luncheon. Let's have apples."

All thought this a good idea. Then someone suggested apples and bananas because that would give choice and they would require little preparing.

They listed the materials they would have to bring—foods and utensils. Then they decided on committees and volunteered to serve on them, writing it all under the title *"Plans."*

Needless to say, everyone was there early next morning and on the job. They were all careful to wash their hands and make sure the utensils were clean. The luncheon was served on time. Not a child said a word about disliking anything. The food all disappeared more rapidly than when they ate in the school lunch department. Suddenly, Billy looked at Keith and said, "I thought you didn't like greens. I certainly couldn't tell it from the way you ate."

"These are better than they usually are," Keith replied. "Anyway, I didn't miss anything, did I Miss Brown?"

"You've been good sports, all of you. But really, didn't you enjoy eating everything?" Miss Brown asked.

All heartily agreed that they had.

When Keith's mother saw Miss Brown, she asked, "How is it you can get my son to eat turnip greens and tossed salad when I try as hard as I can at home and can't get him to consent to taste them?"

"Don't you think it's because he's eating with other children?" Miss Brown replied; "then too, children almost always eat vegetables that they grow and prepare."[5]

Other Forms of Discussion

Buzz Sessions

One discussion technique which can elicit wide participation within a group is commonly known as a buzz session. In a buzz session the class or group is divided into smaller groups of usually no more than six to eight individuals who discuss the problem among themselves for a few minutes and then, through a spokesman, share their thinking with the larger group. Buzz groups can be used effectively to formulate questions around a problem or to define a problem. Then, too, by means of buzz sessions, different aspects of a problem or situation can be divided for refinement or solution as a study develops. The buzz session technique can also be

---

[5] Better Health for Florida's Children. Bulletin 4-E. Tallahassee, Florida, State Department of Education, 1957, pp. 9–10.

followed when airing controversial issues, with each group developing points around a specific aspect of the issue.

When introducing a new unit of study, a teacher may use this device to stimulate interest and widespread identification with the problem or subject. For example, in starting a unit on consumer health, the class as a whole might first establish areas of major interest and then divide into buzz groups to formulate questions from which the study could progress, each buzz group developing questions around one of the interest areas. At a later stage in the project, and after adequate background study, buzz groups might be formed again to summarize points. To illustrate, one area of interest might be on the subject of how quackery could be discouraged. One group might summarize what the consumer himself could do, another what responsibilities the government should assume, and a third what part health and medical authorities should play.

Panel Discussions

In a panel discussion, people holding different views on a subject or problem discuss it informally among themselves in front of an audience. Though the major problems around which the discussion will evolve are usually known in advance by panel members, the discussion itself is spontaneous and unrehearsed. As the discussion moves forward, members of the audience are likely to identify themselves first with one and then with another panel participant. Through this process, they may gain new insights and a better understanding of the many shadings of a problem or situation. At an appropriate point, the audience may be brought into the discussion. From time to time during the discussions, and finally at the end, the leader will summarize points of agreement or disagreement and decisions reached.

Panel discussions are being used increasingly in classroom situations and in assembly programs when subjects of wide interest or concern need special airing. Problems of interpersonal relationships and civic issues lend themselves particularly well to panel discussions. Though the panel members may not reach clear-cut conclusions, their discussion may help to clarify issues and to suggest directions for further study and action.

"Quiz the Experts"

This technique is a variation of the panel discussion. In a typical "production," questioners sit on one side of a moderator and experts on the other. A question brought forth by a questioner is relayed by the moderator to the appropriate expert who responds by giving an answer and perhaps by raising additional questions to which other experts respond. This device has been popular at PTA meetings and other public gatherings, especially when the children are the questioners and health authorities the experts. It could be used with modifications in a classroom situation. When conducted before an audience, it is well to have an adult, such as a teacher or nurse, help the pupils prepare their questions in advance of the meeting.

Reactor Panel

A reactor panel consists of several people who react to a presentation given by one or more individuals. Each "reactor" comments from his own point of view. To illustrate, in one elementary school this technique was used during an assembly program which was the culmination of a sixth grade study of international health problems and programs. Following reports by several pupils, a panel of "reactors," consisting of overseas students from a nearby university, made comments on the points brought forth by the pupils. One pupil reported on water and health in different parts of the world, another on current programs for the eradication of malaria, and a third on the problem of food supplies in developing nations. The "reactors," from Chile, Germany, Nigeria, and Thailand, then discussed both formally and informally among themselves the nature and extent of these problems in their own countries and what was being done by their governments to meet the problems.

DRAMATIZATIONS

Children's experiences with dramatizations may come either through performing themselves or through watching others perform. Both types have their place in health teaching. When the children themselves perform, they may grasp readily the story being told through identification with the characters or the situations being portrayed. Identification is also possible through watching others act. For some, this may be a better way of learning than by taking part themselves.

Children of all ages enjoy dramatizations, but interest runs particularly high in the lower grades. Younger children like to dramatize common events in the home and neighborhood, whereas older pupils may prefer historical events, current affairs, or stories of adventure and success. The fields of public health and medicine provide excellent subject matter for dramatizations at all age levels.

Three types of dramatic experiences, creative dramatics, the puppet show, and role-playing, are discussed here with emphasis on their use in health teaching.

Creative Dramatics

Creative dramatics may be developed by children as a part of regular school work, either to clarify or to accent some phase of study or as a summary. Often dramatizations can be composed in short order and can have much charm and value in their spontaneity.

One fourth grade teacher has described the use of this method as a means of promoting safety understanding. Her report is given in detail to show how creative dramatics can be a vehicle for other kinds of learning experiences including problem solving, discussion, and critical thinking.[6]

Teacher Preparation

In the week prior to the lesson the following news items were located:

1. A boating tragedy that resulted in the deaths of three boys who asked a stranger for a ride. The river was swollen from heavy summer rains.
2. Serious injury resulting from an accident in which a youngster ran into the street in front of a passing car.
3. An article cautioning parents about tooth injuries that increase in the summer when children are playing on playground equipment.
4. A child drowned while swimming in an unauthorized area with two companions. The child panicked and fought off the efforts of his two friends to guide him to a shallow area a few yards downstream.

The teacher carefully read the articles and underscored the points to be read to the class. Although the seriousness of the incidents and the reality of the tragedies were retained, some of the more gruesome details were omitted.

Motivation

To prompt discussion the teacher asked questions:

"Have you ever felt that accidents always happen to someone else?
"How many of you have discussed safety in your classroom studies?
"Have you ever found yourself in situations where you have ignored safety factors and narrowly missed a tragedy?
"I examined the newspaper this past week and found out about some children who weren't as lucky as we have been. They were good children with parents and teachers who did just as much as yours to help them live safe and happy lives. Listen while I read to you parts of these articles. Think about the question, 'What safety rules did these children forget?' "

Each article was read to the class. The situations were real, and the children

---

[6] Reported by Sheila Fitzgerald, Tuttle School, Minneapolis, Minnesota, 1967.

involved in the tragedies were the same age as the listeners, so the class sat with rapt attention. Everyone had something to add to the discussion—comments on the incident, questions on how it could happen, or personal experiences related to the situation. It was a lively discussion, and the children raised points that the teacher had not anticipated, as, for example:

> "My mom told me about crazy things she did as a child. Why do they get so upset when we take chances?"
> "Can teeth that have been knocked out be replaced by the dentist?"

The class was most interested in telling about related incidents they had experienced or read about. The teacher found it necessary to guide the discussion back to the main point—the safety factors that had been ignored by the children.

Planning for Creative Dramatics

The teacher asked the class if these incidents could be dramatized. All of the children were confident of their talents in the dramatic arts because they had had many experiences dramatizing everyday events, poems, and stories. However, now they were going to add a new dimension to their creative skits; they wanted to teach the class as well as present a situation that would be entertaining. It was decided that each group would use as a guideline for its planning the following question: What does this skit teach us about safety? The class would use the same question for evaluating the presentation.

The teacher selected a group leader for each incident, and the leader chose participants to work with him. Each group met for a 15 minute planning and practice session. The usual problems inherent in group work arose: disagreements in interpretation, refusal to accept a certain part in the skit, an overzealous leader, etc. The teacher moved from group to group helping each to understand their disagreements and to praise them for progress and concessions that were being made.

Presentation of the Skits

The skits offered as much opportunity to promote safety understanding as did the motivation of the lesson. Most groups chose to have two acts showing poor and then good safety practices. The first attempts to present the plays were crude and sometimes overlooked important safety factors. One group showed the boys accepting a ride in the boat from the stranger and then showed the same incident again, the boys accepting a ride with the stranger but putting on life jackets! Class discussion brought out the problem, and it was decided that the group should be given more planning time and another opportunity to present their skit for the class. Most of the skits prompted suggestions so three class periods were used before all skits were perfected to the satisfaction of the class.

Evaluation

Class interest is one good yardstick for measuring learning. This approach to safety teaching had a high degree of interest value throughout the three days. The guidance of the teacher was important, particularly in maintaining a focus on safety and how creative dramatics could help to put safety concepts in a more nearly real life setting.

Puppets

Puppet shows have been used extensively in elementary schools. In school systems where they are most successful, the pupils make their own puppets and their own stories, and the device is used along with other teaching procedures. The puppets arouse interest, create favorable attitudes, and provide a means for organizing content material. They also open the way for more solid teaching. In some school systems, ready-made puppets are manipulated before the children to tell some health story. In using puppets for health teaching, facts should not be mixed with imaginative elements so that children become confused. Neither should accuracy be sacrificed for dramatic effect.

Role-Playing

Role-playing is a spontaneous, unrehearsed acting out of a situation by a group or selected members of the group. By identification with a situation or incident through role-playing, the group is often able to gain insights which would be difficult to secure through observation, discussion, or other means. Role-playing is particularly effective for those who are actually playing the roles, but the audience may benefit too. This technique has been successful with disadvantaged children who respond best to physical and visual communication, children who learn through activity.

Role-playing may help a group to understand how people feel in a given situation; it may also make clearer those forces that help or hinder good human relations. It is especially valuable as a technique for effecting change in attitudes. For example, pupils could role-play a parent discovering a son or daughter smoking secretly, a young person turning down an offer of an alcoholic beverage, a trial interview of a resource person, or a baby-sitter upon arrival at a home for an evening alone to care for three young children.

A few suggestions for making role-playing a success are:

1. Role-playing is used more effectively in a natural situation in which a point needs clarifying than in one which is artificially created.

2. The situation needs to be clearly defined by the group before role-playing begins so that each player will know just what is expected of him.

3. Role-players may be chosen by the group or they may volunteer. Either procedure is usually better than to have them appointed by the teacher. The teacher's guidance may be needed, however, to avoid placing a pupil in a role that might produce too great an emotional impact.

4. Reality is enhanced if the stage is set in advance with whatever simple properties are needed.

5. The audience needs preparation so that observations are meaningful. The group may discuss in advance what it will look for.

6. After the scene is enacted, discussion and evaluation are needed to gain full value from the experience.

FIELD EXPERIENCES

Field experiences provide important links between the classroom and the community. They may take the form of visits to places of interest, interviews with resource people, camping experiences, or any number of other activities outside the classroom. Discussion here is limited primarily to one kind of field experience: field trips conducted as part of a learning situation. Many points included in this section could, with adaptations, apply to the planning and conducting of other types of field experience.

A field experience should be arranged only if it can clearly contribute to meeting a specific objective of a learning situation. A field experience may come at the beginning of a project to introduce the project or to arouse interest and curiosity; during the development of a project to help visualize some point under study; or at the end as a summary. A teacher and pupils should decide in each instance when a field experience would be most profitable.

When convenient and possible, the whole class may participate as, for example, through a trip to a farm or a weekend of camping for concentrated outdoor education. At other times representatives from a class may make the trip and share with the group what they have seen or heard by such means as oral reports, on-the-spot video tape recordings, or slides.

Field trips should be taken at periods in the school life when children can profit most by them. This planning can be done satisfactorily only on a school-wide basis. One college student once remarked that she had visited a dairy six times in the course of her elementary and secondary school years. When asked which visit was most interesting to her, she stated that the first one made during the second grade left the most lasting impression. This statement does not necessarily prove that the second grade is the optimum or the only time for such a trip. It does point to the need for serious study by teaching groups as to how to make each trip a profitable educational experience for the children. Every trip should have a purpose, one which ties in with the learning situation at the time. If teaching is being geared to the developmental changes in children, then purposes of field trips will naturally change. Actually, children may go to the same place several times, and each time learn something new and pertinent to their immediate interests and needs.

A few of the places which children might visit are listed here, with suggestions as to what may be observed at each:

1. A dairy, creamery or milk plant—processes in sanitary milk (and milk products) production and distribution.

2. A farm—hygienic care of animals; manner in which foods are grown or produced; farm safety.

3. The health department building—clinic activities; laboratories; people who guard the community's health.

4. A water purification plant—consecutive steps in the purification process. In advance of the visit, it would be well to secure from the plant a flow chart (diagram) of the steps for the children to study so that they will comprehend what they are observing.

5. A sewage disposal plant—consecutive steps in the process. A flow chart would be valuable here, too.

6. An industrial plant—health facilities for workers, such as lunchroom, clinic, recreation, and restrooms; special protective devices from the standpoint of health and safety; how some piece of equipment or some product important from the standpoint of health is manufactured (e.g., toothbrushes, cereals, vitamin products, bandages).

7. Freezer locker plant—how foods are prepared under sanitary conditions for storage; how sanitary conditions are maintained in the packaging of foods; temperatures at which foods are stored.

8. The zoo—how animals are cared for in order to keep them clean and healthy; how baby animals are cared for by their parents.

9. A well-kept home— healthful living conditions in the home; opportunities for recreation; food storage; safety measures. In general, it would be better to select a home comparable to those from which the majority of the children come, and not in the neighborhood served by the school.

10. A modern housing project—provisions for outdoor play area, sanitation, lighting, ventilation. This visit would be more meaningful if conditions in the housing project were compared with those in an area of poor housing. Care should be taken to avoid embarrassment among children who may live in blighted areas. Care also should be taken to avoid any appearance of "slumming" if a visit is made to an area of poor housing.

11. Points within the school.

For the maximum benefit from a field experience, preparation should start well in advance. The teacher himself needs a clear idea of what can be accomplished. This usually means a preliminary visit to the spot and discussions with the host or the authorities at the place to be visited so as to explore potentialities and to arrange details. One or more pupil representatives might also share in these preliminary plans. After these early steps the full class should discuss thoroughly what they hope to get out of the trip; they should do whatever background study is essential so that they are prepared to ask questions and to make intelligent observations. They should work out their own ground rules for conducting themselves safely and in a dignified manner during the trip. On return to the classroom following the field experience ample time should be allowed to discuss the experience and to consider its implications in the larger study of which it is but a part.

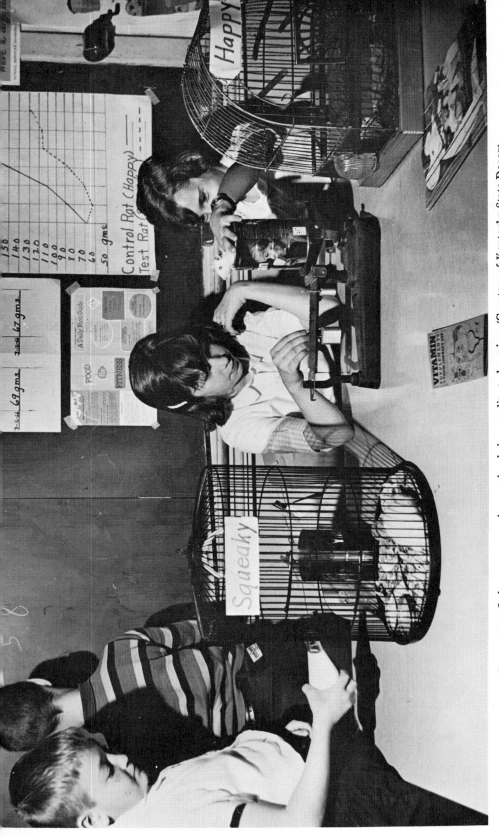

Figure 13. Laboratory experimentation brings reality to learning. (Courtesy of Kentucky State Department of Health, Frankfort, Kentucky.)

LABORATORY EXPERIMENTATION

The laboratory method is especially appropriate in the field of health education, which deals constantly with biological processes and with scientific phenomena. The anatomy and physiology of the human body are best studied through laboratory experimentation, or observation. Such problems as those concerned with lighting, heating, ventilation, and food preparation and care lend themselves to laboratory investigation. Modern health and science books suggest many excellent laboratory experiments bearing on health which can be carried out by pupils in the classroom.

The teacher's function is to provide the basic information needed for investigation or to direct students to sources of such information. The teacher, too, will furnish the essential tools for scientific study or, again, guide students in the search for or development of these tools. Methods of experimentation or observation must be taught. A spirit of exploration should prevail as students seek to discover things for themselves.

If health teaching is to be established on sound foundations, much more attention needs to be given to this scientific method for learning than in the past. Improved procedures over those commonly used under the name of laboratory work are also important. Students should be given the opportunity to carry on exploratory studies and experiments themselves and not merely follow blindly directions in a laboratory workbook. An increasing number of university laboratories and other research centers are providing opportunities for young people to gain experience in research. For some students such experiences have become steppingstones to a health career.

CREATIVE ACTIVITIES

Under this heading one may group a great variety of experiences that defy orderly classification. Many of the learning experiences already discussed in this chapter may be carried out so as to provide opportunity for creativity. Group problem solving, discussion, dramatization, and laboratory experimentation may become creative acts when appropriately performed; they can embody creative thinking and lead to new solutions or discoveries.

Independent investigation is an especially useful form of creativity in health education. Carried beyond an intellectual exercise to the point of application in the life of a pupil, such creative activity can have lasting value. A junior high school student, whose curiosity in modern drug therapy was aroused by current newspaper stories of misuse of drugs, made a detailed investigation of federal laws for the control of food, drugs, and cosmetics and of problems connected with their enforcement. Further, he investigated informally the amount and kind of self-medication occurring among his classmates and their families. Interest and concern aroused by his study led to the clearing out from his family medicine cabinet of all self-prescribed medicines which had been accumulating over the years.

Creativity can be expressed in such apparently mundane acts as planning a balanced daily diet or a daily routine with proper distribution of work, recreation, and rest. The children in the Florida classroom, mentioned earlier in this chapter, were in fact creating something unique and special for themselves when they prepared the meal at school.

Written or oral reports provide opportunity for creative expression. So, too, do various art forms through which pupils set forth their interpretations of health concepts and information.

PARTICIPATION

Participation of pupils in health improvement programs can become an important method of health education, especially when potentialities for education in such participation are fully exploited. Problem solving, already described, is an example of participation which can lead to new learning. Participation through volunteer services is another example. To illustrate, young people who assist at an outpatient child health clinic may learn much about child care as an integral part of their experience. They may learn, too, about health services in their community and perhaps also gain some comprehension of career opportunities in the field of health. Teachers and health personnel arranging for such volunteer services have a responsibility to prepare pupils for their duties and to interpret for them the nature and importance of their activities or observations. One cannot depend wholly upon the experience itself to provide the learning which is inherent within the situation.

SUMMARY

Methods and techniques in health education provide the means by which pupils are helped to move toward desirable health goals. They must be determined in the light of objectives and with an understanding of the learning process.

Problem-solving methods are especially well adapted to health education; they provide a rational approach to decision making and to action. Discussion methods, so inextricably woven within the fabric of our democratic living, are used widely and with great variation in health teaching. Dramatizations, field experiences, and laboratory experimentation are among other methods that can be used effectively.

Opportunity for creativity occurs through these and other experiences, including independent investigations, written or oral reports, and use of various art forms to interpret health concepts and information. Participation of pupils in health improvement programs can become an important method of health education when potentialities for education in such participation are fully exploited.

Methods and techniques are not ends in themselves, but when appropriately selected and used can bring life and meaning to health teaching.

REFERENCES

Beatty, W. H.: Theories of instruction for what? A projection. In Theories of Instruction. Washington, D.C., Association for Supervision and Curriculum Development, NEA, 1965, pp. 114–118.

Bruner, J. S.: The Process of Education. Cambridge, Mass., Harvard University Press, 1961, 97 pp. See especially Chapter 4: Intuitive and analytic thinking, pp. 55–68.

Bruner, J. S.: Toward a Theory of Instruction. Cambridge, Mass., Harvard University Press, 1966, 176 pp.

Fodor, J. T., and Dalis, G. T.: Health Instruction: Theory and Application. Philadelphia, Lea & Febiger, 1966, 176 pp.

Hanna, L. A., Potter, G. L., and Hagaman, N.: Unit Teaching in the Elementary School. Revised Ed. New York, Holt, Rinehart and Winston, Inc., 1963, 595 pp.

Health instruction: suggestions for teachers. Journal of School Health, *34,* No. 10a (Dec.) 1964, 80 pp. (Special issue.)

Martin, E. A.: Nutrition Education in Action; A Guide for Teachers. New York, Holt, Rinehart and Winston, Inc., 1963, 135 pp.

Mayshark, C., and Foster, R. A.: Methods in Health Education. A Workbook Using the Critical Incident Technique. St. Louis, The C. V. Mosby Company, 1966, 121 pp. (See also Instructor's Supplement.)

National Council for the Social Studies: How to Do It Series. Washington, D.C., The Council.

No. 6. Litchen, R. E.: How to Use Group Discussion, 1965, 8 pp.

No. 10. Larkin, M. S.: How to Use Oral Reports, 1964, 6 pp.

No. 12. Howland, A. E.: How to Conduct a Field Trip, 1958, 8 pp.

No. 13. Collings, M. R.: How to Utilize Community Resources, 1960, 8 pp.

No. 14. Gross, R. E.: How to Handle Controversial Issues, 1964, 8 pp.

No. 20. Zeleny, L. D.: How to Use Sociodrama, 1964, 8 pp.

Oberteuffer, D., and Beyrer, M. K.: School Health Education. 4th Ed. New York, Harper & Row, 1966, 534 pp.

Schneider, R. E.: Methods and Materials of Health Education. 2nd Ed. Philadelphia, W. B. Saunders Company, 1965, 372 pp.

Taba, H.: Curriculum Development; Theory and Practice. New York, Harcourt, Brace & World, Inc., 1962, 526 pp.

Theories of Learning and Instruction. The Sixty-third Yearbook of the National Society for the Study of Education. Part I. Chicago, The University of Chicago Press, 1964, 430 pp.

Turner, C. E., Sellery, C. M., and Smith, S. L.: School Health Education. 5th Ed. St. Louis, The C. V. Mosby Company, 1966, 411 pp.

Willgoose, C. E.: Health Education in the Elementary School. 2nd Ed. Philadelphia, W. B. Saunders Company, 1964, 369 pp.

CHAPTER

7

INSTRUCTIONAL MATERIALS AND THEIR USE IN HEALTH EDUCATION

Instructional materials have an important place in the active process of learning. They reinforce the spoken word and are important channels of communication. Through the use of instructional materials, pupils' knowledge and understanding of the world about them can be greatly extended. When created by pupils themselves, these materials provide a means of self-expression and clarification in the organization and presentation of ideas.

Dale has classified the wide range of instructional materials into three major categories:[1]

Speaking (or composing)—Listening	Radio, language laboratories, tapes, recordings
Visualizing—Observing	Television, films, videotapes, filmstrips, 2″ x 2″ slides, overhead transparencies, pictures, photographs, flash cards, flip books, maps, posters, charts, diagrams, bulletin boards, flannelgraphs, dioramas, models, mock-ups and simulation devices, field study
Writing—Reading	Books, newspapers, magazines, pamphlets, self-instructional material, charts, diagrams

Computers and self-instructional devices, he points out, can fit into more than one of these categories.

---

[1] Dale, E.: Instructional resources. In The Changing American School. The Sixty-fifth Yearbook of the National Society for the Study of Education. Part II. Chicago, The University of Chicago Press, 1966, p. 85.

Rapid advances are occurring in the development and use of instructional materials for teaching. Many new kinds of materials are now available, ranging from highly complex media, such as television and self-instructional devices, to simple pupil-made materials. While attention is being focused nationally on the use of the more complex media available through modern technology, we must not lose sight of the many excellent materials which cost little to produce or obtain and which, when properly used, can be exceedingly effective tools of learning.

Communications media, though receiving great emphasis today, are by no means new. Even in primitive times, people learned how to hunt or to cook by watching others perform and then trying it themselves. Many thousands of years ago cave dwellers drew pictures to transmit ideas. Through the years, good teachers have always used audiovisual aids to supplement their teaching. Now, as pupils are constantly being exposed throughout the day to many kinds of media, it is important that we explore carefully the potentialities of these media as tools for health teaching.

Instructional materials are effective at all stages in a learning process. They are often used at the beginning of a project as a general introduction; they are equally valuable at the end for purposes of summary. They may be used to promote discussion, to help clarify points under study, to assist in learning a skill, and to evaluate pupil accomplishment. They may also be used in various combinations for added reinforcement of any part of a learning experience.

In a book of this kind it is impossible to present fully all the information necessary for intelligent selection and use of instructional materials. Such information can be secured best from specialized books on the subject. Therefore, only a few principles which are particularly pertinent to health teaching are given; they are followed by suggestions for making effective use of specific instructional materials in school health education.[2]

PRINCIPLES TO GUIDE THE SELECTION AND USE OF INSTRUCTIONAL MATERIALS IN HEALTH TEACHING

Instructional Materials Should Be Regarded as Educational Tools Only

When a carpenter builds the framework of a house, he uses various tools for the process, including hammer, saw, and the

---

[2] Examples of classroom use of instructional materials are found elsewhere in the book, especially in Chapters 8 and 9. The reader will be helped in locating examples of the use of specific instructional materials by turning to the index.

like. The end product, however, is not the result of the tools alone; it depends fully as much upon the carpenter himself and his technical skills in construction work as upon his ability to use the tools properly. So, too, when a teacher instructs a class, he may use various tools, such as charts, motion pictures, and radio programs. His success, however, is dependent upon his special teaching skills and the manner in which he uses the tools of learning. Since teachers, unlike carpenters, are working with living, changing human beings, instead of with inanimate objects, the analogy between the teacher and the carpenter falls short at one point. In the last analysis, real success in teaching depends upon the kind of experiences the children themselves have, including what they do and how they think through problems. Instructional materials only aid such processes of teaching and learning; they are not the teaching and learning processes themselves.

There is a story of a teacher who was asked by a visitor what she was doing in her health program. "I'm so sorry," she replied, "but I took it off the wall just yesterday." All too often teachers have thought of health teaching in such limited terms. They have considered the teaching complete if the children have occasionally made health posters or have from time to time seen a film on a health subject. For them, the tools have become substitutes for real teaching and learning, and consequently are both sterile and meaningless.

Instructional materials should be used to supplement rather than to supplant other educational processes. When so used, they become extremely valuable adjuncts to learning.

Selection and Use of Instructional Materials Should Be Guided by Program Objectives

Just as objectives help to determine the content and methods of instruction, so, too, should they guide the selection and use of instructional materials. The relationship between objectives and the choice of learning experiences has been discussed in Chapter 5 and will not be enlarged upon here.

A Wide Range of Instructional Materials Should Be Available in School and Classroom

Learning can be greatly enriched when a wide variety of instructional materials is available. Not all children respond in the same way to communications media. With an assortment of materials, the teacher can help each pupil find those most useful to him. While gifted and culturally advantaged children may devour a wide range of materials and comprehend the very complex, slow learners and children from culturally deprived homes may learn best from concrete materials which are adapted to their backgrounds of experience.

It has been stated that children will learn what their previous experiences permit them to learn. Many materials will have little meaning to a particular group because there is nothing in the background of that group's experience to give them meaning. This point has been brought out forcefully by numerous workers in the developing countries of the world where people in some isolated villages have had little or no contact with modern living. In insect control programs, for example, motion pictures, models, and even enlarged photographs of insects are ineffective teaching devices. The villagers are confused when they see these symbols of the real object. In one village where a film on lice was being shown the people remarked, "Maybe there are big animals like that in your country, but not in our country." Health workers and teachers in that village, as in many others, now use the actual insects for teaching purposes. Here is something the people can understand because it is within the realm of their experience.

We need a better understanding of what children actually learn from various instructional materials. This is a field under increasingly intensive study, especially in curriculum projects for the culturally deprived.

Instructional Materials Should Be Scientifically Accurate in Their Content

Health materials should be evaluated carefully for accuracy before they are put to use. Materials available from official health departments and well established voluntary health agencies are usually dependable. Although many materials from commercial companies are equally satisfactory, greater care must be exercised in their selection to be certain of their accuracy and of the nature of their messages.

Schools need to be especially on the alert for propaganda materials, both commercial and noncommercial, which are slanted toward special motives. Materials containing a few inaccuracies or even propaganda do not necessarily need to be discarded. When the deficiencies are recognized, they may serve as a basis for much profitable discussion.

Accuracy is equally important in materials that are prepared locally either by the pupils themselves or by others. In eagerness to have children create their own materials, we sometimes stress originality and forget accuracy. This is unfortunate if there is any truth in the belief that creative activity helps to fix things permanently in the minds of children.

To avoid inaccuracies in both the selection and preparation of materials, teachers who do not have the scientific background essential for evaluating content should seek the assistance of those who do. In a local community the public health nurse working with the schools or a local health officer or physician may help. A home economics teacher may review nutrition materials, and a specialist in environmental health, those dealing with environmental problems. A qualified health educator may assist both teachers and pupils, not only through direct services, but also by bringing them into touch with technical experts. The teacher, however, must determine the appropriateness of the materials as educational tools for his particular group.

Instructional Materials Should Have Good Eye and Ear Appeal

If teaching materials in the field of health are to compete with commercial materials, they must be attractive. Striking color and artistic design should be used in printed matter; radio and television programs should be worth listening to. Many of the larger health agencies now recognize the power of materials with good eye and ear appeal, and produce materials that hold their own with those in the commercial world.

REAL OBJECTS

Lorado Taft, the famous sculptor, once told the story of an experience at his home in the country. A young girl from the neighborhood was with his family one evening at sunset. As they stood on the porch, admiring with awe the shifting colors in the western sky, the girl suddenly broke away from the group and said, "I must hurry home and tell my mother to look; I am sure she has never seen anything like this before." Here was a child of the country who had lived in the midst of beautiful sunsets all her life, but had never really seen one until this particular evening.

Throughout this book many suggestions have been given for direct experiences with real objects. Field trips, surveys, laboratory experimentation, and participation in volunteer services are but examples of projects which provide opportunities for such experience. If these experiences are to have educational value, they must be more than lived; they must be studied critically and inter-

Figure 14. Some first hand objects can be studied readily. (Courtesy of Kansas Health Museum, Halstead, Kansas.)

preted to give them meaning. Like the sunset, their values may even need to be initially discovered or identified.

Some firsthand objects of study can be supplied readily. There should be no difficulty in obtaining a bicycle, air sampler, first-aid materials, foods, equipment for feeding and bathing a baby, and many other objects useful in health teaching. Sometimes, however, it is impractical or even dangerous to provide the real objects. In learning to care for the sick, it would, of course, be unwise and impractical to bring a sick person to the classroom; rather, pupils themselves could simulate the person. In a hospital or nursing home, however, firsthand experience with the real objects needed for bed-side care might be gained as young people under supervision provide volunteer services for the ill.

DEMONSTRATIONS

Demonstrations are valuable in helping students to develop new skills and to understand specific processes or procedures. Demonstrations are often followed by practice periods in which students try out the precedures they have observed. Much of the content of home-nursing and first-aid classes is taught by demonstration and student practice. Instruction in safety precautions, food preparation, and body mechanics is often best given by demonstration. Some forms of laboratory work are likewise taught by this method. Students as well as teachers can give demonstrations and benefit by the experience.

Demonstrations should be conducted in an orderly fashion with ample time allowed for preparation, presentation, performance, and practice.

Preparation

The successful demonstration is carefully prepared. The demonstrator clearly thinks through just what purposes the demonstration will serve and how it will relate to the subject under study. He allows enough time to assemble all of the materials needed for the demonstration and to practice the successive steps until he feels confident of performing the demonstration.

When demonstrating processes which students may later apply, the demonstrator uses suitable and readily available materials. For example, in demonstrating the use of fire extinguishers, an approved home fire extinguisher would be used rather than one designed for institutional purposes.

The demonstration area is arranged so that every student can see clearly what is being shown. When the group is large, there is ample space between the demonstration and the group. Closed-circuit television is available in some schools for transmitting demonstrations to large groups.

The pupils themselves need preparation. This preparatory period is used to orient the students to the importance of the procedure and to arouse their interest. Principles behind the procedure are explained and the value of the procedure made clear. Points to look for may also be discussed.

Presentation

The demonstration is made before the group. As the demonstrator proceeds, he explains what he is doing and why he is doing it. He may use the chalk board, transparencies, slides, or other materials for reinforcement. He remains sensitive to group reactions, encourages questions, and repeats the process when indicated.

Performance

The students repeat the procedures they have observed in the demonstration. They, too, tell what they are doing as they perform. The instructor encourages them, corrects mistakes as they are made, and remains alert to steps in the performance which may require further attention.

Practice

Each student is encouraged to apply the procedure in a natural life situation as soon after the class experience as possible so that there is greater permanency in learning. In procedures which are not likely to be used immediately in a natural setting, as, for example, artificial resuscitation of a drowning person, students are encouraged to follow up class practice with practice at home. A review at the beginning of the next class period also helps to reinforce the learning.

DISPLAYS

The term "displays" is employed here to cover a wide range of instructional materials including bulletin boards, flannel boards, models, posters, and three-dimensional displays. Displays can be either "homemade" or constructed elsewhere and borrowed, rented, or purchased.

Displays are of value principally because they show in a clear tangible way concepts, processes, and other teaching points difficult to understand through words alone. The teacher may show a chart, picture, model, or some other aid, but it is even more important for the pupils to prepare and show their own displays as part of their regular class work. Preparing, assembling, and arranging material for displays can help pupils to clarify and organize their thinking on a subject.

Presentation Boards

Displays discussed in this section are frequently arranged or developed by teachers or pupils within the classroom situation.

Chalk Boards

Chalk boards have the advantage of being the most readily available of all display materials. Ideas developed by the pupils can be recorded on a chalk board and can be easily rearranged as discussion proceeds. Simple diagrams can be placed on the board and explained as they are drawn. When complex processes are being explained, or detailed material presented, key points can be outlined on the board as a reinforcement of the spoken word. Disadvantages of chalk boards lie principally in their abuse. Too frequently the teacher falls back on this means of visualization to the exclusion of other techniques of presentation. Too frequently, also, the writing on the board is unclear. But when a teacher encourages pupil use of the board, its maximum value is assured.

Bulletin Boards

Bulletin boards, like chalk boards, have the advantage of being in nearly every classroom and of providing an inexpensive and effective location for classroom displays. Pictures, newspaper clippings, magazine articles, and the pupils' own work on a subject under study can be placed readily on bulletin boards. In classrooms which foster cooperative undertakings the children may work together in developing bulletin board displays.

Flannel Boards

Flannel boards or felt boards have limitless possibilities for classroom teaching. The base of this display device is a piece of flannel or felt, or a board covered with one or the other material.

Cutout flannel figures, or, if preferred, paper figures backed with flannel or sandpaper, are superimposed upon the background. Among materials which will adhere to a flannel or felt surface without using a sensitized backing are blotters, cotton, balsa wood, sponge, wool, velvet, corduroy, and steel wool. The pupils can make their own figures and construct their own stories on the flannel board to illustrate points under discussion. For example, cutout pictures of foods could be arranged in a variety of ways to tell different stories about food values, meal planning, and food protection. Flannel boards can be used effectively in describing the steps of a complex procedure, such as the process of milk pasteurization, or in showing relationships, such as growth patterns in the life cycle of an individual from embryo to adulthood. When concepts, ideas, or processes are developed step by step on a flannel board, wide class participation can be obtained. Care must be taken, however, that the class does not become more absorbed with the device than with the lesson it is intended to teach.

Magnetic Boards

The magnetic board is used much as the flannel board is used. It consists of a metal backing to which magnetic pieces, or objects to which magnets have been glued, will adhere. Some classrooms are now equipped with porcelain-surfaced chalk boards with steel backing which can serve as magnetic boards. A simple board can be made inexpensively from an automobile oil-drip pan. When painted with chalk board paint, the board can serve a double purpose.

Hook and Loop Boards

The hook and loop board has a nylon surface made up of many small but exceedingly strong loops. An adhesive-backed patch, on which are thousands of minute hooks, is attached to an object which is then placed gently against the looped surface. Quite heavy objects can be displayed in this manner. This is a great advantage in health teaching, for real objects, rather than pictures of such objects, can thus be displayed. For example, primary school children can arrange on such a board equipment needed for maintaining personal cleanliness, such as soap, brush and comb, nail file, toothbrush, and mirror. Even heavier objects can be so arranged.

Models

When real objects are not easily obtainable for display, substitutes can often be found in models or mock-ups. Through hobby shops and school supply houses, manufacturers are now providing kits from which models of numerous objects can be constructed. Common among them are models of the human body, including the different systems and organs of the body. Elementary children enjoy assembling these kits and can learn from the experience, particularly if systematic study accompanies the activity. There are also models which show processes not readily understood through pictures or in real life situations, as, for example, models of the circulation of the blood through the body or of the process of water purification in a water-treatment plant.

Pupils do not need to depend wholly upon readymade models; they can make their own. For example, in a study of urban renewal, they could do a mock-up of a neighborhood slated for improvement, laying out space for play areas, location of street lights and traffic lights, and designing other improvements they think are needed as a result of their studies or consultations with planning authorities.

Posters, Flip Charts

These visual aids are frequently used in health teaching to reinforce the spoken word.

Posters

Posters have long been associated with health education. Well designed posters on many health subjects are available from health agencies and commercial companies dealing with health-related products. Posters displayed in a classroom can draw attention to a health concept; they can create an "atmosphere." They can, moreover, accent a point under study if shown at a psychologically appropriate time. Unfortunately, posters are often hung in the classroom with little thought given to their use as tools of learning; they frequently become gestures only. Readymade posters should be selected carefully in relation to a specific learning situation and shown only for the time for which they were intended.

Pupils often make their own posters. When made in line with principles stated earlier in this chapter they can serve a worthwhile function. Posters produced by pupils provide wide latitude for creativity; they can also be adapted to local conditions. Their limitations lie in the danger of overemphasis on the artistic abilities of the children and underemphasis on what they are teaching. This is particularly true when health poster contests are held and much time is given to perfecting the design.

Figure 15. Displays can develop from a class project. (Courtesy of the Minneapolis Star.)

Flip Charts

A flip chart is a series of pictures and statements arranged in sequence, with a separate chart for each new idea. Flip charts are often used to accompany a talk. They can be made locally at little cost. Flip charts have been helpful in describing visually a series of events or steps in the development of programs. To illustrate, in a class on baby-sitting, students might summarize their studies by preparing a series of charts on points to consider in connection with the different phases of the baby-sitting process. Flip charts do not need to be elaborate; like posters, their value lies in their contributions to the learning process and not in their artistic excellence.

Three-Dimensional Displays — Exhibits

In health teaching the most effective displays are those which are developed as an integral part of classroom learning; however, pupil-made exhibits for school-wide or community-wide display are sometimes indicated. Thus, materials which have grown out of classroom or school-wide projects may be shown in corridors or in the lunchroom if these spaces are large enough so that no traffic or safety hazards are involved. Moreover, as schools become identified with community activities they may carry their exhibit-making into the community, cooperating with community groups in the process.

When preparing, selecting, and arranging exhibit materials for general display, the following points should be kept in mind:

1. The subject should be of interest and concern to the audience, and at its level of comprehension.
2. Exhibits should be carefully planned. The children should write down what they want to show, why they want to show it, and briefly how they plan to show it. A preliminary sketch should be prepared along with the written plan. When all the snags have been removed, the exhibit is ready to be constructed and set up by the children. Such planning will save much time, effort, and materials.
3. The exhibit should convey a single, unified message in a simple, concise, clearly understood form. The subject should be self-explanatory, and able to be grasped at a glance. One idea is enough to include on a single poster. Larger, more comprehensive exhibits should have a central theme to hold them together.
4. Sound principles of design should be followed. There should be plenty of space around the lettering and pictures to set them off properly. Color and line should be pleasing. Lettering should be simple and easy to read.
5. There should be opportunity for audience participation, if appropriate, in the exhibit. This may mean pushing a button or lever to have something work, or taking some other active part in the exhibit itself.
6. Exhibits should be displayed so that they can be readily seen. In the class-

room, they should be in good light and in the line of vision of the children. In some rooms, a corner is set aside for exhibits which are changed as projects change.

FILMS

The motion picture is used widely today as an aid to education. Animation and time-lapse photography are among the unique contributions of this medium to the audiovisual field. Through a film, pupils can experience vicariously many events that cannot be participated in directly. Films taken of their own observations or activities can be relived and studied at a later time. Films make things seem real and provide maximum personal identification; they have the potential for creating a climate conducive to behavior change.

Health films are of many types. They may describe a particular process, such as how food is digested in the body; demonstrate a skill, such as handling a boat safely; give straight information, such as films on human reproduction; or present problem situations with incomplete answers as a basis for pupil discussion. There are also films which dramatize significant events in the field of public health and medicine.

Health films are most valuable when used as classroom teaching aids and for the various purposes outlined earlier. On occasion, they may be shown during assembly programs to help promote some health project of general school interest. The school may also sponsor the showing of educational films to community groups.

Films come in three different sizes, 35 mm., 16 mm., and 8 mm. The 35-mm. films are usually used for movie theaters. Educational films for general school and community groups, exclusive of theaters, are made in the 16-mm. or 8-mm. sizes.

Educational films are either silent or with sound. Though the silent film is being replaced to a large extent by the sound, it should not be considered obsolete. Each type of film has its place in classroom teaching. The silent film is cheaper to produce, and may even be made locally by children or others in the community. The sound film has the advantage of combining both auditory and visual impressions, thus producing a more realistic effect.

Films may be in color or in black and white. The color film is more spectacular and lifelike, but the black and white is cheaper to produce, and often is as good a teaching tool as that in color.

A film with a magnetic sound track, similar to that used on magnetic tape recorders, and a projector, which both records and projects sound film, are available in both 8-mm. and 16-mm. sizes. With the film and recording projector, commentaries may be added to the film and erased and new recordings added as with ordinary tape recordings. Thus, the same film may be adapted to different grade levels and to various community groups simply by changing the commentary on the sound track.

One type of film has only the magnetic sound track upon which the recordings are made. Another type has two sound tracks, one the traditional, permanent track and the other the new magnetic track. It is also possible for silent film to be reproduced on sound film stock which has the magnetic sound track on it. This means that old silent films can be converted into sound films which have up-to-date commentaries. Since an inexperienced person may learn readily how to make the recordings, and since, moreover, they may be made without using a soundproof room, opportunities for teacher and student recordings for motion picture film are many. Some schools are now purchasing for student use completely automatic 8-mm. movie cameras which can have magnetic sound added to the film. These easy-to-operate cameras make it possible for students to capture on film important experiences or processes which they may wish to review or study further at a later time.

Single concept cartridge films (silent or sound) have recently come on the market along with compact projectors which operate with a touch of the button. These films show promise in the health field as libraries of them are developed. The films are particularly adapted to self study or to use by small groups. They run for as short a time as four minutes and the children themselves can load and operate the projector.

The following suggestions are offered for showing films:

I. *Preparation*
   A. Instructor:
      1. Selects a film which he thinks is appropriate for the purposes to be served. If it is necessary to order the film, places order far enough in advance to be assured of delivery.
      2. Previews the film and critically evaluates it. Notes strong and weak points; obvious errors; omissions of ideas; points of confusion; vocabulary; controversial material; suitability.
      3. Determines key points and considers how they may be used to reinforce related learning experiences.
      4. Draws up a plan for the use of the film.
      5. Makes sure that room and equipment are ready for the showing.
   B. Pupils:
      1. May, on occasion, assist in the selection of the film, and, through their representatives, in the preview of the film.
      2. In advance of the showing, discuss key points briefly with guidance of the instructor. Such discussion arouses interest, prepares the pupils to view the film intelligently, and helps them to see the relationship between the film and other learning experiences. Too much advance discussion may decrease interest in the film itself, however.

II. *Presentation*
   The instructor remains with the class during the film showing. He sees

that good ventilation is provided and that the room has approximately $\frac{1}{10}$ foot candle of light. He makes certain that the screen is at least 6 feet ahead of the front row of pupils and that the pupils are comfortably seated.

III. *Follow-up*

At the completion of the showing, the key points are again informally discussed, and are linked appropriately to problems currently being studied. A second showing is sometimes helpful.

Supplementary filmstrips are available with some educational motion pictures. These filmstrips also furnish helpful pivotal points for discussion, and for planning of further activity.[3]

Sources of Health Films and of Health Film Catalogs

Sources of Health Films for Loan or Rent

For teachers in most states, the common sources of such films are:

1. State film library. This may be connected with the state university or the state education department. There usually is a small fee to cover transportation, servicing, and replacement costs.

2. State or local health departments. Films from this source may be borrowed at little or no cost.

3. Local education departments. City and county school systems in some areas of the country have libraries.

4. Voluntary health agencies. No attempt will be made to provide a full list of these agencies, since they vary with communities. Among the agencies at state, county, or city levels which may have films on their particular fields of interest are groups dealing with tuberculosis, cancer, mental health, blindness, heart disease, safety, and social hygiene. Most national organizations lend films through their state or local organizations. For examples of specific agencies, see Appendix A.

5. Commercial film distribution companies. In every city of any size there are companies that rent films.

Catalogs of Film Titles

It is futile in a book of this kind to present lists of health films. Month by month, new films are added to an already extensive supply and old ones become obsolete. Rather, it seems better to familiarize the reader with catalogs of film titles.

1. Library of Congress 3″ × 5″ film catalog cards. Theatrical and nontheatrical motion pictures are indexed by the Library's Card Division. The system, similar to that used in cataloguing books, makes available to teachers much pertinent information about films.

---

[3] Portions adapted from materials prepared by audiovisual education services at the University of Minnesota and the University of Michigan.

2. Film lists from state film libraries, state health departments, and various national agencies.

3. *The Blue Book of Non-Theatrical Films,* published periodically by Educational Screen and Audio-Visual Guide, 415 North Dearborn St., Chicago 10, Illinois.

4. *Educators Guide to Free Films.* Latest annual edition. Educators Progress Service, Randolph, Wisconsin.

5. *NICEM* (National Information Center for Educational Media): Index to 16mm Educational Motion Pictures. Published by McGraw-Hill Book Company, 330 West 42nd Street, New York, N.Y. (First in a series of volumes that will cover all areas in audiovisual materials.)

FILMSTRIPS

Filmstrips, stripfilms, or slidefilms, as these visual aids are variously called, are a series of 10 to 100 still pictures on a continuous strip of 35-mm. film. They are shown through a special projector which is often operated by "push button" remote control so that the pictures may be viewed at any speed desired. They are frequently used with sound. When coordinated with sound, records are played on a phonograph or tapes are used. The record or tape can be stopped at any point for class discussion. Children may make their own tape recordings to go with the pictures.

Filmstrips may be used much as motion pictures are used, that is, as supplementary teaching aids. The instructions given for making full educational use of the motion picture apply also to the filmstrip. Filmstrips should be previewed, and plans should be worked out carefully for their introduction in the curriculum. Pupils should be prepared in advance of the showing so that they will know what to look for, and should be given opportunity to discuss the material after the showing.

There are both advantages and disadvantages to filmstrips. The advantages include ease in operation, low cost, and opportunity to have one's own made. The pictures are unbreakable, compact, and therefore easy to ship and to store. The children themselves can operate the projector. The disadvantages are largely from the standpoint of teaching procedure. Once the filmstrips have been made, the order of the pictures cannot be changed; so it is impossible to adapt a series of pictures to different types of teaching situations. Filmstrips can be cut up, however, and made into 2" x 2" slides.

Filmstrips serve their purposes well in teaching standardized procedures in a standardized way, which is often imperative when procedures must follow a definite pattern on a large scale. The desirability of this type of teaching in public schools has been questioned by many authorities in education. Doubtless, however, there is some justification for readymade filmstrips, especially when teachers are inexperienced and the subject is difficult.

Sources of Filmstrips and Filmstrip Catalogs

Sources of Filmstrips for Loan or Rent

Many of the sources for loan or rental of motion pictures also loan or rent filmstrips. For examples of specific agencies, see Appendix A.

Children may readily make their own filmstrips. Combinations of pictures may be assembled and sent to any one of several companies, where they will be reproduced on a 35-mm. strip in the order desired.

Catalogs of Filmstrip Titles

1. *Educators Guide to Free Filmstrips.* Latest annual edition. Educators Progress Service, Randolph, Wisconsin.
2. Library of Congress 3″ × 5″ filmstrip catalog cards, mentioned earlier under section on Films.

SLIDES

Slides are still pictures projected one at a time through slide lanterns designed for the purpose. They come in two sizes: the "standard" size (3¼″ x 4″) and the 2″ x 2″ slides.

Slides make an excellent supplement to group teaching. The principles suggested for the use of motion pictures and filmstrips should govern the use of slides; that is, there should be a reason for using them and they should fit naturally into the curriculum, according to some plan, along with other learning experiences.

One of the most effective ways to use slides is to have the pupils prepare their own in connection with a specific health project. This type of activity helps to create interest in a subject and, through its high motivational value, aids in the learning process. Pupils can make pictures, for example, of their own activities, of places visited on field trips, of community events, and of scenes before and after carrying out a health project designed to improve a situation.

When readymade slides are secured, the teacher will wish to select from a given collection only those pertinent to the situation, and project them in the order that seems best suited to the group. Since slides can be so adapted to each group, they are much more flexible teaching aids than either the motion picture or the filmstrip.

Slides for teaching purposes in the field of health may sometimes be secured on loan from such sources as health departments, voluntary health agencies, and school audiovisual education departments. In general, however, it is more difficult to find slides for loan or rent than it is to find either motion pictures or filmstrips.

A number of biological supply houses and science companies sell slides. Though the slides are more commonly used for college teaching, some would be suitable for high school health and science classes.

The most satisfactory slides are those produced locally for a particular teaching purpose, as just suggested. Great possibilities exist in the 2" x 2" color slides which children themselves can take. Pictures are taken with an ordinary miniature camera that holds 35-mm. colored film; they come back from the photographic laboratory ready for use. The effect of color slides is impressive—the cost is reasonable. With the newer, completely automatic cameras the process can be greatly simplified. Handmade slides are popular among children who like to see their own work. They may prepare their own tables, charts, titles, and drawings through a variety of processes, using slides of standard size. Materials for handmade slides are available at photographic supply stores.

Slide-making should be carried on more extensively by both teachers and children in health education work. They can learn much from the agricultural extension services that have effectively used locally prepared slides in their teaching of farm and home improvements. Detailed information on how to make slides can be obtained from supply stores and is available in books on audio-visual education.

OTHER FORMS OF PROJECTION

Two types of projection only are mentioned here, overhead projection and opaque projection.

Overhead Projection

This is a useful piece of equipment for presenting material in front of a class. Typed material, drawings, writing, and the like are inscribed on transparent plastic sheets and the image from the sheets is transferred by the projector to a screen behind the teacher. There are several advantages in the use of the overhead projector. The teacher can write or draw extemporaneously on a horizontal surface in front of him (or show already prepared materials) and throughout the process maintain eye contact with the class. A large image of his work is projected behind him and is of such clarity that the room may remain lighted. The transparent plastic comes in a continuous roll that can be moved backward or forward; erasures can be made. The plastic can also be cut into sheets as large as 10 by 10 inches, depending upon the size of the projector, and the sheets viewed separately or on top of each other as overlays. Because of the transparency of the plastic, a series of images can thus be built one upon the other. For example, if a line graph with several parts to it is being studied, a separate sheet can be used for each line so that the lines can be studied separately or in different combinations. In the same way, diagrams of the systems of the body can be studied separately or, if built one upon the other, seen in their interrelationships. A waxed crayon is used for handmade writing and drawings, but special stencils are needed for typed materials. Transparent inks in different colors are also available.

It is possible now to prepare transparencies of typed or printed material by running the material and a projection film simultaneously through certain types of copying machines, just as a letter is copied in such machines. Moreover, colored pictures from magazines can be "lifted" by similar means, the ink from the paper being transferred to the film in the process. Audiovisual laboratories in schools and universities may be able to help teachers prepare the more elaborate materials. Prepared sheets are also available from supply houses. The projectors come in different sizes, some of which are portable.

Opaque Projection

These projectors are found in many schools. Through them, pictures, pages from books, diagrams, and other flat, opaque objects can be viewed by a whole class. Thus, single copies of materials, such as students' written work, which otherwise could not be shown before large numbers, can be viewed readily on a screen without transfer to slides.

RADIO, RECORDINGS, AND TELEVISION

The radio is a potent force in school and community education. Programs are broadcast to schools from local stations or over national networks, and heard immediately in a classroom, or recorded and played to a group at a later time. The radio also carries programs prepared and presented by the children themselves. In addition, public address systems at schools are used for broadcasting information on a school-wide basis, and simulated broadcasts have become a part of regular class work.

Recordings, though newer than the radio, are growing in popularity and are finding many uses in education. Recordings for education are most commonly made on recording discs and tape recorders.

Television in education is a rapidly expanding field. As facilities become more widely available for educational television broadcasts, there is reason to believe that its influence in schools will be as great as in homes and in public places.

Radio Broadcasts

Broadcasts by Local Radio Stations and National Networks

An increasing number of health and safety broadcasts over local stations and national networks can be used in health teaching. Some of these are on school-of-the-air programs; others are sponsored by health and medical agencies. The teacher should secure as much advance information as possible about a broadcast in order to prepare both himself and the children for it. Many educational broadcasts are announced weeks in advance, and some are accompanied by teaching manuals that provide helpful guides to the teacher. When a teacher knows what is coming, he may have the students do advance reading on the subject. As a follow-up, there should be a discussion of the ideas contained in the broadcast, with perhaps additional reading. Often, however, the programs do not fit with what is being taught at the time. It may, therefore, be desirable to make recordings of the programs for future reference. Some of the best programs are given during out-of-school hours. When teachers know about these, they may encourage the children to listen at home and report back later what they have heard.

Pupil-Prepared Broadcasts

All radio stations must devote a certain portion of their time to public service. One type of service is the school-sponsored broadcast in which the children themselves participate. There are many potential educational values in this type of program. Such public performances are strong motivational devices that help arouse interest in subjects of importance, not only among the participating children, but also among their parents and the community in general. If handled properly, they stimulate the children to do careful work. The facts must be thoroughly checked, the wording grammatically correct, the content well organized, and the voices properly modulated. In some of the larger school systems the work is done in radio workshops under the supervision of specialists in the production of radio programs.

School Public Address Systems

School public address systems provide another channel for health teaching by radio. They should be used with discretion, however, and only when the broadcasts are of school-wide interest or importance. For example, health councils may announce plans for new projects and seek support for them over the public address system, or pupils may broadcast talks or plays to promote important health events. Instructions during emergencies, as in epidemics, can be handled partially through the public address system.

Simulated Broadcasts

Simulated broadcasts are widely and effectively used in many classrooms. Children write their own radio scripts and broadcast them over make-believe microphones, often rigged up in the classroom so that they appear realistic. Almost any health subject under study would lend itself to this device.

Recordings

Recordings have become important adjuncts to education in many schools today, and are often used for health teaching. Some schools have phonograph recorders and large playback machines or turntables on which transcriptions available from record libraries can be heard. Tape recorders are now in common use. They produce cheaply, easily, and permanently, if desired, almost any type of program. Portable recorders are available in many schools.

Tape recordings may be secured from recording libraries or may be produced by the pupils themselves. Recordings made on magnetic tape have great flexibility in their reproduction and use. They may be kept indefinitely as originally reproduced or they may be erased partly or entirely, and re-recorded as desired. They may also be rearranged through cutting and splicing of the tape.

There are numerous possibilities for teaching health with the aid of recordings. Teachers or pupils may tape health broadcasts from radio and study them when they best fit into the curriculum. They might record commercial radio advertising bearing on health subjects and then study the materials collected in a unit on consumer health. In other instances the children might make records of their own work as a summarizing experience in a health project. The imaginative teacher will no doubt find many additional ways to use recordings in her work.

Television

The growth of television as a tool in education has been phenomenal. Educational television stations are increasing in number throughout the country and many uses are being found for television in the classroom. Radio and television supervisors are being added to the staffs of the major school systems to handle programming details.

Experiments in numerous school systems have demonstrated that television classes can be conducted successfully by master teachers and used in classrooms as a basis for study and discussion. In a number of systems, closed-circuit arrangements are used for transmitting lectures from one room to others in the same building. The students ask questions and take part in discussions, either with the broadcaster (through a two-way communication system) or with the classroom teacher. As mentioned earlier, closed-circuit television, employing portable cameras, can also be used within a single room to amplify a demonstration or some other process. Some school telecourses are now broadcast to the general public, who not only benefit by the broadcast but also become better acquainted with the school's program.

One of the most important innovations now used by many schools is the video tape recorder. With this compact recorder which captures both sight and sound, pupils can go to any location to take pictures and do on-the-spot recording as well. Moreover, these recorders provide instant playback. The tapes come in both color and black and white and in different widths, depending upon the machine in which they are used. The potentials of this audiovisual tool are limitless. Many of the instructional methods discussed previously can be greatly reinforced through use of this tool, including group discussions, field visits, and dramatizations. The events can be recorded, analyzed, and discussed in greater detail and depth than would be possible as they occur.

The dramatic potential of television makes it a powerful medium for health and safety education. Yet a number of questions need to be raised by thoughtful educators. Few of us would contest the enriching influence of television or its value as a tool for motivation and attitude development. Few would question its effectiveness in bringing into the classroom, with a vividness never before possible, events and information on a wide variety of subjects. From the standpoint of learning, however, we may well ask, can television become a substitute for the more intimate teaching through face to face contacts and the give and take relationships of a classroom? Can facts and skills be soundly taught by someone who cannot see the reactions and the strengths and weaknesses of a particular group of children? Can emotional as well as intellectual needs be met? Can education through a master teacher replace the learning which takes place through teacher-student planning in situations that are meaningful to a specific group? Can such teaching develop the qualities of independent thought and action and the ability of individuals and groups to work out constructively the solutions to their own prob-

Figure 16. Student using a video tape recorder. (Courtesy of the Department of Audio-Visual Education, University of Minnesota.)

lems, an ability so very much needed in the field of health? Perhaps we should even ask, can we set up the protections necessary to avoid the danger of this potent medium becoming a tool that could be used in undemocratic ways? Here are questions for which fully satisfactory answers have not been found. Doubtless one answer is the video tape recorder; others are yet in the future.[4]

PROGRAMMED INSTRUCTION MATERIALS

A chapter on instructional materials would not be complete without mentioning materials now available for programmed learning. Among these materials are textbooks, magnetic tape recordings, and special machines which give instructions to the users. All are essentially self-instruction devices with the information to be learned arranged in sequence and in such a way that the learner is led forward through a series of steps. He may answer a question, solve a problem, or respond in some other way, as the programmed material directs. When he gives the correct answer he is so informed and then directed to proceed to the next logical stage in the learning. Through all of this he can move at his own pace.

Programmed instruction materials are being developed in those subject areas for which there is precise, factual information reasonably constant in nature, as is the case with arithmetic, spelling, geography, and historical data. Scientific phenomena which can be taught in this systematic way are likewise being programmed. At the present time, however, few programmed materials are available for health instruction.

Opinions vary widely on the value of programmed materials. Those who favor these materials point to their value in liberating teachers from the task of purely mechanical instruction, thus allowing them to do the things machines cannot do. Some advocates feel that this method of instruction has proved useful with the slow learner, who now can progress at his own rate, as well as with the more able learner. Arguments against programmed instruction materials point to the fact that they are of little help in developing originality and creativity in pupils—that they provide a lock-step type of learning and might in fact be used unethically to manipulate human beings. Regardless of these diverse opinions, few teachers are prepared to use programmed materials effectively. Those of us who are concerned with emotional health as well as with intellectual development may find meaning in these words of Robert Fleming:

---

[4] For a helpful review of the current status of television in the classroom, see Murphy, I., and Gross, R.: Learning by Television. New York, The Fund for the Advancement of Education, 477 Madison Avenue, 1966, 95 pp.

. . . This period finds some schools, teachers and others wanting to accelerate learning episodes by automated, vigorous, impersonal procedures. Many of these are planned for the "Gifted," "Able," "High I.Q." The machine does not smile, it does not diagnose, it does not really give approval, it is not human. We need much research to help us know how it may be used as a means of helping individuals and of saving the time of teachers for other work with individuals. Much of teaching and learning requires real allegiance to human factors and to human values.[5]

PRINTED MATTER

Under this heading are included textbooks and other reference books; printed booklets, pamphlets, and leaflets; magazines and other periodicals; school newspapers; mimeographed materials; and handwork of pupils.

Printed matter used in schools is of two types: material already prepared and ready for use when acquired, and material prepared at school, or under the school's supervision. Both types have their place in teaching.

The power of the printed word has long been recognized in the field of education. Ideas in writing have a convincing quality seldom matched in the spoken word. This fact makes printed material a forceful tool in health education; it also makes it a potentially harmful tool when the information contained is unsound or misleading.

Printed matter, like all other teaching material, should be developed or selected in relation to specific objectives and in association with various learning activities; it should not become itself a sole basis for instruction. Its place is well established at every step in a learning situation. At the beginning of a project it may stimulate interest; at all points in the development of a project it may provide essential information; and at the end of a study it may serve as a summary.

Materials developed by the students themselves help to organize and summarize concepts that have been learned.

Every elementary classroom should have a reading corner located where the light is good, to which pupils may go at any time. In this library there should be a rich and varied supply of up-to-date health reference materials, including assorted texts, supplementary reading books, periodicals, and carefully chosen pamphlets. Selected classrooms in secondary schools, such as biology, health, and home economics rooms, should be similarly equipped. Children should be encouraged to turn to these materials, not only as references in connection with each health project they undertake, but also during free reading periods.

---

[5] Fleming, R. S.: How children learn. School Lunch Journal,*16*:52 (April) 1962.

School- and system-wide libraries likewise should be stocked adequately to augment the resources of the classroom library. In some schools, library periods are provided so that a class can explore the resources of the larger central library under the supervision of the librarian. These periods could be used occasionally to introduce the group to available health materials. Such orientation, however, should be linked to the interests and activities of each group.

A systematic arrangement of printed materials in a classroom or school library will facilitate their use by both teachers and pupils. Pamphlets should be filed in boxes or filing drawers under subjects appropriate for study by the grade groups using the materials. It is a waste of time to catalog each pamphlet, since such materials become out of date in a short time and are constantly being replaced.

The selection of printed material should be a matter of serious concern; each piece should be studied from cover to cover to make certain that it is adapted to the group and is accurate in content.

Mention has already been made of pupil- or teacher-prepared materials. Most of these materials are transitory, but occasionally will be of permanent enough value for reproduction in mimeographed or printed form. When the students know their materials are to be printed, they are likely to exert special effort to do a good job. Many schools now furnish spirit duplicators, mimeograph machines, or similar equipment for duplication of classroom materials developed by students or teachers.

Pamphlets and similar printed materials are distributed by most official and voluntary health agencies, and by numerous commercial companies. A partial list of agencies that supply materials is found in Appendix A.

SUMMARY

Instructional materials are indispensable tools for health teaching. These materials should be chosen in line with objectives and should be suitable for the groups that will use them. They should be scientifically accurate in their content, attractive in their format, and sound in their educational approaches. Instructional materials may be readymade or may be constructed by the pupils as part of their regular classroom work. A wide range of instructional material is now available. Learning can be greatly enriched when the teacher helps each pupil find those materials most useful to him.

REFERENCES

Beyrer, M. K., Nolte, A. E., and Solleder, M. K.: A Directory of Selected References and Resources for Health Instruction. Minneapolis, Burgess Publishing Company, 1966, 148 pp.

Bridge for Ideas. Austin, Texas, Visual Instruction Bureau, Division of Extension, The University of Texas.

No. 3. Dent, C. H., and Tiemann, E. F.: Felt Boards for Teaching, 1957, 28 pp.

No. 4. Meeks, M. F.: Lettering Techniques, 1960, 34 pp.

No. 6. Meeks, M. F.: Models for Teaching, 1956, 40 pp.

No. 7. Coltharp, J.: Production of 2 x 2 Inch Slides for School Use, 1958, 79 pp.

No. 9. Lockridge, J. P.: Educational Displays and Exhibits, 1960, 47 pp.

No. 11. Lockridge, J. P.: Better Bulletin Board Displays, 62 pp.

Brown, J. W., Lewis, R. B., and Harcleroad, F. F.: A-V Instruction Materials and Methods. 2nd Ed. New York, McGraw-Hill Book Company, 1964, 592 pp.

Dale, E.: Audio-Visual Methods in Teaching. Revised Edition. New York, The Dryden Press, 1954, 534 pp.

Erickson, C. W. H.: Fundamentals of Teaching with Audiovisual Technology. New York, The Macmillan Company, 1965, 384 pp.

Four Case Studies of Programed Instruction. New York, The Fund for the Advancement of Education, 477 Madison Avenue, 1964, 119 pp.

Minor, E.: Simplified Techniques for Preparing Visual Materials. New York, McGraw-Hill Book Company, 1962, 136 pp.

National Council for the Social Studies, NEA: How to Do It Series. Washington, D.C., The Council.

No. 1. Hartley, W. H.: How to Use a Motion Picture, 1965, 8 pp.

No. 2. Cartwright, W. H.: How to Use a Textbook, 1966, 8 pp.

No. 4. Grubola, M. R.: How to Use a Bulletin Board, 1965, 6 pp.

No. 5. Cummings, H. H., and Bard, H.: How to Use Daily Newspapers, 1964, 7 pp.

No. 8. Siggelkow, R. A.: How to Use Recordings, 1964, 8 pp.

No. 11. Wronski, S. P.: How to Locate Useful Government Publications, 1961, 8 pp.

No. 16. Wilson, M. C., and Miller, J. W.: How to Use Multiple Books, 1965, 8 pp.

Thomas, R. M., and Swartout, S. G.: Integrated Teaching Materials. Revised and enlarged impression. New York, David McKay Company, Inc., 1963, 559 pp.

Wittich, W. A., and Schuller, C. F.: Audiovisual Materials: Their Nature and Use. 4th Ed. New York, Harper & Row, 1967, 554 pp.

CHAPTER

8

GUIDES TO HEALTH TEACHING IN ELEMENTARY SCHOOLS

This chapter contains suggestions for carrying on health teaching at the elementary level. Up to this point, the bases for selecting content and learning experiences have been established. Health needs of children and of home, school, and community are discussed in early chapters as a means of directing the teacher's attention to the particular needs of the pupils and the community he serves. Though not identified as such, the needs described in these chapters are suggestive of the broad concepts which should provide the framework for an organized approach to health instruction. Methods of instruction and instructional materials which may lend interest and variety to health teaching are discussed in other chapters.

The material in this chapter is grouped according to three levels: kindergarten, lower elementary, and upper elementary levels. For each level, the following guides to health teaching are given: factors that will help determine what to teach and how to teach it; suggestions for health teaching emphasis; scheduling for health teaching; and suggested learning experiences. These latter, in many instances drawn from successful experiences of teachers throughout the country, are illustrative only of those which might be developed in a class situation through teacher-pupil planning. They are in no sense a blueprint for all teachers to follow. As emphasized previously, *in health teaching, as in all teaching, details necessarily must be worked out locally and in relation to the needs and interests of specific groups of children in specific schools and communities.*

GUIDES TO HEALTH TEACHING IN THE KINDERGARTEN (Age 5)

Factors That Will Help Determine What to Teach and How to Teach It

Health Needs, Interests, and Beliefs Related to the Growth Pattern (see also Chapter 2)

Growth in height and weight. This progresses at a rather slow rate. The well child is expected to add yearly about 4 to 6 pounds in weight and 1 to 3 inches in height.

Eating. The child of this age usually eats two good meals a day. His breakfast is likely to be poor. He prefers simple meals and plain food. He may have difficulty in eating cooked vegetables, especially root vegetables, and cereals. He will accept new foods under favorable conditions. He may need some help in feeding himself.

Elimination. The child usually has one bowel movement a day, which is more likely to be after lunch or supper than after breakfast. He may need some supervision and help to establish satisfactory toilet habits.

Exercise and play interests. A variety of play activities and adequate play space for vigorous free movement are needed for the development of motor skills and for general body development. Through exploring new ways of using the body, through repetition of movements, and through the opportunity for self-expression in dance and play, motor learning takes place.

Sleep and rest. The child of this age needs $11\frac{1}{2}$ to 13 hours of sleep. He may take naps or have quiet rest periods.

Eyes and ears. The child is usually farsighted. Too fine work may bring unnecessary strain or fatigue. Ear injuries and infections are frequent.

Teeth. All 20 deciduous (first) teeth are in. The permanent teeth are forming inside the jaws.

Posture. The child sits and stands with trunk upright, but becomes restless when attempting to maintain a sedentary position.

Illnesses and disease. Such childhood diseases as chickenpox and colds are common.

Accidents and injuries. Accident risks increase in this period of experimentation.

Emotional adjustments. These vary widely among children and within the same child. In general the child is poised and self-contained, consolidating the gains of earlier years. He is generally intolerant of too much change. Child lives in real as well as highly imaginative world. He enjoys a routine. He can assume small responsibilities.

Sex adjustments. Sex interests center largely in the baby and a desire to have one in the home. The child may also be interested in the sex of animals and in animal reproduction.

Interests and Adjustments in Respect to Home, School, and Community Living (see also Chapter 3)

Home. The child's interests center around the familiar—his mother and immediate experiences in the home. He likes to play house.

School. The child usually adjusts easily to his teacher and to the group situation. He enjoys routine in his daily activities at school. He shares in classroom duties and for the most part manages himself in dressing and toileting.

Community. The child is interested in his immediate neighborhood and what happens in it. His comprehension of life beyond the neighborhood depends upon the nature and variety of experiences he has had, as through viewing television, traveling, or moving from one community to another.

Suggestions for Health Teaching Emphasis in the Kindergarten

An analysis of the foregoing factors suggests the importance of placing emphasis in the kindergarten on the establishment of healthful daily routines, and on the development of wholesome attitudes toward health. School life is new to these children, who must learn certain things about living healthfully and safely together during the school day. Among the health problems likely to need special attention are healthful daily routines; development of good eating habits, including enjoyment of cooked vegetables; and safety, especially in the new activities at school. Children should become acquainted with the nurse working in the school. In addition, each group of children will of course have its own special problems.

Scheduling for Health Teaching in the Kindergarten

In the kindergarten, health will be taught informally throughout the day and in relation to events that arise as children live and work together. Frequently the teacher may need to schedule a specific time to take up a health matter of concern to the group. Whether teaching informally or by direct instruction, the teacher must plan carefully to assure that health values are brought out and sound health practices are developed.

Suggested Learning Experiences[1]

Development of Healthful Daily Routines

Healthful practices at school. Kindergarten children will vary widely in their need to learn these practices. Much depends upon home conditions. Many children may be learning the practices for the first time; others may require only a review and application in the school situation. Examples of health practices are: maintaining general body cleanliness, including handwashing after toilet and before eating; care of clothing, such as removing outdoor wraps when indoors and removing or drying wet clothing; using drinking fountains in a hygienic manner; flushing toilets after use; wearing glasses if indicated; learning to relax or rest; and covering mouth and nose when coughing or sneezing.

Among activities which could contribute to the development of these practices at school or at home are:

Demonstrate satisfactory ways to wash hands and face and care for hair.

Study classroom and its facilities and work out ways to live healthfully in the classroom, as for example, by arranging chairs and tables for good lighting, using cleanliness facilities, and taking a regular rest period.

Tour school building, pointing out drinking fountain, toilets, cafeteria, and health room, and if necessary, demonstrating correct way to use the fountain and to flush the toilet.

Draw pictures, or cut out pictures, of articles used for general cleanliness and grooming. Even better, the real objects may be assembled and displayed on a hook and loop board.

Demonstrate proper use of handkerchief or tissue and disposal of used tissue.

Talk about and demonstrate the correct way to brush teeth.

Discuss desirable clothing for current season.

Care of pets. Children may keep a rabbit or some other pet in the school and note the animal's need for regularity in eating, sleeping, and exercising. They may compare the animal's needs with their own.

Room helpers. The children may share in such room responsibilities as feeding pets, adjusting shades, and putting away toys. These simple tasks help develop desirable habits.

---

[1] Many of the activities given in this section would be suitable for pupils in nursery school or Head Start programs. Moreover, the kindergarten teacher will find in the following section descriptions of learning experiences for lower elementary grades which could be developed with kindergarten children.

Playing house.   "Members of the family" may dramatize various routines that illustrate healthful living. For example, they may dramatize getting ready for bed, going to bed, and getting up, and then discuss the importance of getting enough sleep. An individual child may tell about a new baby in the family; he may dramatize what he can do for the baby and what its mother and father can do for it.

Development of Good Eating Habits

Lunch at school.   One of the most direct and effective approaches to better nutrition is through the school lunch program. During the mid-morning snack, at noontime, or whenever food is served at school, the children may discuss what they are eating and enter into the experience as a pleasant, social event.

A "tasting party."   A weekly "tasting party" was used with Head Start children as a means of encouraging good nutrition and better free selection of foods. During the first week of this demonstration project, the children tasted small samples of fruit, including cantaloupe, dried apricots, and grapefruit. The second week was devoted to vegetables, including cabbage, raw carrots, and tomatoes. In the third week they tried foods from the meat and protein group, such as baked beans, tunafish, peanut butter, bologna, and peanuts in the shell. Then came foods from the bread and cereal groups, and after that, the milk products group. Along with this tasting project the children made placemats which they used each day at snack time. Each week a new food picture was added to the placemat. In addition, a follow-up with mothers took place; the mothers were invited to observe some of the nutrition activities at an open house during the last week of the project and to offer their evaluation of the project.[2]

Food and growth.   Children may make flannelgraphs using cutout pictures of infants, preschool children, and school children as a basis for a discussion of growth, including the relationship between food and growth. Early snapshots showing their own growth changes can also be used. Children may keep individual height and weight records to watch their own growth progress.

Safety

School safety measures.   A teacher with the help of pupils may record situations occurring in the classroom or on the playground which require attention from the standpoint of safety. Here

2 Reported by Mrs. LaVonne Fritz, Nutritionist, Minneapolis Division of Public Health, and Mrs. Kay DeRoos, Graduate Student in Public Health Education, School of Public Health, University of Minnesota, 1967.

are items from a list kept by one kindergarten teacher: block throwing; pulling chair out from under another child; carrying sticks on the playground; using hammer and nails; climbing onto the window ledge; building block house too high; fruit skins on the walk; running in front of swings. Each provided a focus for class discussion leading toward improved behavior.

Safety on streets.   Schools in northwestern Ohio reported a program designed to start training tomorrow's drivers at the kindergarten level. The following instructions and activities are a part of this program:

1. In the fall when mother brings child first day to register, give the mother a letter of "reminders" among which are requests to teach child:
   a. Full name, address, and telephone number.
   b. The safest way to and from school.
   c. To walk always on sidewalks.
   d. To cross streets only at crossings.
   e. To go directly home from school.
   f. How to cross streets with red and green traffic light.
   g. Not to go through alleys.
2. Study traffic lights:
   a. Learn colors—red, yellow, green.
   b. Make traffic lights by drawing with crayons or making them with circles of colored paper pasted on shape of traffic light.
   c. Make milk carton models.
3. Take trips and walks:
   a. Walk to corner and watch traffic lights work.
   b. Observe when cars stop and when they go.
   c. Practice crossing street in small groups, using light.
   d. Show where to cross streets, always at corner, not in front of school building.
   e. Practice crossing at corner with "patrol children."
4. Teach safety rules for trips by automobile and bus:
   a. Sit quietly.
   b. Watch signs (help driver look).
   c. Pretend to be the driver (use paper plate); stop at all stop signs; signal for stop; get in and out of car on *right* side.
5. Make large pictures of traffic safety by using opaque projector to enlarge any small pictures the children draw.[3]

Safe toys.   Children in one room cut out pictures of toys they would like for Christmas. Pictures of safe toys (e.g., toy auto with smooth edges, sturdy cart, doll, wooden blocks, telephone set) were pasted on one poster board; pictures of unsafe toys (e.g., sharp scissors, breakable tea sets, water pistols, fireworks, sharp-edged toys, brother's chemistry set) were pasted on another.

Safety with animals.   The teacher may discuss the danger of petting strange animals and procedures to follow when a strange

___
[3] Ohio's Plan of "Safety for Tomorrow's Drivers." Lima, Ohio, Ohio Department of Highway Safety, 1960.

animal comes to school. In this connection she may stress the importance of training household pets to stay home. A discussion of safe ways of handling pets may be profitable, including proper ways of picking them up, avoidance of teasing, and the necessity for washing hands after contact with pets.

Living safely at home and in the neighborhood. Children may dramatize the different things members of the family do in the house to live safely and to protect others. They should learn that in respect to their own practices they should:

Keep floors and stairways free of toys and other objects.
Keep medicines, cleaning fluids, and other dangerous household substances out of reach of younger children.
Use caution when turning on hot water faucet.
Avoid home electrical outlets and cords.
Stay out of leaf piles, snow piles, abandoned houses, and construction areas.
Never touch guns.
Avoid use of streets for playing; instead go to playground or neighborhood house or some other safe area.
Keep yards, sidewalks, and playgrounds free of trash.

Oregon schools propose the following activities in which children may learn safe practices—especially in regard to fire safety.

Demonstrate how to act in case of a home fire, i. e., getting out of building (getting younger children out, too); getting adult help; calling fire department.
Demonstrate how to roll up in blanket or take off clothes if they are on fire.
Invite fireman to visit classroom and talk about fire safety.
Discuss why an adult should be present when near an open fire.
Play "grab bag." Have a large bag which contains pictures of pins, nails, scissors, matches, lawnmowers, and saws. Draw a picture from the bag and tell how the object shown in the picture can help us and how it should be used.
Discuss possible dangers found in local play areas.
Discuss activities they can do themselves and those which require adult help.[4]

Learning to Live and Work with Others

Emotional and social health. Emotional and social health, no less than physical health and safety, are important aspects in the overall kindergarten program. The teacher can do much in guiding the child toward healthy relationships in the family, at school, and in the community. She may help the child to adjust to disappointments, discussing what to do when things go wrong, such as how to adjust to unexpected changes of weather or changes of plans.

Helping at home. Children may discuss what each family member does at home. In a show and tell period they may share freely those things they do at home to be helpful. Through such free discussions the teacher may gain insights which may be useful

---

4 Health Education in Oregon Elementary Schools; K–8. Salem, Oregon, State Department of Education, 1965, p. 14.

Figure 17. Training tomorrow's driver in Safety Village, U.S.A. (Courtesy of Independent Insurance Agents of Greater Tampa, Tampa, Florida. Photo by Graphic Art Productions.)

in helping individual children, while the children may benefit by listening to each other's experiences.

Developing friendships. Pupils need many experiences of being wanted members of a group. They need help in relating in friendly ways with others. Children and teacher can discuss ways of showing friendliness and having a happy time with friends. Pleasure in sharing experiences and materials is an important concept for the child to grasp, and he may be helped to do this by participating in a variety of activities such as dramatizations, group games, and excursions. Children may discuss how they feel when cooperating with others.

Being good neighbors. As children in their social studies learn about different neighborhoods in their community, and the diversity among them, they may gain an appreciation of others who are different from themselves—not only within their own neighborhood but also in other neighborhoods not like theirs. They may discuss ways in which they themselves can become good neighbors, as for example, keeping the neighborhood clean and safe, and being helpful to older people in the neighborhood.

Becoming Acquainted with Helpers in Health

A party for the nurse. One kindergarten group invited the nurse working in the school to a party and had her tell how she helps to keep them and other people well.

Visit to school health center. In touring the school to learn where different things are, the children may visit the health center or nurse's room and learn about her work.

Playing doctor, dentist, or nurse. This is a favorite activity of some children. Inexpensive play kits are available to make the acting more real. The teacher will find many opportunities to help the children look upon these helpers as friends.

GUIDES TO HEALTH TEACHING AT THE LOWER ELEMENTARY LEVEL (Ages 6 to 8)

Factors That Will Help Determine What to Teach and How to Teach It

Health Needs, Interests, and Beliefs Related to the Growth Pattern (see also Chapter 2)

Growth in height and weight. Growth progresses at a slow but steady rate. A yearly gain in weight of 3 to 6 pounds and in height of 1 to 3 inches may be expected.

Eating.   The well child is a good eater and is apt to want between-meal feedings. Breakfast tends to remain the poorest meal. During this period there is gradual improvement in appetite control. The appetite of the poor eater begins to improve as he grows older. By eight or nine years the child develops good control in the use of eating implements.

Elimination.   Habits become more definitely established during these years. One group of children usually functions after breakfast, another after supper. Children may have more than one bowel movement a day.

Exercise and play interests.   An abundance of energy is evident. The child experiments with new motor skills, such as bicycling and ice skating. He perfects other skills, such as climbing and jumping. Imaginative play, rhythmic movements, and dramatizations are popular. The child likes to collect things.

Sleep and rest.   Sleep requirements are 11 to 12 hours for the six-year-old; $10\frac{1}{2}$ to 11 hours for the eight-year-old. The child usually sleeps soundly under proper conditions. The six-year-old may need an hour's "play nap." The children in this age group can take responsibility for their own bedtime schedule.

Eyes and ears.   There is rapid growth in eye development and control. An increasing number of children will need glasses. Eye accidents are a problem. Middle ear infections are common.

Teeth.   This is a crucial period. The four six-year molars (first permanent teeth) erupt, to be followed by other permanent teeth. There is continued calcification of non-erupted permanent teeth.

Posture.   If the general health is good, posture is likely to be satisfactory. By eight years the child becomes aware of posture in himself and in others.

Illnesses and disease.   Younger children have frequent colds and illnesses. By eight years, illnesses decrease and health improves.

Accidents and injuries.   Accidents increase. They include falls, drownings, and automobile and bicycle accidents.

Emotional adjustments.   Transition to school life for the first time may cause emotional upsets. The child becomes increasingly aggressive in his behavior early in this period, but shows less aggression later in the period, except verbally. Younger children are often beset with fears and worries, which apparently decrease as they become adjusted to school. The child gradually changes from a self-centered person to a more social one. He grows in independence and in his ability to reason things out. He responds favorably to praise and approval.

Sex adjustments.   The child may begin early to show curiosity about sex differences and to want general sex information. By eight years he may want more specific sex information. He begins to notice attractiveness in the opposite sex. He adores babies.

Interests and Adjustments in Respect to Home,
School, and Community Living (see also
Chapter 3)

Home. The child's responses toward home life are greatly influenced by patterns of family relationships. In general, he shows strong emotional feelings toward his mother and family and his own place in the group. He will usually help to do his share of the work, though he goes through rebellious periods.

School. The child usually likes his teacher and wants to please her. The younger child makes heavy demands on the teacher's attention. He grows in willingness to help in school routines, and in ability to take part in group work and play. He likes a record, or chart, of his own successes. Children form classroom clubs and share in school councils, thereby learning civic responsibilities.

Community. Throughout this period interest in community widens to encompass areas beyond the one in which he lives. The extent of this interest, however, is dependent upon the nature and variety of experiences he has had, as through exposure to mass media, travel, or moving from place to place.

Suggestions for Health Teaching Emphasis at the Lower Elementary Level

In analyzing the foregoing information, it would appear that the following problems may need special attention through planned instruction: improvement of eating habits, with special emphasis on breakfasts; development of individual responsibility for good sleeping habits; care of the six-year molar; maintenance of health; prevention and control of acute illnesses of childhood; accident prevention as in relation to newly developed skills of bicycling, skating, and climbing; emotional adjustments to school life; understanding of simple facts about human development; and acquaintance with health resources and problems in the neighborhood. Each group of children, however, has its own unique problems and interests that may or may not be similar to those just outlined. In some experimental curricula children in these early elementary years are being introduced to concepts and content customarily taught to older children. They have demonstrated that they can respond to the more complex material. However, educators disagree as to the level of comprehension in their responses. On this point, much more study is needed.

Teaching should capitalize on the child's intense interest in home and family life, and his expanding interest in the larger community, including the world community. Also in line with the child's interests, teaching may utilize dramatizations, make provi-

Figure 18. Children can learn much about life processes by observing pets in the classroom. (Courtesy of the National Education Association. Photo by Carl Purcell.)

sions for collecting things or caring for pets, encourage record keeping, and, as the child matures, provide for management of many daily routines through classroom or school-wide clubs.

Ways of meeting these selected problems through health teaching are suggested in the pages that follow. Other examples, especially for beginners, are in the preceding section of this chapter.

Scheduling for Health Teaching at the Lower Elementary Level

Health instruction at this level, as at all levels, needs to be planned. At times it will be scheduled as direct instruction; at times it will grow out of the events of the day. Often health instruction can be integrated with other subject matter areas. Though not always taught as a separate subject, a time and place must be found to introduce specific health units in the curriculum. Dependence entirely upon informal and incidental teaching is likely to result in but little growth for the pupils.

Suggested Learning Experiences

Improving Eating Habits

To be complete, a study of nutrition will stress well-balanced meals throughout the day. There are times, however, when the teacher may wish to place special emphasis on some specific feeding problem, such as improvement of breakfast habits. Surveys of what children eat and competitive devices based on these surveys should be avoided, particularly if children know what the teacher approves for meals. Such surveys encourage dishonesty and may cause unnecessary tension among children from homes in which inadequate meals are habitually served.

Breakfast at school. An occasional breakfast party at school may create interest in better breakfasts at home. The children can plan the menu, figure costs, and determine how much each youngster needs. Then they can make shopping lists and do their own shopping. To make this a more festive occasion, they may invite mothers to a breakfast party.[5]

Lunchroom menus and lunchbox meals. During a study of teeth, a third grade group became interested in foods. They called upon the home economics consultant to give them information

---

[5] Because of the danger of food contamination, many school systems today discourage the use of food brought from home or prepared by the children, especially if preparation is unsupervised by qualified food-service personnel.

about good foods and proper eating. As they discussed lunchroom menus and lunchbox meals, they realized that many children were throwing away sandwiches. This observation led to the formation of a committee which looked up recipes for tasty sandwich fillings. The recipes were then duplicated for the other children. After a talk given by the school dietitian, another committee worked out a week's menu for the school lunchroom. The children began to talk about the whole digestive process. An anatomical model was borrowed from the high school so the class could examine the organs. In order to appreciate the approximate length of the small and large intestines, the group measured off 20 feet for the small intestine and 6 feet for the large and then cut a string to these lengths. As a culminating activity, parents were invited to a lunchbox party held in the school yard. The teacher felt that, as a result of this study, the children developed better attitudes about food and eating and gained in their ability to select proper foods. They also learned something about digestion and elimination. Correct terms for body functions were also learned.

Picnic garden.   Children in one school raised a picnic garden during the spring months. In it they grew lettuce, radishes, and onions for their last-day-of-school picnic.

Family food patterns.   As children study about diversities in family living patterns within their own or other neighborhoods, and around the world, they may learn about foods that other families enjoy which are different from foods eaten in their own family. They may begin to understand that basic daily food requirements can be met through a wide variety of foods and that choices differ from culture to culture.[6]

Choosing which cereal to buy.   The following project, proposed as an activity in economic education in the Minneapolis Public Schools, could become also a lesson in health education. Using cutout characters of mother and two children as flannel board figures, the teacher tells this unfinished story of a trip to the grocery store:

> We always go grocery shopping with Mom every Friday night because that is the day Daddy brings home his pay check.
> Last night Mom had her grocery list made out and we all got into the car when Daddy came home. We walked into the grocery store and Mom got a grocery cart. She began looking over the list of things she wanted to buy. Tommy and I wandered over to the cereal shelf and began looking at all the puzzles and games on the outside of the cereal boxes. I didn't know what kind of cereal was inside but the games and toys in them looked like a lot of fun. We went to find Mom to show her the three kinds of cereal we wanted. I had seen those kinds of cereal on television. Mom came over to the shelf with us.

---

6 See for example, What Did You Have for Breakfast This Morning? Chicago, National Dairy Council, 1966, 11 pp.

What will Mother decide to do? How should the family choose which cereal to buy?[7]

Sleep and Rest

Ready for bed.   While playing house, children may simulate bedtime conditions. They may role-play a mother trying to get her young son to bed and may discuss attitudes and feelings about going to bed. They may talk about the things they can do to prepare themselves for bed so they will sleep comfortably and soundly.

Unfinished stories.   Teacher or children can make up stories about the daily activities of other children illustrating them with pictures or flannelgraphs. The stories can involve decisions about finding time to rest or sleep and can lead into a discussion of the children's own daily routines.

Learning to relax.   Children themselves may list, discuss, and then practice things they can do to relax. Suggestions include: pretend to be a sack of flour, with a hole in each corner, hanging over a desk, getting flatter and limper. Tense muscles first; then relax (hold tight and let go). Rest with heads on desks. Physical education instructors may help children with other relaxing activities.

Care of Teeth

Though the first permanent teeth may be the focus of a dental education program for the younger children, dental care in general should be the subject of study. Since teeth are still in their developmental stages, the studies on nutrition, as suggested earlier, are important. A positive approach to the mid-morning snack, through the serving of raw vegetables, apples, and the like, may help to reduce greatly the amount of candy and other sweets that are eaten at school.

The children should learn where each of the four six-year molars is located. It is the sixth tooth on each side of the mouth (both upper and lower jaws), if one starts counting from the front toward the back of the mouth.

At the dentist's office.   The following activities are among those suggested by Minneapolis teachers as appropriate for this age level:

Plan with the class a visit to a neighborhood dentist. Assure children this is a visit for the purpose of learning more about having good teeth. Children who have been to a dentist can be helpful by relating pleasant experiences, giving the more timid children a sense of security for the trip. . . . Conduct a discussion period in school following visit.

---

7 White, E. J.: Unfinished Stories for Primary Grades. Minneapolis, Minnesota, Minneapolis Public Schools, Economic Education Project, 1967, p. 7.

Children may build their own dental office with improvised material.

They may cut and color many paper toothbrushes for the play dentists to give to each patient, along with some toothpowder which can be made by the class. The waiting room contains chairs and a table on which, in lieu of magazines, are scrapbooks made by children and other small attractive pictures showing a child washing his hands, brushing his teeth, eating fruits and vegetables, and drinking milk.

As the children play in the dental office, new ideas develop and are utilized in the office. A coat of unbleached muslin for the dentist makes him quite professional. The dental hygienist suggests a sterilizer, and the children remember having seen one in the real dentist's office. A box is labeled "Sterilizer" and so becomes one.

Play dentist, dental hygienist, and patient.

Children are selected by the class to serve as dentist and dental hygienist for periods of a week or less so that all have a turn.

Children should be cautioned not to put fingers or instruments into each others' mouths.

Children from other rooms, as well as teachers, dental hygienist, nurse, other school personnel, and mothers may be invited to make appointments for inspection.

Completion slips provided by dental hygienist may be made for those who visit the office.

Keep a record of dental completion slips returned.

Sterilize the play instruments.

Discuss the importance of reporting the completion of dental work.

Make a toothpowder as follows: Mix one level spoonful of ordinary table salt with three level spoonfuls of baking soda. For flavor, add one drop of peppermint oil.[8]

Keeping Well—Preventing and Controlling Illnesses and Disease

As suggested earlier, instruction here may center around such preventive measures as hygienic living practices and immunization programs. It should place emphasis on keeping well.

We can improve.   One teacher has reported the successful use of evaluation charts. Into a three-pocket folder labeled "good," "better," "best," the child tucks slips noting the areas in which he needs to improve. As he improves in these areas, he moves the slips up the evaluation scale. This self-evaluation method can be very useful in making the child aware of his own needs.

Dressing for the weather.   A weather record was kept by a second grade group. The students cut out pictures of different kinds of clothing needed for different weather conditions and took pride in wearing this kind of clothing themselves.

Protecting others at school.   Children may carry out the following practices and then discuss reasons for them: covering coughs

[8] Excerpts from Dental Health Teaching Units; Kindergarten—Grade 12. Minneapolis, Minnesota, Minneapolis Public Schools. Reprinted 1966, pp. 1–3.

and sneezes, using drinking fountains properly, staying at home when they have a cold, washing hands before touching food, and storing milk in a cool place for school lunches.

Controlling diseases.   To aid in an understanding of communicable diseases and how they are spread, and to develop good health behavior that contributes to the prevention of disease, the teacher may have the pupils engage in the following activities:

1. List methods by which disease germs may enter the body.
2. Learn why the physician wants to check a person's health when he is well.
3. Learn how to look up information on the chart "Communicable Disease Information for Schools."
4. Discuss the signs of the illnesses listed on the chart.
5. Report on some of the following (small group of pupils):
   a. What the public health nurse and the health department do to help keep people well.
   b. What the physician does to help people stay well and some of the things he does when one is sick.
   c. What the hospital does for people.
   d. What the pupils in the classroom do to help control the spread of disease.
   e. Principal causes for absences due to illness in the room during the year.
6. Make a list of the diseases each child has been immunized against. If he has not been immunized against polio, whooping cough, tetanus, diphtheria, and smallpox, have him discuss the importance of these immunizations with his parents. (Note: measles should now be added to the list.)
7. Draw pictures that illustrate how germs spread.[9]

Safety

A positive approach is needed in teaching accident prevention. Children should not only learn to be cautious, as in crossing the street, but in addition, they should develop skill in their daily activities which will minimize the possibility of accidents.

Safety leaders.   Many schools have pupil safety leaders who help to keep the classroom neat and free from safety hazards, and who also help to supervise playground activities. Leadership should be changed frequently so that gradually all children become alert to safety needs.

Safest route to school.   In a large urban area the children of a second grade room made a huge map of the entire school district and filled in streets, the home of each child, traffic lights, and stop signs. The map was kept on the floor, and the children practiced walking from home to school along the safest routes.

Safety practices explained on slides and tape recordings.   A first grade teacher had the children demonstrate their knowledge of safety rules and practices before a camera. Color film for 35-mm. slides was used. As the slides were projected, the different children

[9] Guide for the Montana School Health Program. 2nd Ed. Helena, Montana, The Montana State Board of Health, 1961, pp. 65–66.

explained the practices and these explanations were tape recorded for future use. Kindergarten children were invited to see the slides, which also were shown to parents.

Game—cleaning out the kitchen cupboard. The following game is described as one which children could play as an aid in learning to discriminate between those materials used in the average household which may be poisonous and those which are not.

Half of the children are designated to represent non-edible substances; the other half represent materials which are usually safe to keep around the baby.

Teacher "ad libs" a story about mother cleaning out the materials kept in a low kitchen cabinet near the floor, replacing the ones which might be poisonous on higher shelves, or under lock and key where baby brother or sister can't reach them. As she names each object which mother finds in the cupboard, those who represent "safe" or "unsafe" objects, whichever they may be, get up and turn around, then sit down again.

Objects named might be the following: crackers, shoe polish, pans, floor wax, potatoes, apples, soap, moth balls, dish cloths, furniture polish, silver polish, cleaning powder, carrots, dish towels, soap powder, detergent, cans of soft drinks, bottles of soda-pop, sprays.[10]

Seasonal activities. Safety education lend itself exceptionally well to seasonal emphasis. For example, in preparing for summer vacations, children can talk about their plans and each child can decide what skills he will try to learn so as to enjoy his summer activities without getting into accidents.

Training in traffic safety. The Northeast School, Rockville, Connecticut, introduced a "pilot project" instituted by the Rotarians and the superintendent of schools. Believing that safety cannot be learned too early, the teachers involved undertook a program of safe driving instruction for the first and second grades. Excerpts from the outline of instruction for this project follow:

Good habits and a "safety consciousness" formed early minimize the forming of bad habits later in life and will better prepare the child to encounter the hazards of bicycle riding and teen-age driving. The aim of driver training is to instill in the children such desirable attitudes as: (1) awareness of the rights and privileges of others; (2) willingness to await one's turn; (3) self-control and a sense of responsibility; (4) respect for property; (5) the development of skills and habits which will carry over into future activities, such as habits of observation and alertness, and the ability to prevent accidents and injuries.

In the early stages of the program the pupils make several tours of the community near the school to observe traffic signs and lights and painted lines. They notice particularly the safety devices constructed for the protection of children (fence around school, vehicle entrance and exit, bicycle parking lot, play areas) and they are warned of such hazards as incinerators, balls rolling into streets, and areas in the community where there are no crosswalk lines,

10 A Guide for Teaching Poison Prevention in Kindergartens and Primary Grades. Washington, D.C., U.S. Government Printing Office, 1966, p. 60. (This guide, prepared by the Division of Accident Prevention, Public Health Service, in cooperation with several school systems, contains many interesting projects for classroom use.)

228 GUIDES TO HEALTH TEACHING IN ELEMENTARY SCHOOLS

lights, or signs. In the classroom the children discuss safety rules to observe when playing with wagons, scooters, skates, and so forth. To illustrate more graphically the problems involved in traffic safety, a table course was set up with streets laid out by the teacher and buildings, trees, traffic signs, and simple cars made by the children.

The children actually practice safe driving in the "Phoenix Trainer," a car made in proportion to their size, in which they learn to use the steering wheel, give hand signals, use motive power (proceed, stop, reverse), and manipulate the brake to be used for parking only. The teacher calls instructions to the child in the car; when he is able to follow instructions reasonably well, a temporary driver's permit is issued. When the child has received his permit, he will apply what he has learned so far in the driving area, a space laid out in streets with the proper accessories. Here he will practice driving a planned course, observing such elements of good driving as keeping both hands on the wheel except when signaling, keeping eyes on the road, and keeping within the speed limit. He will learn to stop at the stop bar and to look for oncoming traffic which has the right of way, pedestrians who have the right of way, and clear road ahead to proceed into the intersection. He will practice the proper hand signals for turns and stops.

In addition to the actual driving, the children take turns being traffic officers and pedestrians. In the latter capacity they learn to look for approaching traffic from the curb, not to push and scuffle at the curb, and to *walk* across the street after having checked all directions from which traffic may come. They do not practice being pedestrians until they have adjusted to driving cars and to the presence of traffic officers.

In this program the adult participants have found that the tendency is to expect too much of the children and they believe it is better to go very slowly, making sure that the children can manipulate cars properly before adding traffic officers and pedestrians to the driving area.[11]

Emotional Adjustments to School Life

One of the surest ways to help young children adjust to living and working together is to provide opportunities for them to take part in organized activities. Children who have been rejected by others can often be drawn into school activities and given chances to gain recognition by making unique contributions of their own. In each case the first step is to study the cause of a poor adjustment and then to apply corrective measures in line with the need.

Hobbies can be fun. A child with a hobby finds satisfaction within himself and often contributes to the enjoyment of others. To develop interest in hobbies, children can:

1. Give class reports on hobbies—their own, those of their parents, or those of people they know.
2. Prepare exhibits of hobbies, e.g., collections (rocks, shells, butterflies, post cards), posters, or pictures describing hobbies.
3. Visit hobby shows.
4. Discuss where they can get help on hobbies.

Classroom courtesies. Children may discuss and dramatize what each can do to make others feel comfortable and happy. They

---

[11] Grades 1 & 2 Safety Program, 1962. The Northeast School, Rockville, Connecticut. Submitted by Renwick J. Lewis, Supervising Principal.

may tell how they, as well as others, like to be treated, and consider such character traits as fairness, friendliness, helpfulness, dependability, and the ability to follow as well as lead.

How Living Things Develop—
How We, Too, Grow

In the kindergarten and the primary grades, the teacher may give instruction through answering questions as they arise. The care of pets provides an opportunity to observe mating and the phenomenon of birth. The arrival of a new baby in the neighborhood may serve as a basis for discussions. Teachers should become fully informed so that they can answer questions and use correct terms without embarrassment.[12]

Fourteen babies. A Springfield, Illinois teacher brought a pregnant rabbit to school for her first grade pupils to watch and care for. Marshmallow reproduced vigorously, to the tune of fourteen babies. Mrs. Eberhart, the teacher, used flip charts to tell the story of reproduction. Early in the project, the rabbit refused to eat. A veterinarian came to examine the rabbit and, while in the room, talked about the rabbit's health.[13]

A classroom hatchery. A second grade in New York State decided to incubate four dozen eggs in the classroom. They acquired the incubator, candler, and brooder from the local chapter of the Future Farmers of America and the eggs from a local hatchery. In the process of caring for the eggs, the children learned that:

1. They had to keep the eggs warm and at a certain humidity.
2. They could view the progress of the developing embryo by candling the eggs and could see, even on the third day, the veins and arteries of the embryo.

The most interesting part of the program for the children was the hatching of the chicks, which first "pipped" a small hole in the egg and shortly thereafter fairly popped out of the shells. The children took care of the baby chicks in the classroom for three weeks, watching them learn how to eat and drink, and then those who could took chicks home with them.[14]

Food and growth. To illustrate graphically to the children the facts of their own growth, the teacher may have them keep a record of their height and weight, trace their feet and hands to

---

[12] For background, see Lerrigo, M. O., and Southard, H.: Sex Education Series: (1) Parents' Responsibility; (2) A Story about You; (5) Facts Aren't Enough. Prepared for the Joint Committee on Health Problems in Education of the National Education Association and the American Medical Association, Washington, D.C., and Chicago, The Associations, latest edition.

[13] Reported by Mr. Thomas M. Janeway, Supervisor—Health Education, Office of the Superintendent of Public Instruction, Springfield, Illinois, 1967.

[14] MacDougal, V.: Classroom hatchery enhances learning. New York State Education, *48*:28–29 (Feb.) 1961.

compare sizes at different times, or, as in the kindergarten, collect pictures showing the changes which take place between infancy and their own ages. In all of these activities, the teacher will stress the relationship between proper foods and growth.

Health Problems in Our Community and Who Helps Us with Them

Community studies that are commonly made as a part of the social studies during the primary years provide a natural approach to this teaching.

Community helpers. Through informal discussion, children may tell how they or their families have been helped by the services of a health worker, for instance, a nurse, physician, dentist, policeman, or fireman.

Protecting food at the source. One group of third graders in a rural community visited a well-kept farm near the school. The farmer showed them how he milked his cows so that the milk would stay clean. He also showed them how his well water was protected. On their return to school, the children constructed a miniature farm and located the well at a point where drainage from the barnyard and septic tank could not reach it.

Living in migratory camps. In a unit on home and family life, teachers in one area deal with special health and safety problems known to exist in the migratory camps in the area, as, for example, fire hazards, broken glass in the yard, playing in dumps, insanitary practices, and care of small children under crowded conditions. Emphasis is placed on family unity regardless of the surroundings and on the fact that there are many different ways to live which are acceptable.

Apartment house living. As a part of a social studies unit on housing, city children may discuss ways in which they can live healthfully in apartment houses. For example, they may learn that food should not be left around to attract mice and cockroaches. They must learn to respect their neighbors. They can discuss where they may go outside the building to find outlets for their energy, as, for example, to city playgrounds or to a neighborhood house.

Spoon Full of Sugar Club. A group of San Jose youngsters who learned about the lonely senior citizens in the community decided to form a club to bring cheer to the elderly. With the help of a parent, they invited a social worker to show them slides of the plight of lonely people. This interest led them to write letters, make holiday decorations, and do other things for the elderly living alone or in boarding houses.[15] Though it was not reported that

---

[15] Reported by Mr. George Felicetta, Catholic Social Service, San Jose, California, 1967.

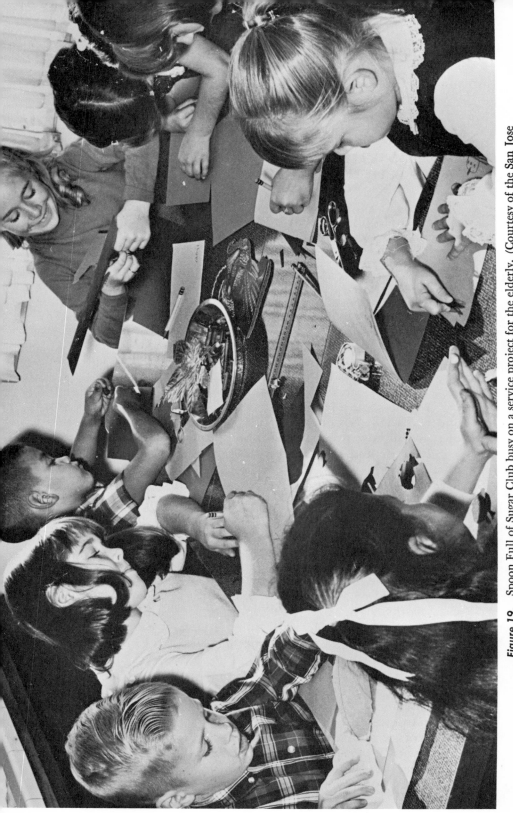

Figure 19. Spoon Full of Sugar Club busy on a service project for the elderly. (Courtesy of the San Jose Mercury-News, San Jose, California.)

these children discussed their project with schoolmates, they may well have done so—to the advantage of all. The project was written up in the local newspaper and also in national publications.

GUIDES TO HEALTH TEACHING AT THE UPPER ELEMENTARY LEVEL (Ages 9 to 11)

Factors That Will Help Determine What to Teach and How to Teach It

Health Needs, Interests, and Beliefs Related to the Growth Pattern (*see also Chapter 2*)

Growth in height and weight. This progresses slowly and steadily. By the age of 11 some girls and a few boys suddenly show rapid growth, evidence of the approach of adolescence.

Eating. At this age he is generally a good eater, and is more likely to think about food than during the earlier years. Girls will read cookbooks and help prepare meals.

Elimination. He has good control over his bowel movements and urination. Bowel movements are most likely to occur outside of school hours, after breakfast, or in late afternoon or evening.

Exercise and play interests. He participates in a great variety of strenuous activity; often does not know when to stop. He works hard to develop new skills. During the latter part of this period he is more relaxed and better controlled in his physical activity. He becomes interested in organized games and constructive projects such as building things. Sex differences begin to appear in recreational pursuits.

Sleep and rest. The 9-year-old sleeps aproximately 10 or 11 hours; the 10- and 11-year-old may sleep less. He is usually a good sleeper. Children at this age are often not given enough sleep. Some show marked fatigue.

Eyes and ears. He gains fuller control of eye movements. An increasing number of children need glasses. Earaches are less common than in earlier years.

Teeth. The permanent teeth are appearing: at 9 and 10 years, the first and second bicuspids; at 11 years, the cuspids.

Posture. When sitting, he is likely to slouch; he assumes unusual postures.

Illnesses and disease. In general, this is a period of good health with fewer diseases and infections. The child begins to take simple responsibilities in disease prevention, as, for example, using his own cup, covering his mouth when coughing, and the like.

Accidents and injuries.   Accidents continue to increase. Children tend to play in dangerous places and in dangerous ways when not given proper supervision or recreational facilities.

Emotional adjustments.   The 9-year-old has himself well in hand, and this ability in self-direction develops markedly under proper guidance during this age period. He is well organized, he is critical of himself, and he learns to appreciate the satisfactions of achievement. He likes hard work and challenging tasks, and needs to feel that older people have confidence in him. Some children may develop physical complaints (headache, stomachache) which can be traced back to emotional disturbances. Emotional outbursts occur, but they are usually temporary.

Sex adjustments.   The 9-year-old is more interested in his own body than in that of the other sex. He wants unanswered questions answered. Sex differences become marked among 10- and 11-year-olds. There is little companionship between the sexes. The 11-year-old girl is likely to be self-conscious in the presence of boys. The well organized girl is a much more mature person than the boy of the same age.

Interests and Adjustments in Respect to Home, School, and Community Living (see also Chapter 3)

Home.   The child is so absorbed in his own activities and friends that he shows less emotional attachment to his parents. He is usually cooperative in home responsibilities, however, and will help do such things as prepare meals or care for the sick. He has only a mild interest in his own daily health routines and may need frequent reminding to carry them out. He is quite capable, however, of planning his own day. He may be quarrelsome with his brothers and sisters. He is frequently torn between loyalty to home and to peer groups.

School.   Social intelligence and an ethical sense become greater during this period. The child enjoys delving into real problems, including those with broad social meanings. He becomes increasingly willing to accept responsibilities. He wants the satisfaction of working independently; he likes to experiment. He can deal more effectively with abstractions than in earlier years.

Community.   The gang spirit is strong; membership in a club, often a secret one, is usual. Age mates set standards of dress and deportment, though indirect guidance of parents and teachers is needed. The child is likely to show increasing interest in other lands and times. He sees his own community in relation to other communities and to the nation and the world. He enjoys using the community as a laboratory.

Suggestions for Health Teaching Emphasis at the Upper Elementary Level

It would appear from a study of the material just presented that special attention may need to be given to the following personal health problems in the teaching program: how to plan a daily program to allow ample time for work, play, and rest; how to prepare simple family meals; how to relax; how to acquire and maintain good posture; how to prevent accidents, especially from the standpoint of dangerous play, bicycle riding, and home and farm safety; how the human body is made, and how it functions; how to maintain dental health; what qualities make a good friend or a good member of the family. Since some children will experiment with smoking during these years, instruction on smoking should start at this time. Each teacher should analyze his own situation, however, to determine whether these or other problems are important.

Although most children have not reached the point at which they are greatly concerned about public health, foundations can be laid during these years for such concern. Many of the concepts of man's relation to his environment, as developed in the social studies and science, for example, can contribute directly to such an understanding and interest.

Children at this age are able to discuss thoroughly the reasons for desirable health behavior and are capable of being critical of their own behavior patterns. When curiosities have been aroused, there is almost no limit to what children may do. Groups given free rein have been known to carry on experiments and to explore problems that would challenge an adult, and they may even delve into materials intended for professional workers. Gang spirit and interest in club activities may be directed into constructive channels by allowing children to set their own standards of health attainment.

Illustrations of experiences in health education for this age level are given in the following pages.

Scheduling for Health Teaching at the Upper Elementary Level

In order that pupils may solve their immediate health problems rationally and arrive at understandings of health in its broader aspects, there should be direct health instruction during these years as well as planned health teaching which is integrated with the different subject areas.

In some states educational laws require that health be taught

Figure 20. Social groups have a strong influence on social development.

a certain number of minutes each week. In traditionally organized schools there has been an unfortunate tendency to set aside weekly the required amount of time for health textbook reading and discussion. Many teachers are discovering that state requirements can be met within the framework of a more flexible program. During some weeks it may be necessary to spend several hours on a health unit while at other times incidental teaching will suffice. The important thing is to plan for health teaching and its incorporation in the curriculum in terms of what needs to be done to accomplish desirable goals for this age group.

Suggested Learning Experiences

Planning the Daily Program for a Balance of Work, Play, and Rest

Pie graphs.   The children may help to plan their own schedules, including the week's program at school. One group made pie graphs on which were marked off 24-hour schedules that allowed time for the different daily routines. Each child then tried to live according to the plan he had set for himself.

Survey of television watching.   Children in one sixth grade classroom complained of being tired. This led to a survey of television watching habits and a discussion of ways in which these habits could be improved to allow for more sleep.

Heroes.   Study ways in which the astronauts, favorite athletes, and other present-day heroes budget their time and get into condition for their work. Such study can lead to a better appreciation of the importance of good health habits. Collect pictures, newspaper clippings, and magazine articles to illustrate points under study.

Children in other lands.   Read and report on customs in other lands which show the universal need for good health practices. Find out through reports from the World Health Organization and other sources what conditions in different countries need to be improved for better health of the people.

The Food We Eat

Food shopping problems.   These shopping problems are proposed by one school system as appropriate for study: Which is the cheapest way to buy orange juice? How much does it cost for a small glass? Which two vegetables are the cheapest to serve and which are the most expensive? (Note: the answer will vary in different parts of the country and at different seasons of the year.)

What cheap protein foods can be used for the main dish for lunch or dinner?

Ideas to try. An interagency nutrition committee in Kansas suggests the following activities:

> Visit school lunch facilities to:
>> Learn how menus are planned.
>> Learn how to determine amounts of food needed.
>> Learn how to figure the cost of food.
>> See kinds of equipment used in food preparation.
>> Learn to recognize good sanitation practices.
>
> Plan a week's school lunch menus:
>> Meeting the Type-A Lunch pattern.
>> Using the commodity foods.
>> Figuring the market order.
>> Staying within the budget.
>
> Make field trip to packing plant, food processing plant and market, to learn about: food production; varieties; care of food; processing; storage; preparation; preservation; sanitation; distribution.[16]

Learning about our own diet through the study of poultry. As a corollary to the study of the formation of the chicken embryo and the hatching of the chicks described earlier in this chapter, the project can be carried further to illustrate various aspects of diet. The children can care for the chicks and feed them a balanced mash diet; they can compare the foods they feed to the poultry with their own dietary needs. They will discover that chickens need whole grains, milk, meat scraps, fish, vitamins, and minerals, in other words, a balanced diet of proteins, carbohydrates, minerals, and vitamins. With the right diet, the chickens will produce more eggs and make good meat. Then the children can check their own diets, comparing them with those of the poultry, and plan menus for breakfast, snacks, lunch, and dinner. At the end of the study the children may prepare their own booklets with correct menus for the different meals during the day.

Good Posture

Physical education classes at this level will include instruction on posture and relaxation. Children may work out their own methods for securing the right kind and amount of exercise for good posture.

Fatigue and posture. One group discussed what happens to posture when we are tired, and they reported on observations of posture of people at work, walking, and relaxing.

Bent branches. On a nature walk, pupils may observe trees and branches which have been bent by the forces of nature, and

---

[16] Nutrition in the School; A Guide for Teachers. Topeka, Kansas, Kansas State Department of Health, 1965, p. 13.

consider what forces or habits may likewise bend their own bodies out of shape. Further, they might try bending a young sapling for a time and then noting whether it returns to its upright position.

Sketching the body in motion.   Make sketches showing good body mechanics in daily activities. (If necessary, consult the physical education teacher.)

Manikins.   Manikins cut out of cardboard with the parts joined together by paper fasteners may be manipulated into different positions to demonstrate good and poor posture.

Dental Health

With the appearance of permanent teeth there is need to extend an understanding of teeth and their care.

The Council on Dental Health of the Ohio State Dental Association, in cooperation with educational and health authorities, has prepared an excellent dental health guide which contains the following suggestions for teaching dental health at this age level:

1. Children should examine teeth in a hand mirror to note different types and structure.
2. Children may make dental health scrapbooks, using pictures from magazines.
3. Children may keep diet lists of everything that is eaten in one week. Compare these lists to charts or lists of foods harmful to the teeth.
4. Illustrate how acids dissolve calcium from teeth. Place one tooth [a baby tooth that has fallen out] in 10 per cent hydrochloric acid and another in plain water. Allow to stand for a week and show softening caused by acids.
5. Make simple dental posters for display in school.
6. Demonstrate how an inexpensive, effective dentifrice can be made by mixing one part salt with two parts baking soda.[17]

How the Body Is Made and How It Functions

Your growth.   In a study of growth and development with fourth grade children, a Champaign, Illinois, teacher asked children to bring baby pictures and also current pictures of themselves. The children placed the pictures on the bulletin board and with colored pieces of yarn arranged a display as follows:

How Do We Grow?

In height and weight—	Picture of growing boy or girl
In skills—	Picture of child in an activity such as swimming

---

[17] Dental Health Guide for Teachers. 1961 Revised Ed. Columbus, Ohio, Ohio State Dental Association, 1961, pp. 29–30.

In responsibility—

                               Picture of a child
caring for a baby
brother or sister or
assuming some other
responsibility

In consideration of others—   Picture of a child
helping an older
person across a
street or performing
another service

The baby picture appeared at the left of the display. The project provided a basis for much useful discussion. It could be extended to include a study of growth rates of different parts of the body and to develop the concept that each boy and girl grows in his or her own way, and that each has a different rate of growth.[18]

Parts of the human body. To aid in the study of parts of the body the children can cut out a large outline frame of the human body and hang it on the bulletin board. Then as they study the various organs, they can trace the organs, cut them out, color them, and put them on the proper place in the frame. The teacher may provide the class with models of the human body or of its various organs, and institute a class project of putting the parts together.

Selected activities from a unit on the structure and function of the human body. Activities which correlated instruction on anatomy and physiology with health practices were reported from a Texas school. Among them were the following:

1. Made a model of cross section of skin, using a block of clay and coloring it. Care of skin was discussed.
2. Used experiments to show how perspiration aids in keeping the body cool.
3. Used model of arm to show how muscles contract and expand. Model had boards for bones, hinges for ligaments, rubber strips for muscles, and string for tendons.
4. Examined an x-ray showing a fractured bone of one of the class members.
5. Demonstrated that we breathe slowly or rapidly, depending on air needed, by counting number of breaths per minute before and after exercise.
6. Children demonstrated how normal growth in height, weight, and body build can vary greatly in children of the same age. Those of the same age stood in rows together to note these differences. Stress was placed on the fact that they were all normal, growing at their own rate.
7. Children helped with tests of eyes, ears, height, weight, and other routine checks.[19]

Human reproduction. A report from Columbus, Georgia, tells about pupil responses to sessions on menstruation for girls and puberty for boys. In a unit for sixth grade pupils during which

---

[18] Adapted from report by Mrs. Leota M. Goldie, Champaign Community Schools, Champaign, Illinois, 1967.

[19] Adapted from Dorothy Isbell, DeQueen School, Port Arthur, Texas. From a report of the Society of State Directors for Health, Physical Education, and Recreation, 1952, pp. 2–3, 5.

films were shown and discussed, such questions as the following were asked: What do you mean, "fertilize the egg"? What causes twins? How many times do you have to mate to get a baby? Do you ever stop menstruation at any age? Why do children look like their parents or some of their kinfolks? How do you have a baby? What is a miscarriage? What is a prostitute? Why am I so small and some of my friends so much bigger; will I catch up? Should you marry the first person you fall in love with? Even more sophisticated questions were asked—a fact which suggests that most schools need to reassess the manner in which they are providing sex education.

The same report tells about plans to introduce fourth or fifth graders to concepts of child growth and development by bringing a "real live" baby to the classroom for a monthly visit over a period of several months.[20]

Hearing.   In a unit on hearing, the pupils may

1. Learn the basic structure of the ear and the common signs of impairment.
2. Understand why objects must be kept out of ears.
3. Understand the basic hygiene of the ears—what to do to prevent damage and to care for the ear.
4. Appreciate the need for regular medical checkups and early care of illness to prevent health problems.

To achieve these objectives, pupils may discuss how sound travels; watch a demonstration of a sound wave in a pan of water; discuss, list, and practice ways to prevent hearing loss; and discuss the types of work in which deaf people and people with hearing loss may be engaged. More actively, the pupils may conduct the following experiment: plug both ears with cotton; observe that voices and noises are more subdued; discuss these observations in relation to the problems which people with a hearing loss have.[21]

Audiometer and vision testing.   At this age, children are ready to learn about these tests—why and how they are given, and what they show. They may participate in testing programs for themselves and for younger children.

The human body in our space age.   As a part of a larger unit on the drama of the space age, pupils may:

1. Investigate provisions made on jet planes for comfortable and safe travel at high altitudes.

2. Find out what equipment is used by astronauts to make it possible for their bodies to function normally in space.

Smoking and Health

Many states now provide teaching guides to help teachers with their instruction on this subject. At this stage of our knowledge,

---

20 Taken from an unpublished paper by Mrs. Herndon Jackson, Health Education Consultant, Muscogee County Health Department, Columbus, Georgia, 1967.

21 Guide for the Montana School Health Program. 2nd Ed. Helena, Montana, The Montana State Board of Health, 1961, p. 195.

most efforts at instruction are experimental and with unpredictable results. Nevertheless, many activities which are promising are being proposed. A few of these activities are outlined here.

A survey of smoking habits.   In one sixth grade classroom, the children made a survey of the smoking habits of their parents and smoking patterns in the school, developed posters, wrote letters to their legislator, and developed a sample bill for him to introduce to the legislature in the state.

Making decisions.   Among the many learning experiences contained in a guide prepared through cooperative efforts in the state of Washington are the following:

> Conduct role-playing experiences in decision making. (Example: Develop a skit with one person trying to get another to smoke. Show social pressures students use to get others to smoke.)
> Develop the following themes with bulletin board displays or displays with pamphlets:
> > a. "I won't start because. . . ."
> > b. "Sports and cigarettes don't mix!"
> > c. "Don't let a cigarette advertisement fool you."
> Collect advertisements; student committees identify the kinds of appeals used. Instigate a counter-advertising campaign.
> Survey students to determine reasons why they do not smoke. Results could be tabulated and graphed.
> Invite a junior or senior high school student leader to discuss the topic, "Smoking and Popularity."
> Find the cost to a smoker of one pack of cigarettes per day for one year. What else could he do with the money?
> Collect and categorize news articles about fires caused by careless cigarette smokers.
> Prepare a school bulletin board display on smoking and safety hazards.
> Show pros and cons of smoking by use of a mobile—how do they balance?
> Interview people who smoke and those who do not smoke for their advice on making the decision to smoke or not to smoke.
> Make tape recordings which summarize what your class has learned about smoking and health. Exchange the tapes with other classes in your school or other schools.[22]

Accident Prevention at Home, School, and on the Highway

Accident surveys.   The children may make spot maps of accidents which have occurred at home, school, or on the highway and then discuss these from the standpoint of how the accidents might have been prevented. The pupils can also make safety surveys around their own homes and neighborhoods to discover unsafe

---

[22] Smoking and Health Guide for Elementary and Secondary Schools. Olympia, Washington, Washington State Department of Public Instruction, 1966, pp. 5–15. (Working copy.)

places to play: dumps, quarries, railroad property, abandoned buildings, new homes under construction. They may present their findings to the class and follow these with group discussion about safe places to play: parks, playgrounds, and so forth.

Practicing good citizenship. A class of fourth graders, distressed by an accident caused by a driver who was confused by red lights on a bridge, wrote a letter to the city alderman suggesting ways in which changes could be made on bridge markings which might prevent similar accidents. The council referred the letter to its safety committee.

Home accidents. A sixth grade class had read about the high death rate for home accidents and decided to learn more about this serious problem. With the help of the public health nurse and the public health educator, the children prepared a home safety check list which they used in their own homes. Each pupil reported accident hazards found in the home and, at a later time, reported the corrections made. The class determined which accidents were major problems and made large posters to illustrate them. At about the same time, the local Junior Chamber of Commerce became interested in the sixth grade project, since the Chamber, too, was stressing home safety during Community Health Week. The health committee of the Junior Chamber of Commerce made contact with the health council at the school and worked out a plan to use the school's home safety project for publicity in the community through newspaper and television. The results of the classroom project were so gratifying that the local health department made a short movie of what the class had done as it learned about home safety. This movie has been shown throughout the state of Georgia.

Accidental poisonings. A midwestern 4-H Club voted to adopt for its health project a program aimed at prevention of accidental poisonings. With the cooperation of the local Poison Control Center, the club members compiled materials to be used in a pamphlet to emphasize the common causes of accidental poisoning, especially in young children. This pamphlet points out why these accidents occur, how to prevent them, and what to do if poisoning has occurred. Since the Poison Control Center has frequent evidence of the need for parent education to prevent these accidents, the club members also provided information to newspapers and radio and television stations on how to prevent child poisonings and on the services of the Poison Control Center. Although this was a 4-H Club project, the same activities could be carried on by a health class.

Safety cadets. Short messages recorded on the tape recorder by safety patrol members of one school were broadcast to the entire school over the public address system. One five-minute taped message reached hundreds of students and teachers at one time. These messages have also had a very positive, creative, and powerful effect when played to parent groups, interested citizens, and civic organizations.

Getting Along with Oneself and Other People

Problems of human relationships come up in the day-by-day living at school which may lead to worthwhile discussions. Current events topics also provide a fine basis for such discussions.

What would you do?   Show a filmstrip or movie to the class which depicts a human relations problem. Stop the film before the end and have the class members supply their own solutions to the problem.

Understanding yourself.   Among concepts and learning experiences suggested for sixth graders in Cleveland to help them understand themselves are the following:

Concepts	*Learning Experiences*
Taking a candid look at yourself is wholesome.	Discuss growing up and getting ready for junior high school.
	Pretend you are turning the camera upon yourself. Decide your greatest personal problem. Keep this in mind for future consideration.
You can learn to adjust to people and events.	Use examples from fiction to show adjustments made to various happenings.
	Suggest endings to an unfinished story read or told by the teacher about some character's problem.
Getting along with members of the family often requires personal adjustments.	Plan some skits showing ways of getting along with siblings and adult members of the family.
	Give book reports emphasizing adjustments made by various characters in stories about families.
You can learn to play and work with others.	Tell of committee work in: science — Boy Scouts; social studies — Safety Council
	Name team games and cite examples of good team work.
Responsibilities increase as you grow up.	Choose an adult whom you admire. List responsibilities expected of that person.
	Consider reasonable responsibilities you would be expected to assume at home and at school.
Your well-being often depends on the personal habits you develop.	Give examples of situations that call for decisions. Contrast wise and unwise decisions and determine which show maturity.
	Discuss the responsibility of the individual in relation to the use of tobacco, alcohol, drugs, narcotics.

Concepts	*Learning Experiences*
As your body changes your feelings toward others change.	Contrast in specific situations the behavior of a little child with that of an adult in considering the needs of others.
Choosing and keeping good friends require sound judgment.	List qualities you want in a real friend. Have a panel discussion or debate about clubs and gangs.
Everyone needs to solve personal problems.	Recall what you selected as your greatest problem at the beginning of this unit. Evaluate your progress in handling this problem.[23]

Improving Public Health

Acute communicable disease control.   The class may engage in some of the following activities, as suggested by the *Guide for the Montana School Health Program*:

1. Read the textbook and supplementary material assignments and increase the general knowledge of diseases as to: causes, common symptoms, methods of spread, prevention, and control.

2. Become familiar with use of the chart "Communicable Disease Information for Schools."

3. Find out how the local regulations for the control of communicable diseases differ from the state regulations, if there is a difference.

4. Study the lives of scientists and the accomplishments they made in the control of disease: Pasteur, Reed, Jenner, Salk, and others.

5. Gain an understanding of the body's defense against disease.

6. Study the various methods for destroying disease-producing bacteria and viruses.

7. Visit the public health office to determine how the personnel assist the community in the control of communicable diseases.

8. Develop a plan for the pupils in the room to follow that should help control communicable diseases.

The individual pupil can list the kind and date of immunizations he has had and determine what precautions are taken at home to control communicable diseases (safety of water, proper sewage disposal, refrigeration and storage of food, individual towels and drinking cups, etc.).[24]

An air pollution unit.   Sixth grade children in Eau Claire, Wisconsin, made an air pollution study during Cleaner Air Week under the guidance of the local health department. Summarizing correspondence which described the project:

A resource unit on air pollution was provided to all sixth grade teachers in the Eau Claire public school system with a packet of reference material. Six miniature Ringelmann smoke scales for grading the density of smoke were included in each packet. . . .

A high-volume air sampler was borrowed from the State Board of Health and its use demonstrated at a principals' meeting. A schedule was prepared and the

23 Excerpts from Teacher's Health Guide; Grades 4, 5, 6. Cleveland, Ohio, Cleveland Public Schools, 1963, pp. 115–120.

24 Guide for the Montana School Health Program. 2nd Ed. Helena, Montana, The Montana State Board of Health, 1961, pp. 67–68.

Figure 21. Studying the results of an air pollution test made with a high-volume air sampler. (Courtesy of the City-County Health Department, Eau Claire, Wisconsin.)

sampler was sent to schools on a weekly basis with a filter, an instruction sheet for operation, and a data sheet in an envelope addressed to the health department. When six of the filters were returned, they were sent to the Occupational Health Division, State Board of Health, where they were weighed and analyzed and then sent back to the local health department. The local health department then returned the filters to the schools with a fact sheet on air pollution findings in the same month from a high volume sampler permanently located in downtown Eau Claire (Eau Claire is part of the federal network) and for urban and non-urban areas across the United States. On completion of the project the sixth grade teachers, in responding to a questionnaire, were unanimous in favor of continuing the program and expanding it.[25]

Opening the door to public health.   This is the title of a 55-page report prepared by sixth grade pupils of Glenridge Elementary School, Clayton, Missouri, as a summary of a six-week project which included field trips and "bench sessions" at which health authorities discussed health problems and programs. Among places visited on the field trips were waterworks, the county health department, the College of Pharmacy, a hospital, and a department store restaurant and kitchens where pupils made their own restaurant inspection. Through observation and discussions during trips and "bench sessions" they learned about the work of the health department; a policeman's view of accidents; care and precautions in the use of medicines, narcotics, and the Pure Food and Drug Act; ordinances and inspections of food handling establishments (including vending machines and itinerant restaurants); and air pollution. The writing of the final report was divided among members of the class, with a committee working on each chapter or area of interest.[26]

Working for better school and community health.   This is an age for doing. With help and encouragement, children are ready to do their share in improving health conditions in school and community. Here are suggestions for their participation:

1. Carry on a clean-up campaign at school or in the neighborhood, enlisting the help and support of others.
2. Write articles for the school newspaper on things pupils can do to make the school a healthier place in which to live.
3. Take part in community health education efforts for such measures as immunizations, improved housing, traffic control, and securing better health services.
4. In an older school building, study lighting and other environmental conditions and participate in efforts to improve these conditions.

Cattle.   In a fifth grade unit on cattle, the following experiences related to health are found:

Watch the vaccination of cattle (while on a study trip).
Dramatize a cattlemen's committee meeting to consider problems such as the

---

[25] Summarized from a report by Mrs. Helen M. Watts, Health Education Coordinator, City-County Health Department, Eau Claire, Wisconsin, 1967.
[26] Information provided by Dr. Virginia Jackson, teacher, Glenridge Elementary School, Clayton, Missouri, 1967.

following: drought, severe winter weather, disease control, wild animals, lack of water.

Compare the safety precautions taken now to assure wholesome, safe meat with the practices of 100 years ago.

Rabies control.   Denver has long been known for its successful program of vaccinating dogs for rabies control, and an important factor in this success is the participation of the public schools. The Denver Department of Health and Hospitals furnishes the teachers with fact sheets on rabies as it occurs in dogs and man along with an outline of the Denver control program. Using this material as a basis, the teachers carry on class discussions and integrate the material into their art work, safety program, social studies, and reading.

Water in our community.   In a sixth grade classroom a boy who was watering the plants suddenly said: "You know, we have not studied at all about water. How is our water kept pure? Where does it come from?" His questions led to a class project devoted to seeking the answers to these and other such questions concerning water, as: How important is water to people? In an effort to determine the usual ways that cities secure their supply, the pupils formed committees, one of which visited city hall to ask the city manager:

1. How is water sold to the people of the city?
2. How much money is invested in our plant?
3. How much is paid in salaries each month to keep the plant going?
4. What problems does the city have in connection with the water supply and sewage disposal?
5. Has our city ever had any cases of illness due to impure water? If so, what were they?

Another committee visited the water plant and a third went to the city swimming pool to seek information.

In order to compare the water situation in their own city with that in others, the pupils studied about water in New York, Chicago, New Orleans, Los Angeles, and ancient and modern Rome. They made graphs and tables and a mural showing the way water reaches the individual from its original source. They also had an assembly program so that the older boys and girls might know about the city water supply.

Two girls were sick.   In a fifth grade classroom the pupils decided to devote some time to the study of safeguarding food, after learning that two of their classmates were sick as a result of eating spoiled salad at a picnic. The teacher asked: "Have you ever thought about the number of people who protect our food?" The answers from the class included the county health officer, the sanitarians, and the food inspectors who check markets, stores, and eating places. In response to a reference to pure food laws, the pupils checked the encyclopedia and were astonished to learn that even in the Middle Ages governments made many laws regulating the adulteration and quality of foods. They read other references on food preservatives, drying, salting, canning, refrigerating, and freezing. While reading, the children were looking for the answers to such questions as: How are foods preserved? What keeps food from spoiling? How do we keep food from spoiling in our own homes? Their reading led to a class discussion in which they reported much helpful information.

Experiments on how germs spread.   Several experiments can be conducted in the classroom to determine facts about germs and how they are spread. Los Angeles City Schools suggest the following:

1. To discover what conditions may affect the growth or destruction of germs (pathogenic microorganisms), take two pieces of cloth approximately the same size and wet both pieces; for a week leave one in a dark, warm place and the other in sunlight and air. The piece of cloth kept in a dark, warm place mildews and has an unpleasant odor, while the other piece smells clean and is relatively free of mildew. The implications of this experiment are that warmth, moisture, and darkness help molds and bacteria to multiply.

2. To discover the presence of germs in a cough, obtain two Petri dishes (or two metal lids), two glass squares, and agar or plain gelatin. Wash, dry, and sterilize the Petri dishes. Dissolve ½ ounce of plain gelatin in 1¾ cups of water and sterilize the solution; pour into Petri dishes. Cover one dish; cough into the other and then cover. Put dishes in a warm, dark place and observe daily for a week. Watch for colonies of bacteria to develop in the contaminated dish. A practical implication of this experiment is the importance of using a handkerchief or tissue to cover coughs and sneezes in order to avoid spreading germs.

3. To discover how germs spread, obtain three oranges, one of which is moldy, and a needle. Push a needle into the moldy part of an orange; pierce another orange with the contaminated needle. Clean and sterilize the needle; then pierce the third orange with the sterile needle. After a week or so it will be seen that the orange that was pierced by the contaminated needle became contaminated. The growth of mold on the orange may be compared to the spread of bacteria in infection. Molds and bacteria may be destroyed by sterilization.[27]

For ideas on other experiments consult bacteriologists, sanitarians, and others in your community.

If Disaster Strikes

Suggested safety precautions.   These precautions can be investigated by the pupils and compiled into a set of instructions for

---

[27] Health in the Elementary Schools; An Instructional Guide. Publication No. EC–201. Los Angeles, California, Los Angeles City Schools, 1959, pp. 272–273.

school distribution. Since conditions vary widely from one part of the country to another, a locally developed list could be most useful. A list developed in a midwestern state included the following items:

1. Tornado—listen to radio or TV for official alert; seek shelter—southwest corner of basement preferred as tornadoes usually move northeast; hollowed or sheltered place in the earth; cover face to prevent suffocation from dust.

2. Hurricane (or cyclone)—listen to radio or TV for official alert; leave low-lying beaches or flood areas early; seek shelter in a well-built house, out of danger of high tide. Fasten storm shutters and brace outside doors. Open a window or door on the side opposite that facing the wind to equalize air pressure as storm passes.

3. Flood—pay attention to flood warning and get to safety in plenty of time. Before leaving home, turn off gas and electricity at the point where they enter the house in order to guard against fire or explosion during or following the flood. Destroy anything such as medicine, fruits, and vegetables that have been under flood water. Keep a good first-aid kit ready with blankets, food and other emergency equipment.

4. Blizzards—never leave shelter if a blizzard threatens. If caught in a car, do not leave the car for any reason. Stuff cracks to keep out wind or cold. If on foot or horseback head immediately for any type of known shelter.[28]

SUMMARY

This chapter deals with health teaching suggestions for the elementary school years. In general, instruction during these years should be related closely to daily living problems and grow out of the events of school and community life. It may be coordinated closely with teaching in other areas of learning, such as the social studies, science, and language arts, in order that concepts may be understood in their larger relationships. The specific learning experiences that finally occur in each classroom should develop through careful teacher-pupil planning.

REFERENCES

Beauchamp, G. A.: Basic Dimensions for Elementary Method. Boston, Allyn and Bacon, Inc., 1965, 340 pp.

Britton, E. C., and Winans, J. M.: Growing from Infancy to Adulthood. New York, Appleton-Century-Crofts, Inc., 1958. Chapter 3: Characteristics of children in early childhood, pp. 33–45. Chapter 4: Characteristics of children in later childhood, pp. 46–57.

Collier, C. C., Houston, W. R., Schmatz, R. R., and Walsh, W. J.: Teaching in the Modern Elementary School. New York, The Macmillan Company, 1967, 310 pp.

---

[28] The Challenge of Safety Education. Circular Series A—No. 128. Springfield, Illinois, The Office of the Superintendent of Public Instruction, 1959, pp. 26–27.

Florio, A. E., and Stafford, G. T.: Safety Education. New York, McGraw-Hill Book Company, Inc., 1962, 382 pp.

Hanna, L. A., Potter, G. L., and Hagaman, N.: Unit Teaching in the Elementary School. Revised Ed. New York, Holt, Rinehart and Winston, Inc., 1963, 595 pp.

How Children Develop. Revised Ed. Columbus, Ohio, The Ohio State University, 1964, 68 pp. (Prepared by the faculty of University School, College of Education.)

Irwin, L. W., Cornacchia, H. J., and Staton, W. M.: Health Education in Elementary Schools. 2nd Ed. St. Louis, The C. V. Mosby Company, 1966, 462 pp.

Jarvis, O. T., and Wootton, L. R.: The Transitional Elementary School and Its Curriculum. Dubuque, Iowa, William C. Brown Company, 1966, 481 pp.

Joint Committee on Health Problems in Education of the National Education Association and the American Medical Association: Health Education. 5th Ed. Washington, D.C., and Chicago, The Associations, 1961, 429 pp.

Lee, J. M.: Elementary Education; Today and Tomorrow. Boston, Allyn and Bacon, Inc., 1967, 308 pp.

McCarthy, R. G., Editor: Alcohol Education for Classroom and Community. New York, McGraw-Hill Book Company, 1964, 308 pp.

Moving into Adolescence; Your Child in His Preteens. Children's Bureau Publication No. 431—1966. Washington, D.C., U.S. Government Printing Office, 1966, 46 pp.

Needed improvements in elementary school health education programs. Journal of Health—Physical Education—Recreation, *38:*28–29 (Feb.) 1967. (Prepared by AAHPER Committee to Focus on the Improvement of Elementary Programs of Health Education.)

Petersen, D. G.: The Elementary School Teacher. New York, Appleton-Century-Crofts, 1964, 570 pp.

Willgoose, C. E.: Health Education in the Elementary School. 2nd Ed. Philadelphia, W. B. Saunders Company, 1964, 369 pp.

Yost, C. P.: Teaching Safety in the Elementary School. Washington, D.C., American Association for Health, Physical Education, and Recreation, 1962, 32 pp.

Your Child from 6 to 12. Children's Bureau Publication Number 324—1949. Washington, D.C., U.S. Government Printing Office, 1961, 141 pp.

CHAPTER

9

GUIDES TO HEALTH TEACHING IN SECONDARY SCHOOLS

This chapter contains suggestions for health teaching in junior and senior high schools. Up to this point, the bases for selecting content and learning experiences have been established. Health needs of youth and of home, school, and community are discussed in early chapters as a means of directing the teacher's attention to the particular needs of the pupils and the community he serves. Though not identified as such, the needs described in these chapters are suggestive of the broad concepts which should provide the framework for an organized approach to health instruction. Methods of instruction and instructional materials which may lend interest and variety to health teaching are discussed in other chapters.

The material in this chapter is arranged according to junior and senior high school levels. For each level, the following guides to health teaching are given: factors that will help determine what to teach and how to teach it; suggestions for health teaching emphasis; scheduling for health teaching; and suggested learning experiences. These latter, in many instances drawn from successful experiences of teachers throughout the country, are illustrative only of those which might be developed in a class situation, whether a health class or one in another subject, such as social studies, science, home economics, or physical education. These examples of learning experiences are in no sense presented as a blueprint for all teachers to follow. As emphasized previously, *in health teaching, as in all teaching, details necessarily must be worked out locally and in relation to the needs and interests of specific groups of young people in specific schools and communities.*

GUIDES TO HEALTH TEACHING IN JUNIOR HIGH SCHOOLS, GRADES 7 TO 9 (Ages 11 to 14)

Factors That Will Help Determine What to Teach and How to Teach It

Health Needs, Interests, and Beliefs Related to the Growth Pattern (see also Chapter 2)

Growth in height and weight. This period is one of rapid increase in physical growth, commonly known as the pubescent spurt. Wide variations in growth patterns occur among individuals and between the sexes. In girls, rapid growth usually starts between the ages of 11 and 14; in boys, between the ages of 12 and 16. By the age of 14, growth differences between the two sexes are less than during the early part of this period. Young people are usually very much concerned about this growth phenomenon.

Eating. Large intake of the right kinds of food is needed for proper growth and development. The healthy adolescent has a ravenous appetite, though he does not always choose his food wisely. The tired, nervous type may have a poor appetite; he may pick at his food and eat too many sweets or snacks that are short on growth-promoting elements. Dietary excesses are common.

Elimination. Faulty eating habits, irregular daily regimen, and emotional strains may heighten the tendency to have difficulties with elimination.

Exercise and play interests. Young people need exercise for proper development, but too great physical exertion during this period of most rapid growth may cause overfatigue. Abilities for physical activity vary widely. The early maturing adolescent may have physiological capacity for strenuous activity that is lacking in the late-maturing individual. There is a growing interest in team play and sports which should be encouraged. Awkwardness that comes from rapid growth and the resultant self-consciousness may cause some adolescents to shun physical activity, however. A varied program is necessary so each pupil may find an activity he will enjoy.

Sleep and rest. The early adolescent tires easily. Although it is commonly stated that adolescents have reached the adult level in respect to the amount of sleep they need, physicians believe that 9 to 11 hours of sleep are needed each night. Apparent laziness may be a reflection of physiological or emotional imbalance or a symptom of poor hygienic habits.

Eyes and ears. Hearing and vision defects appear. Students seem to have an interest in the proper care of their eyes.

Teeth. Permanent teeth continue to replace deciduous teeth. There is continued need for keeping teeth in good repair.

Posture.   Postural difficulties are prominent during these years in which the young person is learning to coordinate his strangely new body. Often he will have good balance in activity, yet poor posture in repose. Nagging the adolescent about his posture may increase his self-consciousness and may even intensify his problem.

Illnesses and disease.   The early adolescent is relatively free from acute illnesses and communicable diseases when compared with his younger brothers and sisters. Many minor illnesses still occur, however. Some of these have an emotional basis. They may be aggravated by too little rest or by poor nutrition. Interest in disease is not great.

Accidents and injuries.   A startling increase in accident rates, especially among boys, occurs in this period. Fatal accidents lead all causes of death, as in earlier years.

Emotional adjustments.   Biological changes that take place during this period may cause considerable emotional concern. Emotional tensions are common, especially among those who mature early or late. Tensions may be manifested by overaggression, withdrawal from the group, illness, menstrual disorders, or too much interest in self. Personal appearance grows in importance. There may be great concern over problems of grooming and of skin conditions, such as acne (pimples). The young adolescent needs adult understanding, and a recognition of his own personal worth. There is need, too, for identification with significant group efforts.

Sex adjustments.   The onset of puberty presents many new experiences to the young adolescent. Among girls, menstruation starts at this time. At first the periods may be irregular, but when once established, they interfere little with normal life. Numerous secondary sex characteristics appear (development of breasts, pubic hair, and so forth). Puberty may start with boys during the latter part of the period, or it may be delayed until later. Sex organs develop, and secondary sex characteristics such as changes in voice and development of hair on face occur. Acne is a common condition at this time. Even when the adolescent is prepared for the changes, he may be greatly worried about them. Interest in the other sex increases during the latter part of this period, but it is usually revealed by clumsy displays of affection rather than by mature responses. Some 12- and 13-year-olds start going steady. Pregnancies occur.

Interests and Adjustments in Respect to Home, School, and Community Living (see also Chapter 3)

Home.   The adolescent has a natural desire to emancipate himself from his parents, though he is usually tied to them economically. He begins to demand adult status in the family. Parents need to help the adolescent gain a sense of dignity and respect for his status as a man or woman. The majority of families can do this with relative success when both parents and children gain an insight into needs. In homes with poor ethical standards, reaching adult status may mean quite another thing, however, Too often parents will condone physical aggression, premarital sexual relations, use of liquor, stealing, and other types of behavior that they themselves have followed.

School.   The seventh grader is likely to be interested in all types of activities. He likes to experiment, to explore, and to delve into the meanings of things. By the eighth and ninth grade he may become very much absorbed in himself and in his relations with others, with the result that, without proper help with his personal adjustments, school work may lag. Gaining status with peers is more important to him than adult approval.

The well-adjusted adolescent throws himself enthusiastically into group undertakings with his fellow students. The poorly adjusted one is likely to withdraw. In general, the adolescent grows in his ability to form judgments on both personal and social problems and to establish values of his own in respect to himself, his family, and society. He develops greater ability to deal with abstractions and ethical questions, though he seems unable to concentrate long on any one thing.

Community.   The young person at this level often identifies himself with some out-of-school club or organization, such as the Scouts, Camp Fire Girls, and 4-H Club. The activities of this group absorb much of his attention. Children for whom such groups are not always available are likely to form their own gangs or cliques.

Some cliques may act defiantly toward generally acceptable adult standards of behavior, though they can be led into acceptable directions under proper guidance.

There is interest in the more colorful aspects of living—dramatic episodes of the past and the present. Toward the end of this period there is a dawning recognition and acceptance of the cultural patterns set by adults.

Suggestions for Health Teaching Emphasis in Junior High School

Generalizations for this period are difficult to make because of differences in the students themselves and also in the curricula. There is little question, however, that the junior high school years are critical ones from the standpoint of the student's personal adjustments. Health teaching, it would appear, may suitably stress individual responsibilities for physical and emotional fitness and should deal with such problems as diet control, healthful exercise, care of skin, grooming, adequate sleep and rest, and an understanding of the changes associated with puberty. Special attention should be given to accident prevention. Boy-girl relationships should receive emphasis. One appeal likely to succeed with the girls, and during the latter part of the period with most boys, is that of personal appearance. The boys, and to a lesser extent the girls, may be led to see the values of fitness in great adventures, such as in aviation, explorations, and athletic prowess. Scientific experiments and investigations have an appeal and should be fostered.

In teaching for greater responsibility in family health, the teacher may utilize the young adolescent's desire to become accepted as an adult member of the family. Emerging interest in the selection of a vocation may provide opportunity for elementary instruction about the various health professions and about the health requirements for different occupations.

Inherent interest in community health apparently does not run high among most students of this age. There is, nevertheless, a need for keeping alive and developing further what interest there is, especially since many students leave school at the end of junior high school. Perhaps one answer here is to encourage participation in community affairs through various group activities.

Schools should make serious attempts to correlate health teaching in the classroom with the community projects now undertaken by such organizations as the 4-H Club, Red Cross Youth, Future Farmers of America, Future Homemakers of America, Girl and Boy Scouts, Camp Fire Girls, and the like (see Chapter 12). The school may also make provision for community projects as a part of its curriculum. Moreover, many of the concepts developed in social studies, science, and language arts should help in the development of interest in community needs.

A broad objective in the curriculum of the junior high school years is that of orienting the young person to his position in the local, state, national, and world community. Health teaching should contribute at every possible point to this orientation.

Suggested learning experiences for this age level are given in the following pages. Additional activities adaptable to this age level are described under senior high schools.

The activities presented here are by no means an outline for a health course; rather they are illustrative of what schools are doing or could do around common problems of the young adolescent. Each teacher will wish to develop learning experiences in cooperation with the students and in terms of local needs.

Scheduling for Health Teaching in
Junior High School

In secondary schools, as in the elementary, time must be allowed for direct health instruction. The adolescent's problems are many and complex. Students at this age have reached a degree of maturity at which they have a right to expect teaching which has sufficient depth to challenge their intellects and sufficient scope to help them meet their many needs. A regularly scheduled health and safety course is essential to realize these expectations.

Many national committees have recommended that a minimum of one semester of direct health and safety instruction be provided in the junior high school. The most frequent recommendations are for daily class periods for one or two semesters. The block plan is used in some systems, with units in direct health and safety instruction alternating with units in physical education. Under this plan, blocks of two or three weeks are recommended—long enough to complete satisfactorily one or more units of study. Least to be desired is the all-too-common practice of having two or three class periods a week alternating with physical education. This arrangement does not allow for unified experience on the part of the students. Then, too, it is difficult to sustain interest in an extended project when the group meets at infrequent intervals. Moreover, some teachers feel that students have little respect for a subject that is given such a minor and unfavorable place in the curriculum. Though some schools find consecutive time harder to schedule, those which place high value on health somehow succeed in overcoming the difficulties.

In addition to direct health and safety instruction, there should be planned instruction through the social studies, science, language arts, home economics, physical education, and other areas in which such instruction can be given naturally.

Suggested Learning Experiences

Improving One's Health

Personal health inventories.   These inventories are popular with adolescents and help to arouse interest in health improvement. Students may use a readymade inventory or develop their own in consultation with teachers and health personnel.

If inventories are used with discretion, they may lead to many worthwhile health education activities. They often reveal needs that should be checked further with the nurse, physician, or guidance counselor. Inventories stimulate questions that could form the basis for much health teaching. They provide facts for evaluation. But most important of all, they may help to arouse students' curiosity about health and put them in the mood for solid health instruction. Pupil health inventories should never be used as substitutes for keen teacher observation, or in place of a health examination; neither should they be used with any thought of diagnosis. If inventory findings are shared, names should be omitted to avoid embarrassment and to prevent false statements.

Time well spent. Each boy or girl may keep a record of how he spends his time over a period of several days and then analyze the record to determine which activities might help or interfere with his best physical and emotional growth. Pupils may also prepare a set of slides or a filmstrip on the subject of a well-balanced day for a junior high school boy or girl.

Comfortable feet. Good foot health may be encouraged by a study of such topics as the relationship of foot disorders to fatigue, poor posture, backaches, and other pains; the effect of ill-fitting shoes on the feet; well-fitting *and* attractive shoes; selection of appropriate shoes for the occasion; and foot cleanliness and care, including "athlete's foot" and how to control it. Students may study models, charts, and pictures to learn the structure of the foot; they may also observe demonstrations of foot exercises and displays of desirable and undesirable types of shoes.

Eye conservation. After a review of information already acquired on eyes and vision, students in Montana are encouraged to extend their understanding of this subject by such activities as:

1. Survey school environment and practices to determine safety hazards to eyes in shops, gymnasium, art room, kitchen, sewing room, laboratory, and playground. Discuss with class and make appropriate recommendations for correction.

2. Measure lighting in library, halls, and stairways to determine adequacy. Report to class, decide on necessary action, and follow through to see if corrections can be made.

3. Visit the offices of specialists in care of services to the eyes (ophthalmologist, optician, optometrist) to gain understanding about vocation or career opportunities and information about tests, methods of examination, types of lenses, and so forth.

4. Send for information on sight conservation and services for the blind in Montana. Prepare a report for the class.

5. Get information about the Montana School for the Deaf and Blind at Great Falls. Prepare a report for class on eligibility, services, training, and so forth, and compare what is done in your own school district or county to help visually handicapped children. Compare reports with others. Are sufficient services available in your community?

6. Select a committee to get information from State Highway Patrol on night driving, head light glare and eye reaction to the amount of available light, and limited vision under different conditions—snow, rain, night, twilight hours, and so forth.

7. Find out how the public health nurse assists people in the community in the prevention of blindness and how she helps those who are blind.

8. Have members observe methods and habits for protection of eyes in class-rooms, library, shops, and science or chemical laboratories at school and report to class.[1]

Quiz the experts. As a change from approaches frequently used in a discussion of personal health problems, the class might formulate its questions for response by a panel of "experts" con-sisting of the school nurse, a physician, and other specialists selected in line with class interests. The questions could be prepared in ad-vance and presented to the "experts" by spokesmen for the class—or some other scheme could be worked out by the class itself. As a modification of this technique, the class could direct questions to committees formed within the group which would then investigate the answers. For example, committees might deal with weight con-trol, diet fads, exercise, personal grooming, smoking and health, health of astronauts, and other subjects selected by the students.

Weight control. Though pupils with serious weight problems will need individual counseling and medical guidance, the follow-ing group activities may be helpful in placing weight control prob-lems in proper perspective:

Discuss some of the handicaps of being overweight and underweight during junior high school years.

List and discuss foods, and an activity and rest schedule which may help under-weight individuals to gain weight.

Calculate the caloric needs of a volunteer underweight student. Compare this with his caloric intake over a week's time.

Calculate the caloric needs of a volunteer overweight student. Compare this with his caloric intake over a week's time.

List and discuss ways in which overweight people might reduce their caloric intake. Emphasize medical assistance for any weight reduction plan other than the general reduction of caloric intake.[2]

Candid camera shots. Colored slides or motion pictures may be taken of class members in different sitting, standing, or action positions to help them analyze and correct postural difficulties. Photographs in newspapers and magazines could be studied, not only for what they show about posture but also about other per-sonal health and safety practices.

Preparing for the job. With the help of guidance counselors and health teachers, students may investigate the health require-ments of jobs which interest them. To gather information they may interview personnel directors or the employees themselves, as well as read about the requirements. These analyses will help to give meaning to many health principles.

---

[1] Guide for the Montana School Health Program. 2nd Ed. Helena, Montana, The Montana State Board of Health, 1961, pp. 415–416.

[2] Adapted from Junior High School Health Guide; Unit IV—Nutrition. Salt Lake City, Utah, Utah State Department of Public Instruction, 1964, p. 10.

Figure 22. Health protection of astronauts can be a subject for study. (Courtesy of the National Aeronautics and Space Administration, Washington, D.C.)

Smoking and Health

Since resource units and other teaching materials on this subject are now readily available from state departments of health and education, and from several of the voluntary agencies, the learning experiences suggested here are limited to a few which have been selected from a number of sources. Many young people start smoking in their early teens; these, then, are critical years for carrying on an educational program which is directed toward keeping them from developing the habit.

Health aspects of smoking

1. Students may form committees to study research and reports on the relationship of cigarette smoking to the following diseases and conditions: cancer of the lungs; coronary artery disease and other heart diseases; circulatory diseases; pulmonary diseases (other than lung cancer), especially chronic bronchitis and emphysema; ulcers; allergy and asthma.

2. Discuss the principal findings of the Advisory Committee to the Surgeon General of the Public Health Service in their report of January 1964.

3. Set up a microscope and show slides that are made with tissue taken from the lungs of cigarette smokers, non-smokers, and ex-smokers. The slides may be borrowed from a pathologist in a nearby hospital.

How do parents feel about smoking?   Selected students may ask their parents the following questions and use the replies as a basis for class discussion:

Smokers: Why do you smoke? How did you feel the first time you smoked? Would you really like to stop?
Non-smokers: What are your reasons for not smoking? Did you ever smoke? If you did smoke, how did you stop?

In the discussion period, students might profit by examining a leaflet of the American Heart Association on "What to Tell Your Parents about Smoking," and consider whether or not they feel they could use it with their own parents—and if so, how?

Gaining insights through role-playing and dramatizations. Here are situations which if acted out may help students to identify more closely with the smoking problem than they could by discussion only:

1. A 14-year-old student tells his parents (who both smoke cigarettes) and his uncle (who smokes a pipe) that they should try to stop smoking.

2. A group urges a non-smoker to join them for a smoke.

3. A family scene in which a son announces that he has begun smoking.

4. A reporter interviews the following people regarding their concern for smoking and health: (a) a tobacco grower, (b) an advertising director of a local television station, (c) a physician, (d) an athletic coach, (e) a person trying to stop smoking.

5. A parent finds cigarettes in his son's room.

6. A boy and girl on a date—the girl is attempting to dissuade the boy from smoking.

The high costs of smoking.   Students can compute the amount of money spent in a year by a cigarette smoker who smokes a pack a day, and by one who smokes two packs a day. They might then figure how much could be saved over a 25-year period if the smokers quit smoking and placed the money spent on cigarettes in savings.

They might also collect data on the cost of advertising cigarettes and estimate the economic and human loss from fires caused by careless smokers.

Understanding Oneself and Others— Emotional Health

During these worrisome years, individual counseling will often be necessary to help with the many problems of personal adjustment. In addition, qualified teachers may give group guidance through classroom work and homeroom activities. Many excellent books, films, and recordings are now available for student as well as teacher use. Problem situations presented in these materials provide good foundations for discussion.

Growing up emotionally.   Class activities coordinated with a television program helped Columbus, Ohio, students in the eighth grade to understand better their own emotional needs and reactions. They discussed such subjects as childish reactions; ways in which your emotions can help you; ways in which your emotions can harm you; ways of handling upset emotions (e.g., anger, fear, worry); how you can tell whether you are really growing up emotionally; local groups which can help you achieve good mental health. They viewed films, wrote reports, and held interviews.[3]

The new arrivals.   In one community, teachers and pupils worked out a series of role-playing situations. Several of the groups chose the "new pupil in the classroom," and others, the "new teacher in the classroom." These and other skits helped to convert a difficult situation into one in which there was much greater concern within the groups for the welfare of each member. Teachers also stated that the pupils were beginning to see them as real persons.

Looking at ourselves and others.   The following activities are suggestive of those which may be used to help pupils to understand themselves better and to develop satisfying interpersonal relationships.

1. Set up volunteer groups to work during one to three class periods to portray a certain situation and some possible solutions, e.g.,

---

[3] Growing Up Mentally and Emotionally. Unit IX for Grade 8. Columbus, Ohio, Columbus Public Schools, 1961. Committee Contributors: Carroll J. Smith and Ralph Van Atta.

A fellow student is seen stealing in the locker room.
A new boy or girl enters school and appears quiet and withdrawn.
A classmate is constantly being rude and interrupting the class.
Friends are gossiping about another student.

2. List and discuss ways in which self-confidence can be developed, e.g.,
Being dependable
Wearing appropriate clothes
Doing one's best
Being respectful to others
Having integrity
Finding out what one does well

3. Ask each pupil to write what he wishes to accomplish in life and to identify his strengths and weaknesses in terms of achieving this goal.

4 Formulate and discuss definitions of success in work, play, home life and friendship.

5. Note various success stories of people who have overcome great odds, e.g., Abraham Lincoln and Booker T. Washington overcame financial problems and became self-educated; Franklin D. Roosevelt, Helen Keller, Roy Campanella, Sammy Davis, Jr., and Henry Viscardi all overcame physical handicaps.

6. Discuss basic emotional needs such as love, acceptance, belonging, security, control, consistency, sense of worth. Interpret the behavior of boys and girls according to the extent to which one or more of these needs may have been met.

7. Encourage each student to keep a personal record of dates, events and behavior. Analyze improvements and areas in which progress has been made.

8. Hold a discussion on how some students have felt concerning rapid or slow growth and ways in which they may overcome this feeling.

9. Discuss how world problems could be eased through respect and understanding of the similarities and differences of others, e.g., religion, customs, financial status and laws. Correlate with English and/or foreign language departments in writing to foreign students regarding these factors.

10. Suggest that students discuss the behavior of teenagers with adults.

11. Hold panel discussions on the various problems and rewards of being with younger children, with adults and the aged.

12. Utilize role-playing: Your best friend invited the person you wanted to take to a dance.—or—You are asked to become a member of a club outside school and your best friend is not.[4]

Preparing for Family Life

Home economics classes may deal thoroughly with this subject, but it is of such great importance that health classes and other subject-matter areas taken by more students should also include appropriate learning experiences.

Biological bases of family life. Anatomy and physiology of human reproduction, prenatal growth and development, and heredity are among subjects which fit suitably into biology or health classes and provide foundations for understanding family responsibilities. There are numerous films on these subjects which can pro-

---

[4] Curriculum Guide for Health and Safety; Part 2, The Middle Years (7–9). Roslyn, New York, Nassau Tuberculosis and Health Association, Inc., 1966, pp. 1–2. (Prepared by a Curriculum Steering Committee which was sponsored by the Nassau County School Health Council.)

vide background for class discussion. This instruction is of such importance that it should be placed in courses taken by the majority of students.[5]

Boy-girl relationships. This subject may be taught in a unit on family life or as a part of a unit on interpersonal relationships. The following suggestions are taken from a guide prepared for use in the ninth grade of Roseville, Minnesota, public schools.

Questions: How do boys and girls react to each other at age 4? 11? 14? 17?
    Is there more trouble at home between brother/sister, sister/sister, brother/brother?
    What are some situations or places where boys and girls are voluntarily or involuntarily caused to associate or speak with each other?
Role-play situation: A young teen-age girl wanting to date but whose mother feels she is too young.
Encourage understanding of individual differences in the development of sex interests and an awareness of the factors that influence one's interest in the opposite sex. How much influence is exerted by physical maturity? parents? your peers?
Ask students to give some of the values in conforming to peer pressure and some of the problems that may result from conformity. List the positive and negative factors in two columns on the blackboard.[6]

Baby-sitting. Classes in baby-sitting are becoming increasingly popular among junior high school pupils who often help care for children. One school incorporated such a course in its seventh grade English and social science classes or in the junior high school core curriculum. The group heard talks by mothers; visited the kindergarten and participated in care of kindergarten children; observed simple first-aid measures; visited homes to watch mothers bathe and feed children; discussed grooming, ethics, and proper action in emergencies. The girls wrote two short plays and presented them to the public to demonstrate knowledge gained in class.

Some schools carry out projects in which students systematically care for young children in their homes or neighborhoods. They keep records of the children's routines and plan a healthful regimen for the children, all the while receiving basic class instruction on child care and family life problems. In projects of this type the public health nurse should be of invaluable assistance.

Accident prevention, handling of emergencies, symptoms of illness, amusing children of different ages indoors and outdoors, feeding children, putting them to bed, and health habits in general were topics included in a course in baby-sitting at Cobourg and

---

[5] For further background, see Lerrigo, M. O., and Southard, H.: Sex Education Series: (3) Finding Yourself; (5) Facts Aren't Enough. Prepared for the Joint Committee on Health Problems in Education of the National Education Association and the American Medical Association. Washington, D.C., and Chicago, The Associations. Latest edition.

[6] Adapted from Family Life Education. A Teaching Guide; Grades Nine and Ten. Roseville, Minnesota, Roseville Schools, 1966, pp. 33–45.

Port Hope, Canada. This course, in which school personnel co-operated, was offered by the local tuberculosis association, Girl Guides, and other groups.[7]

Similar content is often included in health courses or courses in family living.

Sex education via instructional television.   Seventh and eighth graders in the St. Louis, Missouri, schools receive instruction in this subject by means of open-circuit television. Lesson plans placed in the hands of teachers in advance of the broadcast add to the value of the instruction. The lessons are 30 minutes in length with 5 to 10 minutes pretelecast time for class preparation and 15 to 20 minutes follow-up time for discussion. Though changes are made from year to year, the 1965–66 series for the eighth grade is typical of the usual plan. During that year there was one lesson for the girls and another for the boys on male and female reproductive systems, a lesson on prenatal development and birth of a baby, two lessons on venereal disease, and one on sex and social life. A full-time studio teacher, aided by other teachers and members of the community, assists with the planning and conduct of these lessons.[8]

Socio-cultural characteristics of the family.   With schools placing increased emphasis on how people in different cultures live, it would be appropriate for junior high school students to study how families differ in dealing with health problems and family relationships. For example, they might consider what influence the following family structures may have on decision-making on matters of health: the one-parent family; the family in which the mother works; the family with several children; the extended family in which several generations live under one roof or very close together. They may discuss ways in which they themselves can contribute to improved family living.[9]

Home care of the sick.   A unit on this subject is most timely at the junior high school level. A school may develop its own unit or use Red Cross material.

Accident Prevention

Safety surveys.   Surveys of home, school, and community accidents and hazards continue to interest young people. These surveys can be particularly valuable if they form the bases for preventive

---

[7] Health course for baby sitters. Canadian Tuberculosis Association Bulletin, *39:*4 (March) 1961.

[8] For details see Cox, H. M.: Sex education via instructional television. Journal of Health–Physical Education–Recreation, *37:*71 (April) 1966.

[9] For additional suggestions on this and related subjects see Growth patterns and sex education; a suggested program—kindergarten through grade 12. Journal of School Health, *37* No. 52 (May) 1967. (Special issue.)

and corrective measures. Included should be an analysis of available data on accidental injuries and deaths, with special attention given to data for the age group the pupils are in.

Power mowers can be dangerous. Students may collect evidence of accidents which have occurred in their neighborhoods from careless use of power mowers. They may then develop a set of rules as guides in the safe handling of the mowers.

In fields and woods. Hikes and other outdoor activity which take young people to field and woods can be more enjoyable if precautions are taken against poisonous or injurious plants and potentially dangerous insects and snakes. Students can profitably study those forms of plant and animal life in their own locality which may cause harm. The study should include identification of the plants or animals, dangers of each, precautions to take against the dangers, and first-aid treatment which may be applied if necessary. Pertinent information can be obtained from state and local health departments and from cooperative extension services at state universities.

Driver education. In some school systems driver education is introduced at the ninth grade level. Many states now provide guides to such instruction.

Seat belt campaigns. Young people can investigate the benefits of using seat belts in automobiles and can take part in community efforts to promote installation of seat belts.

Safe handling of boats. With the growing popularity of outboard motor boats, there is great need for young people to learn how to handle boats safely. Eighth graders in Norfolk, Virginia, study:

1. Boat handling and seamanship, including, for example,
   a. Proper way of entering boat
   b. Proper way to apply motor
   c. Boat capacity
2. Rules of the road, boating customs and etiquette, for example,
   a. Nautical rules
   b. Fundamental rules of the road
   c. Assisting in emergencies
3. Care of boat, motor and equipment
4. The weather and what to do about it; what to do if caught in a storm
5. The fun of boating, water skiing, cruising[10]

Contributing to Community Health

School surveys. Community health study may begin with the school community. Numerous state departments of health or education now publish check lists suitable for student use. Students

---

[10] Building Healthier Youth. Norfolk, Virginia, Norfolk City Public Schools, 1961, pp. 103–104.

may also construct their own lists with the help of health personnel. It is important to work toward improvement of conditions found through such surveys. Students should provide space on the lists to record progress toward the attainment of goals.

Young citizens in action. A classic example of pupil participation in community health betterment was reported some years ago from Petersburg, West Virginia. Pupils conducted an extensive community health survey through 13 committees set up for the purpose. Each committee explored one particular phase of community health in four consecutive steps: they carried on an investigation and recorded all facts, they made recommendations for the improvement of the phase studied, they informed the public of the findings and recommendations, and they took part in action needed for improvements. In order to prepare the parents and community for this project, letters giving full explanation were sent to the homes and to key adults in the community. The project started with the eighth grade, but before long it included the whole school. As an example of the activities that were undertaken, the seventh grade group, which was studying food handling, took a three-week course on the subject given by the State Health Department. They made field trips to study food handling practices in restaurants and grocery stores, and also observed the practices in their own school lunchroom and homes.

Working for an antipollution bill. Seventh graders in Watertown, Minnesota, concerned about water pollution on the Minnesota and Mississippi rivers, enlisted the aid of other seventh graders of Minnesota schools in getting an antipollution bill passed in the legislature. They mailed 450 letters to other seventh graders urging them to write to their congressmen, the Governor, and others who could help. The news media featured this project. According to the teacher, Mr. Joseph Diethelm, "the class received a dramatic response from these other schools. The antipollution bill was passed and I really believe that we had a significant part in its passage. As a consequence, the campaign served as a good lesson in practical democracy."[11]

A water pollution survey. The ninth grade general science class of Elbert S. Long Junior High School, Chattanooga, Tennessee, conducted a study of water pollution and its abatement in South Chickamauga Creek. Their plan could be copied, with modifications, by pupils in other areas troubled with this problem that is causing increasing concern throughout the country. According to Mr. John W. Schaerer, the instructor, the pupils had become aware of the many uses of surface water and were disturbed by the de-

---

[11] Reported by Mr. Joseph Diethelm, science teacher, Public Schools, Watertown, Minnesota, 1967.

Figure 23. Students engaged in analytical procedures to determine water quality. (Courtesy of the Tennessee Game and Fish Commission.)

plorable conditions of the creek. This concern led to a project which was conducted in three phases, as follows.

Phase I: Organizing trip and collecting samples. The group selected a chairman who then made assignments of pupils to different tasks according to their interests. Background information material from the Tennessee Department of Health was secured and studied. The Tennessee Game and Fish Commission supplied slides, while local professional personnel and news media proved to be invaluable sources of information.

The pupils assembled equipment needed for collecting samples, including boats, buckets, sample containers, and other materials. The publication, *Standard Methods for the Examination of Water and Wastewater,* of the American Public Health Association, served as a guideline for procedures in taking and analyzing the samples. After careful preparation, the water samples were taken at different points along the creek.

Phase II: Determining nature of water samples by analytical processes. Various analyses were made, including those for hydrogen-ion concentration, alkalinity, turbidity, color, and odor. Comparisons were made with surveys conducted by the Tennessee State Pollution Control Board.

Phase III: Assimilating and disseminating data. At this point the pupils consolidated the findings of several subgroups which had worked on the different aspects of the study and made their interpretations. They prepared graphs and otherwise summarized the findings of the study.

As a concluding activity, they presented the findings at a meeting of the Stream Pollution Control Division of the State Department of Public Health. Local newspapers and television stations became interested in the project and publicized it through their media.[12]

Becoming informed on sanitation problems.   One state guide suggests the following activities as appropriate for junior high school pupils:

Have sanitary engineer discuss local sanitation problems.

Investigate methods used in your school, community, and home to dispose of trash, dead animals, and garbage.

Organize a "litterbug" campaign. Secure assistance of newspapers and radio.

If no refuse receptacles are used in your community, try to interest a service club or women's group in providing them. If receptacles are available, have class help in their maintenance.

Send committee to talk to mayor about sanitation problems; visit city engineer to discuss local ordinances related to sanitation.

Have representative of local recreation department talk about problems of safe swimming water.

Have committee of pupils visit person in charge of plant for purification of water. Discuss procedure for providing adequate water supply.

Study milk-borne diseases.

Examine under microscope milk that has been properly kept, milk that is contaminated.[13]

---

[12] Summarized from an unpublished report of the project by Mr. John W. Schaerer, Elbert S. Long Junior High School, Hamilton County, Chattanooga, Tennessee, 1967.

[13] Excerpts from A Guide for Health Education in Indiana Schools, Bulletin No. 219. Indianapolis, Indiana, State Department of Public Instruction, 1956, pp. 173–175.

Refrigerated foods. Students may perform the following class experiment to determine temperature differences between foods stored in large and in small containers. Prepare white sauce or a soft paste made from cooked cornstarch to resemble such foods as potato salad, cooked rice, or meat loaf mixture. Fill (a) a four-quart container and (b) a one-quart container with this mixture. Then, with a food thermometer, take the temperature of the center of the "food" mass in each container. Next, refrigerate both containers on the same refrigerator shelf for four or five hours, or the approximate time which usually intervenes between preparing and serving a quantity of food. Remove containers and again take the temperature of the center of the "food" mass in each container. If the experiment is properly carried out, the students will find that very little temperature change will have occurred in the mixture stored in the larger container. They may carry the experiment still further, using containers of different sizes to determine the point at which a container is too large to cool the "food" adequately for safe consumption. This experiment may then lead to a discussion of safe handling of foods at home and in public eating places.

Our city a healthy city. Why? An extensive study of the contributions of citizens, local health department, and voluntary agencies to the health of Columbus, Ohio, is recommended in a unit for eighth grade pupils. Among topics suggested for discussion or reports are:

1. The lag between the discovery of useful health information and its practical application.
2. In what way does the Columbus Board of Health supervise our schools?
3. A check on sanitary conditions within schools, for example, in kitchen and cafeteria.
4. How a pollen count is made. Consult newspapers during peak season for pollen count.
5. What does the Columbus Health Department do for you and your family?
6. What services now available in the Columbus Department of Health were demonstrated and proved valuable by *unofficial* health agencies?
7. How does the recent trend in bulk handling of milk help to make our milk supply safer?
8. The difference between the Columbus Department of Health and the Ohio Department of Health. How does the Ohio Department of Health use funds to make Columbus a healthier city?
9. How can you help make Columbus a healthier city?
10. Who are the personalities associated with our State and Federal Health Departments? e.g., Secretary of Health, Education and Welfare.[14]

---

14 Columbus, A Healthy City. Unit XIV for Grade 8. Columbus, Ohio, Columbus Public Schools, 1961. Committee Contributors: Frances Louise Dicks, Joan McFarland, John Canfield, Allen Beamenderfer, and Mabel Groner.

Health Careers (see also, Health Careers,
Senior High School)

Charting careers in health science.   In an eighth grade class in Columbus, Ohio, a unit on "Careers in Health Science" has as its objectives: (1) to present to the pupils an overview of the health science vocational field; (2) to make pupils aware of the qualifications and preparations for many careers; and (3) to teach teen-agers techniques for exploring sources of vocational information. To pursue these objectives, the pupils work in committees according to the vocation they have selected. If some pupils choose a career in a field other than health science, they are permitted to pursue it. Students give reports as panel discussions, plays, individually, or in other similar ways, based on a series of questions relating to choice of a career. The unit recommends that only one committee in any class choose and report on any one career. Obviously, only a few careers will be covered, but it is hoped that the pupils understand that the technique for investigation will be the same for all and that they learn how to locate sources of information.

Students may easily prepare their own chart on health careers, using for its basis the following questions:

1. What are some vocations in the health science field? (dental hygienist, dentist, medical technologist, nurse, etc.)
2. What do these people do?
3. What abilities and skills are needed for these careers?
4. What preparation is necessary for these careers?
5. What yearly salaries are paid?
6. What are some advantages (disadvantages) of these careers?
7. From what sources can we obtain further information?[15]

Health Teaching through Subject-Matter Areas

Examples of health problems that may become an integral part of the teaching of certain subject-matter areas are outlined here.

Social studies
1. How can one get along with oneself and with others?
2. How do natural environments in different parts of this country and in the world affect the health of people?
3. How have people lived during different periods in the development of this country, and what are the resultant effects on health?
4. What health assets and liabilities has the industrial revolution brought, such as from the standpoint of physical health, nutrition, housing, and family adjustments?
5. What occupations are there in the fields of public health and medicine, and what preparation is needed for them?

---

[15] Careers in Health Science. Unit X for Grade 8. Columbus, Ohio, Columbus Public Schools, 1961. Committee Contributors: Molly Pugh, Harold Nelson, and Joseph Kelly.

6. What special contributions did certain prominent people make to health during the development of the country? In world history?

Science

1. Where does our community get its water for drinking? What treatment does it undergo before it is safe for consumption?
2. How do plants and animals contribute to human welfare and health? How do they endanger it?
3. What are the common poisonous plants or animals in the neighborhood? How should we protect ourselves from them?
4. What changes have taken place in modes of living, especially from the standpoint of health and safety, since the use of electricity has become widespread?
5. What is the effect of sunlight on the human body and on health?
6. What is the effect of weather on health and efficiency?
7. How does an audiometer work?
8. How must we as human beings adjust to our environment and adjust the environment to us in order that we can live healthfully?

Language arts (writing, literature, and the like)

1. Read books on great medical discoveries, and biographies or autobiographies of physicians, nurses, and other leaders in public health and medicine.
2. Participate in school club activities and, when the need arises, present health problems to the group for solution. Develop skill in discussing these problems with club members.
3. Prepare reports and give informal talks on such health subjects as the following: what I would do if someone I was with became injured in an accident; what we did on a camping trip to guard our health and safety; how to feel at ease at a girl-boy party; how college athletes train for the football season.

Physical education

1. How can physical activity contribute to health and to physical and emotional well-being?
2. What are the values of outdoor activities?
3. What should one know about pulse, breathlessness, perspiration, and muscle cramps?
4. Is there such a thing as athlete's heart?
5. What sanitary and safety practices should be observed in use of swimming pool, athletic equipment, or on the playing field?
6. What precautions should be taken to prevent the spread of athlete's foot?
7. What is meant by physical fitness?

Home economics

1. What foods can be packed in a lunch box?
2. What do we need to know about reading labels on foods, household chemicals, drugs, and the like?
3. How can less accepted foods be prepared and served so they are acceptable?
4. How should frozen foods be prepared, stored, and handled after defrosting?
5. When should children be immunized?
6. What should one feed a sick person?
7. What recreational activities can families enjoy together at little cost?

Agriculture
1. Why should one wash before milking?
2. What safety precautions should be taken in the handling of farm animals? In the use of farm tools and machinery?
3. What are the scientific reasons behind the various health regulations established for dairy farms, creameries, and the like?
4. How may insecticides and chemicals be used in ways that will prevent food contamination?
5. In what ways are nutrient needs of man similar to nutrient needs of animals?

GUIDES TO HEALTH TEACHING IN SENIOR HIGH SCHOOLS, GRADES 9 TO 12 (Ages 14 to 18)

Factors That Will Help Determine What to Teach and How to Teach It

Health Needs, Interests, and Beliefs Related to the Growth Pattern (see also Chapter 2)

Growth in height and weight. During the early part of this period, growth in many students may continue at a rapid rate. Growth rates differ greatly, however, between early and late maturers. By the age of 16, growth rates will have leveled off in the majority of cases. Students continue to be concerned about their stature and weight.

Eating. Caloric requirements remain high. Food excesses, on the one hand, and "picky" appetites, on the other, continue to present problems.

Elimination. Any difficulties with elimination may be attributed largely to faulty eating habits, irregular daily regimens, and emotional strains.

Exercise and play interests. There is an increased interest in highly skilled sports, both group and individual, and greater confidence in ability to participate. Interests vary greatly at this age, however. For those for whom the more strenuous types of activity have little appeal, there should be provided lighter activities, several individual and dual sports and various forms of dances.

Sleep and rest. Many adolescents in this group will still need nine or more hours of sleep.

Eyes and ears. Vision and hearing defects continue to increase. Students appear to have an interest in the proper care of their eyes.

Teeth. All permanent teeth are in except the third molars (wisdom teeth), which appear between the ages of 17 and 21 years. Regular dental care is important.

Posture.   Posture difficulties may continue, though they are perhaps less critical than during early adolescence.

Illnesses and disease.   Minor illnesses continue to prevail. Venereal diseases present a growing problem at this age level. Cancer (malignant neoplasms) is one of the major causes of death from disease. Many young people show increased interest in problems of disease prevention and control.

Accidents and injuries.   Accidents continue to lead all causes of deaths, with an increasing number of motor vehicle accidents and accidents from sports, including hunting. Young workers in out-of-school occupations, as, for example, in farm work, are prone to accidents and have an unusually high accident rate.

Emotional adjustments.   Emotional problems continue during this period of growing into adulthood. Each adolescent needs to feel his personal worth within his own group and his family. Psychoneurotic conditions increase at this age level. Delinquency becomes a special problem among the maladjusted. An increasing number of adolescents smoke and drink. They show great concern about their personal appearance and grooming. Acne, common at this level, may cause much distress.

Sex adjustments.   Some adolescent boys reach puberty with all the accompanying problems of adjustment during the early part of this period. (See ages 11 to 14 years). At this age most young people show intense interest in the other sex. By the latter part of this period, many young people are contemplating marriage and the establishment of a home and family, and want specific information to guide them. Some of them are having firsthand sex experiences, the implications of which they too often do not fully comprehend. Pregnancies occur. They want adult information on their own sex roles.

Interests and Adjustments in Respect to Home, School, and Community Living (see also Chapter 3)

Home.   The adolescent becomes increasingly ready to serve as an adult member of the family and needs to be given the chance for independent action. Many of the conflicts that arise between parents and the adolescent are due to the unwillingness of parents to allow the child to become an adult. The adolescent wants privacy and a chance to pursue his own interests. At the same time, he is willing to share in family responsibilities. Most girls are interested in homemaking and in the care of children.

School.   Throughout this period the adolescent is likely to be very much absorbed in his own personal relations, but by the latter part of the period he may also have considerable concern over the problems of the school, community, and society in general. He usually has wide intellectual interests, though they may not always be well directed. He is greatly influenced by what his fellow classmates think and do.

Community.   There is increased interest in community problems, and greater participation in community affairs. The adult types of recreational activities, such as social dancing and individual sports, are often preferred. Group activities as in clubs, sports, and the like, continue for many young people. Among boys, interest may run high in real adventure. The older adolescent often has a burning desire for social and economic reform. He may have an intense religious interest. Toward the end of the period he is thinking seriously about his future work and education.

Suggestions for Health Teaching Emphasis in Senior High School

The suggestions given for the junior high school are likely to apply equally well during the early part of this period. During the last two years of secondary school, the adolescent is approaching adult stature, and the problems that will concern him most are apt to be adult in character.

Problems of personal adjustment persist throughout the adolescent years. The following problems may need special emphasis: personal grooming for acceptance in the adult world and by the other sex; understanding of the biological bases of health; sex relations and preparation for marriage; use of stimulants and narcotics; and problems of family health adjustments. Among other subjects that may need special attention during these last years of school are accident prevention as it relates to work experiences, the driving of motor vehicles, the use of firearms, and outdoor recreation; consumer health; housing; vocational competence; and community health in general. The adolescent should be appealed to as an adult who is ready to assume responsibilities in an adult world. He should be given the satisfaction of firsthand experiences in the solution of real problems: he should have opportunity to approach health studies from a scientific point of view.

The problems listed suggest, in a general way, the content that would seem appropriate for senior high school health classes. Actually, however, each teacher should work out his own course materials in cooperation with the students, and in terms of the local situation.

In the following pages, teaching suggestions are given to aid the teacher in his planning. Additional suggestions are found earlier in the chapter under Junior High Schools.

Scheduling for Health Teaching in Senior High School

In senior high school, as in the junior high school, time must be allowed for direct health instruction. Such instruction should be of sufficient scope and depth to challenge the older student at his level of maturity. A regularly scheduled health and safety course is essential to accomplish this goal.

Many national committees have recommended that a minimum of one semester of direct health and safety instruction be provided in the senior high school, as in the junior high school. The most frequent recommendations are for daily class periods for one or two semesters. The block plan is used in some systems, with units in direct health and safety instruction alternating with units in physical education. Under this plan, blocks of six to nine weeks are recommended—long enough to complete satisfactorily one or more units of study. Least to be desired is the all-too-common practice of having two or three class periods a week alternating with physical education. It is difficult to sustain interest in an extended project when the group meets at infrequent intervals. Moreover, some teachers feel that students have little respect for a subject given such a minor and unfavorable place in the curriculum. Though some schools find consecutive time harder to schedule, those which place a high value on health instruction somehow succeed in overcoming the difficulties.

In addition to a health course at least once during the senior high school years, there should be planned health instruction through social studies, science, language arts, home economics, physical education, and other areas in the curriculum in which instruction can be given logically and effectively.

Suggested Learning Experiences

Biological Bases of Health

If earlier health teaching has been consistently and thoroughly carried on, students by this time should have some basic understanding of the anatomy and physiology of the human body. Such knowledge, however, should be further expanded so that a sound and rational basis for health behavior continues to be laid. Modern health and biology textbooks and guides contain material on the subject.[16] Science fairs dramatize the students' creative abilities to explore new worlds of knowledge about living organisms.

---

[16] See, for example, American Medical Association: The Wonderful Human Machine. Chicago, Illinois, The Association, 1961, 56 pp.

In teaching the subject, a functional approach should be used. Structure of organs and systems of the body should be related to physiology, and both should be related to the health, disease, and care of each area of the body. In this connection, students may give reports on advances and current trends in the biological sciences, medicine, and health, using the most up-to-date materials available. Charts, models, and teaching films can also be obtained.

Physical and Emotional Health

School newspapers urge better breakfasts. As part of a city-wide nutrition campaign among the young people in Memphis, Tennessee, student editors and faculty sponsors of all local high school newspapers were invited to attend a press breakfast given by the Dairy Council of Memphis. After posing the problem of the tendency of teen-agers to skip breakfast, or to eat an inadequate breakfast, the guests divided into buzz groups at separate tables. Ideas discussed were presented, recorded, and later mimeographed and sent to each editor. These journalists were also challenged at the press conference by an announcement that in the spring the Dairy Council would present a plaque, the "Nutrition News Award," to the high school paper doing the most effective job of putting nutrition in the news during the school year. Among the ideas the young journalists came up with were:

1. Use a roving reporter with a question about breakfast; a "Did You Know?" column giving facts about food and breakfast.
2. Check membership in honor societies against general student body to see if there is any correlation between grades and breakfast. Also, check keeping awake in class vs. breakfast habits.
3. Enlist help of home economics students and advisers for suggestions on do-it-yourself breakfasts to run in paper.
4. Have a student panel present story to a P.T.A. meeting to let parents realize breakfast is often boring.[17]

Youthpower projects. This program, sponsored by food processors and distributors, is designed to improve nutrition among teen-agers, to introduce them to career opportunities in food industries, and to foster leadership in this age group. The Minnesota program, for example, encourages interested young people, ages 15 to 19, to engage in nutrition and career projects with assistance from their teachers. The projects are submitted to the state office, and winners are invited to a state conference. Then selected individuals are sent to a National Food Congress. Among ideas suggested for projects are the following:

---

[17] Excerpts from Shoun, F.: High school papers campaign for breakfast. Nutrition News, *23*:7–8 (April) 1960.

1. Keep a record of the meals and snacks served your family for three days. Include foods eaten away from home. Analyze the meals using the Daily Food Guide (Four Food Groups). Note strong and weak points in the diet of your family. Then take charge of the family meal planning and food shopping for one week, making needed adjustments. Make another three-day study of your family's meals and snacks. Report your findings and any changes that have occurred as a result of your study.

2. Develop an appropriate survey form and have about 20 of your classmates report one of the following:

> Total intake of snacks for one day;
> Breakfast eaten that morning; or
> Lunch eaten that day. (Be sure to include yourself.)

Analyze the nutritional value of the snacks or meals using the Daily Food Guide (Four Food Groups). Report your findings. Make a poster or exhibit to help your classmates if you find they need to improve their food habits.

3. Teenage Food and Fun Party—Organize a party for 6 to 10 guests using highly nutritious foods. Use the Daily Food Guide (Four Food Groups) to help you select foods. Display these foods so that your guests learn that they have high food value. Report your plan, attendance, menu, and reactions of teenagers present. You could have a tasting party to acquaint your friends with teachers. Home Agent, or Food Company Home Economist will have helpful suggestions.[18]

Care of eyes. Suggestions given for junior high school pupils could be used also in the senior high school. In addition, the following learning activities might be developed:

1. Invite an ophthalmologist to the class to discuss visual problems and the conservation of vision throughout the adult years.
2. Diagram on the board and discuss the progressive consequences of glaucoma. Discuss the cause, cure, and detection of glaucoma.
3. Differentiate between the training and services of the ophthalmologist, the optometrist, and the optician.
4. Discuss contact lenses, their limitations, value, and cost compared to regular eyeglasses.
5. Discuss the emotional and psychological benefits of contact lenses to some people.[19]

Man in space. A study of the value placed in the space program on good nutrition and on general protection and care of the human body can add to an understanding of the importance of these health factors. Various publications of NASA (National Aeronautics and Space Administration) describe menus for space flights, microbiological analyses of space foods, measures to overcome circulatory problems resulting from "weightlessness," waste management, and other considerations related to living in space. Inquiries should be addressed to Educational Programs Division, Office of Public Affairs, NASA, Washington, D.C.

---

[18] Youthpower Teen Handbook. St. Paul, Minnesota, Youthpower of Minnesota, Inc., 1967, 4 pp.
[19] Adapted from Senior High School Health Guide; Unit V—Personal Health and Fitness. Salt Lake City, Utah, Utah State Department of Public Instruction, 1965, pp. 10–14.

Making personal adjustments. The following pupil activities are proposed by the Nassau County School Health Council:

1. Discuss the statement—"He has a wonderful personality." Relate the need to understand the popular misconception of the word "personality."
2. Divide the class into two separate groups. Have one group develop a listing of characteristics which they feel are admirable. The other group should develop a listing of characteristics which they feel are undesirable. Discuss methods to develop or redevelop these qualities.
3. Select a biography of a famous person. List the qualities of his personality and show how these qualities shaped his destiny.
4. Discuss family patterns of authority: the authoritative, the democratic and the laissez-faire. What are the advantages and/or disadvantages of each? How does family life affect one's personality development?
5. List the social graces which you would like to see practiced by all members of the class.
6. Have half the class bring in articles that give examples of reacting to an emotion in an intelligent manner, while the other half bring in articles showing undesirable emotional reactions. Compare and discuss.
7. Have each student analyze his or her strong and weak points. Discuss methods of strengthening weak points.
8. Ask the school psychologist to discuss behavioral problems of school children.
9. Discuss how emotions have a valuable influence on behavior.[20]

Emotional maturity. In a course on Problems in Living, eleventh graders in Uniondale Junior-Senior High School (New York) approached the study of mental and emotional health by considering such topics as emotional maturity, factors promoting mental health, anatomic and physiological background, and mental and emotional illness. Suggested methods for studying emotional maturity include:

1. Divide the class into committees of four or five students each. Have each committee prepare a written case history, with related discussion questions to illustrate emotional maturity or immaturity, or both, in teen-age boys and girls.
2. Have each committee present this case history to the class and discuss related questions. Examples of suitable topics are:
   a. How and how not to break the apron strings.
   b. Good and poor sportsmanship.
   c. Good behavior in traffic situations.
   d. The right and wrong way to handle stage-fright and shyness.
3. Use the following as discussion stimulants:
   a. Are your emotional responses inborn or learned?
   b. Are you glad or sorry you have emotions?
   c. What are some of the main differences between emotional maturity and immaturity?
   d. Do daydreams help you get what you want or keep you from getting it?
   e. What is the value of a good sense of humor?

---

[20] Curriculum Guide for Health and Safety; Part 3, The Senior Years (10–12). Roslyn, New York, Nassau Tuberculosis and Health Association, Inc., 1966, p. 8. (Prepared by a Curriculum Steering Committee which was sponsored by the Nassau County School Health Council.)

Figure 24. Learning good sportsmanship helps to develop emotional maturity. (Courtesy of University High School, University of Minnesota.)

    f. Why are emotions such as fear, hatred, and prejudice sometimes called the "destructive emotions"?

    g. Why are emotions such as love, affection, kindliness, and sympathy often called the "constructive emotions"?[21]

Preparing for Marriage and Family Life

As stated earlier, this instruction should be given first of all in the home and by the parents; however, schools need to supplement home teaching in a manner appropriate to the age level and the community. A point of view toward sex instruction has already been expressed in Chapter 2. Case studies, role-playing, motion pictures, and other presentations of family relationships may be the subject of discussion in health classes as well as in other classes. Attitude development is fully as important as the absorption of scientific data and should not be neglected in the different phases of school life.

A coeducational approach.   In Paynesville, Minnesota, family life education is taught to seniors as a required course in social studies. The community is included in the program. During one recent year, a citizens' committee planned and presented a public seminar for parents and a well-known speaker talked before a meeting of the general public.

In the course for seniors, parental responsibilities are stressed, with emphasis on sharing as equally as possible in the early care and rearing of children. A unit on preparation for marriage starts with a discussion of why people marry and deals with such topics as the contrast between shallow infatuation and the slower and deeper growth of love. The unit on dating, courtship, and engagement is covered in a frank but positive manner. Among other topics included in the course are divorce and the broken home, and the unwed mother, her rights and her responsibilities.[22]

The family.   In a study of the family, included within a unit on "Love, Courtship and Marriage" from Muscogee County, Columbus, Georgia, the following activities are among those suggested:

1. Write a theme on "What family life means to me."
2. Invite a panel of parents to discuss their concepts of successful family life.
3. Study the biographies of great men and women to learn about the homes in which they grew up.
4. Find out how community agencies can help families.
5. Watch the paper for accounts of 50th wedding aniversaries. Try to arrange an interview with one of these couples to find out what they consider to be essentials for a successful marriage.
6. Make a study of the initial cost of having a baby and bringing up a child.

---

[21] Reported by Terence McDonald, Health Teacher, Junior-Senior High School, Uniondale, New York, 1961.

[22] Southworth, H. H.: Senior high school course must highlight responsible actions. Minnesota Journal of Education, *47*:24–25 (Dec.) 1966.

7. Find out the cost of rent, food, utilities, etc., and work out a family budget for one month.

8. Write themes on "Why it is a privilege and a responsibility to be a parent"; and "Every child has a right to be well-born."

9. Make a list of changes in the daily life of a family if there were to be a new baby.

10. Discuss the pros and cons of a newly married couple living by themselves or with relatives.

11. Make a list of the factors that should be considered in deciding on the size of your family.

12. Invite a lawyer to explain the protection which law gives to members of the family from birth to death: Marriage and divorce laws; laws concerning contraception, abortion, unwed mothers, property rights; laws for the protection of children; legal responsibilities of the husband; legal responsibilities of the wife; laws concerning adoption; premarital blood law; prenatal blood law; and why make a will.[23]

Smoking and Health

For senior high school, as for junior high, resource units on this subject are available from state departments of education and various national agencies. The learning experiences outlined here supplement those presented under junior high school.

Getting into action. Among a wide range of activities suggested by the Oregon Interagency Committee on Smoking and Health are the following:

1. Invite a representative from the local cancer society to speak to the class about the relationship between cigarette smoking and lung cancer; from the local tuberculosis and health association, to speak about the effects of smoking on the respiratory system; and from the heart association, to talk about the effects of smoking on the circulatory system. (Students may prefer to arrange interviews with these individuals and make the reports themselves.)

2. Analyze cigarette advertisements clipped from magazines or taped from radio and television as to their accuracy and the techniques used to attract attention and get people to start smoking and/or use a particular brand.

3. Write a series of one-minute spot announcements on the deleterious effects of smoking that might be used by local radio stations.

4. Prepare one or two short letters to a junior high school or upper elementary school friend telling him about the coercion that he is about to be subjected to in regard to smoking, and also telling the best way to avoid being "taken in."

5. Students who have established the smoking habit and would like to quit may use themselves as subjects for experimentation on the effectiveness of ways to quit. Decide on the methods to employ and then have subjects keep a diary of what they do, what they feel, and how successful they are in quitting. Following this they may write an essay on why they succeeded or failed.

6. Request school board to take a stand against student smoking.[24]

---

23 Adapted from Love, Courtship and Marriage; Unit for Senior High School. Columbus, Georgia, Muscogee County Health Department, Health Education Service, 1966. For other suggestions see Growth patterns and sex education; a suggested program—kindergarten through grade 12. Journal of School Health, 37 No. 5a (May) 1967. (Special issue.)

24 Adapted from Smoking and Health. Salem, Oregon, Oregon Department of Education, 1967, pp. 16–19. (Prepared by the Oregon Interagency Committee on Smoking and Health.)

Will it work?   Students are currently being bombarded with information on smoking, often with little opportunity to say what they think may or may not work in educational efforts. By senior high school years, they should be given the chance to examine critically some of the attempts to influence people to stop smoking. They might, for example,

1. Conduct a panel discussion on the values of present efforts in the fight against smoking, including the labeling of cigarette packages, the program for 7th and 8th graders sponsored by the PTA in cooperation with the Public Health Service, and the introduction of special instruction on the subject in the school curriculum.

2. Engage in experimental efforts to educate younger children, especially those in upper elementary grades, evaluating their efforts in the process.

3. Investigate laws regarding the sale of tobacco to minors and consider their value.

4. Find out from the local health department, or any other sponsoring agency, what success it is having with smoking withdrawal clinics. Consider alternative approaches to the addicted smoker.

5. Interview adults who have tried to stop smoking to find out what techniques they used, their physical and psychological reactions, and their success and failure rates.

6. Discuss "Who defends smoking and on what basis?" in an effort to understand some of the reasons why change in a long-established custom presents many difficulties.

7. On the basis of their findings, draw up a plan for a school and community educational program on smoking and health which they think might work.

Alcohol and Health

In most school systems basic instruction will have been given on this subject long before high school years. There is a need, however, for a more intensive study from an adult point of view during the latter part of senior high school.

A realistic approach.   The Oregon State Department of Education suggests the following activities:

1. Dramatize a conversation, "Let's Talk It Over," in which athlete, doctor, dentist, nurse, airline pilot, banker, etc., each state how alcohol affects his skills and responsibilities.

2. Conduct panel discussions on:
    a. Drinking customs of man through the ages
    b. Drinking customs in the United States and other countries
    c. Attitudes of various religions concerning drinking
    d. Why people drink. (Class determine validity of reasons given.)
    e. Understanding and treating the alcoholic

3. Compile a scrapbook of news stories and pictures pertaining to alcohol. Have class evaluate this information.

4. Compile a scrapbook of liquor advertisements. Determine how these advertisements appeal to fundamental needs and desires such as success and recognition. Determine facts and propaganda presented. Attempt to determine cost of advertisements.

5. Make a map pinpointing all local or statewide facilities available to help the alcoholic; include A.A., state agencies, and private centers.

6. Make charts, graphs, or posters to show various aspects of the alcohol problem such as teen-age drinking and traffic accidents. Discuss these and draw conclusions.

7. Visit an open A.A. meeting, Al-Anon, or alcohol clinic.[25]

Conferences on youth and alcohol.   Pennsylvania, through its Governor's Advisory Council on Alcoholism and the Council for Human Services has sponsored a series of conferences attended by youth as well as adults. Attitudes of youth were solicited at these conferences. Panels composed of a state policeman, a clergyman, and a physician gave their views on drinking; and adults in attendance, many of them parents, had opportunity to give their views.[26]

Teen-agers and the drinking question.   In a class in New Hyde Park High School (New York), the teacher and pupils prepared a general outline or script for a closed-circuit television lesson. The panel members were selected from the various health classes which were receiving the lesson. The questions and attitudes to be presented were developed by the students during four after-school planning sessions in which they decided on the most pertinent ideas to be considered. The lesson was well received by the other classes and stimulated further discussion in the classrooms.

The following are some of the topics discussed:

1. Drinking habits are influenced by cultural heritage, social and economic status, religious beliefs, drinking habits of others. As an example, one student with a European background reported wine with meals in her home, while others reported that drinks were served at home when there was company.

2. Home environment influences our attitudes toward drinking.

3. Teen-agers are exposed to drinking at home, teen-age parties, night clubs after a prom or special dance, resort areas, public recreation areas.

4. Factors to guide us in making decisions regarding drinking are: Good manners, knowledge of effects of alcohol, laws to protect us, parental supervision.

5. What will be the right decision for you?[27]

Drugs and Health

The wide exposure of students to the drug problem through newspapers, magazines, and television, as well as through personal experience in some instances, makes it imperative that they learn the basic facts about drugs and discuss freely the effects of drug abuse on the individual and on society.

[25] Health Education in Oregon Secondary Schools; Grades 9–12. Salem, Oregon, State Department of Education, 1966, p. 26.

[26] Youth and alcohol. Target, 16:1–2 (Dec.) 1966. (Publication of the Division of Behavioral Problems and Drug Control, Pennsylvania Department of Health, Harrisburg, Pennsylvania.)

[27] Reported by Carolyn Tallow, New Hyde Park High School, New Hyde Park, New York, 1961.

Facts on drugs.   Students may read articles and publications on drugs and report on their findings. A recent publication, *Drug Abuse: Escape to Nowhere*[28] provides helpful background for teacher and student. The Food and Drug Administration also issues material on the subject. Students should learn what happens when narcotics are taken and withdrawn. Drug addiction should be understood. At the same time, they should learn about the contributions of drugs to modern day medical and dental practice.

The high cost of drug addiction.   The following are suggestive studies which students may profitably make:

1. Invite a Federal Narcotics Agent to discuss problems of drug addiction.
2. View and discuss the film "Drug Addiction."
3. Assign student reports on the cost in dollars, lives, and health of drug abuse. (For example, cost to the individual addict; cost to society through loss of merchandise stolen in the process of obtaining money to purchase drugs; cost of legal controls at local, state, national, and international levels; cost to society in treatment and rehabilitation efforts; and cost in terms of wasted human potential.)
4. Students may investigate the health problems which arise when drug addicts live gregariously in shabby quarters, and consider the cost to the individual and society in terms of illness, disease, and the public health measures required to protect others. (Examples of health problems are venereal disease; pests, such as body lice, bedbugs, rats; respiratory illnesses; skin infections; and intestinal diseases due to poor basic sanitation.)
5. Students may investigate the extent to which drug addiction has become a problem in their own state and find out what is being done to prevent and control the problem as well as to treat and rehabilitate users and addicts.

Case studies.   A unit on narcotics may be started with the question, "Why do people become involved with the various illegal drugs?" The students could write the reasons on the left side of a notebook and then as possible solutions are discussed, add them alongside the problems. The unit might conclude with a review of actual police cases. The class could divide itself into smaller groups to study and discuss the cases and present solutions to the full class.

Consumer Health

If taught well, this subject holds wide interest for the senior high school student. It may be taught as a separate unit, or its content may be woven into all parts of a health course and the curriculum in general. In the space available here one cannot do justice to the wide range of possibilities for helping students to be wise purchasers and consumers of health products and services. The Food

---

28 Drug Abuse: Escape to Nowhere; a Guide for Educators. Washington, D.C., National Education Association, 1967, 104 pp. (Published by Smith Kline & French Laboratories in cooperation with the American Association for Health, Physical Education, and Recreation.)

and Drug Administration, the American Medical Association, and state departments of health and agriculture, as well as many other agencies and organizations now have available much useful information on the subject. A few suggestions only are given in this section.

To tell the truth.   Students may collect examples of false or misleading claims for products or services and of sound and ethical advertising. In evaluating the items, representatives from the class should consult appropriate authorities such as the local medical society, health department, chamber of commerce, home economics teachers, and the like.

Commercial interests.   Tenth grade students in one school sought answers to the following questions:

1. What are some examples of commercial concerns that have helped to increase the life span? Explain how. (For example, drug companies, life insurance companies.)

2. How can we tell the difference between false advertising and truthful information about a product? (For example, Consumers Guide, Consumers Research.)

3. What are some books that will help us understand the role of advertising? Review them.

4. What governmental agencies are set up to help prevent the commercial concerns from giving false information? What is their responsibility? (Food and Drug Administration—false or misleading statements in or on the trade package; Federal Trade Commission—regulating advertising in interstate commerce.)[29]

Investing in health.   The following excerpts from a unit on this subject illustrate activities appropriate for young people nearing adulthood.

1. Collection by class or small committee of data on amounts spent by nation on patent medicines, drugs, cosmetics, medical and hospital care, and related items to show importance of problem and its relation to other social and economic problems. Analysis and discussion of the data may lead to a talk by an authority on the problem of the "gullible public" in relation to the price of ignorance in purchasing health products and services.

2. Talk, made on invitation of class, by the school physician, health officer, or a family physician on what health services every family needs (and how to secure the services).

3. Planning by class to have a panel of physicians, businessmen, and other qualified professional persons to discuss a family's need for planning for medical, dental, and hospital care to meet severe illnesses and accidents.

4. Compilation of a list of community, state, and national sources of reliable health information.

5. Development of criteria based on approved standards for selecting a hospital in case of illness requiring hospitalization.[30]

Information learned through instruction in home nursing. Units in home nursing and care of the sick deal in part with con-

---

[29] Reported by Carolyn Tallow, New Hyde Park High School, New Hyde Park, New York, 1961.

[30] Excerpts from Teachers Guide in Health Education for Secondary Schools. Sacramento, California, California State Department of Education, 1952, pp. 61–63.

sumer health problems, such as what to include in the medicine cabinet, how to choose a physician, and how to improvise equipment cheaply and economically in the care of the sick.

Defenses against quackery. The American Medical Association, which is actively involved in educational efforts to protect citizens from being victims of quackery, and at the same time to help them know where to turn for competent medical services, has developed a packet on this subject. A few suggested learning experiences taken from a resource unit for teachers contained in the packet are given here.

Mechanical quackery
1. Suggest that each member of the class locate some advertisements of mechanical aids to health.
2. Require one portion of the class to locate descriptions of some machines proved to be worthless, and the other portion to obtain descriptions of some machines legitimately used in health services. Attempt to develop generalizations by the class regarding the difference between the two types of machines.
3. Suggest that students keep a notebook on all material available in current magazines and newspapers regarding mechanical quackery.
4. Classify all of the devices discovered into these categories: no value; unknown value; of definite value in proper hands.
5. Suggest that the class evaluate the mechanical devices used by their own athletic department and local youth agencies.

Evaluating health services
1. Develop a list of criteria for the selection of a personal physician and dentist.
2. Collect and discuss examples of advertising on radio and television and in newspapers for health treatments and health services. Evaluate.
3. Determine the reasons why medical, dental, and nursing professions consider it unethical to advertise services.
4. List the qualifications a person should possess who is recommending a health service or product.
5. Discuss the reasons why a so-called educated person may not be health-educated.[31]

Health and Safety of the Worker

General instruction on this subject may be given in health classes, but vocational guidance courses, shop courses, vocational agriculture, and other appropriate courses should also give additional instruction.

Occupational health problems. Students may make a survey of the most important industries of their community and the occupational hazards associated with each. They may interview

---

[31] Excerpts from Defenses Against Quackery; A Resource Unit for Teachers. Chicago, American Medical Association, 1966. (Concepts and sample teaching units for the high school and adult groups.)

local health authorities and industrial leaders to learn steps being taken to improve industrial health conditions.

Vocational safety.   Florio and Stafford have suggested numerous ways in which students in shop courses could study accident prevention. At the end of a very useful chapter on vocational safety they propose such activities as:

1. Request a copy of the annual accident record of a local industry and determine the types of casualties most often reported. Secure information concerning the safety program in operation in that industry. Report your findings to the class.
2. Invite a safety engineer to talk to your class on the safety program in operation in his company. Plan a visit to his factory.
3. Invite an equipment manufacturer to talk to your class on "Safety Equipment and Its Use."
4. Study a number of newspaper accounts or radio comments concerning industrial accidents during the past month and discuss before your class the possible causes of these accidents and the measures that should have been taken to prevent these accidents.
5. Develop a safety check list for the school shop, covering lighting, ventilation, housekeeping, protective equipment, and arrangement and use of tools and machines. Use this check list to survey the vocational facilities in a nearby school and report to your class on the hazards discovered and your suggestions for correcting, compensating for, or removing them.
6. Use a similar check list to survey a home workshop. Note especially hand tools. Are they adequate and in good condition?
7. Study the accident record of a high school for a given period and list the most frequent types of vocational accidents. Report your suggestions for avoiding such accidents.[32]

Students in health classes could likewise engage in such studies.

Farm health and safety.   Since many rural youths are engaged in daily work about the farm, and since city and town youths also help on farms during summer vacations and out-of-school hours, this subject may be appropriate for study in many sections of the country.

1. Take inventory of health and safety hazards on farms, and consider ways of removing hazards or of minimizing their effects.
2. Give a style show of safe and healthful clothing for farm wear. For contrast, also show unsafe and unhealthful clothing. Information may be secured from the county agent or the state agricultural extension services.
3. Visit a modern farm to observe firsthand the machinery and other equipment, as well as practices which embody safety principles.
4. Become familiar with poisonous plants, snakes, and insects which inhabit the locality. Prepare exhibits to familiarize others with these.
5. Role-play a farmer interviewing a city youth for summer work on a farm. Have the "farmer" question the youth on his preparation for driving a tractor, handling animals, and other practices which require skill for safety. This may be followed by a discussion of the preparation needed for farm work. Similar activities may be carried out for other types of occupations.

---

[32] Florio, A. E., and Stafford, G. T.: Safety Education. 2nd Ed. New York, McGraw-Hill Book Company, Inc., 1962, pp. 242–243.

Schools may profitably cooperate with groups like the 4-H Club members in North Dakota who are engaged in a program directed toward safe use of pesticides. They distribute decals labeled "Before using this sprayer—STOP" to stick onto sprayers, a first aid card, and an informational leaflet.[33]

Quiz the experts.   A panel of "experts" from local industry and labor as well as from the health department may be invited to appear at a school assembly, and students who have been studying health problems can be the quizzers. How the worker's health is protected, the community's responsibility for the health of workers and their families, and the worker's responsibility for his own and his family's health are appropriate subjects for questioning and discussion.

Health and Safety in Sports and Outdoor Recreation

Alongside the benefits of outdoor recreation are certain health and safety hazards that can become a test of a person's ability to face emergencies. In driving, swimming, boating, hunting, climbing, skiing, and organized sports, young people are confronted with situations that demand skill and judgment. The experienced person knows the dangers of the activity in which he is participating and exercises his skills to avert trouble. The inexperienced or untrained individual is the one who is most likely to take unwarranted chances that can lead to accidents or illness. Within every community there are adults who can help teach young people the skills needed in specific sports and how to enjoy the out-of-doors safely. Moreover, many sports organizations, such as the American Water Ski Association and the National Ski Patrol publish safety hints for their particular sports.

An ordinance drafted by students.   To promote active participation in government, Baltimore Public Schools have supported over the years a Model Youth City Council program. In this program, senior high school students interview department heads, observe municipal activities at firsthand, and after thorough explorations of problems and services, draft model legislation aimed at better government. History, civics, and modern problems classes, as well as English classes, engage in this project. They elect city-wide officers, such as the Mayor, President of the Council, and so on, and then hold a two-day legislative session in the City Council Chamber of the City Hall. Full support for this project is given by the executive and legislative branches of city government. A sample ordinance is presented here:

---

[33] Reported by Mr. Craig R. Montgomery, Assistant Director for Youth, Cooperative Extension Service, North Dakota State University, Fargo, North Dakota, 1967.

AN ORDINANCE to provide for the wearing of protective head gear by both
the driver and passenger on a motorcycle or a motorscooter.

1   WHEREAS, there is evidence of increased traffic injuries and fatalities
2   every year, and
3   WHEREAS, an effort is being made both nationally and locally to stem
4   the tide of traffic accidents and,
5   WHEREAS, fatal accidents and injuries have risen in alarming proportion
6   by the use of motorcycles and scooters, and
7   WHEREAS, more stringent rules and regulations governing the safety of
8   these vehicles are needed, therefore
1   SECTION 1.   Be it ordained by the Mayor and City Council of
2   Baltimore City that every driver and every passenger must be equipped
3   with and wear at all times protective head gear.
4   Which head gear must be approved as satisfactory by the Baltimore City
5   Police.
1   SECTION 2.   Be it further ordained, that this Ordinance should take
2   effect upon the date of its passage.[34]

Warning signs.   Island Lake "Zeps," a 4-H Club in Lyon
County, Minnesota, placed danger signs and depth signs near farm
ponds and swimming areas on a lake. They also cleared trash and
debris from the lakeshore. In addition, they developed a roadside
rest area and placed there a sign encouraging travelers to stop and
"take a break for safety's sake."[35]

Water safety.   Tennessee has over 400,000 acres of big lake
water, thousands of miles of streams and thousands of farm ponds.
Most of these lakes have been created since 1935 by the impound-
ment of waters in the Tennessee Valley system of reservoirs. Thus,
in one generation, a state population that had had little or no experience with water found itself a leading water recreation center
in the country. Aware of the excessive number of drownings in
Tennessee and of the need for safer practices on the water, three
biology classes at Cohn High School, Nashville, Tennessee, undertook an extensive study of water safety. Emphasis was placed on
safety while swimming, boating, skiing, and fishing; administering
first aid; importance of tetanus and typhoid immunization; preventing stream pollution; and preparing for emergencies. Class
activities extended over a six-week period and extracurricular activities for three months. A few of the activities are listed here:

Prepared and administered questionnaires on swimming practices and on
boating, skiing and fishing. Interpreted findings to teachers, student body and
parents.

Sponsored swimming classes at a neighboring community center pool. The
classes were arranged by the Director of Water Safety and First Aid, American
Red Cross, and were taught by volunteer instructors.

Learned from the Red Cross Director about common errors while boating.

---

[34] Taken from 1967 Bill Book, Fourteenth Annual Legislative Session, Baltimore
Model Youth City Council, May 4 and 5. Baltimore, Maryland, Baltimore City Department of Education, 1967. (Ordinance No. 16, introduced by Cheryl McQuillan of Mergen-
thaler Vocational-Technical High School.)

[35] Reported by Carla Larson, Lyon County, Minnesota, 1967.

Planned and gave an auditorium program on boat safety, emphasizing proper equipment and its use.

Demonstrated how to keep afloat when a boat capsizes. A sporting goods store furnished a boat and other equipment and the demonstration took place in the pool at the community center.

Presented a program to the Men's Club on the project and demonstrated how to properly equip a boat and how to use each piece of equipment to best advantage.

Learned how to give artificial respiration. This instruction was given in physical education classes to all students in the school.

Found out how many students in the school had protection against tetanus and typhoid fever and encouraged the large number not protected to receive immunizations. Requested the Davidson County Health Department to provide personnel and facilities for immunizations.

Heard the Director of the Stream Pollution Control Board explain the problems of stream pollution in Tennessee and the plans to improve the situation. Read booklets, made class reports and prepared bulletin boards on stream pollution. The State Biologist also spent a day in the school explaining biology of fresh water and demonstrating various water tests. Studied water conservation needs.

Planned and carried out a Water Safety Day program for the entire school. The program was released to the local newspaper and given publicity over the local television station.

During this project, 25 separate organizations cooperated through supplying materials, speakers, instructors, advisers, and demonstrations. All together, these people donated 198 hours of their time. Ninety students were immunized against tetanus and typhoid fever; 45 learned to swim, or improved their swimming; and over four thousand pieces of literature related to the class activities were distributed to homes and business firms. Recommendations were made for a state-wide education program to teach people water safety and for many other school, community, and state procedures leading to safer and more enjoyable use of Tennessee's waterways.[36]

Health Factors in Housing and Urban Development

Young people will find a study of housing and urban development both interesting and profitable. In social problems and health classes the efforts of cities, towns, and rural areas to plan for better housing and a better general environment can become a subject for study in cooperation with local planners.

Dispersal of people from blighted areas. Students may invite to the class a representative of the city government (health department, welfare department, or city planning commission) who can discuss health factors, both favorable and unfavorable, associated

---

[36] For a more detailed report, see It's a Family Affair, Cohn High School, Nashville City Schools, Tennessee, 1957, 14 pp.

with urban renewal projects. As blighted areas are renewed, is there danger of the blight spreading to other parts of the community? What is being done to help those people who are being dispersed to make physical, emotional, and social adjustments to their changed surroundings? Students will doubtless wish to raise many other questions.

High-rise apartment living. Students may make a study of health and safety factors associated with living in high-rise apartments. Subjects which might be explored include: how young children get their exercise and develop their friendships, accident patterns, provisions for disposal of garbage and refuse, and efforts to stimulate a sense of "community" responsibility within the building or development.

Housing for the elderly. Students may arrange to visit a housing development for the elderly, noting adaptations in design and equipment in kitchens, bathrooms, and around the grounds which contribute to safe and healthful living. They may learn about provisions for recreational activities in these units or in the neighborhood. They may discuss the advantages and disadvantages of separate housing for the elderly.

Architectural barriers. Public buildings, private homes, industrial plants, and other areas where people live, work, and move about often present insurmountable barriers to the crippled or incapacitated. Students may make a survey of the conditions in their own community which prevent many people from engaging in everyday activities open to others. Among common barriers are: steps at the entrance to public buildings; rotating doors; doorways too small for wheel chairs to pass through; public telephone booths too high for a wheel chair user to reach; high curbs; and inconveniently arranged equipment and facilities in kitchen, bathroom, and other rooms of the house. They may then consider private and public measures which would prevent or improve such conditions.

Health Careers

Employment in the health professions has great appeal to many young people who have ideals for community service. An excellent publication of the Department of Labor describes briefly but clearly job opportunities in a variety of health professions.[37] Throughout the country, health agencies and professional organizations are becoming increasingly interested in cooperating with vocational guidance counselors and health teachers in giving information about health professions. These agencies may also offer opportunity for

---

[37] Health Careers Guidebook. Bureau of Employment Security, U.S. Department of Labor. Washington, D.C., U.S. Government Printing Office, 1965, 204 pp.

useful work experience as a means of orientation to the different fields of service. Learning about health careers and participating in community service projects can become an integral part of health instruction at the senior high school level. As suggested earlier, experiences young people are having in community service can frequently serve as case study material in health and social studies classes.

Health career possibilities. As a unit within a health class, students might investigate health career opportunities as follows:

1. Establish committees within the class according to student career interests, as for example, committees on nursing, medicine, physical therapy, public health, and laboratory sciences. Preliminary study of the health careers book just mentioned would help students in locating careers of possible interest.

2. Each committee may then do background reading and, after preparing questions which are pertinent to their field of choice, arrange for interviews with professional workers in that field. Visits to locations where these people are working would lend reality to the study. In addition to committee activity, students with special career interests should be encouraged to pursue their interests independent of the group. It should be pointed out that many of the professional fields are broad in scope and have a variety of specialties within them. It would be well, then, for students to decide which specialties they will concentrate on. Moreover, during interviews students might find out what new career opportunities are opening up as a result of new developments in the health sciences.

3. Since some students in a class will not be interested in pursuing a health career, these students might approach the study from a consumer's point of view and concentrate on the public's image of the professional fields under study, as well as the services available to the public of which people in general are not aware.

4. On completion of committee investigations, each group might prepare its own report as a basis for a final class roundup. In presenting the committee reports to the full class, students might use the reactor panel technique. To illustrate, a student from each committee might give a brief statement, and then a panel of representatives from the appropriate health professions, invited to the session for the purpose, could react to the students' presentations.

Health careers day. The Health Careers Association in Cincinnati sponsors each year a Health Careers Day for high school pupils. On this day boys and girls visit hospitals, research centers, and various offices where health services are performed. In October 1966, 1,030 students took advantage of the day. In addition, most of the eight high schools in Cincinnati have health careers clubs to which any high school pupils may belong.[38]

Junior volunteers. "Chequers" is the name given to a teen-age group of girls who provide volunteer services at the New York State Rehabilitation Hospital. These volunteers were organized through the interest of a teen-age daughter of the Acting Assistant Director of Nursing. After eight hours of classroom instruction, the

---

[38] Reported in a letter from Mrs. Barbara Worrel, Supervisor, Health and Physical Education, Cincinnati Public Schools, 1967.

Figure 25. Providing volunteer service at the Duluth Rehabilitation Center. (Courtesy of the Duluth Rehabilitation Center, Duluth, Minnesota.)

girls go on the wards and give direct patient care. Working only with women, young girls and babies, they help with such duties as feeding, dressing, removing and applying corrective devices, changing diapers, and washing hands and face. Most important, according to their supervisor, they supply that extra "T.L.C." (tender loving care) so necessary for total patient care. Many of the girls are members of school-related Future Nurses Clubs. The schools have referred to this program girls recommended by attendance officers in the hope that through participation in the program they would be motivated to stay in school. Girls may become members of the volunteer group at the age of 13 or 14. They are interviewed personally and before final acceptance must present written permission and a release of responsibility signed by the parents.[39]

From volunteer service to a career in health. The Junior Board of the Duluth Rehabilitation Center is an active group which over a period of seven years has the enviable record of having 33 of its 85 members who have graduated from high school, or 39 per cent, either working in, or working toward, a job in the health and welfare field. Fourteen different professions are represented by this group. The activities of the group are coordinated closely with school-related activities. As class assignments, a number of the Junior Board members have written papers on rehabilitation, the Center, and various health professions. Several of the students have earned school credit by giving talks before civic groups. Other activities, aside from those at or for the Center, include serving as counselors at a day camp for disabled children. Educational programs and field trips are arranged by the Center for these young people.[40]

Community Health

Several suggestions for community health projects have appeared in this and earlier chapters. In addition to learning about the community, many students at the senior high school level can participate actively in community programs.

Opportunities for service projects are increasing as communities see the importance of giving young people experience in citizenship. One of the areas in which community service can be stressed is that of chronic illness, as illustrated in the previous sec-

---

[39] Reported in a letter from Mrs. Regina Biedebach, Acting Assistant Director of Nursing and Junior Volunteer Advisor, New York State Rehabilitation Hospital, West Haverstraw, N.Y., 1967.

[40] Reported in a letter from Miss Mary E. Van Gorden, Executive Director, Duluth Rehabilitation Center, Duluth, Minnesota, 1967.

tion of this chapter. When boys and girls give volunteer service, an effort should be made to provide a period of orientation so they understand the problems they are dealing with and the meaning of the programs of which they are a part. High standards should be set for the service; students should realize that they are often dealing with situations that affect the health and lives of people. Student participation, when coupled with classroom instruction, provides sound and effective education for future civic responsibility.

Students at this age are ready to learn in detail about agencies and organizations which render health services at local, state, federal, and international levels. Their study of these services may be combined with similar studies by parent-teacher organizations, health councils, and other civic groups, as well as with direct service projects. In fact, the school, in cooperation with health authorities, may often provide the leadership for such a community-wide study.

Introduction to environmental health problems and services. Interest in community sanitation problems may be heightened by such activities as proposed in the *Guide for the Montana School Health Program:*

A. Whole group of pupils
  1. Find out what laws affect sanitation: local, state, federal (interstate, ports of entry).
  2. Invite local sanitarian or health officer to talk to the class about sanitation in the community, sanitary science as a profession, role of sanitation in public health.
  3. Discuss rodents and their effect on Montana and the U.S. in terms of losses —financial, health, property, fire.
  4. Discuss effects of stream pollution in terms of health, recreation, conservation of natural resources, aesthetic viewpoint.
  5. Discuss food poisoning and food infections.

B. Small groups of pupils
  1. Visit a training class for food service personnel, report to class.
  2. Attend a community health council meeting, report to class.
  3. Find out from local sanitarian and county agent what assistance is given to rural families to aid in the development of safe water supplies and proper sewage disposal facilities.
  4. Carry out following experiments, report to class:
  Filtration to remove sediment from water.
  Filtering of water through different types of soil.
  Pasteurization of milk.
  Refrigeration of foods to prevent spoilage.
  5. Observe installation of well.
  Observe installation of septic tank.
  Build model of water filtration plant.
  Build model of sewage plant.

C. Individual pupils
  1. Design septic tank and private water supply installation.

2. Observe sanitation practices in one of the following: dairy, grocery store, soda fountain, restaurant.
3. Investigate requirements for college courses in: Sanitary Science, Dairy Manufacturing, Bacteriology, Industrial Hygiene, Sanitary Engineering.[41]

Foodhandlers' school for high school students

A student cafeteria worker with boils on his arms was the impetus for this program. The school nurse, a health department employee, observed the boy and asked to have him taken out of the food service line.

In addition to the question of personal health that this situation demonstrated, the cafeteria supervisor identified several more. Restrooms were some distance from the kitchen, and it was difficult to be sure that students washed their hands. Students did not understand the need for careful food handling and the relationship to food-borne illnesses.

A food handling course was planned, working with the cafeteria supervisor, the school nurse and the district public health educator and sanitarian. The principal was cooperative and agreed to excuse students from class so that they could attend the training during regular school hours.

At the training session, the school nurse explained the need for good personal hygiene for foodhandlers and proper hand washing techniques. The sanitarian discussed restaurant sanitation. To illustrate how any part of the body or clothing can carry germs, petri dishes with culture medium were touched with a student's fingertips, a hair combing, lip print, the cloth of a sleeve, etc. The plates were put on a board and kept on display so that student cafeteria workers could see the bacterial colonies develop.

Two films, "An Outbreak of Salmonella Infection," and "Kitchen Habits," were shown to give students some conception of the seriousness of food-borne illnesses and the good habits which prevent them.

As to the effectiveness of the course, the following is a quote from a letter written by the cafeteria superintendent, Mrs. Edythe Faris, to Dr. J. B. Askew, Director of Public Health.

"In evaluating the benefit of this course at our school, I have noted a marked change of attitude among our student workers, particularly in the daily check of the hand washing procedure. Their attitude has improved greatly, and compliance with the sanitary requirements is now 100 per cent. The students also now understand the importance of their work and take pride in it. Being singled out for special attention has boosted the morale of the entire crew.

"I truly believe that such a class conducted in each school as soon as possible after the opening of school in the fall each year would be of great benefit."[42]

Refuse disposal. Disposal of garbage, rubbish, junk cars, and general litter has become a matter of major concern in our modern society. The nature and extent of the problem in the local community could be a subject for special study at the high school level. Students could find out, too, what the community is doing about the problem and join with community agencies in efforts to improve conditions. Some schools, for example, are engaging in community

---

41 Guide for the Montana School Health Program. 2nd Ed. Helena, Montana, The Montana State Board of Health, 1961, pp. 381–382.

42 Reported by Mrs. Gail T. McLellan, Public Health Educator, San Diego Department of Public Health, 1967.

beautification projects, such as "sweep-ins" to clean up public parks and recreation areas.

In the public schools of Wellesley, Massachusetts, case studies and "games" have been developed to stimulate student interest in the problem and to provide simulated situations as a basis for problem solving. One project involved arriving at a decision on where a municipal incinerator should be built. Using a map of a fictitious town, each student pretended he was the owner of one of the home or business properties plotted on the map. After each student had worked out solutions reflecting his own interests, a town meeting was held to see if the "residents" could agree upon a single solution. Parents were informed of the project and invited to discuss possible locations of the incinerator with their children.[43]

Learning about air pollution.   The following activities are among those suggested for study by science classes. Health classes, too, could engage in similar studies.

1. Visit a plant or factory in your community using coal or oil as a fuel. Observe the variety of activities that can lead to contamination of the atmosphere.
2. Draw up a list of all the human activities you can think of that contribute to air pollution.
3. Vehicular exhaust is a major source of air pollution in many areas.
   a. Observe the effects of automobile exhaust on the rear end of some automobiles or on parking lot walls or vegetation.
   b. Visit a garage that uses an exhaust analyzer for tuning engines. Ask one of the mechanics to explain it to you and/or let you read the literature that came with the instrument.
4. Soot, dust, fly ash, and other aerosols in the atmosphere can be collected and studied. The materials needed are a container or some other device for collection, a hand lens or microscope, and a fairly accurate balance.

Set out on the roof of the school a wide-mouthed collecting jar, greased (Vaseline) plate or sheet of sticky ("fly") paper. Leave the collecting device outside for a day, a week, or some other definite period of time and then examine what has been collected.

Comparisons can be made of the particulate matter present in the air in different parts of a city or between city air and country air by weighing the collected materials on a fairly accurate analytical balance and by examining them under a hand lens or microscope.

5. Meteorological conditions have an effect on air pollution. Observe the weather maps for several days and then discuss
   a. The effects of the vertical and horizontal movements of air masses on air pollution.
   b. The effects of a prolonged temperature inversion on the community.[44]

Students in action for clean air.   Twenty thousand signatures on petitions circulated by students of Cheltenham High School, Wyncote, Pennsylvania, and area-wide publicity in the news media,

---

[43] Courtesy of Wellesley Public Schools Center for Collaborative Learning Media Packages, 1967.
[44] Carr, A. B.: Suggestions for teaching about air pollution. School Science and Mathematics, *64*:229–235 (March) 1964.

resulted from a project conducted under the leadership of Mr. Roy C. Buri, sociology teacher. The students had been studying a unit on air pollution; when the question arose, "What can we do about this problem?" the action began. Several students wrote the petition and others gathered information for a fact sheet on air pollution for distribution as the petition was circulated. Seventeen area captains signed up students to cover every block in the township. In all, 300 students were involved. As students went from door to door to secure signatures on petitions, each student had with him a copy of the local newspaper which had not only printed a story of the campaign but also had printed a copy of the petition. Shopping centers as well as homes were covered in the project. The signed petitions were presented to the Governor; individual citizens, township commissioners, and local, state, and national political leaders sent congratulatory letters. In two months the idea had spread so that dozens of schools, not only in Pennsylvania but in neighboring states, had asked for copies of the fact sheet and petition. On conclusion of the project, an adult education program was being planned and it was hoped that it would culminate in the formation of a local clean air group.[45]

Venereal diseases. The state of Ohio has developed a plan for teaching about venereal diseases which includes correlation of the subject in selected areas of the curriculum as on opposite page.[46] Student activities proposed by the Ohio group include:

1. Prepare graphs and charts to show the incidence of venereal diseases and other communicable diseases in Ohio and your community.
2. Make a collection of current magazine and newspaper articles on the venereal diseases.
3. Develop and fill in charts which summarize the important facts about the venereal diseases. Such facts would include: (a) cause of disease; (b) mode of transmission or spread; (c) common signs and symptoms; (d) damage done to the body.
4. Some pupils may be interested in securing and studying information on the different serological tests for syphilis.
5. Some pupils may want to write brief biographies of the men who have made contributions to the discovery, treatment, and control of the venereal diseases. Such men would include: Fracastoro, Fritz Schaudinn, Eric Hoffman, Albert Neisser, August von Wassermann, Paul Ehrlich, William F. Snow, Thomas Parran, Alexander Fleming, John Mahoney. An encyclopedia should make some reference to most of these men.[47]

---

[45] Summarized from a letter received from Mr. Roy C. Buri, sociology teacher, Cheltenham High School, School District of Cheltenham Township, Wyncote, Pennsylvania, 1967.

[46] Venereal Disease Education. Columbus, Ohio, Ohio Department of Health with the cooperation of Ohio Department of Education, 1960, p. 10.

[47] *Ibid.,* pp. 11–12.

Suggestions for Correlating Information about the Venereal Diseases in Selected Areas of the Curriculum

AREAS OF CORRELATION	HEALTH INSTRUCTION	SCIENCE	SOCIAL STUDIES	HOME ECONOMICS	FAMILY LIVING	GUIDANCE
1. In relation to other communicable diseases, their cause, spread, symptoms, control and prevention.	X	X	X	X	X	
2. In relation to public health and the health department's methods of controlling and preventing the spread of communicable diseases.	X		X		X	X
3. In relation to causes of mental illness.	X		X		X	X
4. In relation to organisms which cause disease such as the spirochete and syphilis, and the gonococcus and gonorrhea.	X	X				
5. In relation to scientific methods of detecting disease. a. the blood test for syphilis b. microscopic examination for syphilis and gonorrhea.	X	X			X	
6. In relation to the discovery and use of antibiotic drugs.	X	X				
7. In relation to scientific discoveries dealing with disease. a. August von Wassermann's discovery of a serology test for syphilis b. Paul Ehrlich and assistant Hata's discovery of Salvarsan, the first cure for syphilis c. Fleming's discovery of penicillin	X	X				
8. In relation to the effects of venereal disease on the history of the world.	X		X		X	
9. In relation to public health laws. a. the premarital and prenatal blood tests b. blood tests for food handlers c. laws against prostitution	X		X	X	X	
10. In relation to congenital syphilis and children.	X	X		X	X	X
11. In relation to the future health and happiness of the family, with reference to freedom from communicable diseases.	X			X	X	X
12. In relation to disease statistics and the incidence of various communicable diseases.	X	X				

Teen-agers interview teen-agers. Washington, D.C., has embarked on a unique project of employing teen-agers to interview other teen-agers about venereal diseases. After a period of preparation, selected teen-agers, armed with a questionnaire constructed as an educational tool, are assigned to recreational areas, and working closely under supervision, interview other teen-agers. In the preliminary experiment, 400 young people were interviewed. If an incorrect answer was given, the workers corrected the misconception and provided the facts. It was found that about 60 per cent of those interviewed made incorrect statements about venereal diseases. Encouraging, however, was the fact that about 40 per cent of those who were interviewed came back for additional information.[48]

Health hints for travel. Students contemplating summer vacations and travel may prepare a set of health and safety hints which will add to the comfort and pleasure of the experience. They may also consider health precautions followed by people who travel (or work) in other parts of the world. Instructions on health now being given to Peace Corps members should be of special interest to the students.

Serving one's local cancer unit. Suggested ways in which the high school student can aid his local cancer unit are:

1. Spread information for local unit through pamphlets, posters, conversation.
2. Put special training to work:
   a. Boys trained as school projectionists might show movies to clubs and organizations.
   b. Boys and girls in speech classes or clubs might prepare and deliver short talks on cancer, become a part of a speakers' bureau for their cancer unit.
   c. Dramatics students might write and/or present skits, sociodramas, role plays for clubs or neighborhood groups.
3. Help families of cancer patients by baby sitting, errand running, delivering supplies from cancer unit to family, making tray favors.
4. Help service committee of cancer unit by making cancer dressings, collecting clean linen for loan closet supply, typing envelopes for cytology notification project.[49]

Background reading can be done on cancer and may include what it is, how it is caused, methods used for diagnosis and treatment, and current research. Teaching guides now available contain useful information as well as suggestions for pupil activities.[50]

Heart disease—prevention and control. Montana youth are keeping abreast of progress in this field through such class activities as:

1. Discussing: How can the "increasing total number of deaths from heart disease" in a general sense measure to some degree modern successes in defeating early death? What are the common diseases of the heart and circulatory system?
2. Giving examples that illustrate the "strength and endurance" of the heart and circulatory system.

---

[48] Reported in a letter from Robert H. Conn, Chief, Health Education and Information Division, Department of Public Health, District of Columbia, Washington, D.C., 1967.

[49] Guide Lines for the Teaching of a Unit of Cancer Education in Health and Biology Classes in the Secondary Schools. Pilot project of the Schools and Colleges Sub-Committee of the Public Education Committee of the American Cancer Society, Ohio Division, Inc., Gertrude Bliss, Chairman, 1961, p. 27.

[50] See, for example, A Teaching Guide to Science and Cancer. Washington, D.C., U.S. Government Printing Office, 1966, 24 pp. (Prepared for the National Cancer Institute by the National Science Teachers Association.) See also, Teaching About Cancer. New York, American Cancer Society, Inc., 1965, 47 pp.

3. Discussing the relationship between obesity and high blood pressure and heart disease.

4. Discussing the value of exercise to persons with "sound hearts." Watching the home demonstration agent demonstrate how housewives can "save energy."

5. Visiting a physician's office and having him explain how he "listens to the heart" (stethoscope) and how he "sees" the heart (fluoroscope); how he uses the electrocardiograph and why; and how he measures blood pressure and what it means; how x-ray aids the physician in caring for a patient with heart disease. Make reports to the class.

6. Visiting the public health nurse; having her explain how she helps patients with heart disease live with limited exertion.

7. Visiting the office of the counselor of the office of vocational rehabilitation; finding out how he places persons with heart disease in "safe" occupations.

8. Investigating the career opportunities in assisting in the prevention, treatment or rehabilitation of persons with heart disease.

9. Explaining the constituents of the blood and the use of each: plasma, red corpuscles, white corpuscles, platelets, antibodies.[51]

Medicare and Medicaid. Students may study about these new programs and become prepared to give information to members of their family or to neighbors and friends who are eligible for participation in the programs.

Teen docs. This name was selected by a group of teen-age boy volunteers who serve the United States Public Health Service Indian Hospital at Sells, Arizona. After a two-month period of orientation and organization this group began work in the pharmacy, kitchen, and medical records department. From time to time they met with Candy Stripers (girl volunteers) for training in such subjects as methods of artificial respiration and how pharmaceuticals are produced from raw products of nature. They were encouraged to discuss with parents and older relatives the plants and natural products which the Papago people have used to treat illness. These youth were able to talk with patients in their own language. They, their parents, and tribal leaders took much pride in the fact that this was the first group of boy volunteers to serve a Public Health Service Indian Hospital.[52]

World Health

A unit on world health would provide worthwhile study for young people who will soon be called upon to make decisions as citizens regarding support for international health programs. It would be well for them to study not only about the serious health problems still plaguing the developing parts of the world but also

51 Guide for the Montana School Health Program. 2nd Ed. Helena, Montana, The Montana State Board of Health, 1961, pp. 145–146.

52 The Teen Docs. Unpublished report provided by Mr. Henry J. Keneally, Jr., Chief, Area Health Education Branch, Indian Health Area Office, Public Health Service, Phoenix, Arizona, 1967.

about those problems of concern to more highly industrialized countries. Current information can be obtained through library research and in correspondence with the World Health Organization as well as with embassies of the countries under study.

Health problems vary by region.   Students may assemble detailed information pointing out how health problems differ from region to region and how they are influenced by the economic, political, and social development of the area. Differences in health problems because of climate may also be explored.

International health agencies and programs.   Committees of students could investigate the work of WHO (World Health Organization), UNICEF (United Nations Children's Fund), FAO (Food and Agriculture Organization) and UNESCO (United Nations Educational, Scientific, and Cultural Organization), all of which function as multilateral agencies. They might be interested in finding out how these agencies function in individual countries, individually and collectively, to strengthen the ability of the countries to provide their own resources and leadership for health improvements.

Contributions of the United States to international health programs.   Students may find out about the contributions our country makes directly (unilaterally) to other countries for health work, as through AID (Agency for International Development), and how it participates in multilateral programs. They might collect data on our financial contributions to these international efforts and compare figures with expenditures in other fields.

Experiences of Peace Corps volunteers.   Students may interview people who have returned from service in the Peace Corps to learn about their experiences. Many of these volunteers have worked at the village level, where they have had intimate contact with villagers. It would be worthwhile to find out about the major health problems in these villages and to learn how the villagers deal with them. There are many outstanding examples in different parts of the world of concerted local action to improve such conditions as nutrition, sanitation, and housing. A comparison between patterns of decision-making in these villages and decision-making in our society might be enlightening. We have much to learn from those parts of the world where through local initiative and leadership striking changes for the better have occurred.

S.W.A.Y. with WHO.   S.W.A.Y., Students War Against Yaws, is a Canadian centenary project initiated by students of Mount Royal High School, Montreal. Through their efforts, high schools throughout Canada have responded enthusiastically to letters sent by the Mount Royal S.W.A.Y. committee. Contributions have poured in from schools and adult groups to a special fund which has been established by WHO to fight this ugly tropical disease which brings misery and suffering to millions but which responds spectacularly to a single dose of penicillin, costing no more than a bottle of pop.[53]

Health Teaching through Selected Subject-Matter Areas

Social studies
1. How have health problems affected the course of civilizations?
2. What contributions to health were made by the early Greek and Roman civilizations?
3. Why may the Middle Ages be called the "dark ages" from the standpoint of health?
4. What governmental agencies are responsible for health protection and promotion, and how adequately do they meet the needs?
5. What evidences are there of the biological oneness of all races?
6. How can we know whether what we read and hear about health is sound?
7. What progress has been made in the areas of health and accident insurance?
8. How may better community planning contribute to health?
9. What progress is being made to improve health of the people throughout the world?

Science
1. What biological and health factors should be considered in choosing a mate?
2. How does life begin and develop?
3. What are the biological bases for good body care?
4. How are vision and hearing tested, and what are the biological and physical science principles involved?
5. How do glasses and hearing aids help to correct defects?
6. What new chemical substances are being used in the treatment of disease? As insecticides? What are potential dangers of these substances?
7. How may the principle of levers be applied to good body mechanics?

Language arts (writing, literature, and the like)
1. Participate in panel discussions on health problems, such as: How can we secure more adequate health services in our community? Should we have compulsory health insurance? Is our school a safe and healthy place in which to live and work? How can community housing be improved? Speeches on similar subjects can be prepared for delivery before both school and community groups.
2. Prepare research papers on such topics as housing and health; the cost of cancer; and how commercial advertisers use the health appeal.
3. Read literature dealing with health and medical progress; human relations; health professions; family life.
4. Prepare articles dealing with health for the school newspaper.

Physical education
1. How will physical activity contribute to personal appearance?
2. How can the body be used efficiently in work and play?

---

[53] S.W.A.Y. with W.H.O. Canada's Health and Welfare, *21*:4–5 (May) 1966.

3. How can one develop one's body so that it will be of the greatest service in all ways? (See also Junior High Schools).

Home economics
1. What should one know about the home care of the sick?
2. How can one budget for health?
3. What effect has poor housing on health?
4. What inexpensive improvements can be made in home furnishings and equipment that will contribute to more healthful living? (See also Junior High Schools).

Agriculture (See Junior High Schools).

SUMMARY

Health teaching in junior and senior years should stress the student's adjustments to himself and others, and his preparation for adulthood, as a member both of a family and of the community. Through this teaching every student should be helped to solve health problems realistically and sanely. Health problems are legion and so important in the life of the adolescent that they can be met only through planned health instruction. There are many suggestions in the chapter for teaching health. In the last analysis, however, the soundest teaching will grow out of teacher-student planning in a specific situation.

REFERENCES

Bernard, J., Editor: Teen-age culture. The Annals of The American Academy of Political and Social Science, *338*:1–210 (Nov.) 1961.

Britton, E. C., and Winans, J. M.: Growing from Infancy to Adulthood. New York, Appleton-Century-Crofts, Inc., 1958. Chapter 5: Characteristics of preadolescence, pp. 58–67. Chapter 6: Characteristics of children in early adolescence, pp. 68–84. Chapter 7: Late adolescence, pp. 85–90.

Clark, L. H., and Irving, S. S.: Secondary School Teaching Methods. 2nd Ed. New York, The Macmillan Company, 1967, 501 pp.

Deisher, R. W., and Mills, C. A.: The adolescent looks at his health and medical care. American Journal of Public Health, *53*: 1928–1936 (Dec.) 1963.

Florio, A. E., and Stafford, G. T.: Safety Education. New York, McGraw-Hill Book Company, Inc., 1962, 382 pp.

Health Problems of Adolescence. WHO Technical Report Series No. 308. Geneva, Switzerland, World Health Organization, 1965, 28 pp.

How Children Develop. Revised Ed. Columbus, Ohio, The Ohio State University, 1964, 68 pp. (Prepared by the faculty of University School, College of Education.)

Irwin, L. W., and Mayshark, C.: Health Education in Secondary Schools. St. Louis, The C. V. Mosby Company, 1964, 402 pp.

Jewett, A., and Knapp, C., Editors: The Growing Years; Adolescence. Fifth

AAHPER Yearbook. Washington, D. C., American Association for Health, Physical Education, and Recreation, 1962, 320 pp.

Joint Committee on Health Problems in Education of the National Education Association and the American Medical Association: Health Education, 5th Ed. Washington, D.C., and Chicago, The Associations, 1961, 429 pp.

Konopka, G.: The Adolescent Girl in Conflict. Englewood Cliffs, New Jersey, Prentice-Hall, Inc., 1966, 177 pp.

Oliva, P. F.: The Secondary School Today. Cleveland, World Publishing Co., 1967, 482 pp.

Rollins, S. P., and Unruh, A.: Introduction to Secondary Education. Chicago, Rand McNally and Company, 1964, 278 pp.

Sherif, M., and Sherif, C. W.: Problems of Youth; Transition to Adulthood in a Changing World. Chicago, Aldine Publishing Company, 1965, 336 pp.

CHAPTER

10

INDIVIDUALIZED HEALTH INSTRUCTION

At times in every child's life, health problems arise which need individual attention. Though parents and health personnel may be expected to assume major responsibility for helping with these problems, an alert and interested teacher can also do much.

The preceding chapters contain many practical suggestions for helping children meet their individual needs through group instruction; this chapter deals with individualized instruction. To carry on individualized instruction effectively, a teacher needs an overview of the entire field of health education. Only with such understanding can individualized instruction be in harmony with the purposes, principles, and procedures of health education. This chapter, therefore, has been placed late in the book. While concentrating here on the face-to-face approach, its close relationship to group instruction should be kept in mind. For most effective results, the two must go hand in hand, each enhancing the other and often leading into the other.

MEANING AND IMPORTANCE OF INDIVIDUALIZED HEALTH INSTRUCTION

Individualized health instruction is essentially the guidance of individuals toward improved health behavior.

The 1955 Yearbook of the Association for Supervision and Curriculum Development, *Guidance in the Curriculum,* states:

With individual differences as our starting point, we view guidance as relating to all those things which adults do consciously to assist an individual child to live as fully and effectively as he is able.

Such assistance on the part of school personnel may take an almost endless variety of forms—from studying some aspect of a child's life to understand him better, to devising learning situations from which he can gain a needed experience, to conferring with his parents to understand their expectations for the child, to being a sympathetic listener when he wants to talk, to giving him the consistent psychological support which encourages wiser self-direction. Guidance involves both helping the child adjust to a required pattern and adjusting the pattern better to fit the child. Since both of these adjustive aspects have the single objective of developing a human being who is capable of self-direction in a democratic society, the child's freedom of choice, commensurate with his maturity, must be protected. Helping each child to help himself and make his own decisions is inherent in such a concept of guidance.

Parents, teachers, supervisors, counselors, and many other people both inside and outside the school share in the child's guidance. The teacher, however, stands second only to the parents in the weight of his responsibility for guiding the development of the pupil.[1]

This view of guidance, when applied to the field of health, suggests that individualized health instruction consists of those functions which will help an individual to take "developmental, preventive, remedial, or corrective measures" resulting in the fullest use of his health potential. As suggested above, these functions assume many different forms. In general, they consist of fact-finding, information-giving, and helping a child toward greater self-understanding and self-direction. The interview method to be described in this chapter is the one most commonly used to fulfill these functions.

Fact-Finding

An initial step in an individualized approach to health is the gathering of facts upon which to base deliberate one-to-one assistance. The physician seeks information from a patient before making a diagnosis and prescribing treatment. The teacher seeks information, however, not to make a diagnosis, but to appraise the situation before attempting to give help or to seek help from other sources. To obtain these essential facts, teachers widely use the interview method, along with observation, study of records, and other procedures.

Information-Giving

In daily contacts with children the teacher is constantly giving information intended to be useful. When this information is given

---

[1] Low, C. M.: Setting our sights. In Guidance in the Curriculum. 1955 Yearbook. Washington, D.C., Association for Supervision and Curriculum Development, NEA, 1955, p. 13.

for health reasons on an individual basis, as through the interview, it may include such facts as where to turn for help on a specific problem, how others have handled this problem, and a summary of alternative choices with the possible consequences of each. Information-giving on a one-to-one basis is likely to be most meaningful, however, when it is an integral part of problem-solving methods directed toward decision-making on the part of the child.

Helping toward Greater Self-Understanding and Self-Direction

An ultimate goal of health education, as indicated in earlier chapters, is to help children, on their own initiative and commensurate with their maturity, to translate health knowledge into desirable health action. Health education, thus conceived, is a leading forth, a guiding of children toward greater self-understanding and self-direction. When carried on through individualized instruction, the teacher assists a specific child to identify his own needs and to take whatever steps are essential for meeting these needs. This procedure involves fact-finding on the part of both teacher and pupil, information-giving by the teacher as well as information-seeking by the child, and decision-making for which the child assumes major responsibility at his level of development. This chapter focuses attention on this third and most far-reaching approach.

THE TEACHER'S ROLE IN INDIVIDUALIZED HEALTH INSTRUCTION

From the foregoing paragraphs it is apparent that the teacher is only one of several people likely to be involved in helping an individual child with his special health needs and interests.

Degree of Involvement

The degree to which a teacher enters into a one-to-one relationship will be determined by such factors as school policies, the teacher's own capacities and work load, availability of consultant services from health personnel, and the complexity of the problem. To differentiate between those specific needs with which the teacher can safely and legitimately deal and those which are primarily the responsibility of parents and health personnel is beyond the scope of this chapter. Judgment enters the picture here: judgment founded on sound health knowledge and a realistic evaluation of each situation.

The teacher is in a unique position to initiate individualized instruction. His intimate contact with a child places him in a favorable position to detect conditions requiring attention and to encourage the child and his parents to do something about these conditions. In cases too involved for the teacher himself to handle, his counseling may be needed to direct child and parents to appropriate sources of help.

The teacher, moreover, is a strategic person to help the child follow through on health recommendations in cooperation with parents and health personnel. When providing such help, the teacher will want to make certain that he is acting in harmony with efforts of parents and health personnel, reinforcing and supplementing but at no time replacing these efforts. If he is the least bit in doubt as to the part it is feasible and wise for him to play, he should discuss his role with the nurse in the school and with the school administrator. One must not tamper ignorantly with matters of health and disease—too much is at stake. A wrong move may aggravate rather than alleviate a child's difficulties and may even be disastrous.

Specific Areas for Individualized Health Instruction

The problems around which individualized instruction may revolve are myriad. They are as diverse as the children themselves. They may range from a fleeting need, such as a seating adjustment, easily dealt with in a casual and informal way, to needs which require the most expert medical attention, such as a chronic heart ailment.

Problems Arising in the Daily Life at School

Many such problems occur regularly in the classroom, on the playground, in the lunchroom, and elsewhere at school. Excessive fatigue is an example. To illustrate, a teacher in one school, noticing that a child was overly tired, thought, "Perhaps he has been staying up too late at night to follow a favorite television program; if so, this is a situation which I should be able to help correct through wise counseling." However, after interviewing the child, the teacher suspected there were underlying physical or emotional reasons for the fatigue. He immediately discussed the child's problem with the public health nurse working in the school. Parents and physician, as well as the nurse, soon became involved until diagnosis had been made and remedial treatment prescribed. Armed with information about the child's situation relayed by the nurse, the teacher soon found himself performing important guidance functions through providing supportive help as the child carried out a modified school program in line with the prescribed treatment.

Illnesses, Disabilities, and Impairments

Deviations from health found through teacher observation, screening procedures, and health examinations must be handled on an individual basis from the point of detection to that of correction or adjustment. The most common of these deviations have been outlined in Chapter 2.

The Disadvantaged Child

Project Head Start and similar programs have directed attention to the importance of giving personalized help to a large group of children from culturally deprived backgrounds. Especially acute is their need for developing a sense of individual identity. Some children from impoverished backgrounds approach school age without knowing their own names and without an awareness of those physical characteristics which give them individuality. Individual attention, as well as group experiences, is imperative for the unfolding of these young personalities.

The Gifted Child

The gifted child whose abilities and interests qualify him to delve more deeply into his health studies than does the class as a whole needs individualized instruction. His needs can be partially met in classrooms which encourage independent study and which provide a wide range of resource materials from which he can draw. When the teacher is not able to provide all of the help the child requires for developing his full potential, he should seek assistance from those who can. Health personnel in school and community, as well as hospitals and medical and dental societies, may be able to provide challenging experiences for such a young person in line with his special aptitudes.

Career Interests

Individual counseling of young people with potential interest in and qualifications for careers in nursing, medicine, or other health fields is important. Though a boy's or girl's interest in a career may have been aroused through group instruction or otherwise, he will need guidance on a one-to-one basis if he is to determine his capacities for the career and learn what preparation is required. Moreover, through counseling on the part of both teachers and vocational guidance personnel, he may be directed to sources of information especially pertinent to his needs.

The Child Voluntarily Seeking Help

Such a child warrants special attention. He is more likely to be receptive to assistance and to act on whatever decisions grow out of an interview than is the child who has been sought out by the teacher or another health worker. The adolescent girl, for example, is often troubled by the physical and emotional changes accompanying pubescence. A teacher who holds her confidence may give invaluable help at this critical time in the girl's life.

THE INTERVIEW METHOD

As indicated earlier in this chapter, individualized instruction is ordinarily given by means of the interview. Interviews conducted primarily for the purpose of leading to decision-making on the part of the child characteristically follow steps in problem solving as outlined in Chapter 6. As the interviewer and the child being interviewed interact, problems are stated and defined, facts are assembled and analyzed, conclusions are reached, and, in successful cases, appropriate action follows. Though attention is directed to problem solving on a one-to-one basis, it is well to remember that significant changes can occur in individual health behavior through problem solving within group situations. This method has been discussed elsewhere in this book.

Suggestions for conducting a successful interview, given here, embody principles and techniques recognizable as sound in all human relationships and particularly in relationships directed toward strengthening an individual's ability to assume responsibility for his own well-being.

Preparing for the Interview

Bingham and Moore,[2] in a useful book, *How to Interview*, have outlined six points to keep in mind when preparing for an interview. Discussed within the context of this chapter, they are:

---

[2] Bingham, W. V. D., and Moore, B. V.: How to Interview. 4th Ed. New York, Harper and Brothers, 1959, pp. 64–65.

Decide What Is to Be Accomplished

If an interview has been initiated by the child, the teacher will be guided in deciding what is to be accomplished by the expectations of the child. As the interview progresses and both teacher and child gain insights, these expectations may change. Expressed needs and interests, though not always the underlying reasons for seeking help, do provide a starting point for a one-to-one relationship and should be honored.

Interviews initiated by the teachers as a result of some health condition observed or referred for attention likewise need clear definition. For example, when a modified activity program has been prescribed for a child recovering from an illness, the teacher has the need and the right to know just what type of activity is suitable and in what amount. Directions from the child's physician, often relayed through the nurse working in the school, should be sufficiently explicit so that the teacher knows what can or should be attempted.

Know the Child Being Interviewed

Daily observation of the child at work and at play, health records, interviews with parents and health and counseling personnel are among the most productive ways of learning about the child to be interviewed. Usually this information is not complete when an interview or series of interviews starts; however, the teacher should secure as much background as possible before the interview. When good relationships have been established with a child and his parents, additional information is likely to come forth as the interview unfolds.

Make Appointments

This suggestion applies particularly when parents are involved. It may also be necessary to arrange with the child himself for a specific time when he and the teacher can sit down together without interruptions.

Provide for Privacy

Health for a child is a very personal matter. Problems he brings to a teacher should be held in confidence. He must feel he can talk freely and without fear of gossip or ridicule from other children. In a crowded classroom and in the midst of a busy school day, a confidential atmosphere may be difficult to attain; however, if a teacher is sensitive to the feelings of children, he will doubtless find ways to talk with those in need of help without doing it in the presence of others.

Practice Taking the Point of View of the Child Being Interviewed

This suggestion applies to all good teaching. It is particularly pertinent when dealing with personal health needs.

The teacher must comprehend the child's attitudes toward the health problem as well as his understanding of its implications. It is well to remember that his attitudes are usually influenced by those of family and friends as well as by his own values.

Important, too, is an understanding of the child's reactions to the teacher or other interviewer—what he really thinks about him and to what extent he is receptive to his help. If he holds the teacher in high esteem, if he believes he can be of help, then the teacher is in a better position to provide assistance than if such esteem were lacking. Yet there are exceptions to this generalization. Sometimes a teacher may be held in high esteem, yet be shunned for individual counseling. The very fact that he is highly respected can create temporary barriers to communication, for a child may want to "put his best foot forward" with such a person and not risk losing face. Then, too, by the very nature of his work, a teacher must often assume an authoritarian role, a role which can easily carry over into the one-to-one relationship. Many children become passive before an authoritarian figure and inwardly resentful if not outwardly so.

Know Your Own Personality

Much has been written about the personality of the teacher and its effect on children. Self-analysis regarding one's feelings toward a child and one's prejudices toward the health condition under consideration is important. Not all children are easy to get along with and not all health problems are pleasant to handle. Conscious and unconscious reactions to situations can subtly influence the effectiveness of the interviewer.

An awareness of ways in which one deals with one's own personal needs within a face-to-face relationship is likewise important. Some people gain great satisfaction in regulating the lives of others. All of us want recognition from our supervisors and administrators for a job well done. We must ask ourselves frankly, "Are these personal needs entering into the relationship? Do they interfere with our sensitivity to the child's needs?" The teacher who recognizes what his personal needs are and has some insight as to ways in which he is handling them will approach a one-to-one relationship more constructively than one who lacks such perspective.

Conducting the Interview

An interview is a two-way process with communication required on the part of both the interviewer and the one interviewed. A few pointers for conducting an interview are given here.

Establish Rapport

The pupil must feel comfortable with the teacher and must believe that the teacher is genuinely interested in him. He must know that the teacher accepts him for what he is and stands ready to help him in whatever way he requires help. The extent to which rapport can be established between the two depends greatly upon the image the child has of the teacher as a result of classroom encounters. In general it may be said that a child will more readily respond to the warm, friendly teacher who likes children and has a basic faith and trust in them than to the teacher who is indifferent, nagging, or so involved with his own personal needs that those of the children go unheeded.

A first step in establishing rapport is recognizing and accepting the perceptions and attitudes a child holds toward the teacher as well as the teacher's own feeling and reactions in the situation. Time and patience may be needed to change those perceptions, feelings, and reactions which interfere with effective communication. The teacher can increase his understanding of sound mental health principles conducive to good rapport through readings in the fields of educational psychology, guidance, counseling, and social work. Several helpful references are given at the end of this chapter.

At the beginning of an interview, the teacher should make every attempt to put the child at ease. General conversation apart from the underlying reason for the interview may contribute to the relaxed atmosphere essential for easy communication. Several informal contacts may be necessary before a mutually satisfactory relationship has been established. Such preliminary overtures are time-consuming but are not time-wasting if they lead to understanding which makes it possible for the teacher to help the child.

Listen and Observe

Careful attention to the child's words will give clues which should be of value to the teacher. In health matters, we hear many

Figure 26. Listening and observing are essential in establishing effective communication. (Courtesy of the National Education Association.)

things from children about illnesses and disease which should be taken in good faith, but not always literally. On the one hand, they may be of little importance, or, on the other, may be symptomatic of more deep-lying problems requiring expert help. Listening becomes a good screening device in separating those problems with which the teacher himself can safely and confidently deal from those which should be referred to others for attention.

Listening with empathy helps a child to release tensions which may impede effective communication. If the child has taken the initiative in going to the teacher with a problem which is bothering him, he will expect a ready ear. Any tendency on the part of the teacher to control the interview at this point may so discourage the child that he will refuse to reveal the purposes of his visit. If the teacher, on his own, or on advice of health personnel, has initiated the interview, the reason for the interview should be explained, but again the child should be given opportunity to present his point of view at the earliest possible moment.

Listening is a skill which must be developed. Few of us listen well. In teaching, particularly, we tend to dominate situations, giving others too little opportunity to talk. Studies have shown that in all walks of life we do selective listening. We hear what we want to hear and distort those things we hear so that they fit in with our beliefs and prejudices. Moreover, we do not hear many things at all simply because our previous experiences have not conditioned us to be alert to these things. Or we hear at a superficial level, not really grasping the full impact of what a person is saying. A classic example of this last is the child who tells his mother at breakfast that he doesn't feel well and wants to stay home from school. Taken at face value, he is sick. But on questioning the child, the mother may discover he is dodging a scheduled test at school. In one such instance, when a mother asked her seven-year-old daughter what kind of a pain it was, she replied, "I have the kind of pain that when I don't want to do something, I don't," a response showing more insight than is usually the case.

Observation during an interview serves several purposes. It may supplement a more casual observation of a health condition which has led to the interview. It should not, however, become a diagnosis. Posture, facial expressions, and other mannerisms and gestures may suggest emotional factors needing attention. They also give the teacher some indication of the degree to which rapport has been established and of the child's attitude toward his part in the interview. When the interview is accompanied by the demonstration of a skill, as in laboratory or field work, observation may reveal faulty procedures which need correcting or well-administered procedures deserving of commendation.

Encourage Forward Movement toward Greater Self-Understanding and Self-Direction

The pupil who has gone to the teacher for help should be encouraged as early as possible to state his problem. The teacher, in turn, should assist him to clarify the problem through raising pertinent questions or offering pertinent information. When the teacher initiates the interview, he too should define the problem in terms that are understandable and acceptable to the child and in a nonthreatening manner. Together, they will grapple for facts which will throw further light on the problem and on possible steps required for its resolution.

In an interview which has greater self-understanding and self-direction as its goal, the teacher should take care to avoid arriving at premature decisions. Moreover, the teacher will refrain from prescribing a specific course of action. Most children are anxious for quick and easy answers and are all too willing to let the teacher make decisions for them. It takes time and effort to think things through for oneself, especially if the difficulties to be overcome, or lived with, are great as so often is the case with illnesses, disease, and handicapping conditions.

A variety of techniques has been suggested for helping with such forward movement toward behavior change. They are essentially the same techniques used in classroom teaching. A few typical examples of techniques adaptable to different age levels are mentioned here.

On an initial contact, questions such as "What have you on your mind?" or "Can I help you?" may help to launch a problem-solving interview. As discussion proceeds and the need for clarification is evident, the teacher may comment on some pertinent thing he has noticed or raise such a question as, "Have you thought of this?"

Throughout the problem-solving process the child should be given essential facts which are comprehensible at his level of maturity. The teacher may possess or be able to secure some of these facts, but sometimes will find it wiser to refer the child to the parent or to the health authority. The public health nurse working in the school is an indispensable link with parent, physician, or other source of health information or counseling.

In giving information, the teacher may use both the direct and indirect approach. An example of the direct approach would be telling a child with vision difficulties that he should sit in the front of the room and should always wear his glasses. An indirect approach might be raising questions about his classroom practices in order to help him recognize on his own that his difficulties in seeing the blackboard may be the result of sitting at too great a distance from the front of the room or failure to use his glasses, and then asking him what he thinks he could do to improve the situation. With the direct approach goes the assumption that the teacher knows best and the child should comply with the teacher's directions. The indirect approach is intended to lead to greater self-direction. Both have their place. In emergency situations when quick decisions must be made, the direct approach is necessary. The indirect approach is something to work toward, but must often be combined with the more direct approach until the child is ready to think and act for himself.

When a child seems anxious or tense and in need of support, a few quiet comments such as "I understand" or "You *do* have a problem" may help to ease the situation. Even a smile, an affirmative nod, or a response such as "Yes" or "Good" or "Right" have been found through studies to provide the encouragement needed for a person to continue toward a clarification or solution of his problem.

Sometimes in an interview there is a tendency to go over and over the same points. Though some repetition, or at least some reviewing of the problems from different angles may be desirable, every effort should be made to move forward toward decision-making. As a step in this direction, the teacher may from time to time wish to summarize what has occurred thus far. When time for decision-making has arrived, the teacher can further help the child to clarify his thinking and arrive at a plan for next steps by stating alternative paths which may be followed, along with possible consequences of each potential choice, and by giving the child support until he has made his decisions. Follow-up interviews will often be necessary to help the child implement his decisions with action or modify his plans as further experience is gained.

Identify and Use Opportunities for Constructive Teaching and Learning

Instructional opportunities in the interview should be used to the fullest. The very process of problem solving, when perceived and used as such, can become an educational experience for the child.

The value of the interview as an educational tool is well illustrated in the case of children with special handicaps. A diabetic child, for example, must learn to follow medically prescribed measures and to make the emotional adjustments required so that he can live a reasonably normal life, despite his handicap. One elementary teacher with a diabetic child in her room found that the child would go to her now and then to talk about his condition and the measures which his parents and he were following under medical orders to control the disease. This teacher, whose help in the case had been enlisted by parents and medical personnel, was able in turn to assist the child in accepting his condition and in planning his day at school within limitations placed upon him. She did not admonish, cajole, or become overly solicitous, nor did she turn personal contacts with the child into formalized and structured interviews. She was a good listener, however, and when necessary, did not hesitate to remind, question, or offer supportive comments which would help the child. Bit by bit the child was able to accept the routines he must follow. Increasingly he was able to understand why these routines were important and how they could be executed at school without interfering seriously with studies or play.

In quite a different context, the interview can be employed effectively as an educational method when helping young people with their career goals. In larger school systems, guidance personnel may be available to counsel the students, but frequently the home-room teacher or instructors in such courses as health, science, and home economics find themselves in a vocational counseling role regarding careers in health fields. Interest in some careers, such as nursing and medicine, may begin even during elementary years. Whenever a teacher discovers a young person who expresses interest in a specific career, he may raise a few well-placed questions to help the person realistically view his own qualifications and his capacity for the required preparation. The teacher will, of course, share what information he has on the career, but for additional information will refer the young person to resource materials and to people engaged in the work. The interview may lead to arrangements for the student to gain experience in a health agency or hospital during out-of-school hours in order to introduce him further to the career and to test his interest and abilities. Helping an individual in these ways may be exceedingly educational for him as well as useful in planning his future.

SUMMARY

Individualized health instruction is essentially health guidance of individuals toward desirable behavior change. This chapter suggests ways in which a teacher, along with parents and health personnel, can provide individualized health instruction by means of the interview. The interview is seen as a means of fact-finding, information-giving, and helping a child toward greater self-understanding and self-direction. Suggestions are given on ways to prepare for and conduct the interview so that it has maximum educational value.

REFERENCES

Crescimbeni, J., and Thomas, G. I.: Individualizing Instruction in the Elementary School. New York, Random House, Inc., 1967, 428 pp.

Drews, E. M.: Self actualization: a new focus for education. In Learning and Mental Health in the School. Washington, D.C., Association for Supervision and Curriculum Development, NEA, 1966, pp. 99–124.

Gardner, J. W.: Self-Renewal; The Individual and the Innovative Society. New York, Harper Colophon Books, Harper & Row, 1965, 141 pp.

Garrett, A. M.: Interviewing; Its Principles and Methods. New York, Family Service Association of America, 1960, 123 pp.

Guidance in the Curriculum. 1955 Yearbook. Washington, D.C., Association for Supervision and Curriculum Development, NEA, 1955, 231 pp.

Hollis, F.: Casework; A Psychosocial Therapy. New York, Random House, Inc., 1964, 300 pp.

Hollister, W. G.: Preparing the minds of the future: enhancing ego processes through curriculum development. In Curriculum Change: Direction and Process. Washington, D.C., Association for Supervision and Curriculum Development, NEA, 1966, pp. 27–42.

Individualizing Instruction. Washington, D.C., Association for Supervision and Curriculum Development, NEA, 1964, 174 pp.

Individualizing Instruction. The Sixty-first Yearbook of the National Society for the Study of Education. Chicago, The University of Chicago Press, 1962. (See especially, The curriculum and individual differences, by F. T. Wilhelms, pp. 62–74.)

Jersild, A. T.: When Teachers Face Themselves. New York, Teachers College, Columbia University, 1955, 169 pp.

Joint Committee on Health Problems in Education of the National Education Association and the American Medical Association: Health Education. 5th Ed. Washington, D.C., and Chicago, The Associations, 1961, 429 pp.

Perlman, H. H.: Social Casework; A Problem-Solving Process. Chicago, The University of Chicago Press, 1957, 268 pp.

CHAPTER

11

EVALUATION

Evaluation occupies an important place in health instruction—evaluation of the results of the instruction and evaluation of the instructional process itself. The thoughtful teacher is constantly searching for evidence that his teaching is leading toward improved health behavior of the pupils or toward health improvements within home, school, and community. Moreover, he is concerned with the manner in which he proceeds with his health instruction—with his approaches in determining needs and objectives and in selecting and organizing content and learning experiences. This chapter is intended to help the teacher with evaluation; it presents a general plan for evaluation as well as concrete suggestions for carrying it out in a classroom situation.

EVALUATION—ITS MEANING, IMPORTANCE, AND SCOPE

Evaluation, as the term is used here, is the process of determining the degree to which instructional objectives are being met. It also involves an assessment of the instructional efforts themselves in the light of generally accepted educational principles and practices. In a classroom situation, evaluation often goes on quite informally as a teacher attempts to determine the progress pupils are making toward predetermined goals. He may ask, for example, How do the pupils feel about this study? Are they really interested and to what extent have they become actively involved in planning and carrying out the various learning experiences? Do they see the application of what we are studying in their own lives? Are their health practices improving as a result of the study? Am I selecting content and learning experiences which will facilitate these attitudes and actions of the pupils?

In working with a particular group of pupils for a limited time, one cannot always hope to find clear evidence of progress or of achievements. Moreover, when such evidence exists, it is often difficult to differentiate between the influences of the school and those of other forces. If teachers depended wholly upon evidence of change in pupils' behavior attributable to school health education, they might become hopelessly discouraged. We know that pupil progress is apt to be slow and difficult to measure in specific, tangible ways. Likewise, home, school, and community changes are slow and hard to measure. Results of teaching are cumulative, often extending over many years. These results cannot be observed fully by the school. While the assessing of progress or achievements should not be abandoned, additional ways must be found to judge a program.

An examination of the health education program itself thus becomes a legitimate part, though only a part, of evaluation. The content of the program, the methods employed, and the materials used can be studied in line with the best health and educational standards we know. Many of these standards have been suggested in this book.

Whether the evaluation deals with progress or achievements or primarily with the program itself, it is important for several reasons:

1. It helps the teacher to know where to place emphasis in teaching. It may show which behavior patterns and which home, school, and community conditions have been improved as a result of teaching efforts, and which need further attention.

2. It helps to show strengths and weaknesses in teaching procedure. When an instructional program has produced results, evaluation may reveal which procedures have proved worthwhile. Conversely, when a program has failed it may show which procedures have been ineffective.

3. Evaluation made by the pupils themselves may help them to find out their own progress in improving health behavior and stimulate them to further effort.

4. Evaluation may be used as a basis for marks. This statement applies only to systematic health instruction and only to schools in which marking systems are used.

5. Evaluation aids health committees and curriculum planning groups in improving the organization of school-wide health projects and in the coordination of school and community health programs.

6. Evaluation gives data which are useful in convincing administrators and citizens of a community of the value of health instruction.

Who Should Do the Evaluating?

Both the teachers and the pupils should participate in evaluation activities; parents, health workers, and others, too, should have a part. Although the most significant evaluations take place informally in day-by-day class work with the pupils as active participants, school-wide and system-wide evaluations also have their place. Health committees, curriculum groups, and teaching staffs in general should make evaluation a continuing part of their efforts.

Outside groups working in cooperation with school personnel may conduct evaluation studies. These groups usually have had special training in evaluation techniques and have funds at their command to conduct studies of this type, which often contribute greatly to our general knowledge in the field of health education.

When Should Evaluations Be Made?

Evaluation should be a continuous process, begun with the initiation of a project, and carried on as long as results are discernible. Young children often take stock of progress and accomplishments at the end of each day. With older pupils, intervals vary widely depending upon the project.

At the Beginning

There should be a base line for every health instructional effort. Before a project starts, pertinent data on the health conditions being dealt with should be assembled so that one can know later what progress has been made. Moreover, specific objectives of the project should have been formulated at the beginning, not only to serve as a point of departure for selecting content and learning experiences, but also as a basis for evaluation.

As a Project Develops

Periodic stock-taking throughout the project, by both pupils and teachers, is necessary in order to answer such questions as, "What have we accomplished so far?" "Where are we now?" "What more needs to be done?" "Which children are responding to educational efforts?" "Which children are not responding to educational efforts?"

At the End of a Project, and Later

Evaluations should be made at the end of a project to determine results and to aid in future program planning. Equally important are those made later when long-term effects can be learned.

STEPS IN THE EVALUATION PROCESS

There are several distinct but closely interrelated steps in the evaluation process. They are as follows:

1. Determining and stating objectives.
2. Listing specific items to be considered in the evaluation (establishing criteria).
3. Recording conditions and events.
4. Developing and using the most effective evaluation instruments for the study of each item under evaluation.
5. Interpreting the findings and drawing conclusions.
6. Using information obtained for improving health instruction.

Each of these steps is discussed in the following pages. An example is then given of their application.

Determining and Stating Objectives

Objectives, as stated previously, should evolve from needs, with recognition of resources and limitations. Moreover, they should be formulated so that they not only identify the behavioral changes that are desired but also define the conditions under which the changes are to occur. Specific suggestions have been given in Chapter 5 on how to determine and formulate objectives and how to use them as a basis for selection of content and learning experiences. We cannot teach intelligently until we know what needs to be accomplished. Neither can we evaluate what has been done without knowing first what our objectives are. Objectives provide the key to evaluation by giving in specific terms the behavioral patterns desired.

Listing Specific Items to Be Considered in the Evaluation (Establishing Criteria)

By breaking down objectives into parts that are small and discrete enough to be examined one at a time, we can establish criteria for evaluation. These criteria define in concrete terms the performances of the pupils which are acceptable in the process of attaining objectives. Similarly, desirable project standards should be determined at this stage.

Recording Conditions and Events

When developing a project it is important to have tangible evidence of changes that are occurring in the pupils and in the conduct of the project. This evidence should be accumulated systematically by means of such procedures as are suggested in the next section. The teacher should keep records from the beginning of a project; they can often become useful evaluation instruments. If objectives have been carefully prepared and criteria for each objective established (as well as criteria for project standards), the teacher will have a basis for knowing what kind of records he should keep. Many teachers have wished, too late, that they had kept detailed accounts for comparisons later. It is well to secure the help of pupils. They, too, are capable of becoming interested in collecting evidences of their own progress.

**Developing and Using the Most Effective
Evaluation Instruments for the Study of
Each Item under Evaluation**

This is a critical stage in evaluation. One must be certain that an evaluation instrument fits the thing being evaluated. In education, we have too often turned to traditional testing devices and given little thought to their suitability. For example, health knowledge tests are frequently used in connection with health teaching, yet proof that a student knows something is no proof that he is putting that knowledge into action in his daily living. If it is the intent of the teacher to provide learning experiences which will result in improved health practices, then instruments which are more discriminating than a health test will be required to determine whether or not the health practices have in fact improved.

Evaluation instruments used commonly in determining progress toward goals in health instruction are listed here. They are similar in many respects to the methods suggested in Chapters 2 and 3 for determining health needs of children and of home, school, and community.

Observation and Listening

Teachers use these procedures regularly in their day-by-day contacts with children. Though subjective methods, they provide much valuable information.

Interviews and Conferences

Personal interviews with the children, and conferences with

parents, health personnel, and other teachers help to reveal evidences of progress.

Check Lists and Questionnaires

These may be used to help determine pupil attitudes, interests, knowledge, and practices. They may also be used in home, school, and community surveys. When given periodically, and under properly controlled conditions, they may show progress in these different areas.

Records and Reports

The health examination records, absence records, and other health and personnel records may provide valuable data from which to draw evidence of progress. In interpreting these data, teachers should take care not to read too much into them. For example, data may show evidences of improvement as a result of better health services, as well as of better teaching.

Anecdotal records kept by teachers, in which are recorded observations and significant events in the classroom, may give valuable subjective evidence of change.

Surveys

Periodic surveys, conducted by pupils, teachers, health councils, or others, when made in terms of program objectives, are another type of instrument commonly used in evaluation studies. In making the surveys, some of the previously listed techniques may be used, such as observation, interviews, check lists, and questionnaires.

Photographs

Pictures of significant points in a project may be taken periodically as a project develops.

Health Tests

Oral and written tests are another common instrument to show progress.

Samples of Pupils' Work

Samples of the creative work of pupils may give evidence that principles and concepts have been learned and applied. Included

Figure 27. Creative work of pupils gives evidence that concepts have been learned. (Courtesy of St. Augustine School, Hartford, Connecticut.)

among these samples may be written work, notebooks, exhibits, charts, and the like.

Pupil Diaries

Day-by-day accounts of activities and thoughts kept in diary form by pupils, particularly in the elementary grades, are often significant materials to use in an evaluation study.

Interpreting the Findings and Drawing Conclusions

This step is essential in any evaluation. Making the evaluation is not enough. The study findings should be analyzed and interpreted if they are to have significant value. Perhaps it will be discovered that learning experiences were not provided which would evoke the changes in behavior which were intended, or that those which were provided were inappropriate. Perhaps new and broader interests of pupils are revealed which suggest possibilities for further study. Or perhaps misinformation or poor practices are evident which need to be corrected as the project develops.

Using Information Obtained for Improving Health Instruction

This step is a natural sequence to the previous step and should be one of the important justifications for attempting to evaluate a project. When the evaluative approach is used throughout a project, it is possible to shift course if indicated and to introduce different and more effective learning experiences. At all times evaluation can lead to improved teaching and learning.

Steps in the Evaluation of a Bicycle Safety Education Project

The interrelationship of the steps just outlined is shown here by using as an example the hypothetical bicycle safety education project discussed in Chapter 5. It is suggested that at this point the reader review pages 123–124 and 130–131 where the project was used to illustrate how objectives may be determined and also to show how objectives may serve as guides in the selection of learning experiences. Thus the interlocking of objectives, learning experiences, and evaluation can be better appreciated than were evaluation viewed alone.

Two objectives only are taken from the list of those developed for the hypothetical bicycle safety project. For each objective, criteria for evaluation are outlined and for each criterion, appropriate evaluation instruments are proposed. A similar treatment is given to an evaluation of the project itself. Suggestions are also made for records to keep in connection with the project.

Objectives

Objective 1. The pupil is able to list the circumstances under which bicycle accidents occur most frequently in the United States.

Criteria
- a. The pupil turns to dependable sources for data.
  Evaluation instruments: observation; interviews; records. A pretest might be given initially to find out what he already knows about sources for data.
- b. The pupil is able to select pertinent data from information that is available.
  Evaluation instruments: observation; interviews; records; sample of pupil's work (list of sources).
- c. The pupil classifies data according to location, age, sex, nature of violation, or by other categories.
  Evaluation instruments: sample of pupil's work; written test on the subject.

Objective 4. The bicyclist improves his bicycle-riding practices.

Criteria
- a. The pupil gives evidence through his individual record of daily riding experiences that he recognizes hazards and takes positive steps to avoid them.
  Evaluation instrument: pupil record.
- b. The pupil demonstrates good riding practices during a bicycle safety test.
  Evaluation instruments: observation; check list; photographs; oral or written tests.
- c. The pupil shows by other means that his bicycle-riding practices have improved.
  Evaluation instruments: observation; listening; anecdotal records of comments pupil makes about his practices; tests; comments of parents.

Project Standards (Selected)

Criteria
- a. The pupil is given time and encouragement to pursue this study.
  Evaluation instruments: class schedule; comments of pupil and teachers.
- b. The teacher has access to pertinent data and directs the pupil to it, at the same time allowing him to find his own information.
  Evaluation instruments: records; making mental note of teacher-pupil relationship; reports from school librarian.
- c. Arrangements are made for the pupil to take a bicycle safety test.
  Evaluation instrument: evidence that test is given.

Examples of Records Which Might Be Kept in Connection with the Project

List of sources to which the pupil turns for data as well as list of possible other sources.

Anecdotal records of comments pupil makes about his practices.

Brief diary of sequence of events kept by teacher and pupil.

Notes on successful activities which might be shared later with other teachers—or used in future projects.

The various samples of pupil's work mentioned earlier.

EVALUATING PROGRESS IN PUPIL HEALTH BEHAVIOR

In evaluating progress in pupil health behavior, the teacher will be concerned with evidences of changes in (1) values, attitudes, and interests; (2) knowledge and the ability to think critically; and (3) health practices. Each of these will be discussed in turn.

Change in Values, Attitudes, and Interests

If a teacher is working toward better health behavior among the pupils, some of the first things to look for as signs of progress are changes in values, attitudes, and interests. These attributes are difficult to define; they are even more difficult to measure.

The most common instruments for evaluating these areas of behavior are observation and listening, interviews and conferences, check lists and questionnaires (including interest studies), and pupil diaries.

A teacher who is sensitive to the children's reactions is constantly judging their values, attitudes, and interests by means of observation and listening. Does their interest in a project grow as the work develops? Do they take increasing initiative in carrying out activities? Are they showing greater willingness to practice desirable health behavior? Informal class discussions and panel discussions are additional means for becoming aware of pupil values, attitudes, and interests.

Interviews and conferences also give clues. A student may make such comments as, "I was always afraid of the nurse during my grade school years, but since I've had a chance to work with her on special projects I have an entirely different feeling. I think that what she does is wonderful, and she is so quiet, patient, and helpful with everyone." Parents' comments, too, are worth seeking.

Check lists and questionnaires have been used widely. Attitude studies and public opinion polls usually seek opinions of people regarding various health matters, but are nevertheless helpful in giving indications of values and attitudes.

Interest studies may be used at different points in a project as it develops. Since interests are by-products of past experiences, of methods of teaching, and of things of momentary concern both locally and nationally, as well as of the maturity level of the pupils, they have meaning only in the situation in which they are studied. To attempt to use the findings of an interest study from another community as a basis for class planning would obviously be unsound.

Improvement in Knowledge and the Ability to Think Critically

One may expect as an outcome of a well-balanced program a gradual growth in knowledge and in the ability to think critically in matters related to health. To learn whether such outcomes are being realized requires periodic evaluation. Evaluation instruments most commonly used to study changes in knowledge are health tests and samples of pupils' work. The use of problem solving situations and case studies may help to reveal progress in pupils' abilities to think critically.

Health tests may be either oral or written. They may be given at the beginning of, during, and at the end of a project or course. They may be subjective (e.g., essay) or objective (e.g., multiple choice or matching). Both locally prepared and standardized tests may be used. For each situation the teacher will need to determine the type of test best suited to the objectives. To illustrate, if the objective is to learn a specific body of health information, then an objective test embodying the health facts taught would be appropriate. If, however, the objective is to develop judgment in the handling of situations and critical thinking, then a better test would be the presentation of problem solving situations for the pupils to work out.

Pretests which give information on pupil knowledge at the beginning of a program may provide a base line for selection of content and learning experiences and for evaluation. They often help to arouse interest among the pupils, and thus such a test becomes a valuable teaching device as well as an evaluation instrument.

In general, it is better for a teacher to make out his own tests so that they will be in accord with program objectives. There are times, however, when standardized tests are preferred as, for example, during special research studies when one group of pupils is being compared with another.

An examination of pupils' work, such as notebooks and exhibits, may reveal the extent to which the pupils are able to apply health principles and to use health facts accurately. The pupils themselves should be encouraged to evaluate their own work under teacher guidance.

Improvement in Health Practices

Improvement in health practices is the goal of all health education. To obtain evidence that this improvement has actually occurred as a result of teaching efforts, then, is a basic part of an evaluation. Such evidence, however, is not always easy to secure. Sometimes one cannot distinguish between the improvements that are a result of teaching, and those that have taken place because of better services and more effective regulations. If we assume, however, that wise use of services, and cooperation in respect to regulations are usually dependent upon education, then most improved practices are the result, at least to a certain degree, of education.

Evaluation instruments most widely used to study health practices, much the same as those for evaluating change in values, attitudes, and interests, are observation, interviews and conferences, check lists and questionnaires, records and reports, surveys, samples of pupils' work, and pupil diaries.

Observation once again is the most common form of evaluation for the study of practices. This method requires no knowledge of special testing techniques and can be used in the daily contacts with children. For example, are more children drinking milk during the lunch hour as a result of a unit on nutrition which stressed milk drinking? Are students in the chemistry laboratory increasing their skills in the handling of potentially dangerous chemicals?

Pupil self-inventories have been used frequently as motivational devices. The same inventories, used periodically, may help to show progress in health practices.

Records and reports, mentioned previously as helpful tools in program planning, are likewise valuable instruments for revealing changes in health practices. For example, well-kept school health records may show the number of pupils who have been immunized or who have had defects corrected as a result of educational efforts. The nurse's records of home visits may tell about changed practices of children in the homes, attributable in part, perhaps, to health teaching at school.

Pupil diaries, also, are evaluation instruments which help give evidence of progress in practices. These are used more commonly at the elementary, than at the secondary, level.

Figure 28. Testing the ability to drive safely. (Courtesy of Harmann Studio, Sturgeon Bay, Wisconsin.)

EVALUATING IMPROVEMENTS IN HOME, SCHOOL, AND COMMUNITY

In this area of evaluation there may be some difficulty in determining improvements that have taken place as a result of school health instruction. In most situations outside the school the pupils will be working with others, and to single out accomplishments that can be credited to pupil activities alone would be presumptuous. However, if the school has taken initiative and leadership in some project, it may be assumed that some of the improvements were doubtless through its efforts.

Health Improvements in the Home

Many of the instruments of evaluation suggested earlier in this chapter may be used to study health improvements in the home. Common among these are check lists and surveys, such as those on sanitation, safety practices, or nutrition, and home-visit records kept by the public health nurse, to suggest a few. Parent interviews may also be helpful.

Pupils may take snapshots of conditions before and after a unit. This makes a good teaching procedure as well as an objective evaluation device.

Evaluation involving home conditions should be made with great care so as to avoid misunderstanding and seeming to criticize parents. It is highly important that the parents themselves assist with such studies in order that their support may be assured.

Health Improvements in the School

Here, teachers and pupils ordinarily may work on safer grounds. Pupils can and do share actively in health improvements at school. The school in many instances has become the laboratory for much valuable health teaching. There is no reason, then, why pupils should not be encouraged to study the results of their efforts, nor why teachers and others should not do likewise. Check lists, surveys, and pictures may be useful instruments to discover evidences of change.

Health Improvements in the Community

What has been said about evaluation studies in the home applies equally well to studies in the community. If current trends in education continue, pupils will have increasing contact with community health programs. They should, however, be considered a part of a larger community team, rather than independent workers. Evaluation of community improvements may often be better made by all participating groups rather than by pupils alone.

EVALUATING IMPROVEMENTS IN THE PROGRAM ITSELF

The point has already been established that an evaluation of a program (or project) itself is a legitimate part of an evaluation study, provided it is not the only means of judging effectiveness. This evaluation should be made in terms of generally accepted standards.

First, is the program dealing with real health needs of the particular group of pupils and the particular locality? This question can be answered only through local study and through consultation with local or state health and medical authorities.

Second, is the program based on sound health principles and accurate health facts? Information contained in Chapters 2 and 3 should be a useful guide to these principles and facts.

Third, is the program based on sound and appropriate educational principles, methods, and procedures? Information contained throughout this book should be helpful in determining this point.

Fourth, are the materials used in the program understandable and acceptable, and are they being used appropriately in relation to program objectives.

An examination of the program from time to time in the light of such questions as those just suggested should be a worthwhile undertaking both for individual teachers and for groups of teachers working on curriculum improvements. Such studies will show weaknesses and strengths and will provide a basis for further program development.[1]

SUMMARY

Evaluation is the process of determining the degree to which instructional objectives are being met. In health education it should include a study of progress in pupil health behavior and of improvements in home, school, and community health. Evaluation also involves an assessment of instructional efforts to determine whether content and learning experiences are sound and appropriate. Evalu-

---

[1] A working outline for a health education survey conducted as a part of a comprehensive school health study in Austin, Minnesota, is given in Appendix B. Though prepared for use by the survey team, it should be helpful to faculty health committees or councils interested in appraising their own programs.

ation should be a continuous process in which pupils, teachers, health workers, parents, and the community participate. It is an essential part of every well-planned school health education program.

REFERENCES

Austin (Minn.) school health study. American Journal of Public Health, 52:290–309 (Feb.) 1962. (Ten short reports on methods and findings of the study.)

Bonnett, R., and Hughes, A. M.: Report of the 1958 Health Interest Survey. Denver, Colorado, Denver Public Schools, 1958, 63 pp.

Cohen, D. H., and Stern, V.: Observing and Recording the Behavior of Young Children. New York, Teachers College Press, Teachers College, Columbia University, 1958, 86 pp.

Evaluation of the Health Program in the Los Angeles City Schools, 1954–1961. School Publication No. 673. Los Angeles, California, Los Angeles City Schools, 1962, 257 pp.

Fodor, J. T., and Dalis, G. T.: Health Instruction: Theory and Application. Philadelphia, Lea & Febiger, 1966, pp. 124–147.

Herzog, E.: Some Guide Lines for Evaluative Research; Assessing Psychosocial Changes in Individuals. Children's Bureau Publication Number 375–1959. Washington, D.C., U.S. Government Printing Office, 1959, 117 pp.

Joint Committee on Health Problems in Education of the National Education Association and the American Medical Association: Health Education. 5th Ed. Washington, D.C., and Chicago, The Associations, 1961. Chapter 14, Evaluation in health education, pp. 339–358.

Knutson, A. L., and Shimberg, B.: Evaluation of a health education program. American Journal of Public Health, 45:21–27 (Jan.) 1955.

NEA Project on Instruction. Washington, D.C., National Education Association. Deciding What to Teach, 1963, 264 pp. Education in a Changing Society, 1963, 166 pp. Planning and Organizing for Teaching, 1963, 190 pp. From Bookshelves to Action, 1964, 32 pp.

Rugen, M., and Nyswander, D.: The measurement of understanding in health education. In The Measurement of Understanding. The Forty-fifth Yearbook of the National Society for the Study of Education. Part I. Chicago, The University of Chicago Press, 1946, pp. 213–231.

School Health Education Study, A Summary Report. Washington, D.C., School Health Education Study, 1507 M Street, N. W., Room 800, 1964, 74 pp.

Taba, H.: Curriculum Development; Theory and Practice. New York, Harcourt, Brace & World, Inc., 1962, pp. 310–342.

Veenker, C. H.: Evaluating health practice and understanding. Journal of Health–Physical Education–Recreation, 37:30–32 (May) 1966.

Veenker, C. H., Editor: Synthesis of Research in Selected Areas of Health Instruction. Washington, D.C. School Health Education Study, 1507 M Street, N.W., Room 800, 1963, 192 pp.

Williams, H. L., and Southworth, W. H.: Stimulating interests in public health problems among high school pupils. Journal of Educational Research, 53:53–61 (Oct.) 1959.

CHAPTER

12

CO-WORKERS IN HEALTH EDUCATION

Health education of the school-age child can be greatly enriched when schools work closely with community agencies that are interested in school and community health. This chapter suggests possible contributions which teachers may anticipate from such agencies. Following a general discussion, information is given on the work of specific groups commonly found in local communities. Among these groups are departments of education, universities, and other school-related groups; public health departments; cooperative extension services; youth organizations; voluntary health agencies; professional societies; civic and welfare organizations; commercial and semi-commercial groups; and coordinating bodies. Since agencies vary widely from community to community, local school people will need to discover their own potential co-workers.

CONTRIBUTIONS OF COMMUNITY AGENCIES TO SCHOOL HEALTH EDUCATION[1]

Among co-workers who may be found in agencies such as those just listed are professional health personnel, as in public health departments; volunteers; and heads of agencies who can facilitate co-operative relationships. Many groups have on their staffs, within their membership, or on their boards, people qualified and willing to assist schools on special health problems. Medical and dental so-

---

[1] For this fifth edition, the material on specific agencies has been reviewed and brought up to date by the agencies.

cieties, nursing organizations, voluntary health agencies, and hospitals are examples of such groups.

Schools will wish to maintain cooperative relationships with these people at all times, and may on occasion enlist their special services when problems arise. Since it is likely that more than one agency will have contributions to make on many school-related problems, ways must be found to mobilize these varied resources for constructive planning and action. School health councils, ad hoc committees, and coordinating bodies as mentioned in Chapter 5 can serve such functions.

To secure consultant help readily when it is needed, teachers should know the proper channels through which to go in each agency. A council might study this subject. For example, the health officer of the local health department is the person through whom schools should work to secure the services of this official body; the executive secretary, or in some instances the chairman of the health committee, is usually the contact person in the medical society; and the executive secretary is the person to approach in such voluntary agencies as those concerned with tuberculosis, cancer, or eye health. Schools that take initiative in seeking the consultant services available in a community will find their own education efforts greatly strengthened through the help they will receive.

A cooperatively prepared statement on health planning by schools and voluntary health agencies suggests the following types of help a teacher, school, or school system might receive from an agency:

> Make available up-to-date health information
> Provide teaching aids
> Offer opportunities for youth to participate in agency activities
> Obtain speakers, consultants, and resource persons
> Help with curriculum development
> Contribute to the recruitment of education and health personnel
> Assist in preservice education of school personnel
> Assist with inservice education of school personnel
> Assist with research studies and special projects
> Conduct demonstrations
> Interpret health needs and programs to parents and communities
> Encourage citizen interest in and support of good school health programs[2]

In the preceding chapters of this book, numerous examples have been given of projects of community agencies in which the pupils have had a part. With close working relationships between these agencies and the schools, there will be little difficulty in locating

---

[2] Guidelines for effective health planning by schools and voluntary health agencies. Journal of Health–Physical Education–Recreation *34*:27 (Sept.) 1963. (A statement from the Society of State Directors of Health, Physical Education, and Recreation.)

projects of value to pupils and agencies alike. By taking their place in programs for community health betterment, along with other members of the community, pupils will grow in their understanding of problems and gain experience in citizenship.

DEPARTMENTS OF EDUCATION

Local Education Departments

School administrators, health service personnel, parent-teacher groups, and school clubs are among the teacher's co-workers in school health education. Each of these contributes to the child's well-rounded development as it relates to health. Some of the contributions are outlined here.

The School Administrator

The school administrator is responsible for the coordination and general supervision of all phases of school health education. The success of a program is dependent upon his interest and support. The administrator's health education functions are both direct and indirect. In his personal contacts with children and parents, and in his public appearances before community groups, he deals with health matters directly. He serves on school and community health councils, and takes an active part in the development of health education curricula. His indirect contributions lie in encouragement and support to teachers, health workers, and the community at large in their health education efforts.

School Health Service Personnel

Types of professional health workers in schools vary widely from community to community. The basic staff, however, usually consists of physicians and nurses working either on a fulltime or a parttime basis. In addition, there may be health educators, dentists, dental hygienists, nutritionists, and related personnel, such as psychologists, guidance counselors, and social workers. Among the nonprofessional personnel whose services affect health are the custodians, lunchroom managers, and bus drivers.

Each of the health workers is in contact with individual children, and to a varying degree with groups of children. Each has important health education functions through such contacts. The professional personnel teach as they perform their services: the physician, the nurse, and the dental staff during individual con-

ferences; the health educator in the capacity of consultant and facilitator of health education activities; the nutritionist through food-
service activities and counseling of individual children; and the
psychologist, guidance counselor, and social worker through personal contacts. In addition, each of these may be called upon to
assist with classroom teaching, either through helping the teacher
in her planning, or on occasion, through meeting directly with
classroom groups. All should share in the development of a complete
health education program.

Nonprofessional personnel, through their services and their informal contacts with children, also perform significant health education functions. To illustrate, custodians may encourage safe and
healthful living practices about the school building. Bus drivers who
drive carefully and insist upon orderly behavior of the children
while riding to and from school are educating by example.

Parent-Teacher Associations

In many schools throughout the country, parents and teachers
are organized into Parent-Teacher Associations (PTA's) for cooperative effort in the interest of the child. These local associations
work through state congresses that are branches of the National
Congress of Parents and Teachers (National PTA). An important
program calls for periodic health supervision of children from birth
through high school, with special emphasis on the first six years of
life and regular appraisal during the school period. The National
PTA advocates that the appraisals be made by the family doctor
and dentist or, if such services cannot be arranged, through the
facilities of a child health center, with its doctor and public health
nurse. The program is an extension of the annual Summer
Round-Up (conducted for over 30 years by the PTA) which is now
part of the larger program of health appraisal.

The role of PTA's in the program is to make surveys of local
facilities for health supervision of children and, on the basis of these
findings, to cooperate with all interested agencies in developing a
program of periodic health appraisal most suitable to the
community.

Study programs are an important feature of PTA's. Sometimes
these programs are dovetailed with similar programs in schools so
that there is a broadside attack on problems by both parents and
children. Each years the National PTA suggests for local study topics
of current, national importance, but each group may choose its own
programs in line with local needs.

Each local organization has its health chairman who encourages membership identification with programs for school and community health betterment. Some associations sponsor health

education efforts through youth organizations, and many participate in community health projects.

School Clubs

In community health projects the school club is an important adjunct to classroom teaching. Many clubs are local and an integral part of the school curriculum; others are affiliated with state and national youth organizations, and may or may not be a part of the curriculum. Among the locally established clubs that have made valuable contributions to health education are those in the fields of science, health and physical fitness, home-making, journalism, and current events, as well as school councils, already discussed in Chapter 5. The nationally organized clubs are discussed elsewhere in this chapter under the heading Youth Organizations.

State Education Departments

Consultant services in health and safety education are provided by many state education departments to local school systems. These services are usually furnished through divisions of health and physical education, but other divisions offer special services, as in connection with school lunches and elementary education. Teaching guides and other curriculum materials in health and safety are commonly developed under the leadership of state education departments. Most departments now work in close collaboration with state health departments and teacher-education institutions; through these pooled services, assistance is becoming increasingly available on content, methods, and materials in health education.

Colleges and Universities

A hopeful trend in education is the more intimate association of educational institutions with the areas they serve. Many of these institutions have on their staffs specialists in the field of health education whose consultant services are used to help strengthen local health education efforts. In some states, working relationships have been developed between teacher-education centers and public schools whereby teachers from the institutions visit schools periodically. These institutions also foster institutes and work conferences on school health. Some areas of the country have access to the staffs of schools of public health and medicine for technical assistance in their health education programs.

Office of Education, U.S. Department of Health, Education, and Welfare

This governmental office supports efforts to improve health education at national, state, and local levels. It conducts relevant studies and through participation in conferences, workshops, and other programs contributes to strengthening health education leadership in colleges and universities as well as at the different administrative levels.

PUBLIC HEALTH DEPARTMENTS

Local Health Departments

A tax-supported health department, with fulltime, professionally trained personnel, should be the backbone of local health activity. A well-organized local health department performs such basic functions as control of communicable disease, promotion of sanitation, protection of health and welfare of mothers and children, collection of vital statistics, laboratory services, and health education. Today health departments, in cooperation with other agencies, are becoming increasingly involved in such areas as mental health, industrial health, school health, chronic illness, provision of safe and healthful hospital and nursing home facilities, home safety, poison control, air pollution, control of radiation hazards, and medical care.

The modern health department is an educational agency in the truest sense. In performing its many regulatory and service functions, it now accepts the principle that these functions must be reinforced by education to bring about lasting improvements in individual and community health. Education, then, has become a primary objective of health department work. Each public health worker, through his own branch of service, performs health education appropriate to the service. A few of the more common health education responsibilities of selected members of the public health team are mentioned here.

Health Officer

The health officer is responsible for the management of the health department. In cooperation with community and other members of the health department staff, he plans and executes the various health programs just outlined. In some communities the health officer also is the school physician, and carries on functions outlined earlier in the chapter.

In all his contacts with the people of the community the

modern health officer prefers to use persuasion rather than coercion. Through meetings, newspapers, and other channels of communication, he keeps people informed of the most critical health problems of the community. He stimulates the formation of, and serves on community health planning and action groups. To these groups he brings his special contribution as a physician and public health administrator.

Regardless of the amount of direct responsibility the health officer is given for school medical services, he should be an active participant in the school health program. He, or someone delegated to represent him, should be a member of school health planning groups. His knowledge of community health needs makes him an invaluable source of information for curriculum committees. His understanding and support of the school health education program, and his contributions to it, are essential for its sound development.

Environmental Health Personnel

Environmental health personnel are concerned with the control of the environment for the protection of health. Among the problems with which they deal are food sanitation, water sanitation, sewage disposal, air pollution, radiation hazards, industrial hazards, and control of animal-borne diseases. Within this category of health workers, one finds public health engineers, sanitarians, and also veterinarians.

In performing their functions, environmental health personnel are an important part of the community health education team. The old idea is passing that they function only to check on sanitary conditions as a means of assuring the enforcement of sanitary codes. In modern public health, enforcement techniques are used as a last resort and only when the public's health is immediately endangered through an infringement of the laws.

These specialists in environmental health are increasingly called on to assist with school and community health education projects. In preceding chapters, several instances of their use have been given. They will be called upon with greater frequency as schools reach out into the community in their health education activities and deal with problems connected with the control of the environment. Without their guidance, many such projects will flounder and accomplish little of permanent value. With their help, activities may be directed into fruitful channels, and procedures that are sound from a technical standpoint may be assured.

Public Health Nurses

Public health nurses are at the very core of a community's public health program. Like the classroom teacher, they have the most intimate contact with the people for whom a program is intended. They serve as family health counselors and deal with problems of family health protection, including help to the expectant mother, care of babies and young children, and care of those ill with acute or chronic disease. In communities where public health nurses carry on school nursing responsibilities, they assist with all types of school health problems, and, in the field of health education, with such activities as those just outlined.

In all that the public health nurse does, she is a health educator of either individuals or groups. In rendering direct service in the home and at the bedside, the well-qualified nurse teaches the patient and his family protective measures and preventive care. Like the medical officer and the sanitary officer, she often meets with groups in a community. She works with volunteers; she may conduct such classes as home nursing and prenatal and child care.

Health Educators

The health educator working in the schools has been mentioned in Chapter 5. As stated earlier, the health educator in the health department works with the health officer and other members of the staff on the many angles of health education for which the department is responsible. His task is that of analyzing situations to determine health education needs and of helping to plan and carry out the educational aspects of health programs.

A community health educator determines appropriate methods and techniques of health education. He assumes responsibility for developing, preparing, and using such mass media of communication as newspapers, radio, television, and printed materials. He plans meetings and opens the way for groups to use the technical health resources of the health department and the community; he assists with community organization for health. In other words, he facilitates the health education activities in the community at large, at times providing direct education services, at times arranging for others to provide the services, but always helping to guide efforts toward maximum use of health education in the solution of health problems.

Schools may expect varying types and amounts of assistance from the health educator of the health department, depending upon his relationship to them and the scope of his responsibilities. At one extreme, his activities may be limited to consultation services only on call. At another extreme, he may have a joint appointment with the department of education and concentrate his work almost entirely in the schools. Regardless of his affiliations and responsibilities, he should help pave the way for many worthwhile school-community health education projects.

State Health Departments

Most state health departments provide, on request, consultant services in the field of health education. In addition, they disseminate information on health by such means as pamphlets, films, news releases, bulletins, meetings, and personal contacts of their technical personnel. In areas served by local health departments, the services are channeled to the public largely through the local staffs; in areas lacking local organization, they are furnished directly by state health departments which customarily work in close cooperation with state education departments in all health education activities involving schools. To an increasing degree, personnel are shared, materials are published jointly, and policies are established through collaboration. This trend toward joining of forces between official agencies is to be commended and encouraged.

U.S. Department of Health, Education, and Welfare

This large and highly complex department of the federal government provides a wide range of services which have a bearing on health education. Three of the units are discussed briefly in this section; the Office of Education was mentioned under "Departments of Education" in the previous section of the chapter.

Food and Drug Administration

The Food and Drug Administration, through district offices scattered over the country, provides educational advisory services to schools on the subject of consumer health. Of special interest is a "Life Protection Series" of teaching guides distributed by this office on such subjects as safety in foods and safe use of drugs. Fact sheets, slides, and films on these and related subjects are also available.

Public Health Service

Numerous offices within the Public Health Service provide help in school health instruction. The Service sponsors studies in school health in cooperation with state and local authorities and publishes materials directed toward improving school health programs. A directory of national organizations interested in school health is available from the Service. This agency is actively engaged in supporting studies and programs dealing with smoking and health as well as many other subjects of current interest to schools. A wide variety of technical and popular health publications and films are prepared by specialists in the Public Health Service. Consultation services in specific program areas may be available in some parts of the country.

Children's Bureau

Over the years the activities of the Children's Bureau have centered around better health for mothers and children. In cooperation with the Office of Education and the Public Health Service, the Children's Bureau has promoted attention to school-child health with emphasis on preventive services. Recent grants for Comprehensive Health Services for Children and Youth are administered through the Bureau. With these funds health and medical services are provided in selected poverty areas for children from birth through school age. Literature of value to teachers and pupils is prepared by the Bureau.

COOPERATIVE EXTENSION SERVICES

Some of the finest adult education programs in the country are conducted through the county extension services under the leadership of county extension agents. These services, aided by grants from the federal government through the United States Department of Agriculture (cooperative extension work) and from state appropriations to land-grant colleges, are used for various forms of education pertaining to farm, home, and community improvement. In addition to adult programs, this extension work also includes the 4-H program which is discussed under Youth Organizations.

Extension services have long promoted education programs in such areas as farm sanitation, family health, and nutrition. Usually these programs are planned with people on the basis of local problems or interests. Emphasis is on learning through participation. Some extension groups participate in school lunch programs; they provide personal services and financial aid as well as materials for classroom study. Extension agents and community leaders have done much in many areas to improve health facilities and services. They have helped communities to survey needs and to learn about government help for obtaining local hospitals, health centers, and doctors.

Also active in movements for rural health improvement are state and local branches of the Farm Bureau, the Grange, the Farmers' Union, cooperatives, and other rural groups. School people interested in health improvement would do well to enlist the support of these alert groups of farm men and women, and join forces with them in community-wide programs.

YOUTH ORGANIZATIONS

Health and safety education holds a prominent place among the activities of most youth organizations, including the Boy Scouts of America, Boys' Clubs of America, Camp Fire Girls, 4-H Clubs, Future Farmers of America, Future Homemakers of America, Girl Scouts, and Red Cross Youth, as well as numerous religious youth groups. A major objective of these organizations is to provide practical training in character building, self-government, citizenship, and community service. They differ principally in detailed program emphasis and form of organization. In some instances, as stated previously, the organizations may be established as an integral part of the school curriculum; in others they function as independent community groups. Features of the health and safety education programs of selected youth organizations are outlined briefly here.

Boy Scouts of America

Health and safety programs center around activities with the Cub Scouts (ages 8 through 10), Boy Scouts (ages 11 through 17), and Explorers (high school age boys). The programs are threefold in emphasis, namely, health and safety protection for the members; education toward developing and applying health and safety knowledge and skills; and service to others, as through emergency service and participation in community health and safety projects. Explorers are particularly active in service-related programs.

Boys' Clubs of America

This organization, which provides opportunities for boys mainly in low economic areas, has always considered health education one of the most important phases of its work. Education activities relate to the detection and elimination of undesirable environmental factors which affect health and to health service programs sponsored by clubs. There is instruction in swimming and life saving, and participation in games and sports. A National Program Committee on Individual Services with health as a major area of concern makes studies of current health practices and aids, and develops programs of health improvement. Small Boys' Clubs, unable to establish a professionally staffed health service, have developed programs that operate through available community resources.

Camp Fire Girls

"Hold on to Health" is a part of the Camp Fire Girls Law. It directs the attention of members to the importance of personal health and healthful living conditions for all people. The Camp Fire program suggests practical ways for girls to develop sound personal health attitudes, to develop good health habits, and to become acquainted with the work of community, national, and international organizations in the field of health.

Health concepts and good health and safety practices are woven into the entire program of Camp Fire Girls. In the Blue Bird program (for girls 7 and 8 years of age), health education is centered on promoting awareness of health and safety needs and problems. In Camp Fire Girls (9, 10, and 11 years of age), greater responsibility is placed on the girls and emphasis is given to applying health knowledge in everyday situations—in the home, at school, and in the group. In Junior Hi Camp Fire Girls, service activities are stressed, and the girl is further encouraged to see the relationship between her own well-being and that of others. The Horizon Club (14 years or ninth grade through high school) gives more extensive information and promotes a widening awareness of personal responsibility and service for others, including knowledge of community health needs and services.

4-H Clubs

4-H Clubs are groups of young people, chiefly in rural and suburban areas, who carry on a wide variety of farming, homemaking, community service, and other projects.

The 4-H program is a part of the national education system of cooperative extension work which the United States Department of Agriculture, the state land-grant colleges, and the counties share. As in the democracy in which they live, 4-H'ers themselves largely run their clubs, elect their officers, help plan and hold their meetings, and select their projects. To guide 4-H'ers, over 500,000 public-spirited men and women, mostly parents, serve as unpaid volunteer local leaders. The leaders are trained, counseled, and assisted by the county agents of the Cooperative Extension Service.

The term "4-H" refers to "Head," "Heart," "Hands," and "Health," which are emphasized in the club program. Health focus for a 4-H member usually progresses from personal health habits to family health, and then to community health. Older members are helped to see that health is a part of personal and social development and good health is an asset for finding suitable careers.

All 4-H Clubs are encouraged to include "health" as an in-

Figure 29. Discussing roadside safety hazard with rural mail carrier. (Courtesy of the Agricultural Extension Service, University of Minnesota, St. Paul, Minnesota.)

tegral part of their yearly programs. The 4-H agricultural and home-making projects give opportunity for the application of health and safety principles as, for example, in relation to care of animals, operating a tractor, food storage, use of the sewing machine, and food preparation. Nutrition improvement for teen-agers is currently receiving major emphasis.

Each state plans a health program on the basis of the major health needs of the young people in each community or area. Emphases shift from year to year. In addition, 4-H Clubs are encouraged to participate in community health activities and in special health and safety projects.

Future Farmers of America

This organization is an integral part of the vocational agriculture program in secondary schools; through it, much of the instruction in vocational agriculture is given. Members of its chapters are boys currently studying the subject or former students in the program. The foundation upon which the organization is built includes "leadership and character development, sportsmanship, cooperation, service, thrift, scholarship, improved agriculture, organized recreation, citizenship, and patriotism."

Students engage in agricultural programs which require sound knowledge and application of health and safety principles, and they enter into community services which likewise may give experience in solving problems of physical and emotional health. FFA activities that have health and safety implications include making community fire hazard surveys, taking part in programs for safe use of farm power and automobiles, and conducting safety and health projects.

Future Homemakers of America

Future Homemakers of America is an integral part of home economics education in the secondary schools of the United States, Puerto Rico, and American Army Post Schools overseas; its membership is composed of students who are taking or have taken home economics courses in the junior and senior high schools. The goal of this organization is to help individuals improve personal, family, and community living.

Members participate in chapter programs which require sound knowledge and application of health and safety principles, and they take part in community service activities through which they learn ways of solving problems which bear on physical and emotional health. They care for young children, give volunteer services in civil defense, work toward prevention of juvenile delinquency, give help when needed in the neighborhood, and carry out projects within their own homes.

Girl Scouts of the United States of America

Health and safety are emphasized throughout the total Girl Scout program for girls 7 through 17. Appropriate factors are taught as they relate to planning for and carrying out all activities. Girl Scouting seeks to supplement and reinforce what is taught at home and school through application in a wide range of activities.

Brownie Girl Scouts (7- and 8-year-olds) learn how to take care of themselves through informal play activities, special projects in personal health, service, and usefulness in the home.

Junior Girl Scouts (9 through 11) improve their skills through health and safety training built into all their activities. Proficiency badges which have special health and safety emphasis are those given for community safety, health aid, home health and safety, and personal health.

Cadette Girl Scouts (12 through 14), progressing in self-reliance, take greater responsibility for their own health and safety and that of others. In their expanding activities girls must think through the health and safety aspects relating to every proficiency badge they earn, and demonstrate appropriate application of these factors when meeting selected real-life situations referred to as challenges. Proficiency badges highlighting health and safety are child care, first aid, home nursing, outdoor safety, and public health.

Senior Girl Scouts (15 through 17) have a wide choice in planning and taking responsibility for their activities. In their Service Aide Projects they have the opportunity to explore careers or to train, under qualified instructors, for community service. Those Aide Projects most closely related to health and safety fields are Aides to Handicapped Persons, Aquatic Safety Aides, Child Care Aides, Hospital Aides, Laboratory Aides, and Program Aides.

Red Cross Youth

Red Cross Youth comprises the youth membership of the American National Red Cross and includes elementary, high school, and college youth. Among the stated objectives of Red Cross Youth are the promotion of health and safety instruction and the encouragement of youth to participate as volunteers in the work of the Red Cross. Youth work within their communities as volunteers in hospitals, homes for the aged, and institutions for the mentally re-tarded. As members of trained teams, they bring health and safety programs to population groups often bypassed by social welfare agencies. Young people who are fully qualified instructors teach life saving and water safety to children and adults.

Through international programs and aid to children in dis-aster areas, Red Cross Youth help to promote international under-standing and to guard good health throughout the world. By utilizing the energy and enthusiasm of well-trained youth the Red Cross is able to extend its health programs to more and more groups at home and abroad.

VOLUNTARY HEALTH AGENCIES

Nonofficial, voluntary health agencies play an important role in many community health endeavors through their contributions in the fields of research, service, and education. These agencies usually function in special problem areas, as, for example, in the fields of cancer, heart disease, and mental health. Nationally, their programs are similar in principle, in organization, and in tech-niques of education; at state and local levels they are more varied in scope and nature, and are determined partially by local needs and circumstances. In the following pages, typical health education activities of voluntary health agencies most commonly found in state and local areas are described. The organizations that have been chosen for this brief summary, though usually autonomous in their programs, are affiliated with, or guided by, their national associations. All regard health education as a major function, and all seek to complement and to strengthen the work of official health and related agencies. A traditional policy on their part is to experi-ment and to pioneer in some new phase of community health im-provement, and then through their channels of education, to encourage adoption by tax-supported agencies of programs that have proved their worth.

The American National Red Cross

This organization is unique among voluntary health and wel-fare groups. Unlike others, it is a quasi-governmental agency whose work in the field of service to men and women in the armed forces, disaster relief activities, blood program, and other services con-cerned with the health, safety, and well-being of the American people is well known.

Wherever local Red Cross chapters are found, in virtually every county in the United States, there, too, will likely be found one or more of the programs of instruction in such fields as home nursing, first aid, and water safety. These classes follow certain basic national requirements as to instructors, content, and methods of instruction, and offer certificates of completion, issued by the national organization. Teachers can obtain helpful source material on safety, first aid, and health from the nationally developed textbooks that are used in the training and are available in most libraries or can be purchased from chapters. Information about blood can also be obtained from the Red Cross. Local chapters assist in community health education activities in various ways. They provide trained volunteers for hospitals, clinics, and other health agencies and participate in community projects related to health. (The work of Red Cross Youth, an integral part of The American National Red Cross, is described in the previous section on Youth Organizations.)

Cancer

Community education activities in cancer and cancer control are carried on by some 3,000 local units of the American Cancer Society. These groups are largely made up of volunteers who are committed to the task of spreading information about cancer and its control and to enlisting citizen support for expanding programs of research, education, and service. They work closely with county medical societies and health department personnel.

Volunteers in the society are trained to carry on both education and service activities. Community education in cancer is designed to reach all groups in the population through mass media, clubs and organizations, schools, business, industries and neighborhood programs.

Essentially, the approach to cancer education is to encourage the individual to act for his own well-being, taking a positive attitude toward cancer control. Local American Cancer Society units attempt to spread basic facts about cancer, dispel unwarranted fears, and facilitate early detection of the disease through encouraging regular physical examinations and alerting people to the danger signals. They also urge and support the establishment of such medical and other service facilities as are necessary in the community. In addition to its educational program for adults and its professional education program for medical and nursing groups, the American Cancer Society provides films, pamphlets, program outlines, teaching guides, and other material designed for use in secondary schools and adult education programs. One current program is the society's teen-age program on cigarettes and lung cancer.

Crippled Children and Adults

Throughout the country there are almost 1,400 state and local societies affiliated with the National Society for Crippled Children and Adults (The Easter Seal Society). The society's program includes (1) education of the public, professional workers, and parents; (2) research to provide increased knowledge of the causes of handicapping conditions and the prevention, care, and treatment of those conditions; and (3) direct services providing care and treatment, education, and rehabilitation of crippled children and adults. Services are based on needs in local communities in the fields of health, welfare, education, recreation, rehabilitation, and employment. Teachers of special classes for crippled children are likely to be members of these societies.

Hearing and Speech

The National Association of Hearing and Speech Agencies (formerly the American Hearing Society) is a federation of approximately 200 community service oriented agencies which provide services to communicatively handicapped persons. The services provided by local agencies range from a relatively uncomplicated information service, through social rehabilitation programs for the deafened, to complex clinical facilities providing programs in depth in diagnosis and rehabilitation. The national office of the association provides field service to presently unserved communities including feasibility studies for establishing new services. The organization has an ongoing recruitment program aimed at recruiting young people into the professions serving the communicatively handicapped.

NAHSA is the only locally oriented national agency working exclusively in behalf of hearing, speech, and language handicapped individuals. It is a forum where lay and professional individuals and organizations combine their interests and efforts toward solving the many problems confronting those with communicative disorders.

Heart

The American Heart Association, Inc., is a national voluntary health agency which joins physicians and laymen in a partnership to combat cardiovascular diseases through nation-wide programs of research, public and professional education, and community services. The association comprises a national office, 55 state and regional affiliates, and their 1,400 local heart organizations. Some Heart Associations provide services to schools, including programs for rheumatic fever prevention, clinics, rehabilitation, and the screening of children for both the identification of heart defects in children and the "de-labeling" of children incorrectly thought to have heart disease. Extensive programs of professional education are conducted for physicians and related professional groups, including nurses and teachers.

Mental Health

The National Association for Mental Health, through its affiliated state and local mental health associations, works for the promotion of mental health, for research, for the prevention of mental handicaps, and for the improvement of care and treatment of persons suffering from such handicaps.

Many of the state and local associations, with their resources in personnel and in authentic materials, assist schools and other community groups in planning mental health education programs. A significant portion of the association effort is spent in working with teachers, physicians, public health workers, clergymen, and law enforcement officers, all of whom are in the closest and most influential contact with members of the community. The local associations collaborate with various professional organizations, official and voluntary agencies, and civic groups on community-wide programs. A Mental Health Careers Program, directed to high school and college youth, provides information about the broad field of mental health as well as the major mental health occupations.

Safety

State and local safety councils, most of which are affiliated with the National Safety Council, are among the leading local groups working with the schools. These councils, and many other local organizations, usually have activity committees including school and child safety, traffic safety, and public information. They offer assistance in organizing junior safety councils, school safety patrols, and other safety activities.

Behind these local organizations is the National Safety Council, a noncommercial, nonprofit association, which serves as the hub of the safety movement in America. Its purpose is to reduce the number and severity of all kinds of accidents by serving as a clearing house for gathering and distributing information about causes of accidents and ways to prevent them. Several of its departments, such as its school and college, home, farm, and traffic divisions, conduct activities related to child safety and safety education in the schools. The School and College Conference comprises sections representing schools and related organizations in which members determine needs and develop programs at all levels of education. Through the Standard Student Accident Reporting System it develops statistics on accidents in community and nation. Other activities include: development of principles of safety education; preparation of educational materials for school use; promotion of driver education; preparation of recommended safety standards; recognition of outstanding school safety programs through the National School Safety Honor Roll and the annual inventory of traffic safety activities; as well as field and consultation services to national, state-wide, and community educational organizations and school systems.

Sight Conservation

The National Society for the Prevention of Blindness and its many state affiliates offer consultant services and educational materials—publications, posters, films and exhibits—to schools, health departments, and local fraternal and civic organizations. Special emphasis is given by the society to vision screening for preschool and school children; school eye safety programs featuring the Junior Wise Owl Club; and improved educational facilities for partially blind students.

Social Health

Over the years the American Social Health Association has been concerned with strengthening family life through education as one means of attacking problems growing out of family and community failure. The specific social ills which concern the association—venereal disease, prostitution, narcotics addiction—are continuing subjects of research, investigation, and action on national, state, and local levels. The association serves as a resource to schools, colleges, and community groups in planning and producing materials and programs designed to meet local and regional needs. It also sponsors and participates in workshops, conferences, and institutes on family life education, working with and through existing interested groups and individuals. Field services are made available through a staff of four regional directors.

Tuberculosis and Respiratory Diseases

The most deeply rooted of all voluntary health agencies are the local organizations (county and state) affiliated with the National Tuberculosis and Respiratory Disease Association. They are influences for good, not only in these specific fields of disease prevention, but also in community-wide health education in general. Leaders in the movement have recognized for a long time that good general health practices are important factors in tuberculosis control and consequently have geared their programs toward broader goals. Specifically and increasingly, the associations have extended their programs to include all respiratory diseases in addition to tuberculosis. Characteristic health education activities of local groups include school and community education in relation to tuberculosis eradication, control of other respiratory diseases, and air conservation; education for complete public health programs; and cooperation with official health agencies and other groups in general health education. An outstanding contribution of many local associations has been financial support to public health agencies and school systems for demonstration programs in health education.

PROFESSIONAL SOCIETIES

Teachers, public health workers, physicians, dentists, nurses, hospital administrators, and other professional groups have local as well as state and national organizations that take varying degrees of interest in the education of the public. Though some have carried on little or no community health education, and others have limited their promotional work to seeking support within the community for their profession, a few have had programs of considerable breadth.

Education Associations

On a local level, teachers, school administrators, and other groups of educators are organized primarily for their own professional improvement, and, as associations, only indirectly play a part in school and community programs of education and health. Representatives of local and state education associations often are called upon to serve on policy-forming and program-planning committees that deal with school health problems, including school health education. Journals of these state associations publish articles in the field of health. State education associations also sponsor health programs at their annual conferences.

In addition to the general associations, with membership from all teaching fields, a few specialized groups deal more specifically with health problems and professional health improvement. Most important of these groups are state and regional associations for health, physical education, and recreation, affiliated with the American Association for Health, Physical Education, and Recreation, a department of the National Education Association. Membership in these groups is drawn largely from physical education and health education, and from physicians and nurses serving the schools. From the ranks of these local organizations comes much of the leadership in local school health education. The national association carries on an active program in health education from the standpoint of policy formation and the provision of consultant services and materials. Officers and members serve on nearly every important national committee that is in any way concerned with school child health, and often initiate health projects of their own.

Potentially helpful for background scientific information in local health education efforts are state academies of science and science teachers who belong to such national bodies as the American Association for the Advancement of Science, the American Institute of Biological Sciences, National Association of Biology Teachers, and National Science Teachers Association.

Professional leaders in home economics, many of them teachers, are members of local home economics associations, branches of the American Home Economics Association. These organizations often have committees on public health that concern themselves especially with problems related to family health and nutrition. Consultant services and materials may be available from them.

Public Health Associations

Locally, public health workers have not been highly organized as separate professional groups. In areas where public health associations have been formed as branches of the American Public Health Association, activities have been focused principally on professional improvement. Nationally, the American Public Health Association is a powerful professional body that seeks to improve the status of public health in the country. Though it does not provide direct, popular educational services to schools and to communities, its influences are far-reaching through contributions to improved public health practice. The American Public Health

Association is organized into sections, including sections for public health education and for school health.

Medical Societies

City and county medical societies are the local component units of the American Medical Association. In a few localities they call themselves district or parish societies, and occasionally "academies of medicine" (a name also given to some city societies). Each city and county medical society, through a committee or through its officers, is encouraged to offer consultation on local medical problems and to participate in community health projects. Representatives serve on local health councils and committees and take part in the development of public health and school health programs. They often are asked to review curriculum materials for technical content. Societies furnish speakers for local meetings, on request, and many sponsor radio and television programs.

Behind the resources of every local medical society stand the state medical society and the American Medical Association. Consultants on school health from the national office are available on request for workshops of teachers and for other state and local programs of significance. The American Medical Association has made an important contribution to cooperative planning through sponsorship of biennial Conferences on Physicians and Schools attended by national, state, and local leaders from the fields of medicine, public health, and education. The Joint Committee on Health Problems in Education of the National Education Association and the American Medical Association has been mentioned elsewhere in this book as an influential body in the field of school health. The association carries on its own nation-wide radio and television programs and now has a National Committee on Radio, Television, and Movies to advise on facts, attitudes and implications in entertainment programs involving medicine as well as in educational programs. Less known to schools, but extremely valuable, is the question-answer service by mail, established at the national headquarters in Chicago.

Dental Societies

Most dentists are members of local dental societies which are component societies of the American Dental Association. These local groups, and their individual members, are committed to a policy of community education in the field of dental health. It is the aim of both local and national groups to make available authentic information, to provide consultation services, to help edit and evaluate educational materials, and to stimulate and take part in cooperative efforts for the improvement of dental health.

Nursing Associations

Local nursing associations include groups affiliated with the American Nurses' Association, the National League for Nursing, or both groups. In the American Nurses' Association, professional nurses work for continuing improvements of nursing practice, the economic and general welfare of nurses, and for the general health needs of the public. In the National League for Nursing, all members of the health team—doctors, professional nurses, practical nurses, nursing aides, interested people in the community, and agencies supplying nursing service or education—work together for the improvement of patient care. Materials for classroom instruction on nursing as a profession and on nursing services and nursing education in general are available from the National League for Nursing and its state and local affiliates. Through the leadership of these groups much valuable community education is accomplished.

Hospital Associations

On first thought, there would seem to be little connection between hospitals and school and community health education. Though education has been for some time one of the major purposes of hospitals, educational activities have been limited until recently to professional groups. The hospital today, however, is increasingly becoming a center for health education. Individual and group instruction, appropriate to the condition, is given to such patients as expectant mothers, diabetics, and presurgery cases, especially children. In some hospitals, the clinics, meeting rooms, and other facilities for health education are housed within the walls; and in a few, there are health museums. Administrators and medical staff are identifying themselves as never before with community health education efforts.

Hospital administrators are organized locally into hospital associations (city, region, and state) intimately related to the American Hospital Association. In addition, some communities have hospital councils, made up of hospital leaders and interested citizens, whose primary functions are to support local hospital activities and to work for closer coordination of hospital services. These councils, as well as individual hospitals, are fostering programs of volunteer

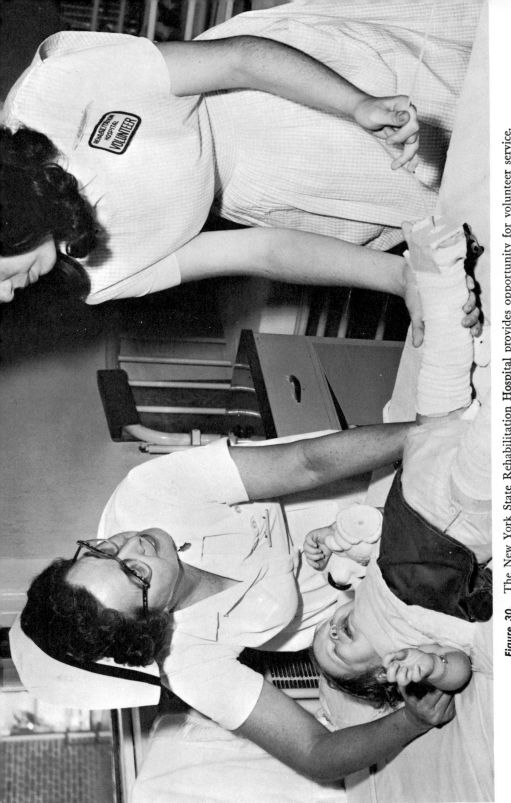

Figure 30. The New York State Rehabilitation Hospital provides opportunity for volunteer service. (Courtesy of the Photography Department, New York State Department of Health.)

service by high school students, as through the Candy Stripers and other similar programs.

CIVIC AND WELFARE GROUPS

Thousands of civic and welfare groups throughout the country are potent forces for community health betterment. Although few of these groups operate primarily in the field of health, their aggregate services are legion. The health education benefits derived through such extensive participation in worthwhile community projects are immeasurable. One may expect that much education is taking place through practical experience in health action programs.

In addition to these civic and welfare groups, many recreational, religious, professional, social, and fraternal organizations take part in community health activities. Labor unions also conduct health and welfare programs among their members and join actively in community programs in cooperation with official and voluntary health agencies, schools, and coordinating bodies. One should remember, too, the newspapers, radio and television stations which give space and time to health matters. And last of all are the many citizens who, on their own time, devote hours to constructive community service.

COMMERCIAL AND SEMI-COMMERCIAL GROUPS

Many excellent health education activities have been sponsored both locally and nationally by commercial groups of high standing. Some of the most attractive popular health literature, including materials for children, comes from such groups. Health education demonstrations in local areas and workshops in teacher training have been carried out with their financial aid. A few of the more prominent have underwritten research studies and curriculum materials for the improvement of school health programs. Chambers of commerce sponsor numerous community projects and are committed to the strengthening of local public health services. Cooperative associations are showing increased interest in health education of their members.

On the opposite side of the ledger are commercial companies which confuse the public with distorted and unsound health facts, companies more concerned with selling their products than with disseminating the truth. Their tactics are changing as the public becomes sufficiently informed to ignore them.

COORDINATING BODIES

This brief review of diverse health education activities reveals a great reservoir of human power behind the school and the community. Millions of people, of their own accord, are participants in programs for the betterment of health. An examination of activities within individual communities, however, often discloses a confused picture. One sees a cumbersome number of agencies and individuals working toward similar health goals, but each proceeding independently. One observes that certain problems are stressed to the exclusion of others of equal importance. This dissipation and waste of human effort, through uncoordinated action, is not peculiar to the field of health alone; it is a common characteristic of much community life. Yet progress is being made in community health work toward a greater unification of planning and action.

There are almost as many different types of local coordinating bodies as there are communities they serve. Perhaps this is as it should be, for each coordinating group should grow out of local needs, and be woven from the resources at hand.

From the standpoint of scope of interest, groups concerned with health problems are of three different types. First in importance are the comprehensive coordinating bodies that include health as only one area—though an important one—of responsibility. These coordinating councils, found at both state and local levels, are becoming increasingly important forces in community life. They are the channels through which citizens in states and counties, cities and towns, and, most important of all, in individual neighborhoods, find opportunity to share in the solution of social and economic problems many of which relate to health.

Second in line should be mentioned councils or committees organized to deal with community-wide health problems. They may perform coordinating functions only, or they may both plan and act in the interests of better community health. These, too, are found at both state and local levels.

The third type of organization is the council established around a specific agency or problem. The school health council, discussed in Chapter 5, is an example of this type. So, too, are the several types of agency councils mentioned in this chapter.

These coordinating bodies differ widely in their functions. Some serve largely as clearing houses for ideas and programs; some do program planning, but refer their plans to member agencies or other groups for action; but by far the largest number combine coordination, program planning, and action.

Sponsorship, too, differs. Health departments, school systems, councils of social agencies, chambers of commerce, civic groups, and neighborhood leaders have all been known to initiate and sponsor coordinating groups. Membership likewise varies. Some groups are composed largely of professional people; some, of agency representatives; and some, of interested citizens in neighborhoods or larger areas. Combinations of these individuals and groups are the most common patterns. Schools may or may not be represented in the membership.

Problems with which these bodies deal are limitless. Many have already been listed in the early pages of this chapter.

In the community of the future, total health education programs are in prospect of becoming a reality. The school, through its proximity to the problems and the people, and through its potential leadership in all aspects of education, will become an increasingly dynamic force in their fulfillment.

SUMMARY

Health education is a function of many individuals and groups within the school and community aside from the teachers themselves. School administrators, school health service personnel, parent groups, and school clubs play active roles. Education is a primary objective and a basic function of public health departments. Youth organizations provide practical experiences in health for their members and, to an increasing degree, stress not only individual health improvement, but also community service. Voluntary health agencies, working usually in special problem areas, regard health education as a major responsibility; they seek to complement the educational efforts of official health departments and schools. Other groups that contribute to health improvement through education are professional societies, civic and welfare groups, and commercial and semi-commercial companies.

This great diversity of activity from many quarters has produced much overlapping and duplication of efforts. As a result, there is a growing demand for coordinating bodies that can help unite health services and education. There also is a growing recognition that such bodies must be formed within the fabric of the community itself, and must grow out of the wishes, plans, and activities of the people. Only as each citizen participates actively in personal and community health betterment, and only as groups learn to pool their resources through unified efforts, will the community's most urgent health problems be met. No one individual or agency alone can accomplish these ends. All must be co-workers on a united front.

REFERENCES

Beyrer, M. K., Nolte, A. E., and Solleder, M. K.: A Directory of Selected References and Resources for Health Instruction. Minneapolis, Burgess Publishing Company, 1966, 148 pp.

A Directory of National Organizations with Interest in School Health. Arlington, Virginia, School Health Section, Bureau of Health Services, U.S. Public Health Service, 1967, 25 pp.

Health Careers Guidebook. Bureau of Employment Security, U.S. Department of Labor. Washington, D.C., U.S. Government Printing Office, 1965, 204 pp.

Health Resources Statistics; Health Manpower, 1965. Public Health Service Publication No. 1509. Washington, D.C., U.S. Government Printing Office, 1966, 182 pp. (Prepared by the National Center for Health Statistics.)

National Conference on Coordination of the School Health Program; Teamwork in School Health. Washington, D.C., American Association for Health, Physical Education, and Recreation, 1962, 32 pp.

Olsen, E. G., Editor: School and Community. 2nd Ed. Englewood Cliffs, N.J., Prentice-Hall, Inc., 1954, 534 pp.

Rash, J. K.: Bridging the gap between school health and public health. Journal of School Health, *30*:10–13 (Jan.) 1960.

Wilbur, M. B.: Community Health Services. Philadelphia, W. B. Saunders Company, 1962, 364 pp.

APPENDIX

A

SOURCES OF FREE AND INEXPENSIVE HEALTH EDUCATION MATERIALS[1]

National Headquarters	*Materials*
Adult Education Association of the United States of America 1225 19th St., N.W. Washington, D.C. 20036	Reprints, lists of references and research reports on adult leadership; monthly magazine, *Adult Leadership;* quarterly journal: *Adult Education*
Aetna Life & Casualty Hartford, Connecticut 06115	Pamphlets and films on safety
Alexander Graham Bell Association for the Deaf Headquarters: Volta Bureau 1537 35th St., N.W. Washington, D.C. 20007	Books, pamphlets, films (for parents) on deafness; magazine: *Volta Review*
Allied Youth, Inc. Rosslyn Building 1901 Ft. Myer Dr. Arlington, Va. 22209	Pamphlets and materials on alcohol and personality development; quarterly magazine for teenagers: *The Allied Youth*
American Association for Health, Physical Education, and Recreation 1201 16th St., N.W. Washington, D.C. 20036	Pamphlets, lists of health literature, teaching guides, journal for members
American Automobile Association 1712 G St., N.W. Washington, D.C. 20006	Pamphlets, posters, teaching units, films —school, bicycling and traffic safety; driver education

---

[1] Materials from these national agencies should be ordered from their state or local affiliated agencies. Discretion should be used in placing orders since many of the agencies can provide materials free only on a limited basis.

National Headquarters	*Materials*
American Cancer Society, Inc. 219 East 42nd St. New York, N.Y. 10017	Pamphlets, teaching guide, exhibits, films, filmstrips, slides, radio and television materials
American Dental Association 211 East Chicago Ave. Chicago, Illinois 60611	Pamphlets, teaching outlines, posters, charts, 2" x 2" slides, films, filmstrips
The American Dietetic Association 620 North Michigan Ave. Chicago, Illinois 60611	Reprints, pamphlets, multilithed material, lists of materials on nutrition. Single free copies to teachers of nutrition education materials. Reprints of articles available at cost
American Heart Association 44 East 23rd St. New York, N.Y. 10010	Pamphlets, films, filmslides, charts, models, exhibits, and transcriptions
American Home Economics Association 1600 20th St., N.W. Washington, D.C. 20009	Monthly journal, free listing of publications, career materials, research reports, bibliographies
American Hospital Association 840 North Lake Shore Drive Chicago, Illinois 60611	Pamphlets
American Institute of Family Relations 5287 Sunset Blvd. Los Angeles, California 90027	Pamphlets on marriage and family life, sex education; monthly bulletin: *Family Life*
American Medical Association 535 North Dearborn St. Chicago, Illinois 60610	Pamphlets, reprints, posters, exhibits, catalogs—health and medical topics, school health; magazine: *Today's Health;* monthly bulletin: *Health Education Services for Schools and Colleges*
The American National Red Cross 17th and D Streets, N.W. Washington, D.C. 20006	Pamphlets, posters, textbooks, study outlines, films, filmstrips, radio scripts —blood program, first aid and water safety, home nursing; teaching guides on accident prevention
American Public Health Association 1740 Broadway New York, N.Y. 10019	Reprints, books, and monographs on technical subjects; journal for members
American Social Health Association, Inc. 1740 Broadway New York, N.Y. 10019	Pamphlets, charts, posters, bibliographies; monthly publication: *Social Health News*
ANA-NLN Committee on Nursing Careers American Nurses' Association 10 Columbus Circle New York, N.Y. 10019	Booklets, brochures, films, scholarship lists, student and counselor packets

National Headquarters	*Materials*
Central Council for Health Education Tavistock House, Tavistock Sq. London, W. C. 1, England	Pamphlets, leaflets, posters, filmstrips, short thematic films, and two quarterly journals which are sold to public authorities, health education agencies, and individuals
Cereal Institute, Inc. 135 South LaSalle St. Chicago, Illinois 60603	Teachers' source books, guides, wall charts, filmstrips, motion pictures
Children's Bureau, Department of Health, Education, and Welfare Washington, D.C. 20201	Pamphlets, booklets; monthly magazine: *The Child*
Cleveland Health Museum 8911 Euclid Ave. Cleveland, Ohio 44106	Exhibits for health education, teaching materials for sex education
Columbia University Press International Documents Service 136 South Broadway Irvington on Hudson, N.Y. 10533	Technical reports of the World Health Organization; UNESCO publications
Equitable Life Assurance Society of the United States 1285 Ave. of the Americas New York, N.Y. 10019	Booklets and leaflets
Food and Drug Administration, Department of Health, Education, and Welfare Washington, D.C. 20204	Teaching guides, fact sheets, slides, films on consumer health subjects, including foods and drugs
The Hogg Foundation for Mental Health The University of Texas Austin, Texas 78712	Pamphlets on mental health (only 5 titles without charge, others at cost; write for publication list)
Maternity Center Association, Inc. 48 East 92nd St. New York, N.Y. 10028	Pamphlets, leaflets, books, charts (Birth Atlas), posters, film
Mental Health Materials Center 104 East 25th St. New York, N.Y. 10010	Packets of materials on family life, human relations and mental health; lists of publications and films on these subjects
Metropolitan Life Insurance Co. 1 Madison Avenue New York, N.Y. 10010	Pamphlets, exhibits, posters, films
National Association for Mental Health 10 Columbus Circle New York, N.Y. 10019	Pamphlets, films, plays, recordings; magazine: *Mental Hygiene*
National Association of Hearing and Speech Agencies 919 18th St., N.W. Washington, D.C. 20006	Bi-monthly publication: *Hearing and Speech News;* monthly newsletter: *Washington Sounds*

National Headquarters	*Materials*
National Commission for UNESCO Department of State Washington, D.C. 20520	Educational materials on UNESCO'S activities
The National Commission on Safety Education, NEA; and American Driver and Traffic Safety Education Association, NEA 1201 16th St., N.W. Washington, D.C. 20036	Booklets, check list, film guide, teaching guides; bi-monthly magazine: *Safety*
National Congress of Parents and Teachers 700 North Rush St. Chicago, Illinois 60611	Manuals, handbooks, pamphlets, including *Keeping Children Healthy* and *Children's Emotional Health;* magazine: *The PTA Magazine*
National Council on Alcoholism 2 East 103rd St. New York, N.Y. 10029	Reprints, pamphlets, bibliographies
National Dairy Council 111 North Canal St. Chicago, Illinois 60606	Booklets, posters, charts, films, and other nutrition teaching aids
National Education Association of the United States 1201 16th St., N.W. Washington, D.C. 20036	Pamphlets on health subjects; monthly professional journal
National Health Council 1740 Broadway New York, N.Y. 10019	Publications on Health Council work and general material on health careers
National Interagency Council on Smoking and Health 8600 Wisconsin Ave. Bethesda, Maryland 20014	Film strip for teachers, newsletter
National Live Stock & Meat Board 36 South Wabash Ave. Chicago, Illinois 60603	Pamphlets, posters, exhibits, films, catalogs—nutrition; price catalog available
National Safety Council 425 North Michigan Ave. Chicago, Illinois 60611	Pamphlets, brochures, posters, film catalogs, exhibit materials, and other teaching aids. Magazines: *School Safety, Traffic Safety, National Safety News, Family Safety*
National Society for Crippled Children and Adults, Inc. 2023 West Ogden Ave. Chicago, Illinois 60612	Reprints, leaflets, pamphlets, bibliographies; quarterly: *Easter Seal Bulletin;* monthly journal: *Rehabilitation Literature*
National Society for the Prevention of Blindness 79 Madison Ave. New York, N.Y. 10016	Pamphlets, reprints, posters, films
National Tuberculosis and Respiratory Disease Association 1740 Broadway New York, N.Y. 10019	Books, pamphlets, posters, films, filmstrips, exhibits, transcriptions, television material

National Headquarters	*Materials*
Office of Education, Department of Health, Education, and Welfare Washington, D.C. 20202	Bulletins, pamphlets, and educational materials
Outdoor Power Equipment Institute, Inc. Suite 400, The Walker Building 734 15th St., N.W. Washington, D.C. 20005	Pamphlets on safety
Paper Cup and Container Institute 250 Park Ave. New York, N.Y. 10017	Informational material on food service sanitation
Peace Corps Washington, D.C. 20525	Information on volunteer services in health professions—overseas
Public Affairs Pamphlets Public Affairs Committee, Inc. 381 Park Ave. South New York, N.Y. 10016	Booklets on timely health subjects; write for catalog
Rutgers Center of Alcohol Studies Rutgers. The State University New Brunswick, New Jersey 08903	Source materials on alcohol and alcoholism
Science Research Associates, Inc. 259 East Erie St. Chicago, Illinois 60611	Guidance series booklets
United Cerebral Palsy Associations, Inc. 321 West 44th St. New York, N.Y. 10036	Pamphlets, films
United Nations Department of Public Information New York, N.Y. 10017	Basic information on the United Nations and its activities
U.S. Department of Agriculture Washington, D.C. 20250	Pamphlets, posters, exhibits, motion pictures, filmstrips—nutrition, family health, sanitation, safety
U.S. Department of Labor, Women's Bureau Washington, D.C. 20210	Materials on health and safety of women at work
U.S. Public Health Service, Department of Health, Education, and Welfare Office of Information, Inquiries Branch 3rd and C Sts., S.W. Washington, D.C. 20201	Pamphlets, films; monthly periodical: *Public Health Reports*
Wheat Flour Institute 14 East Jackson Blvd. Chicago, Illinois 60604	Pamphlets on nutrition
World Health Organization Regional Office for the Americas 525 23rd St., N.W. Washington, D.C. 20037	Leaflets, pamphlets; magazine: *World Health*

APPENDIX

B

WORKING OUTLINE FOR AUSTIN (MINNESOTA) HEALTH EDUCATION SURVEY[1]

A. *Curriculum Plan for Health Education*
   1. Is there a definite overall plan for:
      a. The school system?   Describe
      b. Each school?   Describe
   2. Is there evidence of continuity and progression?
      a. Means of communication to assure fresh approaches?
   3. Is there evidence of planned correlation or integration of health instruction with other parts of the curriculum?
      If there is a planned program,
      a. How much time is allowed at each grade or grade level?
      b. How is flexibility provided for?

B. *Content of Health Instruction*
   1. Is it related to developmental characteristics of children at different age levels?
   2. Is it scientifically accurate and up-to-date?
      a. What consultative services have been used to assure this? How used?
   3. Are specific problems and needs revealed through screening, medical and dental examinations dealt with in the curriculum?
      a. What system of communication is used to keep teachers apprised of these problems and needs?
   4. Is teaching related to environmental conditions within the school? (e.g., sanitation, lighting, safety factors)
      a. What methods are used to identify environmental health and safety needs?

---

[1] Report of Study of the School Health Program in the Austin Public Schools. Part II. Austin, Minnesota, Austin Public Schools, 1959, pp. 214–219.

371

5. Are special programs, such as the school lunch, club activities, and bus transportation, used as a focus for health teaching when appropriate?
6. In what ways are factors in family life influencing the health of children taken into consideration?
   a. National origins, cultural patterns, e.g., food patterns, hierarchy of control
   b. Religious affiliations
   c. Degree of stability, e.g., home owners, migrants
   d. Socio-economic status.
7. In what ways is content adapted to significant factors in community life?
   a. Community health needs
   b. Resources for health and medical care; other resources
   c. Occupations of adult population
   d. Geographic factors, such as climate, proximity to large urban or rural areas or to recreation facilities
   e. Community value systems
      1. How are conflicting value systems handled?
8. What evidence is there of evaluation of content and modification of content to be more appropriate in respect to local conditions and to specific groups of children?

C. *Methods of Health Instruction*
   1. Are methods appropriate to the teaching objectives?
   2. Are methods adapted to the age levels?
   3. What evidence is there of the use of methods believed to contribute to behavior change? e.g.:
      a. Involvement of pupils in the planning of learning experiences
      b. Problem solving
      c. Discussion-decision
      d. Experimentation
      e. Appropriate use of audiovisual materials as tools (e.g., demonstrations, field trips, slides, filmstrips and motion pictures)
      f. Preparation by pupils of their own audiovisual materials.
   4. What evaluation is there of methods?
      a. Is there evidence such evaluation has resulted in modifications of programs?

D. *Resources for Health Instruction*
   1. What textbooks are used? Supplementary reading materials?
      a. How acquired?
   2. What is in each school library for
      a. Teacher references?
      b. Pupil use?
   3. What audiovisual aids are used? and how?
   4. Regarding library materials and audiovisual aids:
      a. How chosen? What criteria are used for their selection?
      b. What plan is followed for keeping them current?
      c. What budget is provided?
      d. What evidences are there that they are used? How are they used?
   5. What teaching units or resource units have been prepared locally to help the teachers? How are they used?

E. *In-service Education*
   1. Is in-service education in health education receiving attention, as through:
      a. Faculty meetings
      b. Scheduled case conferences

      c. Workshops and conferences
      d. Advanced study—summer school, extension?
    2. How is it handled? What is attitude of teachers?
    3. How is it related to broader in-service training plans?

F. *Personnel Qualifications*
    1. Do teachers meet recommended, minimum standards of preparation in the field of health? (Use current reports on standards.)

G. *Administration*
    1. What administrative structure exists for planning the health instruction program?
      a. Where is leadership placed?
      b. To what extent are teachers, administrators, maintenance personnel, health personnel, pupils, parents and community leaders involved in planning?
      c. Is there a coordinating body? If so, what is its structure and what are its functions?
      d. How is the health instruction plan coordinated with
        1. Total curriculum development
        2. Other aspects of school health program
        3. Community-wide health program?
    2. What is the nature of leadership for the health instruction program?
      a. How is it defined? and exerted?
      b. Are teachers clear about it?
      c. Does administration give it continued support?
      d. Is there framework for shared leadership?
      e. How is it related to leadership for other aspects of the school health program?
    3. When staff is hired, what qualifications for health teaching are considered?
    4. How are factors in community life which may influence the program handled, e.g.,
      a. Religious influences
      b. Political influences
      c. Community power structure
      d. Organized medicine and dentistry?

Index of Names

Index of Subjects